Self-Same Songs

Autobiographical Performances and Reflections

ROGER J. PORTER

University of
Nebraska Press
Lincoln & London

Acknowledgments for the use of
previously published material appear
on pages ix–x.

♾

Library of Congress
Cataloging-in-Publication Data
Porter, Roger J., 1936–
Self-same songs: autobiographical
performances and reflections /
Roger J. Porter.
p.   cm.
Includes bibliographical references and
index.
ISBN 0-8032-8767-4 (pbk.: alk. paper)
1. Autobiography.
2. Autobiography—Authorship.
3. Report writing.   I. Title.
CT25.P665   2002
809'.93542—dc21
2001044596

To Dick Rapson and Elaine Hatfield

"And for the few that only lend their ear,
That few is all the world."

Contents

Acknowledgments ix

Introduction: Intentions and Confessions xi

AUTOBIOGRAPHY AND EXILE

1. The Singer in the Song: Autobiography in *The Odyssey* 3
2. The Pleasures of Nostos: Vladimir Nabokov's *Speak, Memory* 17

AUTOBIOGRAPHY AS DEFENSE

3. Filling Up the Silent Vacancy: Edward Gibbon's *Autobiography* 37
4. Unspeakable Practices, Writable Acts: Benjamin Franklin's *Autobiography* 54
5. The Sorrows of Autobiography: Somerset Maugham's *The Summing Up* 67
6. Redemptive Evasions: Edwin Muir's *The Story and the Fable* 81

AUTOBIOGRAPHY AS SELF-EFFACEMENT

7. Autobiographical Writing as Death Weapon: Thomas Bernhard's *Gathering Evidence* and Franz Kafka's *Letter to His Father* 99
8. Figuration and Disfigurement: Herculine Barbin's *Memoirs of a Nineteenth-Century French Hermaphrodite* 117
9. Annulled Selves: Barbara Grizzuti Harrison's *An Accidental Autobiography* and Michel Leiris's *Biffures* 131

AUTOBIOGRAPHICAL POSTURING

10. Romantic Posing: The Life and Death Writing of Benjamin Robert Haydon 149
11. "A Serpent in the Coils of a Pythoness": Self-Dramatization in Eugène Delacroix's *Journal* 166

SELF AS OTHER, THE OTHER AS SELF

12. Conflict and Incorporation: Edmund Gosse's *Father and Son* 183
13. My Mother and Myself: Edward Dahlberg's *Because I Was Flesh* 201
14. Self and Other Is One Flesh: Double Voicing in Nathalie Sarraute's *Childhood*, Ronald Fraser's *In Search of a Past*, and Howard and Arthur Waskow's *Becoming Brothers* 215

Epilogue: Unearthing the Father 233

Notes 237

Bibliography 247

Index 259

Acknowledgments

My greatest debt is to Howard Wolf, for many decades a sympathizer, partisan, and source of unswerving encouragement and goodwill. Harold Bloom and Martin Price provoked my interest in autobiography and set me on course many years ago, and James Cox was a charismatic director of a National Endowment for the Humanities seminar on American autobiography at Dartmouth College in which I participated. Frank Bowman, Albert Stone, and James Olney early on taught me much that I know about the subject. Like everyone working in this field, I have benefited enormously from John Eakin's perspicacity and kindly counsel. I am immensely grateful to Nancy Porter, who inspired me with her literary instincts and her wide-ranging wisdom, and to Howard Waskow, a friend to whom I could look for understanding of the self and of myself—his interpretative power has always been a revelation. Mason Drukman's steady encouragement helped me along the way. Robert Folkenflik and Julia Watson graciously championed my work, giving the manuscript exactly the informed critical reading I needed and sought. Sam Danon's intelligence and wit have been a standard on which to keep a weather eye. Other friends and colleagues whose responses have been valuable include Timothy Dow Adams, Susanna Egan, Dan Gunn, William Howarth, Elinor Langer, Shirley Neuman, and Dick Terdiman.

I also want to acknowledge Reed College for providing me with a sabbatical leave during which I was able to revise much of the manuscript, the University of Nebraska Press, which has been unfailingly cooperative, and Tara Mantel, who meticulously copyedited the manuscript.

I wish to thank the following publications for permission to reprint, in greatly revised versions, material that originally appeared in their pages:

"The Singer in the Song: Autobiography and Time in *The Odyssey.*" *Massachusetts Review* 18.4 (1977).

"Gibbon's Autobiography: Filling Up the Silent Vacancy." *Eighteenth Century Studies* 8 (1974).

"Unspeakable Practices, Writable Acts: Franklin's *Autobiography.*" *Hudson Review* 32.2 (1979).

"Edwin Muir and Autobiography: Archetype of a Redemptive Memory." *South Atlantic Quarterly* 77.4 (1978).

"Figuration and Disfigurement: Herculine Barbin and the Autobiography of the Body." *Prose Studies: History, Theory, Criticism* 14 (1991). Used with the permission of Frank Cass Publishers.

"The Collapse of the Romantic Will: Haydon and Autobiographical Posturing." *The Culture of Autobiography: Constructions of Self-Representation.* Ed. Robert Folkenflik. Stanford: Stanford UP, 1993. Used with the permission of Stanford University Press. Copyright 1993 by the Board of Trustees of the Leland Stanford Junior University.

"A Serpent in the Coils of a Pythoness: Conflict and Self-Dramatization in Delacroix' Journals." *Autobiography, Historiography, Rhetoric: A Festschriff in Honor of Frank P. Bowman.* Eds. Mary Donaldson-Evans, Lucienne Frappier-Mazur, and Gerald Prince. Atlanta: Rodopi, 1994.

"Edmund Gosse's *Father and Son:* Between Form and Flexibility." *Journal of Narrative Technique* 5 (1976).

"Emptying His Sack of Woe: Edward Dahlberg's *Because I Was Flesh.*" *Contemporary Literature* 18.2 (1977). Copyright 1977. Reprinted with the permission of the University of Wisconsin Press.

"Discovery in Morgantown." *West Virginia University Alumni Magazine* 23 (2000).

Introduction
Intentions and Confessions

When we read autobiography we inevitably confront the problem of authorial intention, an issue New Critics tried to banish and poststructuralists have tried to theorize away. But however we focus on an autobiographer's masks and personae on the one hand or on the cultural institutions, language, and genre that construct a self on the other, it is nearly impossible to examine autobiography without raising questions regarding intention: For what purpose has the autobiographer undertaken the task of writing an autobiography? How does the writing of autobiography serve the needs of the writer at the time of the writing? Why has the autobiographer depicted the self in the particular way he or she has, and how does the autobiographical form respond to those claims for identity? What tensions might exist between intentions professed in the text and understandings discerned by a critic? Harold Bloom, modifying Kenneth Burke's query and making it applicable to any author, asks, "What was the writer trying to do for herself or himself, as a person, by writing this poem, play, or story?" (*The Western Canon* 249). Richard Poirier poses an allied and equally important question: "What must it have felt like to do this—not to mean anything, but to do it?" (*The Performing Self* 111). Borrowing Poirier's concept of performance—a writer's energy that projects an ego and expresses a self through, in, or against the chosen form—I will look at a number of examples from autobiographical literature, some well known, some not, that implicitly or explicitly create and "perform" a self. I also take the term "performance" from a question raised by Andrew Parker and Eve Kosofsky Sedgwick: "How is saying something doing something?" (1).

In the texts I examine, where identity is constructed and played out in a wide range of rhetorical performances, the autobiographers, diarists, and even letter writers express a self-consciousness about the act of writing, or in one case, of speaking, as well as an interest in conveying what it is like to compose a self-portrait and to assign the self and the writing a particular significance. The reason for undertaking the writing need not coincide with what he or she felt when performing it, but I attempt to connect the function autobiography appears to serve for a given writer with the activity itself, especially with the ineluctably complex presentation of the pleasures, necessities, sorrows, or reluctances of the autobiographical act. In focusing on writing autobiography *as an activity*, I am less concerned with the process of subject formation outside the text than with how autobiographical writing conduces to the formation of subjectivity, and to the way the language of autobiographers gives them palpability in the act of writing, not just in the constructed image of the life. In her book on autobiography, *Mirror Talk: Genres of Crisis in Contemporary Autobiography*, Susanna Egan asserts that "significant numbers of recent autobiographical works foreground the processes and present time of their own construction" (3). I agree, though such self-consciousness is hardly confined to contemporary texts; indeed, it is found even in *The Odyssey*, where Odysseus's autobiographical tales express a self-consciousness about their making and their narrative function. The works I discuss here validate Elizabeth Bruss's contention that "autobiography typically calls attention to its own devices, to the progress it is making in unfolding its tale." (164). One aspect of this study is the recounting of such moments when the autobiographer tells us what it means to write a life narrative.

Stanley Fish has argued that "meaning is a function of what a particular speaker in a specific set of circumstances was intending to say"; he insists on "the contextual circumstances of . . . intentional production" (11). The intention of an autobiographer may indeed be mediated through any number of impersonal systems that inflect that intention, but even radical skepticism about a self's nontextual existence does not negate the presence of an intention; it merely relocates intention to another realm. Whether we regard the text as a cultural artifact or the product of an individual sensibility, autobiography cannot escape self-referentiality—by which I mean the self-consciousness of the autobiographer in citing more or less directly the reasons for turning to autobiography in the first place. I focus on how the motive for writing autobiography gets expressed and on how the writing serves one or more purposes, even when I suspect the professed intention differs from what it appears to be. I am less interested in how intentions exist *outside* the text via statements in interviews or in letters, for example, than in how they are construed in the writing and understood as a feature of the work that is professing to achieve a particular goal.

Of course the New Critics's attack on intentionality came from a conviction that the best poetry was impersonal. But autobiography can never be deemed entirely impersonal, even if it sounds like that of John Stuart Mill. The most highly intellectualized life-writing, or that most resistant to the expression of emotions, is arguably personal and, as such, is an affair of consciousness susceptible to the scrutiny of intention. William K. Wimsatt and Monroe C. Beardsley's classic essay "The Intentional Fallacy" enjoined the critic from evaluating and aesthetically judging a work, but not necessarily from discerning its possible meanings or interpretations, via the criterion of intentionality.[1] No matter how dubious one might be about human subjectivity or about the self as a center of agency capable of having and acting upon intentions, a depersonalized and stereotypical anti-intentional position cannot hold for the criticism of life-writing. Wimsatt and Beardsley's emphasis on such terms as "voice" and "persona" fits with the notion of autobiography as performance; however, they remain relatively mute on the legitimacy of examining the text to determine reasons for the author's writing the work in the first place. Intentions may not always be clear, but they are never absent. Autobiographers frequently *intend* intentions, and readers may discern them as well as discover counterintentions. Paul John Eakin asks a pertinent question: "How does making something up—a self, a text—answer to the search for self-knowledge? In such an inquiry we do well to begin with the author's own account of the autobiographical act, accepting the text as the author's model for the self and its interpretation" (*Fictions in Autobiography* 27). Eakin quite properly links motivation to a search for an underlying identity, though as we shall see, the search may paradoxically involve an active resistance to a claimed identity. Granted that any professed reasons for writing autobiography might involve self-deception, analysis of linguistic and structural patterns in the work ought nevertheless to yield grounds for assessing such professed intentions.

In this respect I am concerned with what we might call forms of autobiographical desire as they are embedded in autobiographical discourses of self-revelation, self-creation, or even self-concealment. I would argue that intention—or desire—can be discovered through performance even when the activity marshals rhetorical defenses to bar direct understanding of the motives that have generated the writing. By using the term "performance" I suggest that in these texts autobiographical identity is not merely represented but enacted in the process of writing or, in the case of Odysseus, of speaking.

My emphasis is largely on the aesthetic and cognitive issues in subjectivity as they are argued for and conceived in a variety of texts; on the way selves are performed and dramatized in the process of autobiographical composing;

and on the strategies, rhetorical or otherwise, that narrators employ in their stories to construct selves, whether the latter are "coherent" or not. I put that term in quotation marks to suggest that an autobiographer often affirms, or rather constructs, an integral self although critical scrutiny may reveal the emergence of shifting, contentious subjects who speak in a range of discourses. And so I attempt to track the *tensions* in professed *intentions*.

There are numerous reasons why autobiographers undertake the form. Confession of sins or errors with the aim of asserting a reformed and newborn self is one of the original functions of the genre. Such writings often attempt to overcome "misleading" representations, justify a particular course of action, attest to a misunderstood self who aims for legitimacy in the face of public misinterpretation, or argue for an exemplary role validated by the writing of self. These autobiographers seek to seduce, convince, or convert the reader to a particular belief, or at least to an endorsement of the writer. Other autobiographers write to explore previously undetected aspects of their identity and to understand or even to construct the self in the act of writing about it.[2] Several of the autobiographers in this study construct in their text a rational life in the face of a feared irrationality, or create the illusion of an artfully patterned existence in the face of destabilizing contingencies. Writing autobiography in this spirit may confer a sense of power or control, especially to autobiographers whose experience threatens to overwhelm autonomy.

Still others—and here is the focus of much of this study—impose a structure or pattern on the writing to compensate for or to construct something that may be absent in the life as the autobiographer perceives it. Such writers often use autobiography, consciously or not, to construct a particular identity that does not exist, creating a self in language and thereby gaining something that is missing in their lives. Michael Sheringham, in a study of French autobiography, speaks to this motive when he declares that images of form and construction often "express a particular kind of desire stemming, as desires do, from lack and absence. . . . [T]he autobiographer, in redressing a sense of amorphousness, and in response to a desire for shape and definition, may fix on particular manifestations of selfhood and, by a kind of synecdoche, make them stand for an absent totality" (6). I use Edwin Muir's concept of the "story and the fable" from his autobiography of that title as a heuristic model for the genre and as one of its central tropes: autobiographers seeking an informing plan that gives meaning to their lives even as they acknowledge a certain formlessness in them. If the life is fragmented, autobiographers seem to say, then writing the self into coherence testifies to an ability to remake oneself. As Jerome Bruner wittily puts it, "Autobiography is the continuation of living by other means." But this aim inevitably acknowledges the disunity or lack of a fixed center, which is barely healed through or in the writing.

There is no single governing structure of intention in autobiography, despite the insistence of influential critics of the genre such as Philippe Lejeune, doyen of French autobiography scholars, who argues in *Le Moi autobiographique* (The autobiographical pact) that the object of autobiography is always a futile search for one's origins and a hopeless desire to return to one's past; and Sartre, who believes autobiographers write to make themselves significant in the face of obscurity. Given the variety of autobiographical intentions, at most we can only generalize about Eakin's "generative principle," which seems to lie behind all autobiographical projects. I take the "generative principle" to be the autobiographer's forging a self in story that substitutes for the self in life, though Eakin construes this notion less as a model of compensation than of the reproduction of a discovery of identity that originally occurred at an early stage in the life.

I have divided this study into five sections, each representing a different autobiographical intention; my set is hardly exhaustive. I begin with chapters on *The Odyssey* and Vladimir Nabokov's *Speak, Memory*, both texts embodying a trope of exile that is a characteristic of the genre. Autobiography is often concerned with a return to an unrecoverable past along with a focus on the present moment of writing or, in the case of *The Odyssey*, of storytelling. Nabokov, not unlike autobiographers generally, must resist a literal preservation of the past before he can transform it. Autobiography can resemble an exilic condition in that it acknowledges a lost past recoverable only in the imagination—where memory gives way to art, and reproduction of a self gives way to re-creation. Autobiography may be considered an exilic mode in that it cannot escape the disruption of continuity, and as the present or the moment of composition takes over from the reproduction of a past, unity comes to lodge only in consciousness.[3] Nostalgia is thus mediated by presentness, and the autobiography appears to be written and may be viewed with a double perspective that privileges the first term of each dyad: here and there, now and then. In exilic consciousness, as in autobiographical consciousness, memory and the present conspire to create the past.

The next section, "Autobiography as Defense," treats the work of Edward Gibbon, Benjamin Franklin, Somerset Maugham, and Edwin Muir. Though different from one another in many respects, these autobiographers commonly resist acknowledging the irrational or uncontrollable aspects of their lives. The various narrative strategies by which they employ autobiography to create a self in defiance of external contingencies or as compensation give the impression that they have successfully designed and structured their lives. But the various fractures and rhetorical shorings reveal the conscious control that has contributed to the making of a fictional order.

I then move to several figures who turn the genre against themselves, validating their grim perceptions of the world and even achieving a kind of complicity with it. This section, "Autobiography as Self-Effacement," focuses on the way Thomas Bernhard, Franz Kafka, Herculine Barbin, Barbara Grizzuti Harrison, and Michel Leiris dramatize their emptiness and self-annihilating identities using autobiographical narratives that attest to and actually intensify self-erasure. In various ways, from a benign substitution of materiality for a self to a suicidal hunger for obliteration, these autobiographers deliberately use the form to contest the self, in some cases achieving a kind of pleasure in the way their life-writing undermines normative assumptions of the genre.

Next, I examine the autobiographical writing of two visual artists, Eugène Delacroix and Benjamin Robert Haydon, with a glance at Vincent Van Gogh, all of whose characteristic stances I designate as "autobiographical posturing." In different ways these figures perceive themselves as existing in an embattled world where they struggle with rejection, hostility, or loss of confidence by striking notes of self-aggrandizing defiance and by taking on the personae of other artists, writers, or even historical figures. Absorbing an "other" into the self becomes a mode of elevation and a way of contending against oppositional forces. In this section I also look at the reasons why these painters turned with such urgency to life-writing in the form of journals and letters.

Finally, in the section titled "Self as Other, the Other as Self," I look at a number of writers who question the notion that autobiography testifies to autonomy by incorporating into their lives such figures as parents, brothers, family servants, and a psychiatrist. Edmund Gosse and Edward Dahlberg both compose a cross between autobiography and biography, of father and mother respectively. In what I call "double-voiced autobiography," Nathalie Sarraute splits the self into competing and contentious voices; Ronald Fraser argues that his identity cannot be validated solely by himself but must include and perhaps internalize other people's perceptions and interpretations; and Howard and Arthur Waskow cowrite a memoir revealing how their often discrepant views of the past and of their relationship become the subject of an autobiography that is sometimes disputatious yet whose writing heals the rift between them.

Most of the figures treated in this book are white and male, though two are women and one a transsexual; I have not included any writers from racial or ethnic minorities. I realize that few current studies of autobiography pay such scant attention to race, gender, and ethnicity per se. I propose no theoretical grounds for my choice of texts, nor theoretical justification for the absence of others. Rather, as I will suggest in a moment and try to make clear throughout the book, my interest in the figures I do include has much to do with who *I* am. One critic notes, "The starting point for my interpretation of another's selfhood is my own self" (Cohen 3). While the autobiographers I discuss are of course radically different from me, they either address certain concerns that are congruent with my own, or their texts have played significant roles in my life and thus were natural choices for inclusion in this study. The selection makes intellectual sense to me and at the same time seems appropriate to my own narrative and psychological interests. Let me explain.

At the opening of "Experience" Emerson asks, "Where do we find ourselves? In a series of which we do not know the extremes, and believe that it has none" (216). He goes on to image a moment of self-discovery on a stairway, at the top of which is a door where he is given a drink of forgetfulness from the river Lethe, perhaps as a defense against the realization of those extremes. Writing autobiography embodies a resistance to that obliviating act and a corresponding attempt to locate what is significant in ourselves and what produces identity. The question "Where do we find ourselves?" is one I ask throughout this study, and it refers not only to the autobiographer's act of self-locating but to my own, which represents a refusal of that deadly drink.

Like many readers, I find it difficult to read autobiography without reflecting on my own life. Even writing critically about autobiography prompts me to consider my identity and the patterns that constitute my life, and makes me ask why I have been drawn to autobiography, particularly to the texts examined here. I never thought to raise such matters directly until, in the course of writing this book, I recalled a study by Sherman Paul, *Repossessing and Renewing: Essays in the Green American Tradition*. At the end of each chapter Paul includes a brief autobiographical coda in which he gives "an account of one scholar, in his time, finding a usable past" (xiii). In these excursions Paul explains how he became interested in the writer under discussion and describes personal encounters with several of the contemporary figures.

It struck me that a book on autobiography provides an obvious context in which to experiment with what has come to be called—somewhat misleadingly—"confessional criticism." At first I, like Paul, wrote brief codas to my chapters, stating what attracted me to the various autobiographers, why they provoked my curiosity or fascination, and how they influenced my intellectual development. I found it increasingly difficult, however, not to link the appeal of these autobiographers to my life more generally. I gradually sensed a reciprocal influence at work: something in my life generated an attraction to these particular writers who, in turn, had a discernible effect on my thinking and feeling. The more I imagined a relation between self and autobiographer, critic and text, the more I realized I was becoming an autobiographer despite myself. Given my interest in the way life-writing serves a particular function for its author, it seemed inevitable that for me autobiography would elicit autobiography. Even so distinguished an autobiography scholar as Lejeune acknowledges that his passion for autobiography criticism represents a disguised desire to write autobiographically (*Le Moi autobiographique* 31). Gradually I began to amplify the codas, writing about my own life reflected through the issues and themes of each autobiographical text. In some instances it was only after the fact that I realized why I had written about a particular autobiographer, but retrospective understanding of a writer's influence on me hardly rendered the connections less imperative.

These codas, even taken together, do not constitute an autobiography as such: there is no particular structure to them, nor in their entirety do they form a sequence, either chronological or thematic. Each one should be seen as a particular response to the literary autobiography it follows, parallel to but of course greatly different from my critical reading. These codas—stories, fragments of memories, cross-cuttings of experience, attempts to convey something of who I am—are ruminations on various aspects of my life, though it is hard to know whether the reader will think there is too little of me or too much. While something of my character inevitably emerges from these forays into life-writing, I have tried not to fix myself into *a* story, hesitant to create an image that is too coherent or a narrative development that is too inexorable. Perhaps because I have always been a collector, even at times a fabulator, of stories about myself, I prefer writing about telling moments rather than deliberately constructing large patterns. Besides, whenever I feel impelled to view my life as a whole, I'm tempted to diversion, like a trekker in the jungles of the self, overcome by the sweaty effort.

In a recent narrative experiment, Nancy K. Miller, in *Bequest and Betrayal: Memoirs of a Parent's Death*, entwines a critical discussion of memoirs recounting parents' deaths with an account of her own parents, of her relationship with them, and of their deaths. Unlike Miller, I have separated autobiographical material from textual analysis, preferring that the reader attend initially to the critical discussion of each autobiography and only subsequently perceive its intersections with my life. My concern is to see where personal interests and critical responses may have had their origin, to "place" my criticism by exploring factors that shape my reading process and that establish a relation between autobiography criticism and autobiographical writing. Entering into an implicit dialogue with the subject of an autobiographical text represents what Miller elsewhere calls "an . . . autobiographical performance within the art of criticism" (*Getting Personal* 1). If there is any critical arena where such an activity seems appropriate, it is surely that of autobiography criticism. As to why one should be interested in the life of a largely unknown academic, the reader must judge the autobiographical writing itself, which naturally comes in a different flavor from the criticism.

With the hybrid form of this book, I am articulating a normally suppressed subjectivity. "Every textual interpretation," writes Hans-Georg Gadamer, "must begin . . . with the interpreter's reflection on the preconceptions which result from the 'hermeneutical situation' in which he finds himself. He must legitimate them, that is, look for their origin and adequacy" (149–50). Rather than claiming that my interpretations arise inevitably or solely out of the preoccupations that account for my interest in the text, or that the interpretations are entirely a product of autobiographically sited impulses, I am trying to understand what might be called, in line with Gadamer's conception, my "receptivity" to the texts. To explain the genesis of my concern with a given autobiographer is not to substitute the critic's self for the author's text; I claim to do nothing more than to test myself against the texts to understand how a particular autobiographer speaks to me, perhaps even shapes me, and why. Elizabeth Fox-Genovese's assertion that an autobiographical text "triggers or provides the occasion for . . . self-reflections" (73) suggests that far from imposing a disabling solipsism, my inclusion of autobiographical material recognizes the necessary partiality of any critical position even while conceding that interpretation is inescapably contingent.[4]

Autobiographical literary criticism is as polyphonic as autobiography itself, with its liminal zones of fiction and truth, art and artifact, construct and reference. Confessional criticism, or "autocritography," to use Henry Louis Gates Jr.'s term, takes many forms—from the merely anecdotal to an accounting for a theoretical stance toward literary material.[5] Such criticism has been celebrated as a resistance to, even an attack upon, "impersonal" theory and its concealment behind abstraction, or as a testimony to the personal underpinnings of theory itself and a gesture toward saving the subject when it seems obscured by attacks against the personal by structuralism, deconstruction, discourse analysis, or other poststructural technologies. Ironically, the strictures of much critical theory against universality find a home in personal or autobiographically-based criticism. Theory, as Candace Lang both argues and convincingly dramatizes in "Autocritique," need not have an impersonal bias; nor, I would add, does personal criticism inevitably resist being theorized. I will leave it to others, if they choose, to theorize about *my* project. Suffice to say that I believe my stabs at autobiography, however tenuous and fragmentary, represent an attempt to come to self-knowledge and to put that knowledge at the service of an understanding of other selves. Charles Altieri's assertion that autobiography reveals "the ways in which individual lives are woven out of the crossing of diverse discourses" may be applied with equal relevance to autobiographical criticism. Another claim of his applies to autobiography criticism with even greater urgency: "It forces us to confront how determined we are by contingent forces that we cannot control" (57). If this procedure appears to invoke the (vicious) hermeneutical circle, I take heart from James Olney's splendidly convincing words in his magisterial study of autobiography:

> We can understand a text only from a basis of previous self-under-
> standing, but our self-understanding, at least in the context of our
> reading, is contingent upon the understanding we have of the mean-
> ing created in the text; there is thus a correlation and reciprocity
> between self-understanding and text-understanding, and the respon-
> sive reader . . . profoundly implicates a life and an understanding of
> that life in the interpretation of a text and, if the text be one of life-
> writing, in the interpretation of another life. . . . [W]e can begin, say,
> with some small self-understanding, which we bring to a text, and
> from the increased understanding thereby acquired return to a greater
> understanding of ourselves. (*Memory* 224–25)

Writing autobiographically has made me continually aware of the strategies other autobiographers employ in their narratives, or their "performances." I would apply the term "performance" to my own autobiographical writing, for I know full well that my writing is riddled with rhetorical and narrative strategies, distortions, and exaggerations to produce effects and to tell a story in a certain way. If I ever needed validation of what autobiography theorists have long known regarding the genre's discursive fictionalizing, my own attempts at autobiography have rendered it abundantly clear to me. I suspect that gaining such confirmation has not been the least of my aims.

AUTOBIOGRAPHY AND EXILE

1.

The Singer in the Song
Autobiography in *The Odyssey*

> Perhaps the best of songs heard . . . is the resume of them . . . long
> afterwards, looking at the actualities away back past, with all their
> practical excitations gone. How the soul loves to float amid such
> reminiscences. – Whitman, "A Backward Glance O'er Travel'd Roads"

It might seem odd to introduce a book on autobiography with a discussion of *The Odyssey*. I am not claiming that the epic represents Homer's autobiography, or that there are no differences between written texts and the oral autobiographical narratives by which Odysseus is defined and with which he is obsessed. But I choose to begin with Odysseus as a teller of his life-story because his narratives ground the act of autobiography in some fundamental tropes that characterize the genre and raise issues with which I'll be concerned throughout this study.

Autobiography inevitably investigates one's origins and as such returns to the past. But that past cannot be fully recaptured; we might say that the self is somehow estranged, even in exile, from that past, which is as unrecoverable as the land an exile longs to return to but cannot. The exilic autobiographer seeks to recover what has been lost, but concedes it is recuperable only in the imagination or in the stories he or she tells about it. Autobiography expresses a nostalgia (literally a sickness for home) about recovering the past and returning home. But autobiography is also an implicit lamentation for the realization that one cannot go home or to the past again. Writing autobiography is a way of creating the illusion of a return.

Odysseus, as hero of the great epic of exile, "goes home" only through stories, and he narrates his life as compensation for such estrangement. Committed either to wandering helplessly on the sea—adrift and despairing that wandering constitutes his condition—or to lengthy forced stays on islands that mock the home he remembers, he turns to autobiography.

Odysseus's autobiographical narrations serve as interventions in the face of dislocation, or *dépaysment*. Such narratives then become the new "country." Adorno is not discussing autobiography, but his words could well apply to Odysseus's impulse in the midst of his estrangements: "For a man who no longer has a homeland, writing becomes a place to live" (87). We could say that autobiography is, in Edward Said's elegant phrase, "a modest refuge provided by subjectivity" (161). Autobiography represents at once the exile's wish to return to origins and a displacement of that impossibility into the desire to make up a narrative that will stand for the life. As Caren Kaplan puts it in *Questions of Travel: Postmodern Discourses of Displacement*, "For the exile, the site of the authentic is continually displaced, located in another country" (64).[1] That country is the past. Odysseus, in exile from homeland and past, commanding his memory to speak, is the very figure of the autobiographer; telling stories about himself and his origins is as close as he can come to recapturing the past. When home is but a memory, it is crucial to cultivate one's powers of recall.

Odysseus's use of autobiographical narrative demonstrates other significant traits of the genre. Recent autobiographical theory has placed considerable emphasis on the fact that the self who writes or speaks and the self depicted in the narrative are distinct identities, though both share the designation "I." The autobiographer always writes an Other, and the depicted self is markedly different from the writer, who is conscious of that difference. Odysseus plays with this complexity, deliberately confusing his audience about the relation between the teller and the depicted character. His performances throughout the poem have the effect of producing vertigo in his auditors and readers, for while at one moment we perceive similarities between the teller and his autobiographical subject (or between the story we hear and the reality we know), at the next moment we find disjunctions and incompatibilities. What Odysseus practices as an instrument of survival is a hallmark of the autobiographical act.

Odysseus, who can neither be pinned down to truth nor accused simply of lying, dramatizes autobiography's essential shiftiness. His self, or selves, continually disappear into the language of the accounts and, like the stories, are inevitably incomplete, fragmentary, dreamlike, permutable, and often radically unreliable. His elusiveness is a function not just of the plotting of the poem but of the disparate selves expressed by the act of autobiographical narration. Who exactly is telling? Who is the person behind that telling? The inchoateness of the self expressed in and by his narrating implies a problem about autobiography generally. How can we, as readers or listeners, know what is true about the autobiographer, whose ostensible verifications are part of the very self-representation that itself may be dubious? Odysseus is always *re*-representing his life, repeating his story with variations, even contradictions, in order to keep potential enemies off guard and to assert the implicit complexity of a self that cannot be pinned down.

The fact that Odysseus's fictions occur *within* a fiction, that they replicate the very genre into which they are embedded, crystallizes the problem of how to understand autobiography as a purposeful activity. In *The Odyssey*, "autobiography," or perhaps we should call it "life speaking," is such an act, not just a story, and it effects changes in the situation of the speaker, if not his way of conceiving his place in the world. I will be looking at the function autobiography serves for Odysseus, the work it does for him in the world, for it is an *activity*, not just a story of a personal or a collective past. Aside from the practical purpose of eluding those who seek to appropriate him for their ends, why does Odysseus turn to autobiography? I don't wish to make him into a modernist hero of self-analysis, since his narrations are, in the broadest sense, social meditations rather than internal ones. Nonetheless, Odysseus is our first unofficial autobiographer, and though his narrations facilitate the plot of the poem, they occasionally serve a more internal purpose as he struggles to learn about himself in the act of telling his stories.[2] We will see autobiography enacting such an epistemological function throughout this study, even when the autobiography seems evasive, if not downright obfuscating. For the moment, I want to examine the relation of Odyssean self-knowledge and "estrangement," or, put another way, exile as the context in which an understanding of the life unfolds.

Odysseus describes his bow as singing like a lyre or a swallow (Book 21, 404–11). It is appropriate that his weapon have a voice, for *The Odyssey* is essentially a poem about speaking, an epic whose hero is the subtlest of singers, a man who knows how to pitch his tale for the occasion. Odysseus is more skillful at war than most Homeric fighters, but fighting is not where his center of gravity lies. He is a warrior of words, and he uses those words to tell his story. Crafty oration allows him to take total command of his poem in a way that Achilleus never can in the *Iliad*, for Achilleus is too fixated on his own fate to tell his tale. But *The Odyssey* unites story and storyteller, a strategy that magnifies the hero who sings his own deeds, forging his stories as carefully as he does his boat or his bed. Even when Homer reclaims the narrative after Odysseus's long chronicle to the Phaiakians, Odysseus continues to elaborate his "story" as he invents a variety of false accounts and fictive identities, all of which contain truths about his condition as a suffering and enduring hero.

The autobiographical instinct enables Odysseus to control his world and the poem, for he contains within himself nearly the entirety of the poem's experience. Actor and commentator, he interprets the significance of the events for us. Even when he is most vulnerable he understands with a critical perspective, speaks his story, and enhances his stature in the act of telling. In the process of making autobiography out of available material, he forges a new kind of heroism for himself: not merely the wily and rational man, but the poet of his own self. Odysseus is the first great wordsmith, a verbal enchanter and a calculating bard whose stories, whether truthful reports or conniving fictions, allow him to make his way through a precarious world. In an oral culture words are temporary, evanescent; they disappear on the wind. As a result they have great provocative power over listeners, a capacity to spellbind, beguile, and enchant. But gradually we see beyond the practical function of his tales: in the process of reciting autobiography, Odysseus makes what would otherwise be reported legend into a personal relation with his amazed listeners.

One of the principal functions of Odysseus's autobiographical story-telling is to keep his memory alive—in the poem memory is the sole defense against dissolution. Memory and autobiographical narrative are products of the desire to resist death. The fear of being forgotten is analogous to the fear of the natural world that is always in flux, coming into being and passing away, so that memory, which makes autobiography possible, is a phenomenon that resists—or at least permits the comforting illusion of resisting—the time-bound world of change. Memory is what makes Odysseus's narratives possible, and those narratives in turn provide a form for the further remembering that constitutes his identity and becomes a stay against oblivion.

Milan Kundera reminds us that "Forgetting is the great private problem of man: death as the loss of the self. . . . What terrifies us about death is not the loss of the future but the loss of the past. Forgetting is a form of death ever present within life" (234–35). Memory naturally plays a significant role in oral culture. Without a written text the bard has to memorize enormous amounts of material. *The Odyssey* constantly demonstrates the importance of memory, not just as a repository of the culture's wisdom, but as the crucial factor in the making of autobiographical narrative. An autobiographer depends on memory no less than does the bard. Bards remember metrically tailored formulae, shifting them around as the occasion demands; this shifting is exactly what Odysseus does when telling his story, playing with his identities and, like a skillful poet, demonstrating a fluidity not rooted in mere formulae.

In *The Odyssey* there are many stories *about* Odysseus: songs by the bards at Ithaka and Phaiakia, tales by Menelaos, Nestor, and Helen. But the stories Odysseus tells about himself are more complex not just because he has access to fuller and more authentic subject matter but because his motives and his telling differ from those of other narrators. The others fix him into myth, name him as a legendary hero whose image slowly recedes into a seemingly irrecoverable past. Odysseus is a singer of his life because there are so many others who try to tell his story. In effect he must take back the narrative. By telling his own story, Odysseus frees himself from the encapsulation of such other views and reveals a character that changes to fit the necessities of particular circumstances. The stories that Odysseus tells about himself convey his protean quality, and his oral "autobiography" has a complexity that biography and history in the poem can never achieve. That Odysseus tries out various versions of his story, even inventing fictional selves and fabricating a panoply of false personal history, suggests that the truth of any given account is less important than the composite and fluid image that emerges, especially the expression of an imagination that will not be fixed into the archaic rigidity that marks the obsessive behavior of the gods, demigods, and monsters he meets during his travels. The very Odyssean fluidity that even Athene appreciates marks both his character and his narratives, and improvisation characterizes not only his cunning with Polyphemos but his own complex storytelling. Odysseus is *polutropos* (a man of many turns) in his action and his narrations, master of a kind of intellectual mime both in situations calling for physical survival and in storytelling. Trying out roles during the course of his travels is a function of life-preserving cleverness and a way of dramatizing differing conceptions of humanness—especially its forms of vulnerability. The fact that Odysseus is a bardic figure suggests a new emphasis on self-consciousness; he is a hero expressing a sense of wonder at the movements of his mind. Athene says to him, "Your ways of deceiving . . . are near to you in your very nature . . . you are far the best of all mortal men for . . . stories" (Book 12, 294–98); these words are praise not no much for outright lying as for Odysseus's ability to make the self into a fiction.

With Polyphemos, Odysseus lies to protect himself, famously calling himself "Nobody." The false name and the true one that corrects it suggest that Odysseus is always conscious that his identity may depend upon words.[3] One can be nobody or somebody almost at will, thus the magic potency of language. Odysseus is indeed both nobody and "Odysseus," now one, now the other, not only because his situation threatens to obliterate him but because he tries to be whatever he can, even temporarily a self-nullifying absence, through the story he tells about himself. Later his physical disguise and verbal disguise go hand in hand, both strategies of the character who experiments with forms and with himself.

Creatures like Kalypso, the Sirens, Sylla, and Charibdis are governed by brute compulsion, and their lives and actions have a seductive simplicity. But Odysseus has an autobiography, which is to say a dramatized past and the promise of a future. Though he hardly undergoes anything that we would recognize as a serious revision of character, he does discover and acknowledge that he is a being who exists in the force-field of time. By making Odysseus tell the saga of his long return and by having him fabricate accounts of various pseudoselves, Homer portrays a hero whose narrations reveal his broadening perception of the world; each birthing of Odysseus's consciousness represents a further departure from the simplicities and reductions of primordial nature or myth. In telling his story, Odysseus asserts the power of culture against raw nature, insisting that his capacity for remembering and for storytelling constitute his civilized identity. In an oral culture Odysseus must tell his story, for he *is* his story, and narrative *is* his identity.[4]

Odysseus's narrations concretize the poem's expressive duality, particularly as embodied in the singer-hero's identity as king and beggar, godlike hero and weather-beaten victim, scourge and sufferer. The dramatic present and the autobiographically narrated past each reveal a pattern of adversity and triumph, vulnerability and self-assurance. It is not that Odysseus learns how to transcend earlier frailties so much as he discovers that gestures of self-destruction and self-preservation exist in a dialectical embrace, that his life is a struggle between these impulses. The road back from defeat and the return from exile spring from his autobiographical storytelling.

Odysseus contemplates his experience even as he lives through it, his stories giving form to the flux and apparent indeterminateness of the world. Although he comes to embrace the oldest of all consolations—that there is harmony in chaos, an underlying form in a vast sea of confusions—and although he eventually honors the significance of home and sees all else as exile, he nevertheless perceives that every experience is part of a larger destiny in which success and failure, being adrift and being home, mark the cycles of human time. His stories express a life that replicates the relentless rhythms of mixed fortune, rising and falling like the waves on the sea. Even the return to Ithaka is part of a larger rhythm: he will go off and return once again. It is significant that his final journey, after the initial homecoming, involves telling one more story: he must carry a message about the unfathomable ocean to strangers who have never seen it. What can that story of sea and ships be but the story of himself and the meaning of his wanderings?

Odysseus's life is continually turning into story, not merely as an exemplum for others but as an instrument for the exploration of his own mind. In recounting the experiences he has lived through, Odysseus asserts a crucial aspect of the human: an ability to conceive and shape one's past retrospectively and to authenticate himself. In taking over the story of the Trojan War from the Phaiakian bard and telling it himself, he merges in himself hero and poet. Ultimately, autobiographical storytelling is a substitute for action, and when Odysseus becomes his own bard, the rhapsode of the self, at Phaiakia, he asserts the power of narration to be virtually equivalent to action. He also places the evanescent present in a continuum of time, which is precisely the function of exilic autobiography.[5] In the process of telling he endows the bardic function with an unaccustomed heroism. Singer and song, subject and object, become one. When Odysseus repeats his story to Penelope, the narration that creates and validates his heroic identity is succeeded once again by his establishing a parallel identity as poet.[6] We might even speculate that Odysseus's gaining fame via his storytelling and its posthumous guarantee of immortality, as well as his return from the sea (often imaged in the epic as a rebirth), functions as autobiography itself does. That is, while the form can never achieve the closure that the life has, it may serve as a substitute for that completion, a kind of textual survival or generic trope of death and rebirth thematized within the action of the poem.

Walter Benjamin's observation about storytelling seems to fit Odysseus precisely: "The storytelling that thrives for a long time . . . does not aim to convey the pure essence of the thing like information or a report. It sinks the thing into the life of the storyteller, in order to bring it out of him again. Thus traces of the storyteller cling to the story the way the handprints of the potter cling to the clay vessel" (91–92). Odysseus's very being and name survive through the art of personal narrative, whether he is manipulating others or making himself into a form of energy in the world. As one who comes back from the dead, Odysseus makes us see his narratives as assertions of human power that keep him afloat in an uncertain universe. Homer's art of keeping Odysseus's memory alive is thus replicated in Odysseus's own autobiographical tales.

Memory and song are the instruments for self-magnification, but they can be put to devious ends. Odysseus's stories, like his life, are often models of deception. In fact, the prevalence of false tales in the poem parallels the distinction between the narrated past and the present narrator of autobiography. Odysseus's continually fictionalizing his past coincides with the hiatus between experience and story, and his falsifications serve as extreme instances of autobiography's inability ever to achieve pure truth or absolute fidelity to the past. Occasionally the unstable world appears to Odysseus almost as if it were turning into a fiction, and when this happens he answers with silence, tactful speech, and fictions of his own. Odysseus's devices for outwitting, or at least for maintaining his own with his adversaries, are similar to those an autobiographer employs to reveal, conceal, or play with his identity: now withholding, now disclosing his true name (in the autobiographical sense of an authentic self); now deliberately distorting or fictionalizing the past, now representing it as accurately as possible. In a menacing world of strangers, the newly arrived one is always having to say who he is; one's autobiography is literally a matter of life and death, for how the stranger presents himself may determine whether he is dined or dined upon. Odysseus must tell his story with masterful control, holding to his essential desire to come home even while he sometimes dissembles that desire in order to make the goal possible.

Autobiographical storytelling is thus Odysseus's response to exile. It is his way of, for example, connecting his life to the wife he cherishes on Ithaka. The fraudulent personal narratives delivered to Athene, Eumaios, and Penelope are all spoken either when he cannot believe that he has arrived home or when he fears he may never achieve that goal. They constitute a recognition of his desire to end exile, to reconstitute his former roles, and to perceive his life as a form that moves through time, gathering up its own past. All present moments contain both a retrospective element and an anticipatory one, memory and prophecy. Odysseus perceives a continuity in his life represented by the return to Ithaka. Each stab of remembrance opens a vista into a wished-for future; Odysseus's story is fashioned from a need to place events in relation to one another so as to make sense of his life.

If Odysseus's stories establish his image in time, he, like many auto-biographers, faces a discrepancy between his own idealized image and a slowly developing reality. The press of time demands a reassessment, and the way in which Odysseus progresses through the long sequence at Ithaka renders this achievement possible. When Odysseus returns to his island, it is as if he were living through the sweep of his life: the infant child for Eurykleia, the promising son for Laertes, the young master for Eumaios, and the middle-aged husband for Penelope. This movement is analogous to the autobiographer's art of gathering up past selves. Odysseus's lifetime unfolds in layers, and as he senses this movement he seems to inspire in others his own urge to remember and resurrect the past.

Odysseus's need to tell his story is crucial because the threat of anonymity and estrangement looms large. If exile means being cut adrift so that the isolated pockets of culture disappear entirely, then storytelling makes connections across space and time, asserting the power of identity and continuity though the acts of remembering and commemorating. When Telemachus hears stories about his father from Nestor, Menelaos, and Helen, he is not merely receiving information but reaffirming the generational continuity of a pre-Archaic world. *The Odyssey* is filled with stories that assert man's need to locate himself in a social network. In their quite different ways both Odysseus and Telemachus at times forget who they are; hearing and telling their stories are ways of confirming their identities not only for others but for themselves, especially in a constellation of family and history. Appropriately, Telemachus is most often a listener; linked as he is to the image and authority of Odysseus, he has not yet fathered himself, which is a way of saying he has not yet become a self-creator and an autobiographer.

But while the autobiographical narrations are about Odysseus's cheating of death, paradoxically they are also implicit elegies for what he cannot totally recapture. We always feel the gap of the twenty years' separation from Penelope. Like Scheherazade's tales, Odysseus's stave off fatality. Yet his final narrative to Penelope, which recounts the prophecy of his death, concedes his limits. As with autobiography in general, the protagonist does not die, but the elegiac note is struck.

The themes of truth and deception, and of role-playing and auto-biographical storytelling, merge and culminate in the reunion scene of Odysseus and Penelope. This episode shows both lovers tested to the limits of their ability as tactful and cautious speakers, building their stories with suspense and an exquisite awareness of how the nuances of revelation will affect the other person. The past collapses into the present as husband and wife feel the magnitude of what has been lost. Each recalls a separate past, first to test one another, then to bring the other into his or her orbit, and finally to close the circle of communion. The Homeric hero normally defines himself in action, but there are moments when being, not doing, predominates. Such cherished times of repose may correspond to those moments of autobiography when the speaker regards with equanimity and serenity the achieved course of the life, with its defeats acknowledged and transcended in the sheer pleasure of composing the story.

The problem facing Odysseus in his reunion with Penelope is one felt by all exiles upon return: On one hand there has been a need to hold on to the image of the Other in order to remain faithful—to keep the image, as it were, as a talisman or guide. On the other hand, if that image is held too fixedly, the Other cannot match it in reality. A beautiful statement by Martin Heidegger applies to this moment of memory. Heidegger reminds us that initially the word "memory" did not mean the power to recall, but rather a "steadfast, intimate concentration upon the things that essentially speak to us. . . . Originally, 'memory' means as much as devotion: a constant, concentrated abiding with something—not just with something that has passed, but . . . with what is present and with what may come" (140). As Odysseus regards Penelope, he "remembers" her as she is.

Face to face with Penelope, Odysseus needs the flexibility of perception he so often demonstrates in order to accommodate the new reality. In effect the fantasy of Penelope must be held and then broken. Penelope and Odysseus have to change their images of each other just as Odysseus must change his image of himself from warrior to beggar. That he makes this transition signals his capacity not only to improvise but to acknowledge the "baser" role as an authentic aspect of the self; the acceptance is a lesson from his autobiographical narrations. Odysseus and Penelope bring the new image of the other into full being, but each must surrender the idealized image, since all recoveries are imperfect, all dreams flawed, all autobiographical stories partial if not suspect. Each one rescues the other from misconception, draws the other out of an obscuring mist into which he or she has disappeared.

When Odysseus tells Penelope the story of the bed, the autobiographical narration of a past deed gives him title to his identity. But there is one story left to recount, and that is the *entire* story, up to the present and including the prophecy of his future death. Autobiography is a death-haunted mode; it suggests both a staving off of the end and an edging toward that moment, a flirtation with demise in the act of summing up. Autobiography can never be ultimate, only penultimate. At this moment, calmed in his wife's arms, Odysseus experiences great equanimity. "How the soul loves to float amid such reminiscences," says Whitman, "with all their practical expectations gone." The final ease of narrative emerges when at last there is nothing left to plead or bargain for. Mutual dissimulations and mutual testings are complete. The story has almost no burden to bear; it merely *is*.

For once there is a special pleasure in the telling because it has no function for Odysseus other than to separate past from present, to enhance his bond with Penelope, and to assert his joy in the moment. Dangers are past, and just as he is no longer disguised, so the tale is emptied of all deceptive practice. He is shaping his penultimate identity but within the moment there is nothing left to prove. There remains only the sheer hedonism of song, surrounded by lovemaking and sleep. With Penelope the adventures become simply the subject for song, all passion spent. Homer tells the story of Odysseus telling the story of himself telling the story of his life. As tale collapses into tale, and the autobiographical narrative becomes merely story, even Odysseus's art pales in relation to the reunited couple's celebration of life, for Homer moves the emphasis to the "life" that transcends the art of song. In similar fashion the fictions Penelope has been told by others disappear, replaced by Odysseus's presence and by the reality of the moment. As the autobiographical narrative takes on a purely private function, we see the most intimate side of Odysseus: his childhood, the story of his bed, his relationship with his wife. The final storyteller, the singer of his own song, is mere man. We are reminded that the gods do not spin autobiographies.

At home the fabulous world fades into mere reminiscence, a state that ironically may become as nostalgic as home itself once was. The return to Ithaka is cunningly replaced by a return into the past in Odysseus's imagination, a transformation of *nostos*. This movement characterizes a phase of autobiography where, as the narrated past approaches the dramatic present, the telling self and the self told about begin to join. Thus in the scene where Odysseus tells the story to Penelope, past and present seem to merge. But only *seem*, for the account contains a prophecy, which throws the action into a putative future, and we can even entertain a notion that the self from the past whose story the returned Odysseus narrates may only be a fiction or a dream of the poet-voyager. At the end, the autobiographical speaker steps outside his story, and as the past recedes, he looks back on it as story. When he has finished performing, he can finally just listen, turning from the fabulous and timeless world of romance to the time-bound world of family and history.

IN MY FIRST CLASS in my first academic job, after a graduate education at Yale where student teaching was scorned, I came face-to-face with *The Iliad* and a few weeks later with *The Odyssey*. Not only had I no ideas about leading a class other than to avoid the indifferent tyrannies of graduate teaching, I had never before read Homer. My education in the classics was dismal (in the heyday of New Criticism we read Austen, James, and Eliot, not Homer). Reed College requires all freshman to take an interdisciplinary humanities course that devotes the entire first semester to ancient Greece, and when, many years later, the staff dropped *The Odyssey* to give more time to Aristotle, most of my students read it on their own, feeling cheated with only half of Homer.

When I started writing the essay on *The Odyssey* the year those students took their gratifying initiative, I saw that the poem addressed themes of the middle age I was approaching, with its intimations of mortality, its swing between the hunger for adventure and the consolations of ordinariness, and its acknowledgment that some losses are irrecoverable.

I was also writing about autobiography, and my understanding of Odysseus's need to tell stories about himself turned on some of the generic issues I was considering. At the time a significant cultural phenomenon was taking place: young people were starting to write memoirs (Frank Conroy, Frederick Exley, and Willie Morris among them), taking over a genre previously reserved for the elderly, as if asserting their need to capture their experience before someone else—came along to distort it. I considered that Odysseus narrates his life for similar reasons: to get the story right in the face of other characters' narratives that misrepresent him, whether out of ignorance or self-interest. The issues in autobiography I was investigating—identity expressed in the process of constructing narrative, writers incorporating or rejecting depictions of the self rendered by others, autobiography as a form of consciousness, autobiographers exhibiting multiple versions of their self—all seemed relevant to Odysseus's remarkable inventions and storytelling. I wondered if I could relate these generic topics to Odysseus's self-representations without imposing a Modernist conception of self on an Archaic one.

I worked on a version of this chapter during a year when I lived in Europe, and my own separation from home may have led me to regard exile and *nostos* as autobiographical problems. I was hardly exiled, enjoying a cushy enough sabbatical in London, but nevertheless *The Odyssey* reminded me that whatever the pleasures of living abroad, my "real" life awaited me back in Oregon. My life in fact seemed an oscillation between home and comfort on one hand, adventure and risk on the other; and I'm convinced that those systoles and diastoles were responsible for sustaining my attraction to the poem. I have lived in the same house for thirty years, and have taught at the same institution for forty. But I have seldom remained with one romantic partner for more than a few years, and I have probably sacrificed an abiding relation to travel and adventuring. Security has allowed me to take chances; uncertainty and flux have required the security. I have often figured Odysseus as a polestar despite the fact that for me, "home" has not included the family that magnetizes him. Not that the outward-bound movements—teaching in Paris, Egypt, Greece, and Hong Kong, and traveling to locales that scarcely involved real dangers—have been especially courageous. I could always return without risking much loss. Still, I frequently surrender to the Odyssean itch to venture out, testing the world to see what it will yield. That impulse has led me from Fez to Timbuktu to Ubud to Darjeeling to Urgup. A friend tells me that if I were floating in a Tahitian lagoon, I would dream wistfully about the waters of the Caribbean. I have always been restless, and yet a yearning for home draws me just as insistently. Whenever I teach *The Odyssey*, I think of Frost's lines: "I'd like to get away from earth awhile / And then come back to it and begin over. / May no fate willfully misunderstand me / And half grant what I wish and snatch me away / Not to return."

I track down exiles. Recently on Corfu for a conference on the British expatriate writer Lawrence Durrell, I went searching for the house from which he fled the Nazis for the haven of Alexandria. At Alexandria during a year I taught at Cairo American College, I sought traces of the Greek exile poet Cavafy, whose interest in dispossession had influenced Durrell. On Corfu I read Edward Said's memoir, *Out of Place*, in preparation for writing a paper on Egyptian exiles, and in turn remembered having read *Orientalism* years earlier at Cairo American College, only to discover on Corfu that in the 1940s Said was a student at the very place where I once taught—in his day it was called the Cairo School for American Children. I return to distant places to feel more poignantly the nostalgia of the first visit. The far-away becomes a kind of home. Since the real home generates memories that in turn send me back to hunt for the reluctantly relinquished past, how could I not be interested in autobiography, the genre of continually blocked homecoming where memory takes the place of home? André Aciman, a melancholy exponent of *mal du pays*, writes that Odysseus "realizes in fact that nostalgia is not some sort of restless energy that propels him homeward, but that nostalgia is his home. . . . The site of nostalgia is writing and speculating and thinking about nostalgia" (141). When I first went to Greece and wandered on beaches whose emptiness seemed to reflect my solitude, I vowed I would never return, as if to do so would recall my isolation. But once home, nothing haunted me so much as the desire to reexperience what I had felt, impelled back to the "home" that I was beginning to define by the very way it made me restless to return.

The Odyssey has dogged me over the years. Not long ago I led a Reed alumni tour to Greece, discussing the poem in a seminar on the deck of our boat as it plowed through the Aegean, crisscrossing Odysseus's route homeward from Troy. Some years earlier I lived on the Gulf of Salonika, where I had a Fulbright lectureship to Aristotelian University in

Thessaloniki, and my students bore names they hardly recognized, let alone merited: Plato, Penelope, Aphrodite, Zeus; I recall no Odysseus, though the men scarcely needed that name, for they were all wily enough in negotiating their education with the master's guile. More recently I trekked to the beach on Corfu where, I was assured, Odysseus had met Nausicca.

In college I played Odysseus in a production called *Nostia*, a dramatization of the section of *The Odyssey* where the hero, washed up bedraggled and half-naked from the sea, encounters the seductive young girl who momentarily tempts him from thoughts of Penelope. Nausicaa was played by Lisa Commager, the seventeen-year-old daughter of Henry Steele Commager, the distinguished historian who had just come to Amherst. Wherever Commager went outside the classroom—faculty meetings, the college coffee shop, even movies and Amherst football games—he carried three books and read them through, oblivious to everything going on around him. So when the great man dropped by for a rehearsal of the play, he hardly seemed to be watching as he burrowed into his reading. There was a moment when I seized his daughter in my arms, kissed her passionately, and chanted hymns to her body. The rehearsal took place in a small classroom, and the scene had been blocked so that the embrace occurred, to the horror of Professor Commager, directly in front of the flushed paternal face; the quivering father for once abandoned his reading and scrutinized me the way Hamas regards another settlement going up on the West Bank. I sometimes wonder whether, in my critical engagement with the poem, I sought a mastery over it I never felt while acting its hero.

A final personal note: in the opening night audience was the woman, unknown to me at the time and for two more years until we met at Yale, who became, for awhile, my wife. Also in the audience was my college roommate who, four years later as the best man at my wedding, when my bride and I were on the verge of a honeymoon that would take us across the country to my job at Reed, sent us on our way by announcing that Odysseus and Penelope were venturing off together. We may have been that couple for a time, but the marriage was not to be.

2.

The Pleasures of Nostos

Vladimir Nabokov's *Speak, Memory*

In this chapter I want to explore some of the implications of an exilic theory of autobiography for Vladimir Nabokov's *Speak, Memory*. If Odysseus's "autobiography" represents the exile's wish to return to his origins, and a displacement or sublimation of that desire into imagination and art, Nabokov's narrative turns on that notion by transforming a longing for home into an ironic acceptance of, even a luxuriant pleasure in, the displacement. Rather than anguishing over the forced separation from his ancestral Russia, Nabokov assents to it, even revels in it, since it furnishes the conditions for autobiographical writing. For Nabokov, estrangement or distance from home gives birth to the art that only appears to lament that estrangement.[1]

Speak, Memory was to have for its British edition the title *Speak, Mnemosyne*, which recalls the opening words of *The Odyssey*, "Sing in me Muse." Nabokov is an exile who has come home not to his native land but to the shelter of art, and like Odysseus with Penelope, Nabokov has a story to tell his wife Vera, the omnipresent and oft-referred to "You" of the autobiographical narrative. I want to trace the way exile provides Nabokov with an identity, however playful, multifarious, or provisional.[2] Nabokov "goes home" to the origins of his impulse for storytelling; autobiography for him is not so much an exploration of his biographical past but of consciousness, which he defines as the perception of one's self in time—a thoroughly Odyssean recognition. Such a realization allows him to write autobiography that both represents and transcends the workings of time. Much as Odysseus wants both to return home and to avoid too much domesticity in order to perpetuate heroism, so Nabokov, a thoroughly Odyssean modernist, resists regarding Russia longingly, thereby avoiding conventional sentimentality and exploiting his sense of loss for the opportunity it provides for writing. *Speak, Memory* replaces a literal return to homeland. Julia Kristeva declares that the exile "strays instead of getting his bearings. . . . Instead of sounding himself as to his 'being,' he does so [only] concerning his place: 'Where am I?' instead of 'Who am I?' " (8) Nabokov is always in the liminal space between homes, a space we can call the imagination.

It has become a critical commonplace that modernism cannot be understood without considering its writers' need for exile from constraining circumstance; the "artist in exile" has become a defining trope for both modernist perception and literary experimentation. Indeed, narratives representing either voluntary exile or forced diaspora stake out a paradigm of modern and postmodern creativity. In the fullest study of this phenomenon, *Questions of Travel: Postmodern Discourses of Displacement*, Caren Kaplan lists such instances of exile as a "nostalgia for the past; for home; and for a 'mother-tongue.' " (33). Nabokov gestures toward all these signs of nostalgia. Kaplan maintains that the nostalgic impulse is as natural as the desire to be at home, but her claim that "separation from that location can never be assuaged by anything but return" will not work for Nabokov, who is not merely resigned to the impossibility of return but is actually grateful for the exilic state, cultivating it as a blessing. Regarding his family's flight from Russia, he states, "The break in my own destiny affords me in retrospect a syncopal kick that I would not have missed for worlds. Ever since . . . homesickness has been with me a sensuous and particular matter" (*Speak, Memory* 250). While some modernist writers devise a figurative state of displacement and exile to allow for a privileged gain in perspective and creative insight, Nabokov exploits his actual exile to nourish memory and facilitate self-exploration. Not only is the Nabokovian self formed as a result of exile, but exile continues to generate the self by virtue of the autobiographical strategies that constitute his identity. For Nabokov, who never expressed a desire to return to his actual home, the aesthetic turn is not merely compensation for exile, but the welcome result attributable to only apparent loss.

Memory is what the exile possesses as a resource and as a narrative strategy, a way of maintaining a semblance of continuity in time, of harboring the comforting illusion of defeating the time-bound prison of existence, and of confirming a self that, in Nabokov's case, is inseparable from the sequence of generations in his family. He bids memory speak both to awaken and to reproduce consciousness; memory and the art it generates are his only weapons in the struggle against time and amnesia. The exile must maintain an image of the past to fortify himself against being stranded from all familiarity; Nabokov invokes memory to summon his past as the matrix in which he lives his constantly exiled life and which provides him with the conditions for creating art—not so much to combat that exile as to exploit it. *Speak, Memory* is a book about time, always the subject for autobiography to be sure, but Nabokov's text explicitly attempts to control time even as it acknowledges its consequences. It is the impossibility of recapturing the past—the exile's dilemma—that drives Nabokov to memory and to art; the twin obsessions with recall and invention form a dialectic that is the only way Nabokov can confront loss. As he said in a 1967 interview, "When we speak of a vivid individual recollection we are paying a compliment not to our capacity of retention but to Mnemosyne's mysterious foresight in having stored up this or that element which creative imagination may want to use when combining it with later recollections and inventions. In this sense, both memory and imagination are a negation of time" (*Strong Opinions* 78).

A great wanderer, a man never at home, Nabokov cultivates what he terms "retrospective fervor," admittedly his family's most distinctive trait, as compensation for loss. He also cultivates the imagination, which he calls "a form of memory," suggesting that for him truth and fiction are scarcely opposed. He affirms the point when he describes his conception of memory as "the blending of perfect personal truth with strict artistic selection" (*Selected Letters* 85). Through his celebrated playfulness regarding identity and truth, Nabokov creates an identity in the act of remembering and writing; in the course of confronting his exile, he forges an identity that returns to the past in the only way possible—through the imagination.

For Nabokov memory is crucial: it negates the effects of time—his great terror—and stands in as surrogate for any literal homecoming. Michael Seidel notes, "The memory of home becomes paramount in narratives where home itself is but a memory" (11).[3] Memory is especially important for Nabokov, given what he regards as the obliterating effect of the Russian Revolution. But, again, he never regrets the material loss; as he famously reports, instead of seeking to reclaim tangible property, he inherits and cultivates "unreal estate" (*Speak, Memory* 40). By the same token, homelessness is not just a situation historically conditioned but a state of being, something that history cannot ultimately change but only respond to by providing the grounds for a creative rather than a literal renewal. Indeed it may be that "exile" is not quite the right word for Nabokov, since we never sense in *Speak, Memory* that he is eager to return. Even if he wanted to, the return would be temporal, not spatial, discursive not actual. He is obsessed with home only in acknowledging how it has shaped him; he hardly dwells on personal or political grievances resulting from displacement, never expresses anguish nor claims that his present life is merely provisional.

In a moving autobiographical meditation, the Alexandrian self-pro-claimed exile André Aciman adumbrates Nabokov's situation, and though Aciman's description of the exile's dilemma is conceived as Proustian lamen-tation, Nabokov will turn the dilemma to an advantage. Here is Aciman: "An exile is not just someone who has lost his home; he is someone who can't find another, who can't think of another. Some no longer even know what home means. They reinvent the concept with what they've got, the way we reinvent love with what's left of it each time. Some people bring exile with them the way they bring it upon themselves wherever they go" (39). It is Nabokov's reluctance to revisit Russia (not just the impossibility of his doing so) that leads to reinvention of home in textuality. Nabokov's restlessness even in America, his refusal to set down roots, figures in this equation. Nabokov, who never affiliated with any community of Russian émigrés in the United States, fosters an alienation from any present site, secure in a tradition of literary cosmopolitanism that his autobiography goes far to endorse. Nabokov's vaunted political detachment and resistance to nationalism—unlike that of many exiles who, despite or perhaps because of their hatred of the conditions that caused their exile in the first place, retain a fervent loyalty to country—is directly related to this cosmopolitanism, which in turn generates a playfulness and a relentless irony that aestheticizes all experience.

The constellation of exile, nostalgia, and recollection furnishes the themes of Nabokov's entire life, not merely of his forced departure from Russia. At age five, vacationing away from St. Petersburg and missing his home, he recreates "carefully, lovingly, hopelessly, in an artistically detailed fashion," an "inexplicably nostalgic image of 'home'" (*Speak, Memory* 75–76). The autobiography is filled with such memories within memories. These moments cast us into a *mise en abîme*, as when Nabokov remembers his mother remembering, or when he recalls Uncle Ruka recalling his childhood via the same book that Nabokov looks at to recall his own, dizzied by the realization that he is recollecting a recollection of a recollection. Away from St. Petersburg for almost a year, throughout a kind of proleptic exile, the child rehearses "the inexplicably nostalgic image of 'home,'" despite the fact he is barely five years old. "I would draw with my forefinger on my pillow the carriage road sweeping up to our . . . house, the stone steps on the right, the carved back of a bench on the right. . . ." Some years later, when the family escapes Russia for the Crimea, Nabokov "felt all the pangs of exile." Later when he is a student at Cambridge, the university exists "merely to frame and support my rich nostalgia," enabling him to imagine his Russian world, however "artificial" and a product of "careful reconstruction" it may be (*Speak, Memory* 76, 244, 261, 270). In Berlin and in Paris, further points on his route to exile in America, the phenomenon repeats itself. Even his later years in Switzerland bring the same "fertile nostalgia" for America he once felt in America for Russia (*Strong Opinions* 49).

Speak, Memory does contain moments of sorrow, when a sense of separation from the familiar dominates the narrative, and wistful memories of childhood become tinged with the glow of vanished romance. This is especially true when he memorializes his beloved country estate and its parks, or when he recalls his father with tenderness and intermittently refers to his early death by assassination, or when he recalls his mother's affection and his own first love. But the autobiography has a countervailing thematic in which exile from childhood security and nostalgia for childhood bliss provide the possibility for aesthetic revision, the act that turns grief into joy. At such moments he assures himself that he has fortunately escaped a debilitating and tedious "continuity of time, with its primitive absence of perspective" (*Speak, Memory* 250).

The impulse to reconstitute what cannot be recaptured in its original form mirrors the conditions of autobiography itself. Let us look at two episodes where Nabokov rehabilitates the past, shaping his identity and transforming loss into creative triumph. In chapter 12, titled "Tamara," the name of his first love, Nabokov identifies this young girl with Russia itself, which, two years hence, the revolution will force him to leave. His relationship with Tamara comes to a conclusive end when he is in the Crimea, feeling "all the pangs of exile. . . . [T]he loss of my country was equated for me with the loss of my love" (*Speak, Memory* 244–45). This chapter is filled with abandonments, despair that the love affair can hardly be remembered let alone be recaptured. His deepest regret regarding this early romance, however, is that it ultimately yields "very meager artistic results" (*Speak, Memory* 240). Artistic results are what Nabokov is after; they essentially define his identity.

Later, toward the close of the "Tamara" chapter, Nabokov relates an amusing incident that parodies the strategy and design underlying the autobiographer's depiction of the exilic imagination. Nabokov, then about seventeen, and another young woman he met while exiled in the Crimea invent a game in which they "project, as it were, into the future" and transform "the very specious present into a kind of paralyzed past as perceived by a doddering memorist who recalls, through a helpless haze, his acquaintance with a great writer when both were young." So he might say, "I shall always remember the remark V. V. made one warm night: 'It is,' he remarked, 'a warm night' . . . all this delivered with much pensive, reminiscent fervor" (*Speak, Memory* 248). Brian Boyd, Nabokov's biographer, comments on a characteristic technique in the autobiography that this incident dramatizes in a self-mocking way. Boyd says that Nabokov "always considered that to recognize a future recollection at the moment it happened, to know with certainty that this particular moment would later be recalled, was somehow to cheat the tyranny of time" (4). By embedding in the autobiographical narrative the anticipation of a future aesthetic transformation, Nabokov envisions an unfolding pattern in the life (which he says is the purpose of autobiography). This dynamic establishes Nabokov as a man who lives as if his life were continually turning into art. Put another way, he lives as if he were always about to become an autobiographer, for his imagination is both proleptic and reconstitutive, anticipating and refashioning.

How to dramatize continuity within change, a condition that perhaps is this exile's solace? I think the most powerful element (an image, an act, a trope) in *Speak, Memory* that releases Nabokov from any single moment frozen in time, that asserts familial bonds across space and time, and that connects this temporal flux and metamorphosis with art and imagination is the butterfly hunt.

I have mentioned that one edition of the autobiography was to have been titled *Speak, Mnemosyne*, and it is instructive to note that *Parnassius mnemosyner* is the name of a species of butterfly Nabokov chased as a boy at the family's country estate. The appropriateness of a butterfly named for both art and memory is readily apparent. A butterfly first appears in the foreword, in a passage about the general metamorphosis of objects. That butterfly is a hawkmoth, which Nabokov discovered when he was eight at a spot where his father had found a peacock butterfly twenty-five years earlier; at another place in the autobiography he reports his grandfather having collected a similar moth years earlier. Nabokov has virtually hidden the references in his text, composing a temporal puzzle for us to decipher, one that imitates his gradual discovery of continuities—real or imagined—within the generations of his family. By making such connections Nabokov attempts to transcend the disintegrating effects of time. Later he imagines a swallowtail "soaring eastward, over timber and tundra, to Vologda, Viatka and Perm, and beyond the gaunt Ural range to Yakutsk . . . where it lost a tail, to the fair Island of St. Lawrence, and across Alaska to Dawson, and southward along the Rocky Mountains—to be finally overtaken and captured, after a forty-year race, on an immigrant dandelion under an endemic aspen near Boulder" (*Speak, Memory* 120). The image of the swallowtail, oroboral emblem for timelessness, fits with these cycles of discovery and capture; the memory of the past is evoked in the later chase and netting, but completed only in the act of writing, which fantasizes the time-shattering, space-encompassing quest. Butterfly collecting is linked to memory in that the imaginary pursuit violates linear time and substitutes a continuity forged solely in the mind. As Nabokov realizes the significance of an event in a future that seems already to have been imagined, it becomes more important than the actual objects, persons, or events he recalls.[4]

The butterfly is like time—fragile, elusive, and part of a cycle of meta-morphosis. And chasing and capturing the butterfly is like the autobiogra-pher's attempt to recover and pin down the past, which always turns into something barely recognizable, leaving him with the option of making fic-tions. Such fictions constitute a "countermetamorphosis," or transforming invention. Writing, to put one more turn on this, is like the butterfly itself: just as the natural butterfly, when placed in a case, becomes a work of art, so the autobiography is camouflaged, a work of artifice. No wonder Nabokov impels us to shift our interest from the protagonist of the past to the autobiographer of the present.

Nabokov's aestheticism appears to compensate for privation. Nabokov may dream of his childhood or for the locales of that time—say, the parks before nature and history effaced them—but what he inherits, "an exquisite simulacrum—the beauty of intangible property . . . proved a splendid train-ing for the endurance of later losses" (40). The simulacrum becomes the autobiography itself, the intangible artifact that purports to replace what has faded. The artful play with memory emblematizes the radical transformation of his loss.

I don't want to downplay the sense of sorrow throughout *Speak, Memory*. It is paradoxically a text both redemptive and elegiac. Autobiography by nature can hardly be anything but elegiac. Michael Wood, in a fine study, argues that Nabokov is caught between desiring timelessness and acknowledging the harsh effects of time. "Pattern is a redemption of loss, and perhaps the only redemption of loss there is. . . . But . . . that loss is irredeemable, that loss goes on and on" (*The Magician's Doubts* 94). The losses in *Speak, Memory* quickly mount up: his early love cannot be regained, the parks of his childhood home disintegrate, his father is assassinated, war obliterates a generation, his country is ransacked. And yet while Nabokov does not shy from personally tragic experience, he aestheticizes it so that the recall even of trauma may be enjoyed as a private joke, an artful arrangement, or evidence of the author's guile.

Take the death of Nabokov's father, a liberal politician assassinated by

Russian fascists in Berlin in 1922 while the family was in St. Petersburg. There is no conventional screening of this memory, no ordinary refusal to come to terms with the shock of the event. Nabokov does not emphasize the political meaning of the murder, nor even say what it meant for him. Instead, the narrator focuses on the way retrospection can endow memories with a premonitory sense, not to suggest fatalism or prophetic instinct but to show how the writer makes connections across time and sees patterns in the life and the text. As Nabokov announces, "The following of . . . thematic designs through one's life should be . . . the true purpose of autobiography" (*Speak, Memory* 27). He is following the designs in his life by creating or imposing them in his text. The past, even in this terrible instance of a child's grief, serves what we might call a hedonism of recall. Nabokov renders trauma as aesthetically compelling as his butterflies, not unlike the way he transforms the chloroformed specimens in their frame into icons of art.

Let me elaborate. Long before we ever learn directly of the father's death (half the book away), Nabokov gives us a distantly recalled scene in which, through the dining room window of his boyhood home, he glimpses the servants joyfully tossing his father's body in the air. He was "in his wind-rippled white summer suit . . . gloriously sprawling in midair, his limbs in a curiously casual attitude, his handsome imperturbable features turned to the sky." But as Nabokov transforms the figure from buoyant life to the realm of stony death, he transforms the father into a glorious artwork:

> There he would be, on his last and loftiest flight, reclining, as if for good, against the cobalt blue of the summer noon, like one of those paradisiac personages who comfortably soar, with such a wealth of folds in their garments, on the vaulted ceiling of a church while below, one by one, the wax tapers in mortal hands light up to make a swarm of minute flames in the midst of incense, and the priest chants of eternal repose, and funeral lilies conceal the face of whoever lies there, among the swimming lights, in the open coffin. (31–32)

The father is both the soaring sculpted figure and the person in his coffin, which seems to allude to an effigy in repose sculpted on a cathedral tomb. "Conceal" is the crucial word in the passage. Nabokov has concealed the father's body from the cathedral funeral, just as later he will dimly allude to the assassination, telling us only that while reading a Blok poem to his mother, the telephone rang. There is no explanation of what the phone message contained, and we must sift through the text to discover hints and clues as to whether it brought news of the killing. The representation of the actual death is deferred to late in the text, where it becomes part of an artful pattern, like the excessively intricate patterns on butterfly wings that Nabokov ascribes not to camouflage but to artistic enchantment, deception, and exuberance. Nabokov finds pleasure in the patterning of the past regardless of the disturbing content; he takes special delight in imagining how the concealed and puzzling pattern will gradually be discovered by both writer and reader. The premonition of the murder becomes, in the process of retrospective memorializing, a kind of narrative gratification. The pattern is more than a sheer pleasure-giving device; it may be a form of redemption for loss, indeed redemption, *through* form.

Nabokov acknowledges that there is trickery, even knavery, going on, for his self-consciously conceived fictions are covers for anguish. We can't quite tell if the refusal of directness is a defensive strategy, a way of softening the harsh impact of death invading a serene childhood. But for Nabokov, even pain accommodates the compulsion of art. The details surrounding the news of the father's death are vivid, but they are assimilated to a design by which loss is metamorphosed into beauty. The blending of defeat and narrative triumph is analogous to separation and imaginative return as foundational themes in *Speak, Memory*.

There is no getting around the fact of the father's death, especially given the hints that it is inexorably coming despite what the child wishes or what the adult seeks to postpone and then to refashion. But while Nabokov can't alter experience, he is masterful in revealing how he has gained new perspectives on the tragedy and survived it, so to speak, through writing. Throughout the autobiography, Nabokov freezes the past: "Everything is as it should be, nothing will ever change, nobody will ever die" (*Speak, Memory* 77). For Nabokov, autobiography is a form of wish fulfillment. He is at once resigned to sorrow and sanguine about his ability to nullify it. In this regard we might recall Foucault's apothegm: "One writes in order to become other than what one is" (182). Foucault implies that autobiography is the genre that allows one to become whatever one wishes.

Nabokov has an abundance of narrative strategies through which to transpose loss into another register. The principal strategy is to find connections among people or events, taking comfort that the world makes sense. Nabokov begins the autobiography, for example, by peering into the darkness before he was born and, horrified by that void (represented by a home movie made shortly before his birth that shows an empty and waiting baby carriage), establishing his existence via his awareness of continuity within the family. He ends the autobiography on the brink of World War II, as he, his wife, and their young child make their way to the ship that will take them to America—an act that asserts further

continuity and the sequence of generations via the child who will eclipse
Nabokov's own second darkness in death. As if to clinch the case, Nabokov
inserts a fanciful episode in which he imagines that a pottery shard that his
son discovers on a French beach replicates a similar discovery he himself
made years before, as well as a previous one made by his mother and a
still earlier one by his grandmother, "and so on until this assortment of
parts, if all had been preserved, might have been put together to make the
complete, the absolutely complete bowl, broken by some Italian child, God
knows where and when, and now mended by these rivets of bronze" (*Speak,
Memory* 308–09). Modernist fragmentation and randomness are banished
in Nabokov's autobiography. The bowl is, like Wallace Stevens's jar, the
aesthetic object that becomes the autobiographical text. By imagining a
recurrent or patterned action, Nabokov conjoins the past before his birth
to the future his son will enjoy, riveting together the fractures of time
through the imagined connections.

But these patterns also imply that a certain fatality orders his life. Wood
raises an important issue when he says of those patterns, "The purpose
behind the purpose of autobiography, perhaps, is to tell us what the tracing
of designs can't do for us" (*The Magician's Doubts* 96). Still, these patterns do
insist on the power of the writer's imagination, and to round on this issue
once more, Nabokov appears to dwell on loss and discontinuity exactly
in order to overcome them. This lingering naturally dictates that he will
be obsessed with loss and feel a sweet pain in discontinuity, making these
deprivations less of a burden than a challenge. He cultivates privation in
order to overcome it, just as he envisions the "operations of the creative
mind" in an author who sets up for himself "certain nightmare obstacles
that he surmounts, with the zest of a deity building a live world from the
most unlikely ingredients" (*Speak, Memory* 290–91). Nabokov celebrates
a performative will, which can deflect sorrow with elegant and sensuous
appeal.

An amusing incident captures the struggle Nabokov experiences in
aligning life and art. When he remembers his boyhood drawing teacher, he
thinks of him as an elderly gentleman; only later does he realize that the
teacher married about the time Nabokov himself did, and that the teacher
was just a few years older than his pupil. "When I learned these later
developments, I experienced a queer shock; it was as if life had impinged
upon my creative rights by wriggling on beyond the subjective limits so
elegantly and economically set by childhood memories that I thought I
had signed and sealed" (*Speak, Memory* 93). Memory plays queer tricks,
which makes it useful for the transformations he wishes to effect upon

time, history, and relations. But these things will not sit still; life is unruly, and so it must be (narratively) tamed. Of course he knows it will not be, and this is exactly what makes it rife for fictionalizing. We are urged to comply with the narrator's belief that his past might take a certain desired shape, but we see exactly how he forces it to come out in a certain way. What Paul Jay writes of Proust applies equally to Nabokov: memory is not "the source of insight and renewal but . . . the point of departure leading toward . . . creation in the artist's own imagination" (148). Memory, in short, is (an) art.

While Nabokov's childhood memories come effortlessly, recollections of adolescence are more tenuous, since from adolescence on, self-consciousness takes over and memory cannot be distinguished from arrangement. As an adolescent, Nabokov responds to his mother's "retrospective fervor," a family trait that "provided a splendid training for the endurance of later losses" (*Speak, Memory* 40). Inheriting this trait not only allows Nabokov to get back to (a version of) his past, but allies him with the past in the figure of the mother. The mother, like practically everyone in the autobiography, counts because of her symbolic weight, which is defined by the symbols the narrator attaches to her. In a passage that parallels the one about joining the chips of majolica into a composite bowl, Nabokov describes his mother's valise. Purchased for her wedding trip in 1897, the valise held jewels when the family fled St. Petersburg in 1917, transported crystal and silver to London, and traveled with Nabokov "from Prague to Paris . . . to New York and through the mirrors of more than two hundred motel rooms . . . in forty-six states" (*Speak, Memory* 143). The valise resembles a prop in the famous motel journeys from *Lolita*. Is it a real item in the inventory of Nabokov's possessions or a fabulous piece of fiction? It is hard to say; we can note that the traveling bag is like not only the bowl but the peripatetic butterfly, or like an emblem of memory itself—an emblem that cannot be contained by truth but is invoked to create an image of the past as he wishes it to be. Yet at the same time Nabokov makes us see the faded, battered pigskin case, the emblem of sad truths as well as magical imaginings.

Speak, Memory is thus a meditation on writing as much as the story of a life. The title reminds us that the subject of the autobiography is speaking as much as it is remembering. ("Speaking" should be understood as tantamount to writing, not mere verbalizing.) In fact, Nabokov downplays the memories in favor of the *process* of remembering: in *Strong Opinions* he claims that "I am an ardent memorist with a rotten memory" (140). No wonder the act of writing always reveals Nabokov's animus against linear time and unmediated recall.

Several significant images represent Nabokov's stance toward writing: a giant fake pencil that symbolizes the nonrealistic nature of his art; a pen holder evoking memories that are always provisional (when it shows up in a 1929 photograph of Nabokov at his writing desk, the pen holder represents his teasing alternation between realism and play); and the ship taking the family to America, "the ungenuinely gigantic, the unrealistically real prototype" of the boats his child played with in his bath. Each recall of the past, by emphasizing the process by which the recall comes about, suggests that Nabokov views writing as the interplay between the material and the imaginative, a process that derives from a very early impulse to turn his life into narrative and to be self-conscious about making meaning. Such transformations of experience, which correspond in narrative terms to the biological metamorphoses resulting in the butterflies, constitute Nabokov's emergence as the self-conscious narrator of the process of memory.

Even while he lives his life, he seems to be making up a story about it, the inner or "textual" world always embedded in the outer or lived one. It is this emphasis that renders Nabokov a kind of meta-autobiographer, one who writes more about the process of writing and reading (or interpreting) than about "a life" back then and out there. Just as the memories tell us how Nabokov's imagination works, so everything in the text functions like a gestalt-interpreted dream, which is to say everything becomes a representation of the boy and, as we can see in the title under which the book first appeared in America, *Conclusive Evidence*, of his having existed.

How does this process relate to exile? *Speak, Memory* is a form of homecoming for Nabokov, the devoted memorist with a bad memory. As an act of love dedicated to Vera and as a homage to his son Dmitri, who ends the text and sends us back to the child Vladimir who begins it, the autobiography repairs exile in the only way Nabokov knows—through language. In the foreword, he summarizes the complex history of the text, calling the present version a "re-Englishing of a Russian re-version of what had been an English re-telling of Russian memories" (*Speak, Memory* 12). Such a "multiple metamorphosis" implies that only on distant American shores can he finally authorize his past. The linguistic turns show us how he continually approaches and departs from his home(land) until he can see it only with the perspective of distance and time. In the process he is changed like the Russian butterfly who finally alights in the Rockies to be caught and turned into art. Nabokov's muse cannot stay put any more than he can, for wandering, or at least a form of diaspora, is the necessary condition for artful memory. Just as Nabokov appears, in a childhood photograph included in the book, dressed in a sailor suit, so the little Dmitri ends the book gazing at a gigantic ship. "What the Sailor has lost can be found" in the puzzle that is the text—a text that, like Nabokovian consciousness, only the imagination can concoct, unravel, and reveal.

ONE OF THE PLEASURES of reading and teaching certain autobiographical texts is the way their appeal changes at different stages of my life. More than any other autobiography I know, *Speak, Memory* provokes my own, Nabokov's voice quickening mine to ever shifting responses and stirring me in ways I couldn't have imagined when I was first making myself and my students familiar with the work's complexities. When I began to teach *Speak, Memory*, it was mainly to demonstrate how the self is constructed through the language and the playfulness of art and to argue that Nabokov's resistance to mimesis lay at the heart of any reasonable theory of the genre. I continue to teach *Speak, Memory* that way, for it remains an engaging text with which to make the theoretical point. But as I returned to the book over the years, other issues moved to the fore, issues that were less matters for classroom discussion than for openings to more personal rumination. It is difficult for me not to read autobiography autobiographically, and *Speak, Memory* is richly enticing in that way. However preoccupied he is with style, artifice, and mandarin embellishment, Nabokov's insistence on the workings of memory, even a canny and inventive one, prompts my own process of remembrance and makes it impossible for me to remain a detached reader.

The more I read the work the more I focus on the child who emerges at its conclusion and becomes the sign of continuity and the defeat of time. In this respect *Speak, Memory* causes me to reflect on a haunting emptiness. As I grow older I am burdened by the absence of children in my life, and I have come to connect this impoverishment with a sense of exile. Perhaps "exile" is too portentous a term; there was certainly nothing forced about my abandoning the East Coast at twenty-five to settle in Oregon. I left because I got a good teaching position, and it was with a spirit of adventure, not regret or even nostalgia, that I journeyed across the country with a crammed station wagon and a new wife. This was no expulsion from Eden; westering voyages are traditionally toward, not away from, paradise, and who ever regarded New Jersey as Edenic, Garden State though it may be? Arriving in Portland in the early 1960s, I felt it was a cultural wasteland, but I was too immersed in a new job and a new marriage to brood on that deficiency. I joked that Portland's great lack was its absence of irony, and as long as I amused myself about its vacuities and my deprivations, I got by. Oregon's fabled landscape was almost compensation enough.

But something more important did get left behind: not just my widowed mother, two aunts, an uncle, and a few cousins—the relatively small family I could lay claim to—but something of which I was scarcely aware at the time: call it a sense of family, family as an idea and a way of life. Maybe I romanticize family, given that there is now so little of mine remaining (I'm down to a few cousins). Indeed, when I was growing up I was curiously unaware of family because, despite my having felt loved as a child, we lacked anything like a cohesive family bond, say "a Porter way of doing things." Our small immediate family (I was an only child) did splendid things together, but I had little consciousness of ourselves *as a family*, even of some idea of "just the three of us." So from what do I feel exiled? Less from a specific way of life than from a situation where family ought to have seemed natural and inevitable. As my family shrank, I did not seek to replenish it with one of my own; I never consciously thought in such terms, nor did I feel either urgency or deficiency. And finally it was not to be. Only now, with the realization that I will not have children, do I connect that void with a peculiar version of exile—from the very idea of family. The word "family" seems like a vague abstraction, at best a memory trace.

My reading of *Speak, Memory* came increasingly to center on the work's homage to the concept of generations, especially in its commemoration of Nabokov's absent father, of the mother gifted with "retrospective fervor," and of the son Dmitri, now his father's translator. Each rereading of the work affected me with what Nabokov calls a "stab of wonder"—when something perceived one way suddenly metamorphoses into a new thing. Gradually, *Speak, Memory* became new for me: a crucible of loss and a reminder of my exile from "the natural." This understanding has little to do with any dying out of my line and name, but rather with a dawning realization that not having children plays havoc with one's sense of time and therefore of one's very self.

Without children I've lost an awareness that aging is normal and has its place in the order of things. When parents die, the child becomes starkly aware that there are no further generational barriers between him and mortality. Metronomic inevitability takes over, and the countdown begins. But without children at the other end, the process of aging seems even more unnatural and unfair than usual, for the law of succession, however painful it may be, at least makes a kind of natural rhythmic sense. For all the certainty of displacement, children at least place you in time and history, help prevent the illusion that you have stood still. I thought that the death of my parents would make me aware of history and time and passing, but those deaths didn't do the work. I look at friends with grandchildren and wonder how those friends suddenly got to be so old. I see a slightly younger colleague with a twenty-year-old son and cannot imagine that she has been a mother so long; after all, I say to myself, she is only fifty-five.

Nabokov narrates a family plot. Who will put me in the family plot? Who, if I were to lament in the ways of the Fathers, will be my Kaddish? Given my implacable secularism, this is not really a concern; I am more troubled by a gap in the bedrock experience of a life than by Jewish eschatology. Not books written nor plays directed, nothing—for all the culture's metaphors of creativity as offspring—serves as children do to clarify who we are. Without them, far more even than with a partner or spouse, this much at least is lost: understanding that someone who is deeply a part of your life is ultimately separate from you.

How do I know this? Intimations only, during a period of four years when I was down on my knees with teddy bears and toy tea sets, living with and helping to rear the daughter of a woman friend. I know this from the continual thrill—ordinary and astonishing—of watching each day bring to that child unexpected new skills and awarenesses: one day at four years old answering the telephone with the tact of a receptionist, another day speaking with adverbs, yet another day ordering from a Thai menu. Now, without this child in my life, it is not clear to me what exactly I mourn, but I suspect it is something like a capacity for love that was drawn from within me and which cannot be expressed in another relation in quite the same way. No other experience in my adult life has made me both think *like* a child and learn *from* a child.

But there are other, even contrary, realizations. One of my close friends has six grown children from two joined families. The kids regularly check in with their parents, and it's not uncommon for each of them to return home several times a year, the six children stringing their overlapping visits throughout an intensely crowded month. I can scarcely imagine a house of such comings and goings, so many voices. Being childless has made my house a place of quietude, and there are days when my voice is the only one heard. A shift of mere centimeters in the placement of a chair or a sudden unfamiliar noise registers with seismic magnitude. The quiet has allowed me—forced me at times—to listen to inner thoughts that the world often drowns out. And as I get older, spending more time alone seems less threatening, less a sign of deprivation than when I was younger. Still, the opportunity to uncover feelings in solitude is sometimes

offset by the worry that alone in the quiet my ego may be empty. I
understand Doris Grumbach's fears in *Fifty Days of Solitude*, her account of
voluntary isolation: "Searching for the self when I was entirely alone was
hazardous. . . . When I went looking, I was playing a desperate game of
hide-and-seek, fearful of what I might find, most afraid that I would find
nothing" (18)

To combat this suspicion, like many people who live alone, I converse
with myself. I've discovered that I do some of my best thinking when I talk
aloud even if, Beckett-like, I'm the only listener. (I seem to use the first
person for introspection, the second person for inspiration and rebuke.)
An eavesdropper might think I was one of those bedlamites who haunt
Manhattan streets, vehemently chattering to themselves.

When I'm alone I become an oral autobiographer, committed to nostalgia and to spelunking in those caverns of the past that St. Augustine images
as the haunts of memory. While I hardly live in my past, I am probably
more comfortable with it than with the future. I am not a natural planner,
in the way that some people envision a future and then attempt to bring it
into being. When a therapist once asked me to imagine my life five years
hence, I was paralyzed. But when she asked me to make a time line of
things that had happened to me over the previous twenty years, the past
rushed into my brain, and I was able to recall it, year by year, with startling
precision. When I listen to my internal voices, they often speak of the past;
I am a collector of my selves, a reflector on my reflections. Children make
this difficult: they put a salutary lid on free-floating narcissism. Were I to
have had children, would I be less self-absorbed with my past? Perhaps, to
speak oxymoronically, I'd be more a memorist of the present.

It may be that our self in the past is the self we really believe in, especially
as we grow older. Just as the elderly have more vivid memories of their
distant past than their near past, it is possible that our earlier self has
a credible power that overwhelms all else, which is why we return to it
so eagerly. What makes me homesick, and what is it I hold on to in my
memory? Saturday afternoons at the Elmora Theater with the weekly serial,
the cartoons, the news, the coming attractions, the double feature—all of
which never seemed to tire me and my friends. Stickball in the street,
when we regarded a passing car like the tank of an invading army. Selling
door-to-door the plywood signs with reflecting house numbers I made,
more fascinated by furtive glimpses into each house than with sales levels.
Ebbetts Field with my father to see Jackie Robinson and the Dodgers, and
the evening at Toots Shor's restaurant storming into the men's room to
get Branch Rickey's autograph. (Just as the Great Mahatma lumbered out

of the stall, I thrust my scorecard at him as he pulled up his pants, and inquired, "Mr. Rickey I presume?") My first soulful kiss with the inaptly named Faith, down in the little grassy hollow beneath the peach tree in our family's backyard one smoky summer's eve when I was thirteen.

For all Nabokov's playfulness and artifice, his vaunted unreliability, and his emphasis on self-consciousness, *Speak, Memory* honors family and generations, the images of metamorphosis always connected to the cycles of family life. For me the poignance of his autobiography arises from the culmination of Nabokovian experience in the child, generating a story not just of origins but of resumptions. Perhaps my interest in autobiography grows from the need to witness that process at work and to serve as my own *aide-memoire* by revisiting childhood, the academic subject allowing me to grasp and then to surrender my own past. If so, then, for one who came to maturity playing Odysseus, autobiography has all along been my Telemachus.

AUTOBIOGRAPHY AS DEFENSE

3.
Filling Up the Silent Vacancy
Edward Gibbon's *Autobiography*

Modern theory has resolutely insisted that the self in autobiographical texts is both subject and object, the "I" who speaks and the "I" spoken about.[1] That congruence does not mean that the one who utters the discourse and the one who is the object of that discourse are necessarily identical. Though both conventionally go by the same name and by the same first-person pronoun, the narrator and the one narrated may be quite different from one another. Not infrequently the autobiographical narrative expresses a difference in sophistication and understanding between the two versions of "I." Frequently autobiographies open an ironic distance between the two— a distance rooted in differences in age and discrepancies of accumulated experience, wisdom, and self-understanding. As Paul John Eakin notes, paradoxically the "simultaneous double reference as speaker and subject of its speech both makes possible and subverts" the common identity of · author and object of discourse (*Touching the World* 64).

Edward Gibbon's *Autobiography* movingly dramatizes this procedure. From the outset the narrator is congruent with the depicted figure, both of them exhibiting self-assurance and ease in the world. What the younger Gibbon attempted by way of image-building and a focused career, and what the autobiographer writing about his early life attempts by way of defense for an existence he views as exemplary in its rational planning, are analogous. But the autobiographer cannot sustain such congruence. Despite its elegance and rhetorical refinement, Gibbon's *Autobiography* begins to manifest a destabilizing shift from satisfaction to regret, and the narrator's vision becomes ever less sanguine as Gibbon enumerates the accumulated losses suffered and felt by the older self.

What interests me about Gibbon's autobiography and those of the other writers I discuss in this section—Franklin, Somerset Maugham, and Edwin Muir—is their investment in strategies of rhetorical defense. Gibbon attempts to stand against revelations he ultimately cannot resist, but the narrator of the *Autobiography* gradually realizes that the self he initially regards as predictable and consistent is subject to surprising changes and vulnerable to loss. Order, harmony, and rationality prove difficult to sustain, and they entail the sacrifice of even more important gratifications. Gibbon defends against a range of unsettling discoveries that question the elegance, confidence, and poise on which the narrator has so depended, and the autobiography portrays a mind struggling to accommodate unforeseen realities even as it prides itself on having resisted them for so long.

I will read Gibbon's text in a way that emphasizes what Eakin describes as a "shift from a documentary view of autobiography as a record of referential fact to a performative view of autobiography centered on the act of composition" (*Touching the World* 143). In borrowing these terms, I mean to indicate that Gibbon moves from a focus on the externals of his life—believing initially that they confirm agency and control—to a more private focus as his confidence in his power to shape experience erodes. Gibbon's progressive self-understanding *in the text* reminds us that autobiographers establish the self in writing as much as they ground the self in history. Gibbon struggles to demonstrate his ability to make the life conform to his desire. Tracking his shift from confidence to doubt allows us to see the *Autobiography* as a text dramatizing the gradual process of self-discovery—more so than has previously been acknowledged.[2]

Gibbon begins his work convinced that he can locate the core of meaning in his life and that it has been predictable from the start. His famous sense of self-assurance in the opening pages, where the phrases "personal merit," "gift of nature," and "glorious achievement" sound the notes of personal satisfaction, corresponds to his belief that the life can be known in retrospect because its direction, even its achievements, appear to have been inevitable. In an earlier memoir, Gibbon implies that the self is fixed and fully formed, needing only to be uncovered: "Such as I am . . . I owe my creation to Lausanne; it was in that school that the statue was discovered in the block of marble" (*Autobiographies* 152). The Michelangelesque figure expresses the notion that there *is* a predetermined, essential self to be revealed. But as the work unfolds, Gibbon's contentment about his accomplishments begins to diminish, and the autobiography becomes something other than a celebration of the life. Step by step, Gibbon uncovers new awarenesses and an unexpected sense of himself, as he learns to accommodate more unknowns and complexities than he had imagined. The initial note is that of a confident self, as Gibbon organizes his life around his vocation as historian; here we find his characteristic themes of restraint, order, and prudence, qualities that are self-congratulatory if not compensatory. He initially displays a surface of ostensible calm, even serenity, where his famous ironies suggest a good-natured adjustment to the harsher aspects of existence. But as the autobiography proceeds, he gradually establishes a countertendency that is more private than public, more skeptical than optimistic, even melancholy if not thoroughly elegiac.[3]

The further he explores, the more complicated and surprising Gibbon becomes to himself. The question his work raises is whether the contingencies that he invokes signal merely annoying interruptions in his progressive march to success or a profound disruption of self-image. It is hard to say, for Gibbon's ironies can be so protective as to defend against admitting uncertainties. In tracking these shifts in the *Autobiography*, I will explore the way he constructs a favorable view of himself to guard against acknowledging the disturbing complexities.

Gibbon's text suggests that the very search for a design with which to order his life has been its paramount fact. The form he imposes on his past may not be the exact one that determined and guided him, but that he believes it to have been so, or that he tries to convince the reader it was so, is crucial. Gibbon became an autobiographer for the same reason he became an historian—to see a pattern in what might appear to be a welter of haphazard or contradictory experiences. If the life appears predictable and inevitable, it is largely because Gibbon benefits from such a vision, creating an image of restraint and coherence as he marshals his life toward a predetermined conclusion and shapes it into a form granting mastery over experience.[4]

Providing a model of rational selfhood demands vigilance, and the narrator molds himself to conform to the values he and his society celebrate. Numerous passages in the *Autobiography*, where Gibbon yearns for "the best company" of men and manners befitting a civilized order, bear out this judgment. In an early draft, Gibbon had written of his intent to review "the events of a private and literary life," but he struck out "events" and substituted "simple transactions": his life is a negotiation with society, where he accepts its demands for order and in turn makes himself into the epitome of poise and rationality. Gibbon claims he had to build his career prudently, exercising self-control and a steady sense of direction, lest he fall into indolence or chaos.

Gibbon's description of his forced exile in Switzerland following his conversion to Catholicism and his withdrawal from Oxford is an instance of such self-mastery. He undergoes a rigid indoctrination into Protestantism, and not only reconverts but sets himself on a disciplined course of historical study. "My religious error fixed me at Lausanne, in a state of banishment and disgrace. The rigid course of discipline and abstinence to which I was condemned invigorated the constitution of my mind and body." (*Autobiography* 110). Gibbon's rhetoric suggests that he can exercise his mind within a rational discipline to achieve a life of deliberation. Catherine N. Parke argues that Gibbon's characteristic effort in the *Autobiography* is to turn adversity into gain. She cites the way Gibbon transforms his exile at Lausanne into the basis for a "second education," dedicating his life to "perpetual exile" (the terms are Gibbon's own) and gaining a new identity in the freedom from normal constraints. It may not be accidental that when he wrote the *Autobiography*, Gibbon was living in Lausanne, the place of an earlier humiliation that he had overcome. Gibbon returns to the site of exile to compose the autobiography that he hopes will celebrate the life he wished to have.

Building a self equal to the task of writing *The Decline and Fall* was a project demanding emotional restraint. It has often been remarked that Gibbon's abandonment of his fiancée, Suzanne Curchod, was a concession to his father, but Gibbon comes to believe, or at least wants us to believe, that the decision was nonetheless a fortuitous one, as if marriage would have interrupted his freedom and drive to success. One of the uses of autobiography for Gibbon is the depiction of this self-preparation and its rejection of extraneous involvements. Gibbon's portrayal of his character and career involves an ironic perspective that clarifies his sense of purpose. When he reports falling in love with Suzanne and falling to the Catholic Church, he uses a similar tone of comic bluntness: "I saw and loved"; "I read; I applauded; I believed" (*Autobiography* 109, 84). He parodies Caesar to demonstrate his awareness of the young man's pretensions to Classical authority, and also to mock the young man's rapidity and lack of control, his near automatic actions. Such ironic self-regard reveals a distinction in awareness between the precipitous youth and the knowing, but not totally unsympathetic, autobiographer. Gibbon condemns the imprudent enthusiasm of this youthful haste and, in the account of his brief love affair with Suzanne Curchod, denounces with self-ridicule what he sees as unrestrained enthusiasm.[5]

Gibbon begins his account of "the delicate subject of my early love" by denying two connotations of the word "love": "the grosser appetite" and "the polite attention of the gallantry . . . which has originated in the spirit of chivalry and is interwoven with the texture of French manners" (*Autobiography* 108). And yet a confidante of Suzanne Curchod writes that Gibbon went about the fields near Lausanne like a quixotic madman, demanding that some peasants agree on point of death that Mlle Curchod was the most beautiful lady on earth (Low, *Edward Gibbon* 77). In his first letter to Suzanne, Gibbon lays his soul at her feet, counts the seconds of his exile from her, and portrays himself as an oriental prince whisked from his throne to a dungeon; in later correspondence with her, Gibbon repeatedly expresses self-pity and contemplates suicide. But if the younger Gibbon exhibits passion even in abandoning the affair, the older man looking back has a more complex attitude. He repeats some of his earlier passivity ("I yielded to my fate"; "I obeyed as a son"), but now takes a more witty tack: "My cure was accelerated by a faithful report of the tranquility and cheerfulness of the lady herself." (*Autobiography* 109). Gibbon had been blamed for betraying Suzanne, and now he ironically mocks himself to show us that *he*, not she, suffered by his change of heart. Thus Gibbon answers the accusations of his critics by citing the advantage Suzanne gained by her new alliance with the prosperous Jacques Necker, director of finance under Louis XVI. The gentle self-ridicule disarms Gibbon's detractors by displaying his pleasure at her obvious success.

His concealment of the disruptive aspects of the affair could be viewed as simple propriety, the same kind embodied in the notorious phrase, "I sighed as a lover; I obeyed as a son" (*Autobiography* 109), where the private lover yields to the publicly acceptable form. In this case the Ciceronian balance demonstrates an ironic self-assertion that shows his understanding of all he has had to resist, the elegance of his diction portraying a man aware of what must be concealed or overcome. His letters to Suzanne show an indecisive boy unable to cope with the claims of both love and filial obedience, and the forebodings about his father's dismay reveal Gibbon's uncertainties, which upset his cherished equilibrium. But in the autobiography the writer achieves an equipoise through the self-irony, preserving both Suzanne's esteem and his own freedom.

Gibbon's disdain for "enthusiasm" unchecked by reflection establishes an important pattern in the *Autobiography* of powerful emotions calmed into order and tranquility, thus imposing a design upon experiences that otherwise appear uncontrollable. He suppresses his initial enthusiasm about Suzanne Curchod, as "love subsided in friendship and esteem" (*Autobiography* 109). Later he reports that "the love of study, a *passion* which derives fresh vigor from enjoyment, supplies each day, each hour, with a perpetual source of . . . rational pleasure" (*Autobiography* 204).[6] In describing his library, Gibbon jests, "My seraglio was ample, my choice was free, my appetite was keen" (*Autobiography* 201). The reference to his abortive love affair is obvious: the sublimation of his feelings turns Gibbon's library into a room of love where appetite may be satisfied with books. And in a letter to his friend Georges Deyverdun he translates sexuality into bibliophilia: "J'ai mille courtesanes rangées autour de moi / Ma retraite est mon Louvre, et j'y commande en roi."

Gibbon looks back on his life with pride, asserting that every choice and act was deliberately undertaken to contribute to his work as historian. Nevertheless, the loss of his fiancée must have been devastating, however much his witty narration seeks to minimize the emotional impact. Gibbon's preoccupation as historian with catastrophe, collapse, and decay may well have a grounding in his early personal loss.

To understand why Gibbon is compelled to justify order and control, we must examine several images of human nature that occur throughout the *Autobiography*. Gibbon views the world as filled with barbarism, ignorance, and poverty; all statistics affirm a gloomy view of human existence. At first, however, he believes his life counters such misery; amid the inevitability of decaying mental and physical faculties, debt, discomfort, and anonymity, he poses the fact of his success. But he also acknowledges how much material is impervious to control. As a counterpoint to self-congratulation, Gibbon sounds a refrain of fearful precariousness. His grandfather was a director of the South Sea company, "but his fortune was overwhelmed in the shipwreck of the year 1720 and the labors of thirty years were blasted in a single day" (*Autobiography* 38). Even stoicism cannot contain his anxiety before the workings of chance: "As a philosopher I *should* mention without a sigh the irreparable loss of above ninety-six thousand pounds, of which in a single moment . . . I have been ultimately deprived" (*Autobiography* 41). His father's fortunes were continually on the decline, and only his stepmother's lack of heirs warmed Gibbon to her. Gibbon's precarious health is a constant theme, and he is haunted by the death of friends as well as by the fear of his own dwindling powers. Johnson's remarks in *Idler* No. 73 must have forcefully struck Gibbon: "Of riches, as of everything else, *the hope is more than the enjoyment* . . . no sooner do we sit down to enjoy our acquisitions than we find them insufficient to fill up the vacuities of life." Gibbon seizes the image of "filling up" life's emptiness in his own way. At the outset he explains a function of the mature mind: "Our imagination is always active to enlarge the narrow circle in which nature has confined us. Fifty or an hundred years may be allotted to an individual; but we stretch forward beyond death with such hopes as religion and philosophy will suggest, and we fill up the silent vacancy that precedes our birth by associating ourselves to the authors of our existence" (*Autobiography* 27–28).

Life is a void waiting to be filled, a defense against emptiness, deprivation, or disorder; and the circle image expresses Gibbon's desire to encompass as much time and space in his life as possible. If he can devour enough information and fill up enough pages ("Scribble, scribble, another fat book, eh, Mr. Gibbon?") the fears will not loom too large, or he may not have to confront them too closely. Much of the autobiography insists that his mind "has expanded to its proper form and dimensions" (*Autobiography* 98), the preoccupation with career and achievement weighing against his fears that he cannot control all the factors in the game.

At times he acknowledges that success has depended upon a happy chain of circumstances: "My lot might have been that of a slave, a savage, or a peasant; nor can I reflect without pleasure on the bounty of nature, which cast my birth in a free and civilized country, in an age of science and philosophy, in a family of honorable rank and decently endowed with the gifts of fortune" (*Autobiography* 49). He might have ended otherwise had he been much richer or poorer: "Yet I may believe, and even assert, that in circumstances more indigent or more wealthy I should never have accomplished the task, or acquired the fame, of an historian, that my spirit would have been broken by poverty and contempt, and that my industry might have been relaxed in the labor and luxury of superfluous fortune" (*Autobiography* 171). This common eighteenth-century view of the happiness of the middle state of mankind, avoiding both unwanted disruptions or luxurious indulgences, finds its psychological analogue in Gibbon's claim for rationality and finds its rhetorical analogue in the ironic, balanced narrative. This view also marks Gibbon's sense of human limits, allied with a comic view of his earlier self and of human limitations. For the eighteenth century, the poet is not a heroic will withstanding poverty and neglect, but a man whom too much suffering will disable and whom too much ease will distract. Gibbon is one who plans well, flatters himself with the belief that he has guided all, and yet steps back with sufficient detachment to see that he has had to take his chances. He makes an order, though he never claims an abundance of moral heroism for himself. There is control, but he does not give it excessive weight because he is so aware of contingencies.

A dramatic instance of Gibbon's acknowledgement of good fortune occurs in the reaction to his father's death:

The tears of a son are seldom lasting. I submitted to the order of nature, and my grief was soothed by the conscious satisfaction that I had discharged all the duties of filial piety. Few perhaps are the children who, after the expiration of some months or years, would sincerely rejoice in the resurrection of their parents, and it is a melancholy truth that my father's death, not unhappily for himself, was the only event that could save me from a hopeless life of obscurity and indigence.

As soon as I had paid the last solemn duties to my father, and obtained, from time and reason, a tolerable composure of mind I began to form the plan of an independent life most adapted to my circumstances and inclination. . . . My new situation was brightened by hope, nor could I refuse the advantages of a change which had never (I have scrutinized my conscience) which had never been the object of my secret wishes. (*Autobiography* 168–69)

Gibbon appears to be forthright in his admission of restraint, nearly presenting himself as a scoundrel. Only an insistence on his independence keeps him from viewing his father, whose financial irresponsible threatened to ruin the family, as a mere sacrifice to the son's vanity.[7] The speaker opens himself to charges of impiety, but Gibbon offers a providential explanation of his father's death, so that it becomes a necessary condition for his writing *The Decline and Fall*. Nevertheless, Gibbon cannot say outright that his father had to die for the historical work to be born; instead he cloaks his thoughts in detached generalizations. The categorical phrase "tears of a son are seldom lasting"; euphemistic terms such as the "order of nature" and the "duties of filial piety"; the dubious parenthetical assertion "not unhappily for *himself*"; the overprotesting of "I have scrutinized my conscience"; and the repeated phrase "which had never" all suggest Gibbon's antagonism toward his father. Again, however, the rhetoric disarms disturbing emotions; disquieting impulses must be repressed to create the illusion that emotional life operates without risk.

The passage might seem like Gibbon's attempt to convince himself that sustained grief is never expected of children, thus implying the concealment of other feelings, such as resentment toward the father for the Suzanne Curchod episode. There is a tension between two voices: one is impersonal and generalizing, asserting that grief can be dispelled by the knowledge that parents inevitably die, that time heals all, and that filial piety is discharged when we acknowledge that few children wish for the resurrection of their parents; the other is more honest, suggesting that despite all the denials, Gibbon genuinely resented his father's irresponsibility and the resulting constraint on his own freedom. This tension is resolved by the notion of providence, which allows the historical project to get under way. Gibbon thus mediates between unctuous abstraction and forbidden impulse by hypothesizing a rational order to events. His understanding of the combined workings of chance and will prevents him from having to erect the self into a moral absolute.

Martin Price, in his discussion of eighteenth-century orders, notes that they provide "the assurance of living in a world that makes sense, of living within a system that has a unity such as might have been imposed by an intelligence like our own" (*To the Palace of Wisdom* 1). This description precisely fits Gibbon's account, for he portrays his world as comprehensible and comfortable exactly because it has turned out as if his hand has guided everything. Gibbon's structuring of his life demonstrates what he calls "a rule of prudence," a concept implying an acceptance of limits, an ability to profit from accident, and an awareness of what must be done to complete a desired design. "Correct writing" produces "the appearance of art and study" and constructs an even more providential—indeed artful—order than the life itself had. This strategy acknowledges that things are not so tidy. Art is needed to shape the autobiography into a design giving the life an appearance of controlled purpose. Gibbon does not want to press the point: describing *The Decline and Fall*, he crosses out the adjective "laborious" and replaces it with "successful."[8] Yet the urge to impose order is compulsive; the very fact that he attempted six different versions of his memoirs undermines his claim that the writing was done "without labor."

Gibbon's fear that the irrational might overwhelm him emerges in a description of his childhood:

> From my birth I have enjoyed the right of Primogeniture; but I was succeeded by five bothers and one sister, all of whom were snatched away in their infancy. They died so young, and I was myself so young at the time of their deaths, that I could not then feel, nor can I now estimate, their loss, the importance of which could have been ascertained by future contingencies. The shares of fortune to which younger children are reduced by our English laws, would have been sufficient however to oppress my inheritance. (*Autobiographies* 28)

The elegant style disguises neither the self-congratulation at having beaten the odds to survive as his brothers did not, nor his fear of an uncertain financial future.

But there is even greater precariousness. In a remarkable paragraph, Gibbon writes with evident melancholy:

> The death of a newborn child before that of its parents may seem an unnatural, but it is strictly a probable, event, since of any given number that greater part are extinguished before their ninth year,

before they possess the faculties of mind or body. Without accusing
a profuse waste or imperfect workmanship of nature, I shall only
observe that this unfavourable chance was multiplied against my
infant existence. So feeble was my constitution, so precarious my life,
that in the baptism of my brothers my father's prudence successively
repeated my Christian name of Edward, that in case of the departure of
the eldest son, this patronymic appellation might be still perpetuated
in the family. (*Autobiography* 53)

The assertion at the end is patently false. Of his brothers only one, not
five, was named Edward.[9] Gibbon's desire to perpetuate his name and
immortality was stronger than the truth, and a fear of extinction was present
not only in the child but in the older man. Since his father continually
tyrannized him, Gibbon must have felt the need to mobilize his forces
against him: five Edwards arrayed against the father in a dramatic replication
of the self. Making a name for himself becomes making five *similar* names
for himself, a gesture to defeat sibling, father, and death.

Gibbon's vulnerability focuses on the death of a child before it possesses
any faculties of mind. "The first moment of animal life may be dated from
the first pulsation of the heart in the human foetus; but the nine months
which we pass in a dark and watery prison, and the first years after we have
seen the light and breathed the air of this world, must be subtracted from
the period of our rational existence" (*Autobiographies* 113). Whatever is not
rational is dark, even imprisoning. He deducts the fetal months and early
years from the sum of rational existence, as if they were too frightening to
contemplate. And so he builds a rational structure to offset the chaos of
childhood and the uncertainties of existence but, in so doing, ignores his
own "warm desires and long expectations" that do not answer directly to the
historian's task. Similarly, he builds a world in which his mind is master, but
recognizes at the end of the *Autobiography* that rationality cannot provide
the entirety of self-knowledge or happiness. Nor can the autobiography
sustain the illusion of a pattern that hedges against all uncertainties.

With the death of his great friend Deyverdun, an inescapable loneliness
comes upon Gibbon, who by this time has returned to Lausanne to
complete *The Decline and Fall*. He writes to Lord Sheffield: "Since the
loss of poor Deyverdun I am alone; and even in Paradise solitude is painful
to a social mind. When I was a dozen years younger, I scarce felt the weight
of a single existence amidst the crowds of London, of Parliament, of Clubs;
but it will press more heavily upon me in this tranquil land, in the *decline*
of life" (*The Decline and Fall* 191). The word "decline" reminds us that

Gibbon often viewed his life in terms of the Roman Empire. "The life of the historian must be short and precarious": as Gibbon saw it, within the Empire there were always seeds of decay, and within the life of the historian a gradual awareness of declining health, freedom, and prosperity (*Autobiography* 195).

Near the end of the book, when revolutionary rumblings from France threaten Europe's tranquility, Gibbon feels the familiar world receding. It is appropriate that his evocation of the past and the general summation of his life come immediately after the expressed fear of social and moral change. His closest friend is dead, Europe seems to be dying, and he is far from the active London world. We are left not with the historian or the celebrity but with simply a man thinking ahead to the "abbreviation of time and the failure of hope," and back on a life that held more promise than he believes it fulfilled. Gibbon does not seek more fame than he received nor is he disappointed in his monumental labor. But beneath the successful life of scholarship a genuine remorse is apparent, and the melancholy tone of the final paragraph sways between the consolation of false hopes and the anticipation of nothingness: "The warm desires, the long expectations of youth, are founded on the ignorance of themselves and of the world. They are gradually damped by time and experience, by disappointment and possession; and after the middle season the crowd must be content to remain at the foot of the mountain, while the few who have climbed the summit aspire to descend or expect to fall" (*Autobiography* 207). Gibbon achieves fame and success, but other desires remain underground, arising now and then to fill him with a sense of incompletion. The melancholy tone cannot be suppressed even though Gibbon's famous balance is beautifully maintained: the historian assured of his achievement in the world, the man aware that experience can never match his hopes. Gibbon's theme in the *Autobiography* is not simply the intellectual growth of a mind that has written *The Decline and Fall*, but also the precariousness with which any life is lived, even one plotted with deliberation.

A somber tone breaks Gibbon's meditation on his career: "In old age the consolation of hope is reserved for the tenderness of parents, who commence a new life in their children; the faith of enthusiasts, who sing hallelujahs above the clouds; and the vanity of authors, who presume the immortality of their name and writings" (*Autobiography* 207). Gibbon has no children (much of the book is an implicit lament for that emptiness), his belief in an afterlife is dubious, and the sarcasm about "enthusiasts" is in line with his satire on religion in *The Decline and Fall*. All hope would seem to hinge on the immortality of his writings, yet the elegiac tone of the last paragraph points even there to uncertainty, raising questions about whether his achievements provide sufficient consolation in the face of imminent decay and, because he has built his life on the denial and rejection of needs, whether he has fully acknowledged the cost.

"After the middle season the crowd must be content to remain at the foot of the mountain, while the few who have climbed the summit aspire to descend or expect to fall." This is the most dismal note in the final passage: there is no triumph at the climax of a life devoted to ascent, only resignation to defeat or the poignant oxymora, "the golden mediocrity of my fortune" and "aspire to descend." (In eighteenth-century usage, "aspire" meant "rising up.") Gibbon struggles to preserve optimism, juxtaposing the somber tone with one characteristically rational and analytical: "This day may *possibly* be my last, but the laws of probability, so true in general, so fallacious in particular, still allow me about fifteen years." (His pessimism was truer: he lived only two years beyond this writing.) Even at the end, as he tabulates his life and settles his record, he is still qualifying himself into hope. The facts of mutability and of failed hope merely "*tinge* with a browner shade the evening of life." Here again is the voice of moderation, keeping all within the limits of human accommodation, and the self-controlled figure who never rages against experience but never accepts it passively either. He acknowledges what must be, and then refocuses his vision ever so slightly to modify what otherwise appears terrifying.

The Decline and Fall opens with the grandeur of extensive frontiers and vast peoples and closes with a consideration of the short perilous life of human existence. "The art of man is able to construct monuments far more permanent than the narrow span of his own existence; yet these monuments, like himself, are perishable and frail; and, in the boundless annals of time, his life and his labours must equally be measured as a fleeting moment" (305). Gibbon applies both to individuals and to empires oft-repeated phrases from *The Decline and Fall:* "The instability of human affairs" and "the vicissitudes of human life." He speaks of the history of fortune, "which spares neither man nor the product of his works, which buries empires and cities in a common grave." This last phrase resonates with the conclusion of the *Autobiography,* where Gibbon sees in himself "the common history of the whole species." The *Autobiography* is indeed the "history" of Edward Gibbon, largely because he perceives the span of his own life, arching from triumph through suffering to frustrated hope, as paralleling that of the kingdoms and empires, which display the same natural laws of prosperity, adversity, decay, and a dreaded obscurity. Gibbon's voice in the *Autobiography* is more intimate than the historian's public one, but the autobiographer's voice internalizes those grand public, historical themes. Gibbon's perception of himself as the paradigm of Augustan grandeur turns against him, as the elegiac assertion of natural laws invokes the twilight discovery that those same laws apply to him as well as to the figures who stride through *The Decline and Fall*. His desire to become like the ancient Romans he admired—Julian, Cicero, Tacitus—finally narrows into an awareness that he is like them in a sense undreamed.

As Gibbon looks both forward and backward, he virtually declares what autobiography means for him: a way of realizing and defining the self not in retrospect, but at the very moment he writes the final pages, when a crisis of selfhood is revealed. The end of the *Autobiography* represents not just reminiscence but a new stage of self-knowledge. For one who has staked so much on his rationality, the admission of uncertainty is testament to an uneasy though more profound sense of self, one aware of the limits he faces in the final paragraph. Gibbon's attempt to enlarge "the narrow circle in which nature has confined us" may not be enough, but even to know this is to learn wisdom.

THIS CHAPTER STANDS AT THE BEGINNING of my thinking about autobiography. When I was searching for a way to see autobiography as doing more work than simply recording experience, I turned to eighteenth-century versions of the genre, thinking I would find a dialectic of revelation and subterfuge, writers using autobiography to uncover an identity as well as to evade disclosure. The French are better at this duality than anyone else, and I was interested to read an English writer who plays similar games of confession and concealment. In working on Gibbon I wanted to understand how an autobiographer employs rhetoric to seduce readers and gain their sympathy.

My interest in autobiography goes back to my days as a graduate student at Yale. Harold Bloom urged me to write a dissertation on biography, but I was more drawn to writers who authored their own lives. I treated the thesis as an experiment with a genre to which few people paid significant attention at the time, and began it in Milford, Connecticut, where walks on the snowy beaches of Long Island Sound and conversations with my wife, Nancy, helped me think about my subject. It was not easy in the waning days of New Criticism to take nonfiction prose for serious study. I had had a course with William Wimsatt, and as the dominant critic of intentionality, he unintentionally caused me to grapple with the subversive question of why anyone might write an autobiography in the first place. I wanted to know why and how writers transformed their lives into texts (we called them "books" once upon a time), and whether we could investigate them with the detail and precision with which we examined novels. The New Critics's interest in personae suggested to me that behind the speaking "I" lies another "I" with perhaps more fears than the narrator can express, or with intentions other than the ones enunciated in the text. Gibbon seemed like a central figure to study in this regard, one whose turns and tricks are as deft as those of any eighteenth-century novelist or playwright.

The larger question is why I got involved in autobiography in the first place, aside from wanting a subject that was fresh and might provide me with a corner in the profession. My interest sprang from a desire to understand a relation between language and self: how language defines and gives shape to personal experience and how metaphor and identity are intertwined. I suspect my interest was a rebellion against some of New Criticism's shibboleths, however much I was a devotee of its methods at Amherst, where I had been an undergraduate. There I had taken a famous freshman English course whose doctrinaire assumption was that our insights make sense only when we find language to express them, creating the "reality" of our world through the words we use to describe it. But that English course discouraged us from making any direct connection between our language and our selves. We talked only about words, the elimination of our "selves" corresponding to the discounting of writers' lives in the critical orthodoxy. Mired in a 1950s resistance to subjectivity, Amherst could hardly approve of the questions I wished to ask even then, though it taught me to see how a writer utilizes the instruments of form and language for literary representation.

In a way that none of us could know, that course anticipated postmodern theory in its belief that reality and the self were principally linguistic constructs. Autobiography criticism seemed rife for the application of such ideas. And yet the importance in the 1960s of such educators as Carl Rogers and such psychologists as Erik Erikson made me suspect that while it is through (autobiographical) language that we relate to the world, there is another voice in addition to the "I" who narrates, a more private voice under the crafted public one with which we commonly engage the world. In effect, studying autobiography allowed me to bridge the '50s and the '60s, to think about the intricacies of language and the desires of the mind, body, and heart. The dialectic between these two attitudes—a belief in autobiography as a fiction of a self that cannot be fully articulated except through metaphor, and an insistence on biography, even history and culture—came to drive much of my thinking about autobiography.

Those questions about identity arose early and have deepened, and that fact itself intrigues me because of its suggestion that autobiography may be the way we perceive ourselves as creatures in time. Reading autobiographies of others became the "madeleine" into my own life, their acts of memory eliciting my own. Reading autobiographies also makes me aware how many different selves one has, or has been; part of me believes there is a discernible pattern to my life, but part of me knows I have a multiplicity of selves, some of which no longer exist, some of which now seem like fantasies, and some of which I've tried to discard as vexations or encumbrances, however much they cling like burrs. I wonder if I can hold those various selves together or if I should try to make that ragtag bunch of *personae non gratae* go away. Like the eels that won't stay put in the cockney's pie in *King Lear*, some of those selves rise up from time to time in these musings and I want to cry, like the horrified baker, "Down, wantons, down!"

One of those selves occasionally doubted I had the necessary insight, the power of reasoning, or the relentless will to pursue evidence that is demanded of anyone studying literature. When I began graduate school I lacked the bulldog tenacity I saw in my fellow Yalies. As an undergraduate writing a thesis on Ezra Pound, I feared I'd never make sufficient sense of the *Cantos*, so I retreated to the earlier, easier poems. But even there I faltered. Stuck over an interpretation of "Hugh Selwyn Mauberley," I dreamed one night that Pound himself came to me and offered a definitive analysis of the poem. I knew his reading was brilliantly on target, but even in the midst of the dream I realized that I would need a concerted effort to retain the interpretation or it would be gone by morning. I bore down hard on Pound's exegesis: "Remember me, remember me." But when I woke, Pound's words had vanished. "Serves me right," I remember saying to myself of my dream, "it would have been plagiarism."

I have different selves, but do they add up to a pattern? I consider myself a deeply loyal man, but I have often let friendships lapse, love relationships dissolve, projects wane. Distracted by novelty, drawn to what I lack, seduced by what I know I can't have, fantasizing I am another person who might fit the bill better than I, and with eyes madly darting, I lack the Zen-repose of many Portlanders in their West Coast sanctuary of satori. A restless man, I skitter on surfaces like a water bug: theatre critic, restaurant critic, food writer, travel writer, founder of a theatre in Portland, director of plays, teacher at universities abroad, lecturer in Cairo, Leningrad, Shanghai, and Chiang Mai. I've got twenty courses in the teaching repertoire because nothing satisfies me for long. In the midst of any moment I imagine what's next. When I read Gibbon I think about the way obligation often checks desire, producing in me both satisfaction and discontent.

Reading Gibbon also makes me dwell on the way the private life confounds the public man. I have never been a public man: when a roving reporter intercepted me on the street and asked my opinion about the oil crisis of the early 1970s, I went blank, then recovered to mutter a banality and an apology for being badly informed. When my stutterings and stumblings made it on the news that night, any public career I envisioned felt doomed, not that I ever sought one seriously, though I did flirt with becoming a cultural affairs officer in the foreign service. The only public history my family made was when my father ran for the New Jersey state assembly, but he came in dead last without a recount. I have a newspaper photo of him at the time giving a little speech to my second grade class; perhaps he should have restricted his campaign to listeners eligible to cast a ballot or at least able to spell the word.

I was debating whether to be a lawyer like my father or a professor like the men I admired in college and finally made the decision by telling myself I didn't want to give up reading, by which I meant fiction, not legal briefs. I had recently completed my first year in graduate school, which I considered an experiment to see whether I would stay on or transfer to law school. One day, driving home from summer school at Colby College, where I had studied German, I passed a huge oil refinery. That one could build, manage, or understand something as complex and unfathomable as that refinery—or indeed anything so solidly in the world—seemed beyond my imagining. Though I didn't know it at the time, that fleeting glimpse of excessive and tangible worldliness may have ultimately decided things.

Teaching is when I get to put on a more public face. Still, however much I love the give-and-take, even the public lecture, the classroom is not the world, and I am usually restless to be a flâneur, a man *in* though not necessarily *about* town. I have always liked that Kafka, that most private-seeming of writers given to bedeviled introspection, had a gregarious social existence. My public life may have reached its modest apogee when I canvassed in Boston for Eugene McCarthy during the palmy days following LBJ's decision not to re-run. I did antiwar work that year and sat in on the Spock trial, which, along with the rallies on Boston Common after the assassination of King and Bobby Kennedy, made Boston such a heady environment in the late 1960s. I preached antiapartheid in a Xhosa church in South Africa (more about that later), but I've never really been comfortable rallying troops for a cause. To some of my colleagues I appear to have a public face, and it's true that I was a restaurant critic for the *South China Morning Post* and once occupied a regular slot on a television program discussing food. But I have usually gone for the private voice, the quiet confession, the whispered intimacy. I'm most comfortable with one other person, which is why a therapy session is more to my taste than a faculty meeting, let alone a political rally. "Truth" seems more likely to emerge in conversation and rumination than in public discourse. Unamuno tells us that "consciousness is a disease," but I don't believe it for a moment. Among my happiest moments are when I am alone reading Proust, or with a loved person listening to those intimate musical forms: a string trio, a violin sonata, or the dialogue between voice and piano in a Schubert *Leid*.

4.

Unspeakable Practices, Writable Acts

Benjamin Franklin's *Autobiography*

In his seminal essay on American autobiography, James Cox asserts that Benjamin Franklin's decision to write autobiography at sixty-five led him to "embark . . . upon what one wants to call his greatest invention—the invention of himself, not as fiction, but as a fact both of and in history" (16). My discussion of Franklin's *Autobiography* will attempt to demonstrate how that "invention" plays out in the language delineating Franklin's self-conception, but my focus, despite Cox's demur, will be on the way Franklin does indeed create himself "as [a] fiction," although the fiction is inevitably tied to both Franklin's biography and our national history. Franklin's desire to manipulate the reader's sympathy is not so different from Gibbon's; neither are his inclinations to conceal unruly issues that could undermine the projected image, and to interpret his behavior with tidy and rational explanations. Franklin's work is another instance of autobiography employed to frame a self by resisting impediments to a particular vision of identity.

Paul John Eakin has shown that while self-awareness begins when one first employs the language of identity, in effect says "I," a further stage of self-knowledge comes with the writing of the autobiography (*Fictions in Autobiography* 181–278). Though in his later study *Touching the World: Reference in Autobiography* Eakin stresses the referential aspects of autobiographers' lives, the conditions in which they live out their existence and how experience and beliefs shape their self-conceptions, he has never surrendered his notion that language is a key determination in the achievement and understanding of identity. Daniel B. Shea declares that "the real drama in Franklin . . . is a rhetorical one" (39), and G. Thomas Couser, in a discussion of the authority Franklin claims for the text, contends that when the audience of an autobiography is "not divinity but posterity, its credibility" will be less a function of spiritual honesty than one of "rhetorical skill and negotiation" (*Altered Egos* 38). Following this line, I want to argue that Franklin's employment of rhetoric is an activity entered into for purpose of self-definition, which I regard as his desire to convince us that he has brilliantly controlled his own destiny.

Franklin is so concerned with the act and the fact of self-creation that he makes it exceedingly difficult to perceive a real, historical self behind the reflections of his various constructed personae. Everywhere in the *Autobiography* events serve to reflect "Franklin," as if he had recruited them for self-enhancing purposes. Franklin is neither interested in the truth of what happened historically nor especially concerned with portraying an authentic self, as an autobiographer writing in a Puritan confessional mode would necessarily be. Although he speaks of his spiritual models, particularly *Pilgrim's Progress*, he has secularized the religious narrative and shaped the self-image strictly to his advantage. Freeing himself from conventional forms of confession, where the inauthenticity of a sinful life gives way to a renewed and authentic postconversion self, Franklin writes without interest in such claims. Instead of viewing himself as guided by God, he represents himself as subject to his own self-policing control. Referring to himself as if he were a text (he can correct his errors in a second edition of the life), he becomes first the writer, then the editor, of his own life. As a printer he can reset the letters of type, and as an autobiographer he can redesign present and past, authoring and authorizing them at will—just as he engages (in both life and text) in continuous acts of self-transformation. Early in the autobiography Franklin composes his epitaph, comparing his body to "the Cover of an old Book, / Its contents torn out, / And stript of its Lettering and Guilding." (*Autobiography* 44). References not just to his *interest* in books but to his being virtually *synonymous* with them proliferate throughout the text. I want to examine the reason why such a correspondence between self and text might interest Franklin, and how it forms the basis for his defensive mode of self-writing.

As I have noted, a compensatory theory of autobiographical intention holds that the writer represents the life with an artful shape, sense of purpose, and predictable order it may not have had in actuality. Such a strategy underlies Edwin Muir's autobiography, whose original title is *The Story and the Fable*, "the story" denoting life in its messy and contingent ordinariness, "the fable" denoting the design he wished the life had achieved. Muir's text compensates for what the life could not attain by way of form. Here is a succinct expression of this view:

I believe that most autobiographers create their discourse in order to conceive and sustain a self other than that which they have established—or which they have failed to establish—in their engagement of actual experience. The autobiographer, I believe, typically undertakes to press the resources of language in ways in which he has been unable to press the resources of history. . . . For such beings the act of writing autobiography declares itself not . . . as a hymn to peace and plenty but as a final, extraordinarily inventive attempt at therapy. (Glassman 140)

Such a theory would hardly seem to work for a man as successful, confident, and self-confessedly exemplary as Franklin. No one in our national life has more grandly "press[ed] the resources of history"—as statesman, diplomat, inventor, scientist, educator, editor, printer, philosopher, and public benefactor. Franklin's motive for writing cannot be explained by any desire to understand and clarify mysteries in the self (the "dark forests" that D. H. Lawrence lamented Franklin had excluded from his account); nor would it seem to be found in narrative compensation for any felt emptiness or incoherence in the lived experience. On the contrary, no autobiographer begins with more assurance and self-congratulation: "Having emerg'd from the Poverty and Obscurity in which I was born and bred, to a State of Affluence and some Degree of Reputation in the World, and having gone so far thro' life with a considerable Share of Felicity, the conducing Means I made use of, which, with the Blessing of God, so well succeeded, my Posterity may like to know, as they may find some of them suitable to their own Situations, and therefore fit to be imitated" (*Autobiography* 43). And yet Franklin's *Autobiography* expresses confidence and ease only by revealing the constant surveillance he had to apply to his life and by a continual effort *in the writing* to make the life appear as frictionless and effortless as possible. This strategy may not imply precisely a compensatory motive, but it does suggest that Franklin sought to portray himself as unproblematic and his life as controllable. Cox remarks that Franklin's account is notable for its absence of crises and dramatic turning points (17). Franklin speaks, appropriately for a printer, merely of innocuous "faults" he considers harmless "errata" to be corrected in a "second edition" (*Autobiography* 43, 44). Difficult moments are smoothed over by the application of tact or, in textual terms, euphemisms. Potentially troubling episodes that beg for exploration and analysis are passed by with a rhetorical equanimity and comic self-irony that belie the problem of self-evaluation that they inevitably raise. For Franklin to be exemplary demands that he not chance too much introspection; the risks are taken largely in the social and political domains, where private fears may be skirted or at least held in check, and where civic government coincides with self-government.

For Franklin, introspection represents an indulgence that runs counter to the more pressing needs of a rough and tumble existence that threatened to overwhelm the precarious civilization of early eighteenth-century Philadelphia. Franklin several times mentions incidents involving relatives and acquaintances who suddenly experienced a frightening loss of stability in their lives. His friend James Ralph leaves family and country only to become dependent on Franklin's charity to avoid financial ruin; another friend succumbs to drink and wastes his life; still another leaves for Barbados, never to be heard from again. In these cautionary accounts Franklin assures us that the only way to avoid a similar fate is through the proper application of discipline, tact, and control. Where life is chancy and chaos threatens at every turn—or where Franklin *perceives* matters that way—he cannot turn inward without fearing to squander his energies: self-questioning proves distracting if not irrelevant. Instead of engaging in an exploration of private matters, Franklin turns to the public world—first of collective wisdom and shared moral assumptions, later of public service and community enlightenment.[1]

The centerpiece of the *Autobiography* is Franklin's project of arriving at moral perfection: the famous lined notebook pages with the days of the week listed across the top and the initials of the thirteen virtues—"temperance," "order," "industry," and so on—listed down the side; the "little black spots" that mark a fault committed against those virtues on any given day; and Franklin's progress in eliminating vices charted by the erasure of the black marks (again significant for a printer, for whom black smirches on a clean page would be anathema and who proudly tells us of having returned borrowed books "soon and clean"). Franklin prizes the unspotted page of the virtues and the immaculate book of the life. Eradication of black marks becomes a metaphor for life and writing: if the darker aspects of experience are not dwelt upon, they will appear hardly to have been there at all. This plan stands for an entire conception of self in the *Autobiography:* life as a grid, where external behavior is primary, where faults and virtues may be plotted and balanced, and where the self, or at least its darker urges, may be transformed into a value. Franklin's autobiography dramatizes the application of these virtues to the smoothing over of difficult moments in the life and to the success that results from keeping unruly emotions at bay. But he does not tell too much, believing that revelations of what cannot be managed would convey an impression of failure and of excessive strain necessary for even the illusion of success. His autobiographical plan is not

simply to convert inner passion to usable history but to show how control
and rules signal the appearance of effortlessness.

I will not speculate on the psychoanalytic implications of Franklin's
obsession with sweeping the streets clean, or his loathing of mud, dust,
and slush, or his preoccupation with removing from gaslight fixtures the
grime and smoke that hindered the lighting of Philadelphia's streets. He
is pleased to enlighten the city with his new inventions, whether a stove,
electricity, or a better lamp. Nevertheless, getting rid of dirt, black marks,
and, as we will see, Native Americans is in Franklin's calculus, all of a piece:
the elimination of what cannot be controlled and contained, the fearful
threats to culture and to the self.

Here Franklin describes his experience with Native Americans who had
been given rum as a reward for signing a peace treaty:

> We found [the Indians] had made a great Bonfire in the Middle
> of the Square. They were all drunk Men and Women, quarrelling
> and fighting. Their dark-color'd Bodies, half naked, seen only by
> the gloomy Light of the Bonfire, running after and beating one
> another with Firebrands, accompanied by their horrid Yellings, form'd
> a Scene the most resembling our Ideas of Hell that could well be
> imagin'd. . . . At Midnight a Number of them came thundering at
> our Door, demanding more Rum; of which we took no Notice. The
> next Day, sensible they had misbehav'd in giving us that Disturbance,
> they sent three of their old Counsellors to make their Apology. The
> Orator acknowledg'd the Fault, but laid it upon the Rum; and then
> endeavor'd to excuse the Rum, by saying, "*The great Spirit who made
> all things made everything for some Use, and whatever Use he design'd
> anything for, that Use it should always be put to; Now, when he made
> Rum, he said,* LET THIS BE FOR INDIANS TO GET DRUNK WITH. *And it
> must be so.*" And indeed if it be the design of Providence to extirpate
> these Savages in order to make room for Cultivators of the Earth,
> it seems not improbable that Rum may be the appointed Means.
> (*Autobiography* 198–99)

Franklin's discomforting irony grants him license to eliminate whatever
threatens his well-being and to justify his position by recourse to providence
and cosmic order. Underlying his stance is a fear of violence and savagery,
not just of others but of his own. On numerous occasions Franklin recounts
his violent impulses but backs off from any probing discussion of them.
In one significant account, he pitches overboard into the Delaware River a
drunken friend who has refused to help row their boat; Franklin will not

take him back into the boat until the man is waterlogged, exhausted, and repentant. Several such episodes occur, but Franklin mentions them only in passing, creating the impression that unruly passions need not be deeply considered. He keeps control of himself, just as he greases the paths of his march to success and, in the writing, conveys an image of one who has avoided the "dangerous Time of Youth and the hazardous Situations I was sometimes in" (*Autobiography* 115). Too much revelation is dangerous for a man compliantly making his way in society. Franklin never lets us see the pressures generated within the self, and the prosaic tone of his narrative belies any inner struggle.

Life is a morality play for Franklin, and threats lurk everywhere. The *Autobiography* emphasizes escapes from dangers, allowing him both to avoid disorder and to keep his world flexible and free. Nothing terrifies him more than a drunken Dutchman who falls into the sea and almost drowns, or a friend whose frugality barely allows him to "keep his Head much longer above Water" (*Autobiography* 112). Later he describes himself as a "graceful and easy" swimmer who makes his way in the world "swimmingly." When his father discouraged Franklin from writing verses, he "escap'd being a poet" (*Autobiography* 60), a state he viewed as equivalent to that of a beggar. Only discipline allows him to avoid a liaison with thieving prostitutes on a boat, only his famous industry to elude financial ruin. Caution and control, or at least the impression that he has exercised them to resist a balky reality, always predominate.

Mostly, Franklin asserts that his life can be constructed rationally. He strives to convey not merely that existence is providentially secure, even less that it is arbitrarily fortunate, but that through his energetic will he can achieve anything he wishes. Franklin poses no problem about his identity, feels no impulse to take the self *as* a problem, since introspection is the sign of a man sidetracked into debilitating self-consciousness. Too much frivolous dwelling on the self is the greatest seduction of all, worse than the thieving prostitutes, for it robs him of the ability to project himself actively into the world. Cultivation of the self is justified only as a way of expanding its gains in public terms. The project to arrive at moral perfection does not stop in the realm of the private: soon after its formulation, Franklin announces his plan to create an organization to be called the "Society of the Free and Easy," which will disseminate his methods of achieving virtue.

This is doubtless why the book never rises to an emotional climax, but is accretive in its structure: for Franklin all experiences and activities— street cleaning and diplomatic negotiation, say—are equally important. In a text written over a period of eighteen years and on two continents, the very fact of a plain style combined with a structure of equivalent moments displays a disarmingly casual approach to the self. Since there is no strenuous overcoming of obstacles, merely the exercise of cautious discipline, there are no crises to narrate. The autobiography softens whatever anxiety or self-doubt Franklin might have felt about himself. These fears are present in the images of men disappearing or going under or remaining in obscurity; but Franklin conveys his insouciance by displaying a witty and outwitting side. To manifest too much urgency or intensity might acknowledge an anxiety he is at pains to dispel.

The writing, in its unadorned, chronicling mode, suppresses any identity sufficiently particular and distinct to contest the democratic ideal through which the common man may achieve what Franklin himself has. The autobiography ends with events in 1757; an account of the later career, when Franklin's preeminence was lofty, might have blurred the focus on the open-eyed youth and the rising public figure, making the protagonist a hero too formidable to emulate. Just as he viewed the worst sin of living as isolation from others, the worst sin (or erratum) of writing would be the cultivation of an effect so singular and idiosyncratic it might undermine Franklin's brief for democracy. If the rhetorical manner were unique, not a borrowing from such available models as Bunyan, Defoe, and the *Spectator*, Franklin would appear as *in*imitable. He fears claiming too much for himself, so he practices a simple, inelegant, and casual narrative style. He seems to make up his story as he goes, just as he is the American hero as self-made man. Cox notes that Franklin can stop where he wants because he is not trapped by a need to see his life whole. I would add that while the *Autobiography* occasionally shifts perspective, Franklin's story is all of a piece, and each piece resembles every other one.

Franklin's tone reveals a man enormously pleased with himself and delighted by the public's reception of his character and work. He is always knowing and ingenuous at the same time, a combination that permits him to take things just as they come.

> In order to secure my Credit and Character as a Tradesman, I took care not only to be in *Reality* Industrious and frugal, but to avoid all *Appearances* of the Contrary. I drest plainly; I was seen at no Places of idle Diversion; I never went out a-fishing or shooting; a Book, indeed, sometimes debauch'd me from my Work; but that was seldom, snug, and gave no Scandal: and to show that I was not above my Business, I sometimes brought home the Paper I purchas'd at the Stores, thro' the Streets on a Wheelbarrow. Thus being esteem'd an industrious thriving

young Man, and paying duly for what I bought, the Merchants who imported Stationary solicited my Custom, others propos'd supplying me with Books, and I went on swimmingly. (*Autobiography* 125–26)

The narrator never seizes the obvious openings for a discussion about appearance and reality, external image and interior selfhood. The content of this passage is conveyed by a poise that cannot afford much self-questioning. And its success, like so much of the *Autobiography*, depends upon a reader not raising too many questions. But that is exactly what we are inclined to do, impatient with the frictionless bearing of the text. Ultimately, we are left not so much with the self-congratulating, pompous Franklin of Lawrence's caricature, but a subject who knows just how fragile the self really is. That Franklin conceals or denies inner conflicts, mocking his own formulae for success, keeps the *Autobiography* from being as egotistical a document as it might otherwise have been. Franklin knew he had an abundant capacity for vanity and luxuriant pleasures and that the exercise of these tendencies would render his life meaningless. It is not, as has been claimed, Puritan caution or Quaker reticence that lies behind such fears, but rather a wily view of himself and a pleasure in the act of mock self-effacement.

Franklin engages the reader even as he refuses to give much away, trying out a series of roles, and enjoying the posturing. The *Autobiography* exhibits the performances of a skilled con man. Just when we think we know him, he escapes our grasp; at one moment Ben Franklin appears the rank optimist and proud booster of civic virtues, at the next moment he has a dark vision of human rapacity and sees how much manipulation is necessary to effect even minimal social gains. But the autobiography will not settle into any comfortable conclusions about human action or personal awareness. We continually hear the voice of an ironist whose strategy is to undercut himself even as he applauds himself. We might well wonder who is the real Franklin.

In a passage that closes part 2 of the *Autobiography*, Franklin shows how emotions can get out of hand; what is important here is not just his need to subdue his passions, but the way he survives with credit whether he subdues them or not: "In reality there is perhaps no one of our natural Passions so hard to subdue as *Pride*. Disguise it, struggle with it, beat it down, stifle it, mortify it as much as one pleases, it is still alive, and will every now and then peep out and show itself. You will see it perhaps often in this History. For even if I could conceive that I had compleatly overcome it, I should probably [be] proud of my Humility" (*Autobiography* 160). Even as he narrates his failings, Franklin manages to triumph. To be "proud of [his] Humility" might paradoxically seem like a fault, but it turns out to be a claim for honesty and an appeal for understanding. Though he plays the opposite game in the next example, he is the same verbal trickster when, in his catalogue of virtues, his command to himself under the rubric "Humility" is "Imitate Jesus and Socrates." A man as clever as Franklin may often be hard to trust but he is not hard to admire.[2]

Franklin knows that the self may be created as much in the writing as in the process of living. The life has prepared the writer to compose the self, and for Franklin this lesson takes the specific form of circumspection, guile, and in both senses of the word, craft. In the deliberate act of frustrating our desires and keeping us at bay, "now and then peep[ing] out and show[ing]" himself, Franklin asserts that autobiography is less a retrospective genre than a continuous engagement between author and audience, and a witty and rationalized construction of self that may well conceal the effort he expended to achieve identity in the life.

I BEGAN THINKING ABOUT Franklin during an idyllic leave at Dartmouth College, where I was a National Endowment for the Humanities fellow, along with eleven other college professors, in a year-long seminar on American autobiography. In the snowy wilds of Hanover, we met weekly to discuss autobiographies, and the bracing atmosphere both in and out of our library seminar room was a constant stimulation to our work. We turned to Franklin early in the year, and most of us had the conventional Laurentian response to the text, dismissing Franklin's writing as so much puffery and self-inflating propaganda. James Cox, the coordinator of the seminar, prodded us with ludic inversions in order to help us find more searching positions, and when I began to place Franklin's autobiographical strategies in relation to those of Gibbon, both of them virtuosi of rhetoric, defensive rationalists, and self-image makers, I could see my way into a clearing.

It may seem odd that I don't give more attention to Franklin's Americanness, for most critics emphasize his original role in the nation's history, whether as fact or as autobiographical strategy. Although I was educated in New England (at Yale—home of Jonathan Edwards and Robert Penn Warren) and at Amherst—(home of Emily Dickinson and Robert Frost), I never felt so fully in the center of American literary history as I did that year at Dartmouth. I lived across the Connecticut River in Thetford, Vermont, which seemed to me to be what Concord must have been like in the 1840s: a place where writers, artists, teachers, and musicians all thrived. But I was more interested in Franklin's cunning and canniness than in nationalism, and the silence and stillness of Vermont winter life focused my thoughts not on history but on the workings of the mind. Call it the Emersonian influence of that climate.

Cox was also a strong influence on us that year. What he mainly got us to see was that, as he put it, "making a life is not the same as making one up." I began to think that writers craft their lives in relation to what is valuable about their living and that we cannot look upon the narrated story completely aside from the life that produced the need for a particular representation. Every gesture, every sign, every metaphor in the text derives from desires produced by the life, which demands to be told in a certain way to fill specific needs, even though some of the life remains unwritable.

When I read Elizabeth Bruss's *Autobiographical Acts*, which argues that autobiographical writing is not just a form but an act with deliberate work to perform—rhetorical strategies, plots, created identities, and addresses to the reader—all designed to will that reader into a particular response, I felt that what I had done with Gibbon had merit and that Franklin, his contemporary, had been similarly engaged with problems of disclosure and evasion. I became interested in Franklin's work in part because of how the narrator resists threatened encroachments on a life of rational control, indeed defies whatever cannot be understood rationally. I suspect that my interest in Gibbon and Franklin's strategies comes from long residence in the academy, whose culture has generally regarded those aspects of experience that disturb Franklin—the personal, the inner, the irrational—as threats to its concerns, and where phrases like "rational discourse" and "value-free inquiry" are often invoked to deny the importance of the emotional life in the classroom and certainly in scholarship.

In the 1960s, my institution was on its guard against what some colleagues saw as dangerous breachings in the wall surrounding academe; it especially felt the presence of "the Other" within, which seemed even worse than pressures from outside, as if one part of the mind had risen against another. Any invoking of the "I" was looked upon as subversive to disinterested scholarship and dangerous to intellectual work, and was all but banished from discourse. There was considerable skepticism about a symposium I proposed in autobiography studies, for in some quarters the term "self" was thought to be a code word for indulgence, even for anti-intellectualism, and autobiography not merely a genre of little consequence, but a threatening and illegitimate object of study. To explore autobiography was to compound subjectivity with impressionism. The conservative faculty at Reed enunciated these positions, and nothing aroused their defenses against perceived irrationality like the demands in the early seventies for

Vietnam moratoria and the suspension of classes for teach-ins, even after the watershed events of Kent State and the bombing of Cambodia. During one such overheated debate, a young faculty member, barely twenty-five, pronounced that if he could permanently stop the war by canceling his classes for only one day he would never do so, for "too many important values in Western civilization would go down the drain." The speaker of this Franklinian utterance is now the president of a major American university.

Some of us protested against this colleague's stance, and a friend of mine announced on the floor of the faculty that Reed would be more concerned about the loss of a few books from the library than the death of fifty thousand North Vietnamese from napalm raids. The conservatives heard his remarks as a call to firebomb the building, and spent the night in the stacks to guard the collection against Molotov cocktails. Wherever the custodians of Reed looked those days, they saw the forces of irrational darkness in their midst. In a staff course that mandated a single paper topic for all four hundred freshmen, several instructors offered their students alternative topics. Even though the topics were on the same text, all of the instructors were fired for disunity if not apostasy, a paradox for an institution that had courageously stood firm against loyalty oaths during the McCarthy period. But now the culprits of the irrational were deemed to lie within: as the conservatives saw it, the "family" was spawning heresy, and one thought of Goya's engraving "The dream of reason produces monsters." But the truth felt different to me: if large universities are like corporations, small colleges are like families, and in those days Reed was a classically dysfunctional one. When a number of us on the left staged a reading of Aeschylus's *Agamemnon* as an anti-war play and wanted the actress wife of a colleague to play Clytemnestra, he, who had advocated nuking Hanoi, forbade his wife to join in any form of anti-war protest. One faculty member, who elsewhere trumpeted the fabled student-faculty relations at the college, had recently returned from setting up a political science program in Africa. When confronted by curricular demands from Reed's black students, the faculty member railed against their supporters: "You're just a bunch of student lovers," he sputtered, perhaps mocking a pamphlet of the times titled "The Student as Nigger." The next day, the man's wife accused me of "giving up scholarship for relevance," as if there were an inevitable distinction. It was clear that the institutionality of the institution could tolerate no dissent from tradition. Was I learning about Franklin's attempt to contain the demons by watching my colleagues at work?

At the time I was reading Franklin in the Dartmouth seminar, I was also directing three Beckett plays—*Play*, *Happy Days*, and *Not I*—and was struck by an unexpected connection between autobiography and drama. I thought of Franklin as a clever actor, perhaps not so histrionic as Boswell in his journals, nor so stagy as Cellini in his autobiography, but someone able to perform multiple roles at will—wearing masks, scheming, concealing his identity, then strategically assuming another one for his own ends. Autobiography is an implicitly theatrical genre, something like an overheard soliloquy, and my interests in autobiographical role-playing and in theatre have nurtured one another, which may be why Beckett's plays, with their characters' incessant need to make up, stage, and tell their stories (I had also directed *Endgame*), helped me think about the strategies and illusions of self-revelation. In a curiously roundabout way, my involvement in theatre owes something to Franklin's autobiography and its narrative, even dramatic, performances.

It was when I participated in a Rockefeller Institute seminar in autobiography studies at Reed (the program was finally approved) that I first thought of fulfilling a persistent desire to direct plays. One of the visiting lecturers at the Institute that year was Robert Sayre, who had written the first study of American autobiography, including an influential essay on Franklin. Sayre and I were strolling through Portland's Washington Park Rose Gardens, next to which was a sloping hillside with groves of stately pines. He remarked that it would be a wonderful place to set *A Midsummer Night's Dream*. I was teaching Shakespeare at the time, and had recently begun work on the relation of text to performance. I inquired at the Parks Department about producing a Shakespeare play outdoors and, Portland being the accommodating town it is, without much ado was given a three-night stand on a summer program at the same arena-like hill, where three thousand people gathered each night for *Midsummer Night's Dream*. I directed *The Tempest* the next summer and eventually cofounded and directed for the Portland Conservatory Theatre.

I last staged a play in Egypt, where I taught for a year and directed at a new theatre on the campus of the Cairo American School. I proposed *Mother Courage* as an Arab-Israeli antiwar play, with the heroine pushing her cart across the Sinai, but the suggestion was not well-taken. There were mutterings about my coming home in a body bag, so I did *The Crucible*, though the Muslim Brotherhood grandparents of a young Egyptian girl I cast as Abigail did not take kindly to a daughter of Islam being touched, let alone called "a whore," in public, and they withdrew her from the production. That year I lived next to a mosque, whose *muzzein*, or call to prayer, sounded every morning at five o'clock, invariably rousing me from sleep. One night, at the time of rehearsals for *The Crucible*, I dreamt that I was invited to direct *Hamlet* at Stratford-on-Avon, and was naturally delighted and flattered. Suddenly the *muzzein* jolted me awake, shattering the fantasy. I managed to push myself back to sleep, hoping to recapture the dream, but, as if my unconscious were demanding retribution on behalf of the offended grandparents or perhaps exercising a Franklinian caution against arrogance, when the dream started up again I was told to direct the play in Arabic.

Whenever I imagine having a different career, it's always as a theatre director. I like the fact that in fairly short order you can create something large and definite, shaping an idea into concrete reality that just as soon vanishes into thin air, its very ephemerality driving you to do it once again. But after I directed productions of Aeschylus and Shakespeare, the theatre I helped found in Portland collapsed from disastrous financial planning just as the *Volpone* I was directing was about to open. The cast and the production generally was all I had hoped for, and I had made one person extremely happy. *Volpone* calls for a dwarf, and to cast the role I had auctioned someone recommended by the Portland chapter of The Little People of America. This particular little person was reasonably good, but I hesitated to cast him because he was an almost-statuesque four-foot-five, and I was looking for a true midget. When I told him the reason for my reluctance, he wept; no one had ever said he was too tall—for anything! But cast him I did, and like all of us in the production, my prodigious dwarf fell victim to unscrupulous management. As the theatre closed its doors before he could perform, he wept again.

5.

The Sorrows of Autobiography
Somerset Maugham's *The Summing Up*

In a study of confessional practice and narration, Jeremy Tambling argues that the impulse to lay bare one's secrets attempts to "make behavioural issues a matter of personal (i.e., sexual) identity and further, to assume that identity is something that can be spoken—both that it can be known and the way to know it is through speaking" (178). From Tambling's perspective, Somerset Maugham's 1938 autobiography, *The Summing Up,* would not simply demonstrate the writer's reluctance to confess or his refusal to address innermost thoughts; Maugham's very identity, despite his ostensible self-assurance, would be in question. What might seem like mere discretion or protection from others' criticism points to an alienation of the speaking voice. However transgressive Maugham may be in desire, his autobiographical self is either so cloaked in silence or so usurped by a predominantly public voice as to render problematic any authenticity he claims for himself in the text. As I will attempt to show, a resistance to confession reveals Maugham's anxieties regarding his literary status and his fear of superannuation.

My argument about Maugham hinges on the belief that confession (I speak in literary, not religious or legal terms) is the mark of a self with complexity and depth, attested to in the act of writing. Autobiographers tend to assume not only that confessional speech reveals an inner self and some kind of inner truth but that there is an inner self worth speaking about in the first place. We generally believe that autobiographical writing does—or perhaps ought to—bear some resemblance to psychoanalysis in that the latter enterprise is constituted in a *search* for self-definition, and that the process asks not just "who am I?" but "what are the aspects of my life, conscious or otherwise, that express the particular self that I claim to be?" We expect a certain intimate revelation before we can say that the self has made itself known to us. Peter Brooks, in a work

on confession and guilt, claims that the confessional impulse requires a
degree of introspection and articulation about what one has discovered.
Self-examination "promotes metaphors of innerness, depth, recesses within,
where one can track the self in its life of desire, its ruses, untruths, failings—
as well as its aspirations to wholeness and betterness." Brooks asserts that
confession and the acknowledgment of inwardness are mutually linked, and
without each of these concepts it is difficult for us to postulate the other.
"If we cannot imagine . . . confession absent a deep, recessed, secret self . . .
it is equally true that we cannot imagine this self absent the imperative to
scrutinize and . . . articulate it" (111). These terms are helpful as a basis for
understanding Maugham's reticence and how he writes autobiography to
resist our discovery, and perhaps his own, of such an inner self.

   The Summing Up manifests a peculiar self-fashioning that Maugham
has perfected: not that which we commonly take to be a mark of freedom
or autonomy and not that which testifies to the depths of innerness we
expect from a commitment to self-exploration. The autobiography is a
work conforming largely to what he believes others expect from him.
Maugham writes a publicly acceptable autobiography suppressing any
revelation of an inner self, refusing to represent, in Sidonie Smith's words, a
"self-identity [that] emerges from a psychic interiority, located somewhere
"inside" the narrating subject" ("Performativity, Autobiographical Practice,
Resistance" 17). Confession, when it emanates from within, not when it is
enforced by external agents, depends on one's certainty that there is a self
to be confessed, even if the confession brings shame. Maugham's identity
consciously constructed for others questions whether there even is a private
self to be confessed.

   The Summing Up comprises seventy-seven sections of varying lengths,
many of them brief essays on such topics as writing for the theatre,
professional authorship, spirituality, and aesthetics. The work contains a
great deal of autobiographical detail, but whenever Maugham appears about
to analyze personal aspects of his life, he retreats into silence, generalization,
or equivocation. Just as Maugham describes how, as a playwright, he
virtually pandered to his audiences (though he can also show contempt for
them), so in *The Summing Up* he depicts the character he imagines readers
expect, suppressing any self-revelation he fears will discomfort or scandalize
his public. What he cannot acknowledge autobiographically he projects
onto *fictional* characters and is thus "disembarrassed of his subject . . . free
from the burden that oppressed him" (*The Summing Up* 191).

   Strong autobiographical writing emphasizes complex formal structures
that mirror the patterns of a life, whether single or multiple, unified or

fragmentary; narrative and discursive features that signify an individual "I" that belongs to this and to no other being; rich and subtle metaphoric registers that suggest how language is linked to identity; a conception of motivation—enunciated or not—that expresses the need for self-revelation in the first place; and a demonstrable relation to a reader that involves rhetorical strategies to elicit a desired response. In short, we expect auto-biography to exhibit complexity of expression and aesthetic control. We no longer believe that the act of establishing (or creating) a self is immune from distortion or from a degree of fictionalizing; but when we think of self-conscious explorations in autobiography, even from such masters of deceit and artifice as Rousseau and Nabokov, we assume that the writer takes the self seriously, however much the representation depends on a degree of literary performance.

Such expectations might make us uneasy with the many equivocations that dog *The Summing Up*: Maugham's adamant refusal to describe his marriage to Syrie Wellcome and to characterize his relationship with their daughter; his reluctance to discuss his widely known homosexuality, let alone his relationship with his long-term lover, Gerald Haxton, who is mentioned on rare occasions only as "a companion" accompanying Maugham on his journeys; and perhaps more frustratingly and tellingly, because no conventions of historical propriety or social necessity can be adduced in defense of their absence, Maugham's silence on such matters as loneliness, fear, love, and joy. In the following melancholy rumination, for example, Maugham refuses to account for his position, basing it only on general human truths. We want to know what in his life led to this position, but instead he gives us only abstractions without their origins in the concrete density of lived and personal experience.

> I believed that we were wretched puppets at the mercy of a ruthless fate; and that, bound by the inexorable laws of nature, we were doomed to take part in the ceaseless struggle for existence with nothing to look forward to but inevitable defeat. I learnt that men were moved by a savage egoism, that love was only the dirty trick nature played on us to achieve the continuation of the species, and . . . that, whatever aims men set themselves, they were deluded, for it was impossible for them to aim at anything but their own selfish pleasures. (*The Summing Up* 72–73)

Maugham's autobiography emphasizes his beliefs about writing far more than explorations of consciousness. As for the form of the book, it is discursively random, lacking any structural design that mirrors or expresses a conception of an evolving self. And we have no indication that Maugham came to understand himself in the process of writing the text. At every turn we confront a writer resistant to disclosure. What interests me about Maugham's text, then, are the strategies of defense and concealment he employs, and the evident strain revealed in the process of his resistance.

Granted the first sentence of *The Summing Up* protests: "This is not an autobiography nor is it a book of recollections" (1). Early on he declares, in thoroughly anti-Rousseauean fashion, "I have no desire to lay bare my heart, and I put limits to the intimacy that I wish the reader to enter upon with me. There are matters on which I am content to maintain my privacy. No one can tell the whole truth about himself." In context, however, the last sentence implies not the *impossibility* of full revelation but its *undesirability*. Maugham explains this resistance to the personal: too often the exposure of one's private life is commensurate with the revelation of "bad" actions and "[un]redeeming qualities," such that one "appears only weak, unprincipled and vicious" (*The Summing Up* 10). *The Summing Up*, he suggests, represents less the narration of a complex self than a description of values and general beliefs, presented from a somewhat detached point of view. Well and good, but we want to know more precisely why he takes this stance.

At the outset of his autobiography Maugham voices a hope it will not be his final work: "One does not die immediately one has made one's will" (*The Summing Up* 9). Wills are settlings of accounts, not opportunities for confession, and Maugham comports himself with the formal staging appropriate for the recitation of a last testament. His concern for good breeding ("have we not . . . been told that good prose should be like the clothes of a well-dressed man, appropriate but unobtrusive?" [*The Summing Up* 38]) implies he will not disturb the image we might already have formed of him. He will confirm the impressions he trusts we have, fearful of upsetting assumptions and expectations through any surprising disclosure. Michael Wood has written that "[Maugham's] most famous contribution to the moral life of our century is probably his diagnosis of love itself as, above all, humiliation" (Introduction to *Mrs. Craddock* 10). It follows that he organizes his life and writing to suggest that he had them under control, thus deflecting ridicule. Maugham's inhibitions are screening phenomena not unlike the frequent use in his fiction of adultery as a transgressive act to mask his homosexuality. There are occasional moments when he speaks openly about himself, but such moments address his limited sympathies, his dislike of being physically touched, his eschewing of strong feelings, his embarrassment about love, and his inability to surrender to private emotions. Maugham ironically has it both ways: he appears to come close to intimate revelation, but since the revelation concerns the impossibility of intimacy, he can back off, having justified the procedure with an apparent display of the very emotions he claims he is unable to sustain.

This text purports to be Maugham's most definitive exploration of how he shaped his life. But it would be a mistake to argue that his emphasis on his writing and his life as a writer can be completely separated from his inner life and desires, however much he tries to evade them. Maugham frequently employs the term "pattern" as something he both deliberately set out to construct and was able to perceive in retrospect. But what is the function of the pattern for Maugham? Does it mask turmoil and complexity? Or is it a plan of action that, like Gibbon's, allows Maugham to conceive of his life as if it were as well composed as a work of art, thought out in advance and designed to avoid too much messy reality? Or is it less a preconceived structuring than one retrospectively applied, affording him a self-satisfying sense that things have essentially turned out as he wished and furthermore, that if he emphasizes the pattern, he needn't probe beneath its surface?

His phrase "self-realization tempered by a lively sense of irony" (*The Summing Up* 279) captures what is at stake: the self is always qualified by Maugham's subjecting it to the patterns he claims to have pragmatically staked out an an early age, and that his career has fulfilled. The "irony" hinges on a compact he makes with the reader, whom he expects to probe no more than he has. Note how he disowns even his impulses: "Here it is not I that speak, it is the craving within me, *which is in every man*, to persevere in my own being" (*The Summing Up* 277, my emphasis). The "lively sense of irony" is Maugham's wink at the compact with the reader, a compact he trusts will bring satisfaction despite, or perhaps because of, the autobiographer's reticence.

Maugham avoids any emotions that could threaten his sense of direction, and the pattern is something he devises early in his life to keep him on track, which means the avoidance of spontaneity and a focus on the future rather than on the present. In establishing the pattern, he even proposed the number and the sequence of works he planned to produce during his lifetime. He envisioned such a pattern to provide coherence and certainty, his identity depending wholly on his ability to follow and fulfill that pattern. Indeed, it appears that his identity is defined and subsumed by the pattern. Robert Calder, Maugham's biographer, notes that Maugham had read Hazlitt's essay "On Going a Journey" and would have been attracted to Hazlitt's ecstatic cry: "Oh! it is great . . . to lose our importunate, tormenting, everlasting personal identity . . ." (*The Summing Up* 176). Personal identity threatens to break lose from the vigilance of pattern-making, and so Maugham's writing of his identity is tied to his cultivated stereotype of the wry, detached, cosmopolitan British man of letters who declares he would burn his papers before anything untoward was discovered that might undermine the image he wishes to create. The act of summing up constitutes the completion of the pattern, an account suitable for a life that fears surprise, eschews internality, and evades any disclosure that constitutes humiliation.

"I am incapable of complete surrender," he says, referring to love and passion, and thus "it is impossible that my work should have the inti-macy . . . which the greatest writers alone can give" (*The Summing Up* 76, 78–79). The autobiography as well lacks surrender, as if Maugham's "physical repulsion" for "sexual congress" were repeated in his revulsion for the *writing* about personal matters (*A Writer's Notebook* 357). Nevertheless, in *The Summing Up* evasion and revelation exist in a complex, enmeshed relation, and Maugham's prevarications frequently reveal a more interesting self beneath them, as he struggles between several modes of self-presentation even while he believes he has reconciled the conflicts. It is this unresolved tension that suggests how difficult it was to be Maugham and that makes *The Summing Up* a more complicated autobiographical text than appears at first blush.

As Maugham looks back on his life, one of the autobiography's primary themes emerges in the opposition between his sense of superannuation and the compensatory satisfactions of age. Time and again he confronts the transience of age and his flagging reputation with wistful resignation. By 1938, at the time of the writing, he knows he is a conservative if not obsolescent figure vis-à-vis literary modernism and that critics are generally indifferent to his work; but he also emphasizes the writer's need not to bow to currents of fashion: writing to satisfy external imperatives rather than internal impulse is for him anathema. But the autobiography tends to blur that very distinction. One of Maugham's principal conflicts is between his desire for public approbation via the writing with which he felt most comfortable (traditional storytelling with a minimum of nar-rative complexity), and his desire for serious critical approval. Maugham knew his limitations, and pleasing a general audience was ultimately no different from pleasing himself; pleasing academic critics like Edmund Wilson, however, was another matter. In *Classics and Commercials,* Wil-son derided Maugham as a mediocre novelist and philistine critic, but Maugham systematically disregarded such detractors, either out of fear of not matching their standards, or feigned indifference to their opinions. Maugham's justification in 1938 for not having written to the norms of either modernism or agitprop might look like emancipation from external demands, yet because he admits he will not be successful unless he gives the public what it wants, he once again seems to be pandering to popular taste: "the more individual [the playwright] is the harder he will find it to achieve [public success]" (*The Summing Up* 136). His resistance to an originality he fears will offend his public is analogous to his resistance to self-revelation. He is prepared to accept his limitations, although he knows he disappoints more severe critical opinion by acquiescing to standards regarded as journalistic or commercial. And *The Summing Up* gives his general readership exactly what *it* wants: the autobiography's underlying theme is that Maugham's own limitations have perfectly coincided with the readers' tastes, just as his moral outlook has never threatened or even challenged their ethical standards.

But Maugham never shows us the psychological ground of his need to be well-respected by the public. I would argue not that he could have been a different kind of writer yet held himself back for the sake of popularity, but that he will not speak of his fierce need for recognition because he does not want us to see him struggling with writing. He prefers to have us believe that writing is an easy and natural act. Just as he made a career out of hard work but disavows it to give the impression of control and ease, so, as Gore Vidal has claimed, he virtually invents the figure of "W. Somerset Maugham" as a poised, unruffled, genteel man of letters (241). I would add that writing the autobiography is a further act of self-creation that entails the suppression of the more anxious, personal aspect of things—the side of Maugham that Calder calls "Willie" (as Maugham was known to his close friends).

Emphasizing the surface of his life in a way that corresponds to the *writing* of surface, proud of his success and guarding against impropriety, Maugham will not claim too much for himself ("from the standpoint of common sense, I am of no consequence whatever") nor too little ("to myself I have always been the most important person in the world"), thus providing a buttress against failure as well as assuring credit for his triumph ("On his Ninetieth Birthday" 266). Although Maugham asserts that fame can rob a writer of individuality and produce a soul-destroying complacency, he is nonetheless proud of that success, which validates his decision to have followed the public's demands. Whatever he has sacrificed by way of idealism, the image of the crowd-pleasing artist prevails and justifies his subordination of the personal. Maugham rationalizes evasions on the grounds that he has always placed his career ahead of integrity. But in resisting the personal Maugham recognizes, perhaps sorrowfully, what is being sacrificed.

In the midst of a discussion of the theatre and his public acclaim, Maugham states bluntly and proudly, "The intelligentsia, having passed judgment, ignored me, but I was securely fixed in the public favour" (*The Summing Up* 120). But he soon turns against the very audiences who have made him famous: "I found myself, notwithstanding, growing more and more impatient with that section of [the public] that makes up the theatrical audience. . . . The feeling that a mass of people were seeing my plays became a sort of horror of distaste." Hints of this distaste occur earlier in the autobiography, when, describing how an audience can be collectively mesmerized by a performance, he speaks of the "current that passes infectiously from one person to another" and of the "contagion" that spreads among them. The audience, which demands a certain propriety and depends on theatrical conventions, indeed the entire theatrical process, suddenly become tedious to Maugham. "I sighed for the liberty of fiction" (*The Summing Up* 153, 136, 154). What he seeks in writing novels is privacy rather than collaboration. He relishes the solitary creator speaking to a solitary reader. The desire to be alone recurs throughout the text. The importance theatre still holds for Maugham, despite his pleasure at fiction writing, makes comprehensible his struggle between inner versus more public modes of expression. As theatre becomes too public an art form and he retreats into the world of fiction, he recognizes a loss and yet accepts himself as a private figure unwilling to express the values he has come to associate with gossip and histrionics. Ironically, the more private turn does not lead to the autobiographical representation of a private self.

I am scarcely claiming that Maugham practices a hermetic life. Indeed, few other writers led so public an existence, or so relished hobnobbing with celebrities. The list of guests at his villa on the Riviera reads like a catalogue of the famous men of the twentieth century. But his move away from theatre corresponds to an even greater self-concealment. And certainly the word "distaste" in the passage above carries the full weight of his antipathy toward the masses, whose taste he questioned even as his fame and fortune depended on satisfying it.

Such issues are not easily resolved. Throughout *The Summing Up,* Maugham veers between democratic and elitist inclinations. Or perhaps we can say that Maugham finds individuals occasionally fascinating but dislikes people in the mass. Groups—whether they be crowds, people designated by class, or categories like "mankind"—distress him. As much as Maugham attempts to find redeeming qualities in ordinary people, it is always civility he lauds: "to write good prose is an affair of good manners," and "good prose should resemble the conversation of a well-bred man." Writers he admires "attach importance to the refinements of civilization" (*The Summing Up* 37, 38). Occasionally he acknowledges, however begrudgingly, the lure of the primitive and its freedom from civilization. But the people of the South Seas, exotic though "often dull and stupid," hold his interest only if he can use them in stories. However fascinating their character, "I never doubted that it was I who gave them the idiosyncrasy that I discovered in them, and so I decided that there was no further profit for me in travel" (*The Summing Up* 205). When he alleges that life in a hospital, with its range of human types, is good training for a writer, we understand that strangers appeal to him largely for what they yield as literary material. These "others" represent what Maugham will not allow himself to be. The people of the South Seas and the figures who inhabit a class different from his own are analogous to the self he will not explore in *The Summing Up*, not because they are inherently alien from him, but because they are too like his own nonacceptable self.

At one point he announces baldly, "I have never much liked men." Shyness? Misanthropy? Snobbism? It is hard to say precisely, but the sentiment is at the heart of Maugham's autobiography. *The Summing Up* is a text emptied of other people. He asserts that the claims of others make self-realization difficult, and to achieve it he must often ignore other people's desires. Yet he is not insensitive to their misery, and knows that ignoring their needs is evil. This conflict comes to a head during his meditation on "a great work of art." Confronting a masterpiece of art or literature, he experiences "a feeling of well-being in which I seem to discern . . . a liberation from human ties; at the same time I feel in myself a tenderness which is rich with human sympathy" (*The Summing Up* 300–01). At another moment he laments that while he has often loved, he has never experienced requited love; yet in the same paragraph he allows that he finds intimacy almost impossible. Such ambivalence about maintaining and jettisoning personal bonds, combined with his pleas for empathy toward others even as he writes autobiography devoid of such empathy, marks the book's detached point of view and remote tone.

Occasionally he seems ready to launch a searching analysis of himself, but he unfailingly shifts into the impersonal mode. "The writer," he states tantalizingly, "is not one man but many" (*The Summing Up* 229). Yet instead of an account of his own many-sidedness he tells us merely that a writer's multifarious personality permits him to create many characters. There is even a moment when he seems on the verge of narrating his intimate life but says only that those "who possess an aesthetic sense of unusual delicacy diverge sexually from the norm to an extreme and often pathological degree"

(*The Summing Up* 299). The cliched observation hints at but ultimately masks his own sexuality, while the rhetorical excess of "an extreme and often pathological degree" appears to erase any self-reference.

What I find to be the most intriguing element in this opaque text is that Maugham struggles against himself and understands the losses in both life and autobiography. As he brings his work to a close, he offers a long rhetorical defense: "I have never quite lost the sense that my living life was a mirage in which I did this and that because that was how it fell out, but which, even while I was playing my part in it, I could look at from a distance and know for the mirage it was. When I look back on my life, with its successes and its failures, its endless errors, its deceptions and its fulfilments, its joys and miseries, it seems to me strangely lacking in reality. It is shadowy and unsubstantial" (*The Summing Up* 308–09). "When I look back on my *life*." The actual life Maugham deliberately and famously constructed is not so far from the literary artifact. In both lives there is great satisfaction, but there is also a troubled desire for the unexpressed and the inexpressible. Maugham will not say precisely to what in his life the word "unsubstantial" refers. As a result, there is a corresponding insubstantiality in the autobiographical text, an emptiness or gap that we long to see filled in.

For Maugham, as for Franklin, autobiography creates the impression that his life was relatively frictionless. It also fosters the illusion that any secrets could remain as such without ruffling the calm surface of his existence or diminishing his creative energy, just as he renders the impression that his creativity in no way derives from suppressed incidents or feelings. Maugham refuses a representation of his life based on fantasy or secrets or dark episodes, denying that the life is a mystery to be unraveled or even interpreted. It appears as an easily comprehended form, for to suggest otherwise would necessitate a narrative whose ambiguities might raise too many questions. Maugham's self-protective autobiography traffics in euphemisms and as a result arouses our suspicions that significant material has been suppressed. Ironically, the less he reveals the more we imagine that *The Summing Up* conceals a life whose meaning may be more inexhaustible and mysterious than he wishes to acknowledge. As we witness Maugham's fear of revelation and his desire for narrative control, we realize how, no doubt inadvertently, he has placed the reader in just the situation he has labored so hard to prevent.

IN HIS BIOGRAPHY OF THE WRITER, Robert Calder mentions the Japanese Maugham Society and speaks of his high regard in Asia. While working on this chapter, I went to Japan to meet several faculty members from Wasada University in Tokyo, with whom I was planning a course on representations of Japan in American literature, theatre, and opera that we would teach together that summer. My Japanese colleagues confirmed their country's adulation for Maugham, even among younger readers. I thought there must be something in the famous Japanese reticence—its concern for elegant surfaces and the deliberate evasion of depths, seducing us to the container to prevent our inquiring into the contained—that provokes the Japanese fascination with Maugham. Compatriots in evasions and withholdings, they share a resistance to the exposure of vulnerability and a common belief that one's demons are best kept to oneself. Modern Tokyo might have distressed Maugham, with the blaring glitz of the Ginza and the Kabuki-cho red light district, where you might see a man cross-dressed as a nun in spike heels cracking a bullwhip. But the tranquil temple retreats of Kyoto would surely have appealed to his decorum.

Immediately after my return from Japan I gave a paper on Maugham at a conference on his work at Baylor University. I flew from Kyoto to Waco, Texas, to discover that Waco was the far more alien of the two places. Signs on the edge of town proclaimed "You have a choice—burn in Hell or join one of Waco's 94 Baptist churches," and a column in the Waco morning paper criticized the attempt of a local church to keep handguns out of its sanctuary with a sign urging "Blessed are the Peacemakers." The columnist reminded readers that "The Peacemaker" was a famous Colt revolver in the 1880s. During my stay in Waco, Baylor finally permitted dancing on campus after a 140-year ban.

What was a Maugham conference doing at Baylor anyway, in Marlboro country that would have rendered him more furtive and taciturn then ever? Texas, it turns out, is the center of Maugham research. A former English department chairman at Baylor had amassed a horde of nineteenth-century British literary manuscripts, built a mausoleum-like structure to contain the collection, and amplified it with modern British writers. The sepulchral marble vault, with its stained glass allegories of the virtues, housed the conference. A reverential note was struck when a cleric pronounced the benedictions of God and Jesus upon our scholarship. At the opening reception a professor from a nearby Baptist institution asked about my students at Reed. I told him how smart and committed to rigorous intellectual inquiry they are, but he interrupted to say that he was really interested in their religious affiliation. When I replied, "About 70 percent atheist, 25 percent Jewish," he stopped me and said, without a trace of irony, "I thought you said they were intelligent." Incensed, I told my favorite Reed story to plague the man. A senior I know, mentoring a new student, became close to him during the week of freshman orientation. The new student, feeling the upperclassman was a sensitive type, admitted he was gay. "Oh," replied the senior, nonplussed. "Why are you even bothering to tell me? What difference could it conceivably make? This is a tolerant campus, and I couldn't care less what you are." Relieved, the freshman opened up even more. "I have something else to admit. I've never read Hegel." "Oh my God," came the horrified reply, "that's shocking and unthinkable; I'm aghast."

Struck by the inquisitional hand of authority, or goaded by a therapeutic imp of the perverse, as Maugham's decorous tone came across approvingly in paper after paper I had the urge to dredge up secrets from my life and shatter the gentility in a tempest of crazed confession. Dark thoughts of manic disruption gradually calmed into the recall and rehearsal of minor mortifications, incidents that at the time I would not have dared reveal but have since become stories I recite with a certain mordant relish.

So, in a thoroughly un-Maughamish mode, I'll start with an old and slightly nasty memory. When I was bar mitzvahed and received scores of presents, I rated the gifts by putting them into three columns: a set of matched luggage—"A"; a fifty-dollar savings bond—"B"; a tie—"C." In an effort to minimize the greed implicit in this scheme, I took into account and adjusted for what I imagined to be the relative wealth of the giver. That at thirteen I should presume to know such a fact strikes me as a troubling bid for maturity. I suppose I had taken on my parents' cynicism toward the event itself. When a family friend who was national chairwoman of Hadassah, the Jewish women's organization, gave me the autobiography of Chaim Weitzman, the founder of Israel (it was probably a low "C"), my overassimilated parents mocked the predictable Jewishness of the present, though few gifts could have been more appropriate (my day fell on the first anniversary of the State of Israel) or, as it turned out, more proleptic of my future literary interest. Amid the radios and cameras and baseball gloves, an elder statesman's autobiography held no more interest for me than a plumbing repair kit, and I assimilated the family derision. It was probably the first autobiography I owned, but it went unread and finally disappeared when we changed houses. My parents' cynicism was infectious: on the pulpit I tried to imitate the cantors I had heard, chanting and wailing the Torah with plaintive devotion, my goal to bring the grandparents first to admiration, then to rapture and tears (and finally, no doubt, to an "A plus").

Another embarrassment that I kept to myself until it became a self-ironic narrative concerned a high school debate tournament on Communism that I participated in during the early 1950s and that was televised on a local New Jersey television station. I did my homework on the subject but focused only on Russia and the countries behind the Iron Curtain. The moderator asked me what I thought of Joseph McCarthy. I had never heard of him despite the daily headlines. I noticed that among the four judges were a nun and a priest, and since I surmised that McCarthy, whoever he was, could confidently be regarded as Catholic, I guessed he was a favorite of at least half the panel. "Mr. McCarthy," I portentously intoned, "is one of the great men of our time. He has contributed more to civilization than most people ever dream of doing, and we are all hugely in his debt. He is a shining example. . . ." And on and on, eulogizing McCarthy with such smarmy ignorance and unctuous hyperbole that the beaming judges awarded me the prize. When I returned home, a twenty-five-dollar savings bond in hand, I anticipated my parents' swooning congratulations. Instead, my father, a civil libertarian who foresaw the dreadful era about to unfold, looked at me with the disgust a man might feel for a bastard child from some distant land who one day appears on his doorstep to claim paternity and inheritance.

The secret life contains more deplorable tendencies: the slight tang of pleasure I have sometimes felt when a friend failed at something or didn't get the thing he dearly wanted, the pledge to confidentially I have broken to ingratiate myself with another person.

And then there are fantasies, which Maugham is a master at suppressing. Once during the late 1960s, I found myself in the midst of a body-painting session in the studio art building at Reed. A self-proclaimed Dionysian professor of art, had run into me on the campus and urged me to join him and his students. Despite the countless reasons why I ought not to get involved, curiosity overcame discretion. When I arrived at the studio, about a dozen students were nude and slathering one another into fauve sculptures. In keeping with the times, no one seemed the least disturbed by the participation of an equally naked faculty member; the students were either too cool to mind or too high to notice. But for all my fantasies, the session was disappointingly tame, kitsch aesthetics transcending kinky erotics. The only shocking moment occurred when the professor painted his own body to depict a gaping wound in his side, and lay down on a table while one student mimed eating his flesh and another snapped Polaroids. I showered and left to teach *Pride and Prejudice*.

When I was sixteen I wished for a twin sister to make secret love to (proof of course that I had no idea what sisters are), and for several years my favorite readings involved sororal incest: Thomas Mann's "The Blood of the Walsungs," Ford's 'Tis Pity She's a Whore, Byron's Manfred. At least I knew how to sublimate. When at the time I asked my parents why they never had another child, it was a supremely self-interested question, as if they could have custom-designed a sibling to my lustful specification, much like those parents who produce a new child to supply an older sick one with needed bone marrow.

What is the appeal of telling such things? A desire to turn distant indiscretions into amusing narratives? To show how I once tried to be as hip as my students? To indulge the fashionable millennial impulse to speak the unspeakable, as the obsessive confessions on television talk shows demonstrate the democratic credo that by telling our stories we all become at least narratively equal? In Getting a Life: Everyday Uses of Autobiography, Sidonie Smith and Julia Watson speak of the "telling and consuming of autobiographical stories, this announcing, performing, composing of identity [that] becomes a defining condition of postmodernity in America"—a cultural condition Somerset Maugham would have despised. The satisfaction of confession resembles a delight in being "bad": years ago I tried to flout the image of the obedient boy impressed on me throughout childhood, and used to think my getting a divorce represented a deliberate defiance of conventional expectations. I can well imagine the exhilaration that might come from a truly shocking revelation like Kathryn Harrison's account of voluntary incest with her father in her infamous memoir The Kiss. Though Maugham is not among them, autobiographers occasionally invent dark deeds and darker thoughts for the thrill of appearing the worse, which in turn creates the illusion that they appear all the better.

6.

Redemptive Evasions
Edwin Muir's *The Story and the Fable*

Edwin Muir, the modern Scottish poet, would seem to represent the case of a pure autobiographer, one who writes for the sheer pleasure of evoking the past. And clearly one of Muir's pleasures in writing autobiography consists of the summoning up of a lost time that exists only in memory, a time that seems special to him exactly because it is unrecoverable. But beyond the sensuous appeal of the past and the impulse to recall what he regards as a lost paradise, Muir, who saw his life as having been corrupted by time, believes that eliciting the past will allow him to achieve in art what he cannot in life. Faced with the erosion of childhood innocence, he is drawn to recreate his past because for him it was irradiated with a mythic meaning and a magic that no longer exists.[1] I want to examine the nature of that myth and suggest that Muir, in constructing a utopian, Edenic vision of the childhood, has imposed a largely compensatory conception on his life, a design that allows him to structure his life with a comforting idealism, albeit one that cannot be sustained and ultimately unravels.

Muir belongs among the autobiographers who design their texts to defend against various phenomena, whether they be the irrational, a life of unwelcome complexity that threatens to undermine patterns of orderliness, behaviors unwilling to be acknowledged, or complexities of consciousness simplified to accommodate an overarching pattern. Muir's emphasis on what we could call the "cosmic" dimension of his life, its imbrication in a destiny he sees as both religious and archetypal, seems at first to be of a different order from the life-writing of the highly secular Gibbon, Franklin, and Maugham; still, I see all of them employing autobiography to create images or figures of self that attempt to resist questions a reader might put to them concerning the fragile constructions in the life and in their texts.

Muir begins his autobiography by summoning the past as a time apart, a special moment preserved in the mind, one that gave harmony to his life. He seeks a return to the past, for he views his childhood as a world of timeless bliss and his later life as a tragic fall from that Adamic world. In the process, Muir writes autobiography as wish fulfillment, creating in the text an order he could not achieve in his life. In the two versions of his autobiography— *The Story and the Fable* (1940) and *An Autobiography* (1954)—he reveals how he struggled without success to retain a sense of his past as a continuously nurturing one and to preserve it against the destructive rush of history. No other autobiographer in this study appears so self-conscious regarding the way the genre constitutes rather than replicates the past. If he cannot go home again, he attempts at least to endow the past with a redemptive "plot," in the process composing a defensive and self-protecting story of the life.

The Story and the Fable takes Muir up to age thirty-five, in 1922; *An Autobiography*, written five years before his death in 1959 at the age of seventy-two, is essentially the earlier book with several new chapters that bring the account up to date. I want to begin my discussion by examining the significance of the first work's title. Early in the text, Muir makes a crucial distinction between "story" and "fable," and I quote the passage at some length.

> It is clear that no autobiography can begin with a man's birth, that we extend far beyond any boundary line which we can set for ourselves in the past or the future, and that the life of every man is an endlessly repeated performance of the life of man. It is clear for the same reason that no autobiography can confine itself to conscious life, and that sleep, in which we pass a third of our existence, is a mode of experience, and our dreams a part of reality. In themselves our conscious lives may not be particularly interesting. But what we are not and can never be, our fable, seems to me inconceivably interesting. I should like to write that fable, but I cannot even live it; and all I could do if I related the outward course of my life would be to show how I have deviated from it; though even that is impossible, since I do not know the fable or anybody who knows it. One or two stages in it I can recognize: the age of innocence and the Fall and all the dramatic consequences which issue from the Fall. But these lie behind experience, not on its surface; they are not historical events; they are stages in the fable. . . .
>
> I know something of the society which dictates many of my actions, thoughts, and feelings. I know a little about history, and can explain to myself in a rough-and-ready fashion how that society came into

being. But I know all this in an external and deceptive way, as if it were a dry legend which I had made up in collusion with mankind. . . . This external approach, no matter how perfect, will never teach me about them or about myself. (*An Autobiography* 48–49)

For Muir the fable is a mythic state that lies behind ordinary events and phenomena. It is a history beyond history, an idea that joins him with other human beings however their specific, concrete experience may differ. When Muir refers to the Edenic myth of his childhood, he is speaking from a belief that there is a common element, a transcendent state, that all children share. Childhood is not *like* paradise, it *is* paradise; it does not *resemble* myth, it *embodies* or *partakes of* myth.

Muir disavows the possibility of recapturing the fable. He feels his inadequacy in conveying anything but the story—his external life, the facts, phenomena, and contingencies of ordinary existence—and he begins his search for the meaning of the past acknowledging the writer's limitations. This reservation is not just a common autobiographical misgiving, a reluctance to explain the self by satisfying one's idealized conceptions; the misgiving is rather that he can never discern his life so long as he treats only its story and not the underlying fable. Muir wants to write a deeper vision of the life, a "plot" that is not merely an accumulation of discrete episodes describing the life in its literal details. But he is uncertain whether such a "supraplot" will falsify his life even more than a telling of the story. And if he cannot live the fable, how can he write it? Nonetheless, he attempts to push autobiography beyond the recitation of actual events, what he terms "dry legend," even as he insists on the near-impossibility of representing something so intangible as life as myth. Muir's problem is how to express and represent in autobiography such intuitive glimmerings of what is felt but unseen.

This myth is close to the unconscious, or what he wishes his life might ideally be (at first he seems naively optimistic about what a probing of the unconscious might reveal). But an obvious impediment and its attendant frustration occur: Muir assumes that while a novelist can concentrate on the fable side of a life, subordinating ordinary experience to desire, an autobiographer is bound by facts, the *donnée*, the story.

If I were recreating my life in an autobiographical novel I could . . . show how our first intuition of the world expands into vaster and vaster images, creating a myth which we act almost without knowing it, while our outward life goes on in its ordinary routine of eating, drinking, sleeping, working, and making money in order to beget sons and daughters who will do the same. I could follow these images freely if I were writing an autobiographical novel. As it is, I have to stick to the facts and try to fit them in where they will fit in. (*An Autobiography* 48)

Muir trusts that the "intuition of the world" will emerge from the facts, that the fable will arise naturally from the story: "We act [the myth] without knowing it." He attempts to show that every event in the life fits into a greater structure, the significance of which it will be the function of his autobiography to explore. Muir retrospectively structures the life to correspond to larger figurations of myth and Christianity, especially themes of harmony and fall, innocence and experience. Equally important, he believes that that structure is endlessly repeated in his life, which reenacts the earliest disillusion and the desire to regain lost joy.

Whenever Muir stands at a crisis in his life, he invokes the fable. When, for example, he is about to leave the peace of his childhood farm in the Orkney Islands for the squalor of Glasgow, the move becomes analogous to the expulsion of Adam. And when, after a period of deep depression, he turns to Socialism, he describes a vision of humanity in Adamic terms: "There are times in every man's life when he seems to become for a little while a part of the fable, and to be recapitulating some legendary drama which, as it has recurred a countless number of times in time, is ageless. The realization of the Fall is one of these events, and the purifications which happen in one's life belong to them too" (*An Autobiography* 114). At such moments, Muir sees the fable informing the story, as if the life were always in the process of becoming myth. Muir once had a dream consisting entirely of the punctuation mark the colon; the mythic meaning, or fable, of the writing and the life lies to the right of and beyond the colon.[2] Harold Bloom's description of myth is appropriate for the autobiographical Muir: "To make a myth is to tell a story of your own invention, to speak a word that is your word alone, and yet the story is so told, the word so spoken, that they mean also the supernal things and transcend the glory of the ego able to explain itself to others" (*The Visionary Company* 3). Muir's work involves a subordination of individual identity to a more transcendent way of seeing, the self becoming greater than the sum of his particular, unique circumstances. It is understandable, given this belief, that Muir attacks the notion of "personality" as a distortion of one's nature: "Our real task is not to cultivate but to get rid of personality" (*An Autobiography* 181). Such a goal is commensurate with the kind of autobiography he seeks to write, for it questions the primacy of an autonomous ego.

The autobiography is dedicated to recovering a self that time and history have effaced; Muir perceives this self as immortal, timeless, what he calls "the Eternal Man." In so doing he raises the inescapable epistemological problem for autobiographers: How can I know myself? He admits the impossibility. This lack of self-understanding appears to derive from Muir's claim that the process of self-discovery cannot be sustained. But, as I will argue, the work defends against self-understanding largely because of its mythic bias.

Muir was born in 1887 on a small farm in the Orkney Islands and enjoyed a serene boyhood in the isolation of what he considered a rural paradise. Muir grounds every subsequent feeling and thought in the reveries he narrates in the evocative first chapter. In *The Story and the Fable*, he views existence as cyclical, which allows him to quest for a renewal of his Edenic past. *The Story and the Fable* moves from an original Eden of childhood to chaos, disillusionment, loss of selfhood, and finally a presumed recovery of a paradise through memory. There is a conventional narrative progression from childhood to middle age, but the child is conditioned by what he imagines his life will be, and Muir's sense of himself *as he writes* determines the expressed view of childhood. Turning backward is both the method and the subject of the book; Muir is conscious of carrying a sense of time within him and of time as the substratum of his entire existence. The decision to write autobiography follows his desire to unify the life by measuring all later attitudes in terms of the earlier ones. This is what he means when he says that he not only reexperiences his childhood but that his present life "came alive too as that new life passed into it; for it was new though 'old'" (*The Story and the Fable* 193).

Daniel Hoffman, in an essay on Muir's poetry, has this to say in defense of the story side of things: "The Fable needs at every point the Story, to dramatize its incarnation and make its action relevant to human life. The Story must redeem the Fable from Abstraction. When there is no historical reality in which the Fable is both concealed and revealed, no tactile world, no solid landscape, no living creatures nor believable chimeras, in short no story, there is only the Fable.... But when Muir fuses his Fable with his stories . . . the shape of life and the meaning become clear together" (425). But Muir believes that were he to dwell merely on the story, he would distort its significance and limit his autobiography to anecdotal narrative. The power of autobiography for Muir is that it allows him to connect experience across time, so that even if he cannot fully recover the past he can at least sense its continuity in the present: to effect this continuity the fable must predominate.

The account of Orkney begins with the child's closeness to the natural world.

> I can see the rough grey stones spotted with lichen on top of the Castle . . . but I cannot bring back the feelings which I had for them, the sense of being magically close to them, as if they were magnets drawing me with a palpable power. Reasonable explanations can be found for these feelings: the fact that every object is new to a child; that he sees it without understanding it, or understands it with a different understanding from that of experience—different, for there may be fear in it, but there cannot be calculation or worry; or even the fact that he is closer to things, since his eyes are only two or three feet from the ground, not five or six. (*An Autobiography* 20)

Later, Muir speaks of a child's intuitive wisdom as "a state in which the earth, the houses on the earth, and the life of every human being are related to the sky overarching them; as if the sky fitted the earth and the earth the sky." This Wordsworthian "fit" depends upon a silent covenant that the child makes with nature: the child is wisely passive, feeling joy in merely being surrounded by a familiar scene. A "completer harmony of all things with each other than he will ever know again" results from what the child possesses only for a few brief years, especially his diminished height and the geographical insularity of his home (*An Autobiography* 33). The child's stage provides a source of familiarity and comfort. In addition, the island is like the child's mind—a repository of dreams and a place where all things are related to one another.

His mother, an "environing presence," acts like the island itself, protecting the child by granting him a peace that antedates his sense of time. Having faith in the restorative power of these early images helps Muir explain how the child's experiences become part of the fable. Muir's parents, for example, are "fixed allegorical figures in a timeless landscape . . . a stationary pattern, changing, yet always the same"; each day is a mirror image of the previous one, as if there were only "one day endlessly rising and setting." Life is a series of recurring episodes: Muir's father rises "out of changelessness like a rock out of the sea" (*An Autobiography* 24–25), and this image, which makes a kind of island of the father, connects security and insularity. The simple elements of Orkney life come together in celebration of the ongoing power of that life, a place from which Muir can observe the seasons in their unalterable cycles. Every act participates in these cycles: "When a neighbor came to stick the pig it was a ceremony as objective as the rising and setting of the sun" (*An Autobiography* 36). This ceremonial orientation to experience assures the boy that his actions have a transcendent significance and express a sacramental conception of life, allowing the child to accept even disturbingly violent experiences.

These aspects of Muir's childhood, as well as the legends that envelop his archaic community, help define existence as a fable. "The Orkney I was born into was a place where there was no great distinction between the ordinary and the fabulous; the lives of great men turned into legend" (*An Autobiography* 14). Muir suggests that our unconscious life goes back to such an archaic age, and that any present event can be understood only when we realize the significance of its first enactment in mythical time—similar to Eliade's "eternal return." Muir strives to banish linear time, or duration: the early stages of the autobiography express a belief that nothing new happens in his life, for everything repeats earlier experiences just as those experiences conform to prototypes in the life of humankind and of nature. Muir's perception that life re-creates primordial experience is given concrete form in a text that continually circles back to the childhood. Muir's assertion that he spent his later life attempting to recapture an Edenic perspective suggests he is a "natural autobiographer": much like Wordsworth, he lives his life dedicated to its recovery in memory and imagination, and then to writing about it, a further act of recovery. What Paul Jay has said about Wordsworth may be applied to Muir's autobiographical impulse: Wordsworth's " 'saving moment' back into time is paralleled by the retrospective movement of the poem's writing." (*Being in the Text* 74).

But Orkney is not without elements that counter its harmony. The island possesses attributes of the outside world Muir will confront later, and his need to internalize a paradisal vision results from knowledge that place alone can never suffice. Parallel to a hopeful myth of the childhood idyll runs a negative myth of fear, guilt, and joylessness, of potential fall in the child and the land. The tension between "an unknown glory" and "an unseen tragedy being played out around me" provides the drama of the early chapters (*An Autobiography* 133). The child is terrified by the realization that nature can distress as well as soothe; certain flowers can be trusted, others "took on a faithless look." His confidence in the Edenic myth is shattered by the intrusion of a poisonous substance into the garden, and when Muir's father places a sack of toxic sheep-dip in a field and gives his son strict orders not to touch or go near it, the child's fear that he *may* have disobeyed creates a troubling tension both within him and between himself and others.

I went about in terror. For my hands might have touched the sack. How could I know, now that the sack was gone and I had no control over the boy who might have touched it or might not have touched it, being quite unable to stay his hand in that other time and that other place? . . . I had actually gone away into a world where every object was touched with fear, yet a world of the same size as the ordinary world and corresponding to it in every detail: a sort of parallel world divided by an endless, unbreakable sheet of glass from the actual world. For though my world was exactly the same in appearance as that world, I knew that I could not break through my fear to it, that I was invisibly cut off, and this terrified and bewildered me. (*An Autobiography* 34–35)

The child's imagination causes his self-imposed exclusion. The double world—one on each side of the glass or bubble—will haunt Muir for many years, becoming a motif in the autobiography. Cut off not only from the world outside himself but also from the familiar recesses of the self, he creates a fantasy world that testifies to his alien state.

As nature arouses within the child disturbances of which he had not been aware, thus provoking self-consciousness, the autobiography asserts pastoral's "counterforce," a feature of Muir's childhood that "brings a world which is more 'real' into juxtaposition with an idyllic vision."[3] As the island phase draws to a close, Muir portrays the breakup of his family, which signals the end of a unified and confident self. The autobiography takes the form of a quest, as Muir moves outward from the shelter of childhood to the urban chaos of Glasgow and to Communist Prague, where he reaches his deepest conviction of man's degradation. Describing Glasgow, Muir returns to the image of glass enclosures: a bone factory where he works oppresses him with its stench of rotting flesh, and separates Muir from a freer world beyond. He repeats the imagery of isolation: "I moved in a crystalline globe or bubble, insulated from the life around me, yet filled with desire to reach it, to be at the very heart of it" (*An Autobiography* 149–50). Muir simultaneously searches for something buried within and desires to escape from himself. The glass bubble cutting him off from the world is symptomatic of the loss of his childhood myth, and he attempts to close the gap between present and past by plumbing the depths of a preserving memory. The problem for Muir is to conceive of past and present in some sustaining relationship. He attempts to bridge an older, romantic vision that locates significance in a transcendent order of the universe with a newer, modern vision that displaces the self from any such order. Muir must come to grips with typically modern threats to the self: mechanized power, impersonal forces, and spiritual doubt.

A passage from Jung's autobiography *Memories, Dreams, Reflections,* which Muir greatly admired, suggests what the latter was searching for in his representation of a life: "What we are to our inward vision, and what man appears to be *sub specie aeternitatis,* can only be expressed by way of myth. . . . I have now undertaken . . . to tell my personal myth. I can only make direct statements, only 'tell stories.' Whether or not the stories are 'true' is not the problem. The only question is whether what I tell is my fable, my truth. . . . In the end the only events in my life worth telling are those when the imperishable world irrupted into this transitory one" (3–4). Muir had read Jung avidly as his theories were being published in the journal *New Age;* like Jung, he traces his plot to a collective unconscious beneath the individual one, subduing his personality. A series of conversions to Socialism, Jungian anthropology, and finally Christianity all signal Muir's submersion of self into one form or another of collectivism. This process involves Muir in a profoundly unsettling loss of selfhood and a fear that he may possess only a series of empty, even inauthentic, selves. Muir's several conversions ultimately appear inadequate, for they offer facile alternatives to self-discovery. In the central section of the autobiography, Muir focuses on his psychoanalysis, but he is reluctant to face up to his new discoveries regarding the inner life. A wave of dread and disgust comes over him, as his idealized version of self falls away, revealing a core of "sensual desires and thoughts . . . unacknowledged failures and frustrations . . . self-hatred . . . shame and grief" (*An Autobiography* 158). He labels his unconscious "a treacherous spy," torn between evasion and disclosure but ultimately resistant to intimate revelation.

Muir includes several of his dreams, which he sees as expressing a timeless state of existence or the Fall,[4] and they correspond to the way he represents himself at the conclusion to *The Story and the Fable*: "In living that life over again I struck up a first acquaintance with myself. Till now, I realized that I had been stubbornly staring away from myself. As if I had no more choice than time, I had walked with my face immovably set forward, as incapable as time of turning my head and seeing what was behind me. I looked, and what I saw was myself as I had lived up to that moment when I could turn my head" (*The Story and the Fable* 193). But when Muir does turn back and looks against the flow of time, he does not explore his inner life so much as he underscores the "timeless" nature of life, asserting once again that the self is less important than the mythic patterns that lie behind any individual destiny. Muir insists that any given experience has meaning only when it is embedded in the past, but he resists probing the relation between individual identity and transcendent pattern, instead reverting to the pattern. Muir claims he will explore the relation between the story, which threatens, and the fable, which sustains, but instead he seeks to transcend the crippling facts of time by looking beyond personal experience.

At times the fable refers to the design or pattern of Muir's entire life, while at others it refers specifically to the childhood. Muir's desire to return to his past (i.e., to see his life under the sign of the fable that guided his childhood) fosters his decision to write autobiography. If the childhood generates Muir, the autobiography regenerates him. Paul Jay describes how Freud, in *Beyond the Pleasure Principle*, associates the compulsion to repeat "with an organism's desire for regeneration, the urge to 'restore an earlier state of things'" (75). Freud's claim—when a desired state is interrupted, we try to recreate it through compulsion—applies precisely to Muir, whose attempt to return to the past results in his seeing his life as a continually repeated version of the original fable.[5] The "story and fable" model is itself an instance of life-long repetition, a chain of memories of memories that privileges the transpersonal.

After Muir's psychoanalysis in London, he journeyed throughout Europe during the 1920s and '30s. Several elegiac chapters describe his wanderings in a world out of joint, marked by political and social upheavals. Because Muir thinks of these years as a pilgrimage, even his most casual journeys become quests. Stephen Spender, in his autobiography *World Within World*, says about his meetings with Muir, "On each occasion I was struck by the integrity of purpose in his work and life, which made him seem a pilgrim from place to place rather than a wanderer like myself. Indeed he had the purpose which converted a line of shifting jobs into a spiritual pilgrimage" (290). Nevertheless, Muir does seem lost and adrift; the only hope for change comes with two incidents that leap over the accumulated futilities of his wandering years. Both may be thought of as returns from exile and acts of unconscious memory of childhood and the fable. The first occurs in 1939, when the sight of two children playing marbles recalls his own childhood and seems to promise "a timeless renewal of life" (*An Autobiography* 246). The other takes place in Rome, after the war, when Muir experiences a spiritual rebirth and reclaims a natural innocence he has long sought to recover.

Robert D. Newman provides a compelling insight applicable to Muir. Newman states that "we might view memory as a narrative of homecoming." (3). For Muir memory is a result of both the conscious effort entailed in autobiographical writing and the intuition entailed in viewing life as fable. "Homecoming" seems an appropriate concept to invoke because Muir regards his later life as a form of exile characterized by the wanderings in Europe, which appear like a prelude to a homecoming—literally to Scotland, and metaphorically to the fable. In claiming an exilic imagination for Muir, I don't wish to deny the conflicting desires of the exile: the need to return home and the need to wander or, in Muir's terms, the need to weave together the fable and the story. Nevertheless, the final repair of exile comes in the writing of *An Autobiography*, a homecoming that places the story fully under the aegis of the fable.

The question I wish to raise is whether Muir's method is ultimately conducive more to evasion than to revelation. He claims in *The Story and the Fable* that he realized a need to write autobiography in order to gain "a first acquaintance with myself" (193). But has he really done so? Muir completed *The Story and the Fable* within a year of the first of his intense religious experiences. And on the last page of *An Autobiography*, he declares that his development has been brought about by spiritual forces rather than by conscious intent. "As I look back on the part of the mystery which is my own life, my own fable, what I am most aware of is that we receive more than we can ever give; we receive it from the past, on which we draw with every breath, but also—and this is a point of faith—from the Source of the mystery itself, by the means which religious people call Grace" (*An Autobiography* 281). As Avrom Fleishman points out, one of the important influences on Muir's decision to add material to *The Story and the Fable* and to give a more Christian shape to his fuller autobiography stemmed from his reading of Augustine's *Confessions*, which Muir took to be the "encompassing norm for autobiography" (378). But Muir's tone in the material he added to *The Story and the Fable* is profoundly impersonal, ironic because impersonality is the very condition against which he protests in his denunciation of political collectivities. He quotes from his diary: "I can see men and women as really human only when I see them as immortal souls. Otherwise they are unnatural, self-evidently not what they are by their nature" (*An Autobiography* 246).

The discussion of religion toward the conclusion of *An Autobiography* raises a problem concerning autobiographical strategy. Is the ascent into faith, even though Muir disavowed any particular denomination, sufficient to the earlier complexity? All along Muir struggles between Eden and the fallen world, joy and guilt, hope and fear. Even with a presumptive cure in psychoanalysis, darker elements remain within him, arising whenever events in the world threaten disaster. At the end Muir tries to obliterate the previous doubts and uncertainties in a moment of revelation, and in so doing he simplifies the character he has constructed in the earlier autobiographical narrative, resolving too neatly his earlier anxieties. Muir's leap of faith distinguishes the new sections of *An Autobiography* from *The Story and the Fable*, both in tone and theme. The earlier work (which represents about two-thirds of *An Autobiography*) centers on the consciousness and the unconsciousness of the writer; the new section centers on society and religion more than on self, and Muir is less concerned with his own psychological complexity, especially his inner darkness. In his effort to defend against the revelations that beset him, he turns away from the self to the external world.

Muir is most convincing as an autobiographer when he acknowledges how unsettled and dislocated he may be and how committed he is to the exploration of the inner life, especially his demons. But in the later sections of *An Autobiography* all struggle and process are gone, and autobiography is no longer a mode of analysis, only a record of achieved conviction. This is not to question the *authenticity* of his orthodox religious experience, but to say that we no longer see what Irving Howe calls "the turnings and distensions of sensibility" (32), for Muir's triumph forecloses further introspection. There is a profound estrangement between the voice of the first autobiography and that of the second, one that points to Muir's fear that the earlier version of the fable cannot be sustained, and indicates his need to discover a substitute, external arrangement.

In his insistence on the figural aspect of his life (what else is the fable but life *as* figuration?), Muir comes very close to self-evasion. Despite his assumption that memory is the key to self-knowledge, an Augustinian belief that in memory he will meet himself, Muir finds numerous ways—mostly by turning his life into myth—to defend against too much personal discovery and revelation. By turns moving and frustrating, Muir's autobiographical work comes closer than most to meta-autobiography, but even as his autobiography promotes a theory of the genre (the fable undermined by contingencies and recuperated by the mythic structure), Muir withdraws from the revelations his portrayal of childhood seemed to promise. He has negotiated the genre to avoid too much examination of his demons, relying instead on the fabled structure to serve as a defense against the invasion of "personality." In the process Muir asks his life-writing to undertake a great burden of work: it must uncover the self formed by the modern world outside the early paradise and simultaneously defend against the fear of meaninglessness by subordinating that self to a transcendental vision and rhetorical structure, thus undercutting the modernism he has cultivated and occasionally invoked. The autobiographical intention is confounded by the performance, as the pattern threatens to overwhelm the pattern-maker.

BEFORE I READ *The Story and the Fable*, my only knowledge of Muir came from his translations of Kafka; I was curious to understand why a writer so different from Kafka would be drawn to him, and to see in what ways, if any, Muir's autobiography might reflect that influence. I assume Muir's post-Orkney experiences of guilt, desolation, and a sense of helpless exile doubtless contributed to an interest in Kafka; perhaps he saw his own depression mirrored in Kafka, and because Kafka's pessimism seems the embodiment of everything Muir sought to avoid, the "influence" must have been largely by way of warning. Although Kafka writes about the destruction of the individual by impersonal structures, he like Muir is resistant to pure solipsism, though his longing for a sense of community is doomed to be forever out of reach, a distant hope "but not for us." Muir, in his more optimistic way, sets out to "correct" Kafka, but cannot.

There were other reasons why Muir interested me. Walter Pater has a mordant passage in the Conclusion to *The Renaissance* that speaks to something Muir felt keenly: "Experience . . . reduced to a swarm of impressions, is ringed round for each one of us by that thick wall of personality through which no real voice has ever pierced. . . . Every one of those impressions is the impression of the individual in his isolation, each mind keeping as a solitary prisoner its own dream of a world" (196). Pater urges us to listen for genuine voices emanating from other individuals and to open ourselves to those authentic voices; he fears that solipsism will cut us off from a relational community, creating the grounds for alienation. One way to regard Muir's autobiography is to see that he believes in the subordination of self to the fable and to a larger whole that doesn't show much regard for specific individuals, himself included. I read Muir for the first time in the mid-1960s, a decade that held community in greater esteem than individualism. Critics had not yet come to privilege "self-fashioning," and the author (or "author") was coming to be viewed with skepticism. While the '60s often appeared to celebrate a romantic, individualistic freedom, in fact the era typically put that freedom at the service of more collective ideals. Though a moralized religion, such as the one Muir advocates, seemed almost archaic by the '60s, a more socially directed spirituality certainly was making a comeback. The particular terms Muir invokes when he renounces selves as pure subjects feels foreign to me, but in the '60s his idealism did strike a chord.

Muir's work forced me to confront a paradox about autobiographical writing: it is at once the form that elevates individuality yet cannot avoid emphasizing, sometimes even giving priority to, the other individuals, collectivities, institutions, and historical and cultural forces that have formed

that individual. The problems many of us wrestled with in the '6os concerned the relation of institutions to the new freedom we sought for the self.
At times we were cynical about all organized life, trusting only ourselves to
form our destinies and identities. But at other times we felt our only hope
lay in something outside ourselves, whether in our relationships or in the
communities that offered a vision that like-minded persons could share.
The rub was in that "like-minded," and there were many times when we
were less tolerant than we gave ourselves credit for.

One of such communities I participated in, though fairly briefly, was
"The Learning Community," which was begun by a group of Reed faculty
members, some of whom did not get tenure or had been fired for behavior
thought to be dissident and antithetical to Reed's educational culture. In an
effort to keep a group of friends together in Portland a number of professors,
some of us with tenure, joined with the dispossessed and with a surprisingly
large group of students to form an alternative community of learners and
teachers. I thought the experiment a noble one, but I was probably too
middle class to surrender as much as I felt I'd have to, and I drifted back
into a situation in some respects more comfortable, but in others, at least
for a while, more conflictual.

I dislike Muir's orthodox conclusion, partly because my own religious
experience has been so negligible. On my first trip to Europe I spent more
time in cathedrals than I ever had in synagogues. Several years after my
Bar Mitzvah, the first time I found myself at a pulpit was in South Africa,
where I had gone with a friend at the end of our junior year in college.
Driving one day along the Umzimbuvu River, he and I took a turnoff to
a missionary's church and eventually made our way into the little wooden
chapel the pastor and his wife had built in the veld. I was dressed in a
seersucker jacket, my friend in Bermudas, looking no doubt like a couple
of Duane Hanson sculptures. A shaft of light illuminated us among a tribe
of ocher-painted, red-blanketed worshipers. One of the elders interrupted
the service, speaking in Xhosa, and another slowly translated his words into
English: "We would be pleased to have you, who have brought the word of
God to us, address our congregation." I sprang to the little platform, and
as I spoke of the terrible effects of apartheid I had seen in the two months
I had been in the country, I could feel the excitement of the moment even
as I could also step outside my body and watch what I was doing, much
as, at thirteen, I had amused myself with my own performance. But now
more seemed at stake. "My people have taken away your land. You must
never stop fighting for what is rightfully yours, and one day this beautiful
country will belong to you again. Do not be passive, but stand up, and

use whatever means it takes, peaceful or not, to throw off the shackles of oppression." My words came back in Xhosa, sentence by sentence, and I could see my listeners looking incredulous, perhaps even with fear. I finished my impassioned sermon, swept down from the pulpit, and without another word we drove off leaving a cloud of dust. In my fantasy I like to imagine Bishop Tutu, Nelson Mandela, and the African National Congress owing everything to that moment—my favorite delusion of grandeur. Certainly no other religious experience in my life has delivered equally sublime exhilaration. Years later, when Reed refused to divest its holdings in South Africa, I wanted to summon up my private canonical moment.

However far South Africa may be from Edwin Muir, what followed immediately after that impromptu homily was crucial for my life. My friend and I made our way to Kruger National Park, a huge game reserve, where we stayed several days in a rondoval, or thatched roof hut, inside a tourist camp, making forays during the day to see lions and zebras and the dreaded black mamba. The cluster of dwellings was fenced off to keep out wild animals, though I could distinctly hear the cry of hyenas in the night air. I had planned to take a course on Joyce, Yeats, and Freud in my senior year, and C. L. Barber, the extraordinary professor teaching the course, suggested we get started on some reading over the summer. So late into the African night I sunk into Yeats's poems and *Autobiographies* by kerosene lamp. I was aware that the romance of the exotic setting was a compelling and seductive force, but I knew that literature was more important to me than law, the other interest that had been tugging on me for years; as I read through much of the night, poems seemed more meaningful than appellate cases could ever be. If there was one moment that seemed to close the case for literature, it was Yeats's melancholy rumination in *Reveries over Childhood and Youth*, "All life, weighed in the scales of my own life seems to me a preparation for something that never happens." I feared that if I did not embrace the reading and writing of books, something fundamental to me might indeed never happen, and I would betray whatever was speaking from within. Yeats may be referring to an irremediable absence, but as my reading wore on that night, the lamp a consolation in the eerie dark, I knew I could not turn from that inner voice.

Though it felt as if I were weaving a design that had been slowly forming for years, I never thought, then or later, there was anything destined about my decision, and Muir's terms for a transcendental pattern would have seemed utterly foreign. If anything finally decided me on my course, besides the early death of my father that loosened me from family ties to the law, it occurred one night several months after the African adventure. Robert Frost joined my thesis advisor and my two roommates and me in our dormitory room for a remarkably intimate five hours of conversation (or rather a five-hour Frostian monologue). When I mentioned my talk to the Xhosa, Frost commented that the tribe probably dated a new calendar from that day on. And when I told him about my reading Yeats in the glow of the jungle hut, and he replied with stories about his own early encounters with Yeats in London and his role in helping spring Pound from St. Elizabeth's hospital in Washington, the bargain was sealed.

AUTOBIOGRAPHY AS SELF-EFFACEMENT

7.
Autobiographical Writing as Death Weapon
Thomas Bernhard's *Gathering Evidence* and
Franz Kafka's *Letter to His Father*

In the critical discussion of autobiography, there are two principal voices. One argues that despite a narrator's evasions, lapses of memory, and conscious or unconscious selectivity in the name of self-enhancement, autobiographical writing expresses the writer's authentic identity; and that the text represents as well as embodies the subject's coherence and wholeness, the writing a testament to those aspects in the life itself, at least the life as the autobiographer wishes us to perceive it. The other voice argues that it is impossible to represent in writing any form of authentic, individualized selfhood; that only textuality is achieved, the subject necessarily displaced by conventions of rhetoric, laws of the genre, and social codes—"languages" that construct a self rather than reproduce an already-existing reality; and that the precariousness of representation inhibits a fully realized identity.

These descriptive models roughly correspond to two ways of regarding authorial motivations. The first, exemplified in different ways by the autobiographers of the previous section, claims that autobiographical writing brings the life into retrospective harmony and builds a coherent design or pattern that the life may have lacked in its engagement with the world. The other, related to a scepticism concerning the ability of language to represent any definitive truth or a self other than discursively, argues that certain autobiographical texts dramatize not merely the difficulty of capturing an authentic and individuated self but, far more radically, an *erasure* or a *canceling* of the self. In this latter model, writing does not become an act of recuperation but a continuous undermining or decomposition of the self.

Thomas Bernhard and Kafka not only deny that their writing can express a true self but in fact set out to repress the self altogether. Neither writer is convinced there *is* an inner self beneath the false selves that have been shaped by external forces, and their autobiographical writings, far from attempting to establish a more authentic self, reject altogether the possibility of attaining any self. Both writers acknowledge they have been deprived of voice or threatened with muteness, and in their self-writing they obsessively condemn themselves to rehearse this condition. Most ironically, however adversarial these writers are to their culture (for Bernhard that culture is National Socialism, Catholicism, and the Austrian bourgeoisie, for Kafka it is Czech nationalism and the more intimate culture of the family household), their autobiographical writings, far from resisting oppressive social judgment, appear to welcome that judgment in order to concede and even to celebrate nonentity. Bernhard and Kafka ruthlessly contravene traditional humanist notions of selfhood, use the form against themselves, and make their autobiographical work into acts, or pacts, of suicide.

Bernhard has collected five short autobiographies, published between 1975 and 1982, into a single volume titled *Gathering Evidence: A Memoir.*[1] The volume takes him from age eight to nineteen, when he barely escaped with his life from a sanatorium, having contracted tuberculosis and undergone several harrowing operations. The work is a jeremiad against his social-climbing mother, his oppressive teachers, the political malevolence of the Austrian middle class, the horrors of Nazism, the cruelty and oppression of the Church, and the mindlessness with which parents destroy their children's creativity. But Bernhard's severest attack is the one against himself. Obsessed with a sense of failure, Bernhard describes his attempts at suicide, his fascination with corpses following the Allied bombardment of Salzburg, his conversations with the dead in cemeteries, and his desire in the sanatorium to have his sputum tests return positive so he may join the fellowship of the hopeless. He celebrates his "degradation," cherishes his sickness, and actively cultivates a sense of shame. What seems to be an indictment of external forces ultimately becomes an assault upon the self, an extended death wish. It is not an exaggeration to say that Bernhard feels like a dead man, writing less as a survivor than as a voice from beyond the grave.

Bernhard's assault upon himself takes the form of an autobiography with only five paragraphs, one per volume. Bernhard's prose continuously circles back over his obsessions to produce a narrative drive that incises the pain, and he obsesses over the past like a Beckettian narrator. He speaks about his "packet of failures": "I packed it all together again and tied it up. But I could not leave this firmly tied packet lying around: I had to pick it up and take it with me. I still carry it around with me, and sometimes I unpack the contents, then repack them and tie the packet up again." Early in the work Bernhard describes an incident when, as a young child, he crashed his bike in a distant town and had to be rescued. Anticipating punishment, he totes up an "account" against himself "from top to bottom." "The sentence that would be meted out to me" is the first of many he imagines being directed against himself, and it inaugurates a lengthy series of such judgments by the world, some real, some imagined, some anticipated, that he eventually internalizes. Acknowledging that "everything I write . . . is a source of trouble and irritation," he never relinquishes the death wish of the earliest episodes (*Gathering Evidence* 302, 6, 159).

The autobiography is a tallying up of broken relationships, sadistic authoritarianism, physical degradation, and humiliation. Typical of his lamentation and vituperation is this passage on Salzburg:

> Of Salzburg and the existence it afforded him at the time, he has— to put it neither too crudely nor too lightly—nothing but dismal memories, memories of experiences which darkened his youthful development and cast a fatal blight over his whole subsequent experience. In the face of lies, slander, and hypocrisy, he has to tell himself as he writes down this account, intended as an indication of what he experienced, that this city has shaped his whole nature, determined his whole way of thinking, and always exercised a malign and injurious influence on his mind and temperament, above all in those two decades of despair in which he was drilled and hectored into maturity, being constantly punished, directly or indirectly, for crimes and offenses of which he was not guilty—decades in which any sensitivity or sensibility he possessed was ruthlessly trodden under foot. (*Gathering Evidence* 77–78)

But Bernard actually welcomes his condition: "It is here that I am at home, here on this lethal soil" (101). The autobiographer embraces what he most loathes, just as the boy sought out bodies torn apart from Allied air raids. As soon as he suspects that his life is improving, he plunges into an account of further degradation, uneasy with any good fortune. He invokes his grandfather's dictum that experiences which debase us are essential for our lives; the grandfather's central authority in the autobiography—especially his belief that we should suffer illness or produce it artificially in order not to evade reality—accounts in great measure for the self-lacerating tone of Bernhard's narrative. Indeed, Bernhard feels more authentic when he fails: "It would not be at all fanciful to say that . . . I fell in love, perhaps deliriously in love, with my own hopelessness but clung to it with absolute tenacity. . . . [The sanatorium] was where I belonged, a place where . . . people had to give up and cease to exist. . . . I had embraced the wretchedness of humanity and did not want to be deprived of it by anyone or anything" (*Gathering*

Evidence 286–87). Although Bernhard momentarily changes direction and admits he wants to live, the text ends on a fully self-destructive note: violating his doctor's orders, he suffers a life-threatening embolism and refuses to return to the sanatorium for further treatment.[2]

In expressing contempt for life-affirming behavior, *Gathering Evidence* rapturously embraces dissolution. Through an avid welcoming of despair, Bernhard counters any suggestion that he might transcend the nightmare. Every moment of hope leads to a belief in its futility, until the impossibility of escape produces terminal exhaustion. The autobiography itself refuses closure; it simply gives out, as if text and life were one long anticlimax, Bernhard's autobiographical obsessions mirroring his felt sense of meaninglessness. In a 1971 interview he commented: "There should be no more totality, one must chop it to pieces. Something finished, something beautiful is becoming more and more suspicious" (Anderson 82). This position helps explain why the text has no paragraph or chapter breakdowns; the forward momentum of the prose deliberately avoids the illusion that his life has a controllable shape. *Gathering Evidence* recalls a Beckettian monologue: the penultimate act of a life that approaches, but can never reach, silence and finality.

Bernhard thus makes problematic a description of autobiography that John Freccero sees as fundamental to the genre: "The death of the self as character and the resurrection of the self as author." Freccero is describing conversion autobiographies, but he suggests that given the separation of the figure being told from the figure doing the telling, autobiographies generally take the form of such narratives. In his reading, the rebirth or conversion of the object of writing into the author is metaphorically "a simulacrum of death in its ending and a simulacrum of survival in its very existence" (17, 20). The narrator replaces the narratee; the self that *is* takes the place of the self that *was*. The problem with Freccero's enticing formula, as far as Bernhard goes, is that the latter narrates himself as if he were *already* dead. Instead of regarding autobiographical writing as a remaking of the self, Bernhard depicts a self in the act of *decomposition*, indeed questions the significance of composition itself.

Early in the work, his grandfather tells him, "man's most precious possession" is the freedom to kill himself. For Bernhard, autobiography is a synonym for suicide; by the end of the work we've had numerous accounts of his attempts at suicide and continuous meditations on suicide: "The time of one's life spent in learning and study is above all a time for thinking about suicide." In the harrowing final volumes, his attraction to death predominates. He goes to the sanatorium, a "death factory," "in order to contract the severe lung disease"; he elects to stay in the death ward and falls "in love . . . with [his] own hopelessness . . ." (*Gathering Evidence* 80, 267, 286). It seems natural for him to be there because death *is* his condition. *Gathering Evidence* ends with Bernhard evoking one more time the catastrophes that have made his morbidity so palpable, even though rehearsing them intensifies his condition. Not only is redemption a meaningless concept to him, but he attempts to rob his autobiography of all significance by denying that anything matters, especially autobiography itself. He constantly asserts that his life is "a mere residue of existence" and that he is "more or less indifferent to everything," including the text he has just written. A frequently repeated phrase, "nothing matters," pertains not merely to the life but to the account as well: "There are times when we all raise our heads and believe ourselves called upon to tell the truth, or what seems to be the truth, and then we lower them again. That is all" (*Gathering Evidence* 207, 212–13).

We take it on faith that autobiography leads to self-knowledge, but Bernhard rejects even this fundamental assumption: "We go on searching for ourselves and never find ourselves, however frantically we search." Attempts to discover and reconstitute the self in language are as pointless as they are in life. The autobiography that begins with the child embarking on a bicycle journey with the world before him ends as he shuffles across the sanitarium floor, acknowledging his insignificance and the sham of all recuperative impulses. Bernhard writes only to nullify the self.

Richard Poirier has commented that "passages of writing, even as they call for self-erasure, unavoidably call attention to the self as a performative presence in the writing" (*The Renewal of Literature* 185). Poirier means that with narrative performance the self engages in a rescue operation: even when its subject is self-dissolution, storytelling may overcome incoherence, insubstantiality, or self-destruction. But not all performativity gives birth to a self. Kafka's *Letter to His Father* is one of the great self-effacing performances in autobiographical literature, one that almost makes a mockery of the phrase "life-writing." In it, Kafka performs on a tightrope stretched between attack on the father and aggression against himself, but the balancing act cannot disguise how profoundly he has internalized the father's accusations of his nothingness. At every juncture, Kafka's justification for his behavior turns against himself, every gesture toward freedom a further entrapment into the reiterated dead end of nullification. Kafka blocks all the escape routes from the father's domination. Accepting rather than refuting negative assessments of himself, he writes the letter to intensify, not to relieve, that vacancy.

Kafka's letters are typically performances of obliteration; thus, he writes to Milena Jesenska: "You forget, Milena, that we're really standing side by side watching this being which is me down on the ground; but in that case I who am looking am then without being" (*Letters to Milena* 208). The obliterating selves of Bernhard and Kafka dramatize their erasures in quite different ways.[3] Bernhard is obsessive in his denunciations, placing himself in the line of his scattershot vituperation; no one, least of all himself, is spared his denunciations. Kafka is more ironic, which is to say both more self-loathing and more narcissistic. His own psychic process is a matter of continuous fascination for him. Walter Benjamin declares: "There is nothing more memorable than the fervor with which Kafka emphasized his failure" (145). I think here of a passage in *The Letter to His Father*, more wish fulfillment than fear, where Kafka is being spewed out of his *Gymnasium*, much to the jubilation of his classmates who are liberated from their nightmare that *is* Kafka.

I will focus on the *Letter to His Father* because this document is the single most sustained piece of self-analysis Kafka wrote, and it may serve as a substantial autobiographical text. The *Diaries* and the letters to Felice in their entirety constitute a fuller record, but I am interested in Kafka's mind as it circulates through a discrete piece of writing, especially since this text is so encompassing in its thematic reach and so complex in its ambivalence about the object of his aggression.

Correspondence, let alone a single letter, does not establish the discursive continuity we associate with deliberately composed autobiography, where the writer foresees an outcome and presides over the narrative unfolding from a retrospective vantage point. Letters are even more occasional than journals or diaries, and we lack the retrospective, historical purchase on a life we seek in autobiography proper. Even when an autobiography plays with chronology, de-emphasizes or ignores teleology, or relies on associational or fragmented narrative, it is not so circumstantially contingent as even an entire correspondence addressed over a considerable portion of a lifetime to a single attentive and responsive recipient.

Nevertheless, Kafka writes the *Letter to His Father* with a constant awareness of how it relates to and virtually becomes his life—not just in the subject matter but as a performance dramatizing his deepest concerns. Kafka makes us see how even a single letter can *be* a life, not just a reflection or an expression of it. The sixty-page text written to his father is both summation and prolepsis; virtually everything that Kafka did in and felt about his life he himself had prophesied, and his life is lived as a self-unfulfilling prophecy of erasure.

The letter was written in 1919, when Kafka was thirty-six and still living at home. It represents the cumulative experience of a lifetime of fear, and his attempts, always undermined by his own resistance and guilt, to emancipate himself from his father's laws. Because it covers Kafka's entire life in short compass, because it treats issues so fundamental to him as school, family life, work, writing, marriage, and religion, and because it demonstrates Kafka's typical rhetorical moves and psychological process, it seems appropriate to treat the letter as autobiography. The letter's instrumentality, the work that it does for Kafka, has little to do with its being a letter in the normal communicative sense. Kafka gave the letter to his mother, whom he describes in the letter as dedicated to protecting her husband, but must have known she would not pass it on to Hermann Kafka. In fact she did not, returning it to her son. The letter seems written for Kafka himself; in it he talks and listens to himself. Part of its interest arises from a tension between that fact and a letter that purports to be a communication; yet both the text itself and the sheer fact that it does not "get through" contravene communication. During the course of his voluminous correspondence with Felice, he laments that he can never make his feelings clear to her; nevertheless, he cannot cease writing: "I must not lay down my pen, though that would be the best thing to do; instead I am compelled to try again and again, and again and again it is bound to fail, and to collapse on top of me" (*Letters to Felice* 246). In a similar way, the *Letter to His Father* is overdetermined as failure (whether the father sees it or not); at best it will change nothing between them, at worst it will aggravate Kafka's suffering and reinscribe his self-laceration (as if his psyche were being written upon like the body of the prisoner in "The Penal Colony").

Two passages in letters to Felice and to Milena assert Kafka's gloom regarding the efficacy of letters and, I believe, cast doubt on any presumption that he composed the *Letter to His Father* with the hope of mending fences, let alone of reclaiming an authority previously eroded. To Felice he recounts his attempt to mail a letter to her: he takes it to the railroad station, but because the box is on the platform and he has no ticket to enter that area, he is frustrated, until an old man appears out of the gloom and offers to mail the letter. Kafka is not sure he can rely on the stranger, but already it is too late—both the man and the letter have disappeared. Significantly, a friend later sees Kafka, and Kafka tells him, "jokingly," that the letter contained a proposal of marriage; in the subsequent letter to Felice where Kafka recounts this entire episode, he adds, concerning his marriage proposal, "one really can't say anything more unbelievable." Letters may not reach their destination, and affirming an epistolary bond with another, let alone a marital one, is pointless. To Milena he is yet more cynical. Letter-writing brings misfortune, his own letters deceive even himself, and communication by letter is impossible: "Writing letters . . . means exposing oneself to the ghosts, who are greedily waiting precisely for that. Written kisses never arrive at their destination: the ghosts drink them up along the way. . . . [The ghosts] will not starve, but we will perish" (*Letters to Felice* 272–73; *Letters to Milena* 223). In the face of these dismal prophecies, it is difficult to regard the *Letter to His Father* as anything but an exercise in futility. The image of the letter-writer perishing connotes more than a lack of communication ("intercourse with ghosts"); letter-writing is a suicidal act, inevitably written against himself. Each gesture of self-representation asserts there is ultimately no self to represent, and each affirmation turns into its negation, whether concerning the rhetoric of the letter or letter-writing as an act.

The *Letter to His Father* inscribes a series of contradictions undermining the self it purports to validate. To Milena, Kafka writes that the *Letter* is a conspiracy against himself, but in fact he defends and accuses the self at the same time. In an analogous contradiction, after alleging to Felice that his parents are deeply a part of him, he goes on to write, "I stand facing my family perpetually brandishing knives, simultaneously to wound and to defend them" (*Letters to Felice* 526). That defense is less a matter of affiliation than of self-abnegation, for the only way he defends them in the *Letter* is by his turning the accusation upon himself. Much as if he were experimenting with the question raised in a *Diary* entry of 1922—"how would it be if one were to choke to death on oneself?" (416)—Kafka implicitly asks in the *Letter*, "How would it be if I were to judge myself as my father has judged me?"

A passage from Rita Felski's *Beyond Feminist Aesthetics: Feminist Literature and Social Change* captures by analogy the issue we find everywhere in Kafka's nonfictional prose: the impossibility of liberating himself from his father's judgment, which produces the active cultivation in the writing of self-annihilation, an internalization of his father's judgments pushed to the extreme of self-dissolution. Here is Felski:

> The "authentic" self is itself very much a social product, and the attempt to assert its privileged autonomy can merely underline its profound dependence upon the cultural and ideological systems through which it is constituted. The more frantic the search for an inner self, for a kernel of meaning untouched by a society rejected as oppressive and alienating, the more clearly subjectivity is revealed to

be permeated by and dependent upon those very symbolic constraints from which it seeks to liberate itself. . . . [T]he production of ever more writing as a means to defining a center of meaning merely serves to underscore the alienation of the subject even as it seeks to overcome it. (104)

Substitute "father" for "society," "patriarchal" for "cultural and ideological," and we have Kafka's situation perfectly. For all Kafka's attempts to separate himself from his father and to carve out a free, autonomous life, he compels himself to assert his own nothingness. The self-evisceration is so complete that death for Kafka would be mere anticlimax; as he laments in the *Diary*, "To die would mean nothing else than to surrender a nothing to the nothing" (243). Each attempt at emancipation demands approval from the father, since emancipation cannot be a willed act by the son, only an undeserved gift from the older man. The alienation Felski invokes is Kafka's alienation not from the father but from himself, his disgust that even the most feeble gestures of autonomy involve dependence. When he writes to Felice that communication by letter "is the only kind of communication in keeping with my wretchedness," and we see that letter after letter urges her to abandon him, it becomes clear that writing is not an emancipation from, but a magnification of, his emptiness (*Letters to Felice* 197, 304).[4]

Critics have underscored Kafka's ironic assertion in the *Letter* that although he tried to break with his father by turning to writing, since all his writing was *about* the father, freedom was a delusion. Rather than making writing into a cathartic act, Kafka sees it as the inescapable confirmation that he is chained to childhood dependence. As long as he relies on the father for his subject matter, Kafka remains infantalized and nullified. Furthermore, in the *Letter*, Kafka validates his father's contempt for the son's weakness, perpetuating the very image he seeks to erase. The most striking figure in the text is that of the father stretched diagonally upon the map of the world; Kafka can live only in those regions not covered by him, but there are not many of those. The father has appropriated all of Kafka, has worked his way into the writing not merely as subject but as defining principle.

I mean by this that every act of justification ironically becomes a gesture of propitiation, even self-abnegation. Kafka feels he undeservedly owes his life to his father's mercy; as a result, and since he continues to disappoint his father, he feels worthless in his own sight and guilty for any kindness shown to him by the father. When not punished, he accumulates a greater debt and concomitant guilt. Plagued by a fear of failure and by his father's threat that he will fail, he fails, thereby corroborating his father's worst opinion of him so as not to incur further wrath. He disappoints so as not to disappoint. When he escapes punishment through a mysterious grace, his indebtedness increases. These double binds are internalized versions of a phenomenon that occurs in the letter: the father brags about his own success in having early on attained independence and distinction, and castigates his son for weakness, ingratitude, and disobedience. In effect he asks Kafka to become an adult at the same time he infantalizes him.

Stanley Corngold has shown that for Kafka, writing is always about death (8). Indeed, for Kafka writing *is* a kind of death, an act tantamount to disintegration despite his occasional attempts to view writing as redemptive: "Writing is only an expedient, as for someone who is writing his will shortly before he hangs himself—an expedient that may well last a whole life" (*Letters to Friends, Family, and Editors* 289). To try to escape the father through autobiographical writing—ultimately an impossibility—is to decline into death. To Felice he writes: "What I need for my writing is seclusion, not 'like a hermit,' that would not be enough, but like the dead. Writing, in this sense, is a sleep deeper than that of death, and just as one would not and cannot tear the dead from their graves, so I must not and cannot be torn from my desk" (*Letters to Felice* 279). Kafka seems already dead, and cannot awake *from* his writing nor *through* it. An even more powerful image in a letter to Max Brod reveals Kafka anguishing over the futility of writing: "I myself cannot go on living because I have not lived, I have remained clay, I have not [through writing] blown the spark into fire, but only used it to light up my corpse" (*Letters to Friends, Family, and Editors* 334). (We might think of this image in relation to Kafka's notorious request to Brod that the literary executor burn the corpus). When Kafka is removed from the world, even though engaged in the sole practice that justifies the withdrawal, he cannot sufficiently assuage the despair attendant upon his renunciation. His father's usurpation has so tainted the writing that Kafka forever questions its usefulness except as it backlights his nothingness. "The writer in me will die right away, since such a figure has no base, no substance, is less than dust" (334). He is empty when he does not write, and he empties himself out when he does. How could the *Letter to His Father* possibly give life to the self?

In one of the most powerfully felt passages in all his letters, Kafka explains to Felice how every sight of the parental bed renews his wretchedness.

> At home the sight of the double bed, of sheets that have been slept in, of nightshirts carefully laid out, can bring me to the point of retching, can turn my stomach inside out; it is as though my birth had not been

final, as though from this fusty life I keep being born again and again in this fusty room; as though I had to return there for confirmation, being—if not quite, at least in part—indissolubly connected with these distasteful things; something still clings to the feet as they try to break free, held fast as they are in the primeval slime. (*Letters to Felice* 525)

We might view this rebirth as a metonym for the *Letter* itself—not a rebirth from paternal tyranny, but an endlessly repeated return to the state that produced the self-doubt and self-loathing in the first place, a state that writing the letters reproduces. Most disturbingly, only by being drawn back to the paternal realm does he confirm his existence. The strategy is a quintessential Kafka paradox: rebirth is a kind of death, and confirmation of his existence is ultimately confirmation of his nonbeing.

Kafka's vision of his parents' matrimonial bed inevitably raises the problem in the *Letter* concerning marriage. He claims that were he to marry, he would reproduce his father's familial situation. Marriage is an act that might conceivably grant him power, but he cannot imagine emulating the father and entering into the older man's world; if by some miracle he were able to do so, he would lose his distinctiveness. The *Letter* emphasizes his resultant nullity (it frequently employs the term "a mere nothing" ["*ein solches Nichts*"]), while contrasting this state with that of the father, who is All Self. "Nothingness" means that Kafka is robbed of any confirmation of his existence, but by marrying to gain back that existence, linking himself with his father, he would immerse himself in an alien world, ironically another form of death.[5] And yet Kafka appears to welcome death: "In the death enacted [in the fiction] I rejoice in my own death" (*The Diaries* 321).

Writing to Milena, Kafka refers to the *Letter to His Father* as *Vater-Brief*, which can mean a letter to his father, a letter about his father, or a father-like letter, that is, one employing traits of his father. The latter meaning signals another way of regarding the internalization of the father into the son's writing and mind. In this reading, the letter is neither an act of defense nor an attack against the father's hegemony, but rather an incorporation of the father into the self (*Letters to Milena* 63). In *Franz Kafka, the Jewish Patient*, Sander Gilman has argued for this way of construing the relationship between father and son, claiming that the son fears he will become like the father—not the all-powerful but the inevitably decaying, humiliated father. Gilman sees the process as "the Jewish masochist's internalization of the stereotypical representation of the Jew in *fin-de-siècle* culture." By showing how late nineteenth-century anti-Semitic tracts argue that Jews are incapable of assimilating and of becoming true Germans, Gilman captures Kafka's problem in attempting to distance himself from the father: according to German anti-Semitism, "The more [Jews] try to change, the more they reveal themselves as fundamentally defective" (43, 13). In this calculus, Kafka has once again internalized his detractors.

Kafka's attack on himself culminates in a passage at the end of the *Letter* where he writes his father's putative reply. It appears to be a moment of even-handedness, as Kafka allows his father to respond to charges. One might even argue that the son trumps the father by showing the latter to be merely a construction of Kafka's language. But the rejoinder to Kafka's self-defense comes of course from Kafka himself, and so is another turn of the screw against himself. By making the most severe accusation in the letter appear to emanate from the father, Kafka ironically identifies with the father for the sole purpose of turning on himself. The response is a whirligig of conflicting identities: "You maintain . . . I have been the aggressor, while everything you were up to was self-defense" (*Letter to His Father* 121–23). The father's aggression against the son for aggressing unfairly against "him" becomes the son's aggression against himself.

One way to regard the insertion of the "father's" reply is via J. L. Austin's distinction between the "constative" and the "performative" aspects of discourse. In the *Letter*, the constative aspect asserts that Kafka wishes to defend himself against the father's accusations, excusing or justifying himself wherever he can. But the performative aspect says in effect, "I am really guilty after all, and nothing I can say will relieve me of that guilt; in fact my entire existence testifies to the appropriateness of your judgment. Even my attempts to state my case, however feeble, indict me, whether for their feebleness or merely for my ridiculous arrogance in attempting the justification." Moreover, Kafka's performative states not simply that he believes he deserves punishment but that he seeks it, as if to validate his father's authority and worst opinions about the son, which are the son's very own. As Peter Brooks notes in *Troubling Confessions*, "Talmudic law has recognized for millennia [that] confession may be the product of the death-drive, the production of incriminating acts to assure punishment or even self-annihilation" (21). We can indeed think of the *Letter* as a form of confession rather than of self-justification or self-excuse. Kafka attempts to answer his father's accusations exactly because he needs to interrogate and indict himself, thus assuring punishment. The performative nature of the *Letter* is most apparent in that the text is not merely stating something but *doing* something.

The conclusion, as Kafka appears to cede the last word to his father, has him say, "You maintain I make things easy for myself by explaining my relation to you simply as being your fault, but I believe that despite your outward effort, you do not make things more difficult for yourself, but much more profitable." By writing the father's words, Kafka appears to refute the father's claim to be the master interpreter, but following this passage, where the son interprets the father's interpretation of the son's interpretation of things, the house of cards collapses. The son's own voice returns with an admission of "self-mistrust, which you have bred in me" (*Letter to His Father* 121, 125); the son cannot rely on his own interpretations, for they have been infiltrated by the father's. The son cannot even claim ownership of his self-mistrust, which, like the hermeneutical act, is entirely the product of the father's realm. We have the curious situation in which an autobiographical document appears to be written by someone else who the autobiographer claims, nonironically, is the more prescient interpreter.[6]

In an essay on Edmund Gosse's autobiography, Cynthia Northcutt Malone argues that the inclusion of the elder Gosse's letter at the end of the son's autobiography, where the father's accusation turns the son decisively against him, makes that letter into an epigraph, for in framing the text it initiates the entire debate that *is* the autobiography (29). Something similar occurs with Kafka's inclusion of the supposed response from *his* father, but Kafka's strategy, rather than generating the son's emancipation as in Gosse's text, instead confirms and replicates the fear Kafka announces in the very first sentence of the *Letter*—"you asked me recently why I maintain that I am afraid of you" (*Letter to His Father* 7)—where his fear keeps him from responding fully to the charges. Turning against himself reinscribes the fear, and Kafka's attempt to emancipate himself through writing replicates the conditions of his own coercion. The father is a projection of Kafka's voice of self-criticism. By inventing the father's discourse, Kafka implies that his father has generated the entire letter (and in a sense his "autobiography") and that every attempt at becoming a self exposes the extent to which he is created by an Other, obliterating any attempt at separateness and autonomy.

In a theoretical discussion of letters, though one concerned with epistolary fiction, Janet Gurkin Altman takes up the issue of how the "internal," or implied reader, of the letter becomes as important as the writer: "The internal reader's interpretation of the letter . . . is . . . a determinant of the letter's message." What she calls "the epistolary experience" is necessarily reciprocal, regardless of whether the intended recipient even receives the letter, for the recipient is implied in the position and the tonal address of the writer. The letter writer composes by imagining the recipient's act of reading, and each member of the correspondence "reads" the other (88, 189).

Altman claims that the "*I* becomes defined relative to the *you* whom [the writer] addresses," and with this insight we can understand how Kafka and the father create identities for one another. The "I" is partly a creation of the "you" that the "I" has also created. The irony is that in creating the "you" who is the father of the letter, Kafka creates himself as a function of how he believes his father sees him, which is to say how he sees himself.[7] In this process, the pun in "correspondence" has ominous significance: in Kafka's stratagem against himself, he "corresponds" to the version he believes his father has established—his self is created by the internalized father in an act of conspiratorial self-destruction. The *Letter* is a labyrinth in which every plausible escape route is blocked by the writer's compulsion to find the counterargument. Indeed, every way out of an impasse results in an enlargement of the impediment. It is a process not unlike that found in Kafka's letter to Felice's father, where he both asks for her hand in marriage and simultaneously adduces a dozen reasons why her father should turn him down.

Frequently in the *Letter*, Kafka refers to their relation as "a trial"; the conclusion is indeed a kind of conspiracy in which the two men, formerly prosecutor and defense attorney, team together as judge. In a text where the words "judgment," "charge," "confess," "trial," and "guilt" reverberate throughout, the narrator cross-examines himself. In his biography of Kafka, Frederick Karl argues that the son prosecutes the father (4). But this is a misreading: it is Kafka himself who stands indicted, and it is he, not the father, who puts Kafka on trial, tormenting himself for allowing the father to colonize him. The *Letter* is hardly the act of rebellion, the "kill" that Karl claims it to be, for the son grants himself the power and the will only to delegitimate any self-realization.[8]

We might characterize the law of the *Letter* as: "Where tyranny was, there self-hatred shall be." Kafka's Oedipal situation involves not so much a son's desire to defeat the father as it does the realization that the father has attempted to carry out infanticide. Even more striking is Kafka's autobiographical procedure that internalizes the father's murderous desire, so that writing, as I have argued, gets associated with the realm of death.[9] "Writing is a sleep deeper than that of death" (*Letters to Felice* 279). The destruction of the son that the father almost effected through his actions is reproduced as self-representation. "I am nothing but one single word," he famously writes to Milena, "that word being literature." But the transformation of self into literature is not salvation nor even sublimation. In Kafka's case the disappearance of the author into the act of writing is a death warrant signaling that the father has succeeded in penetrating fully into the filial sphere.

A well-known instance of Kafka's self-effacement occurs when he closes a letter to Milena with his name crossed out several times: "Franz wrong, F wrong, Yours wrong, nothing more, calm, deep forest" (*Letters to Milena* 25, 119). This gradual dissolution corresponds to the very subject of the letter, namely the ineffectiveness of Kafka's mere fifty-five kilograms to move the "monstrous scales" of the world or even to force them to take notice of his puniness. The ultimate gesture in this direction was his plea to Max Brod to burn his entire body of writing, including his "autobiography," thus destroying his work—his corpus—and his self. But autobiography is already Kafka's instrument for self-destruction. Ernst Pawel, Kafka's best biographer, calls the diaries "a fetishistic instrument of self-mutilation" (213), and this notion might put us in mind of an excoriating passage in them: "Every day at least one line shall be directed against myself." Why does he invite such trouble? Perhaps only by admitting his nothingness does he believe he can appease the father, but appeasement produces no more freedom than defiance.

The father is both the instigator and the repressor of speech, one who engenders selfhood and disables autonomy. The *Letter* shows how autobiographical self-realization slides into self-denial, and self-justification into silence. For Kafka, writing is a place of emptiness that no expressed claims *within* the writing can ever fill. If he *is* literature, and literature is the expression of "the wretched remnants of my remaining powers" (*Letters to Felice* 461), Kafka, not unlike Bernard, has disappeared into a text that expresses the impossibility of expressing a presence.

WHEN I SET OUT TO WRITE about Kafka's *Letter to His Father*, there was scant material on letters as literature, let alone as a form of autobiography. I had read a luminous essay on Keats's letters, "The Awkward Bow of John Keats," by Robert Bagg, who wrote the play about Odysseus I recounted at the end of the Homer chapter. Bagg sees Keats in his letters responding to the flux of experience, sometimes playfully and sometimes sorrowfully, conscious of the role letters play in his life and how they give shape to it. Soon after reading that essay, I decided to teach Kafka's *Letters to Milena* in a course on modern fiction, deliberately stretching the boundaries of the genre. I meant to suggest that Kafka's letters, despite their contingent and circumstantial origin, told an intelligible story and that we could see in their totality something like a narrative design, though in typical Kafka fashion his self-abnegation always threatens to undermine the identity the letters attempt to construct.

As e-mail makes the personal letter ever more obsolete, I imagine that one day I will reread all the letters I've received over the past thirty years, which I have boxed in vaguely decadal order. As for my own letters, I have been writing my dear friend Howard Wolf for all of that time, and while working on this chapter I reread his voluminous correspondence to me—well over seven hundred items. His files contain roughly the same number from me, and when he turned that pile over to me not long ago, I went through all my letters in chronological order, an uncanny way of excavating one's past. I felt as if I were the biographer of both Howard and someone else who bore my own name. I saw, as if from the outside, that those men had engaged in a forty-year conversation about marriage, work, relationships, books, teaching, travel, family, and the friendship itself. The letters gave both of them a narrative continuity and formed a kind of composite autobiography.

What did it mean to have that extraordinarily faithful exchange? I think there was an implicit commitment on each person's part to let the other into the interstices of his life, and thus an assurance that close friendship would be enhanced. Those letters became an important aspect of our lives, and it would have been difficult to imagine *not* having them, for the correspondence provided opportunities for each of us to try out nascent ideas and get thoughtful responses. We have each counted on the other, like a couple of Beckett characters, to keep the dialogue going, never regarding the letters as merely a set of solitary reports. As college roommates we once said that there would be a lifetime of talk before us—sophomoric self-importance no doubt—but that writing has kept us on our epistolary toes for almost forty years.

When my mother died several years ago, I discovered at the bottom of her dresser drawer a cache of letters from me that she had accumulated since I began writing from summer camp, beginning with the summer of Hiroshima. The counselors enforced weekly letter-writing to assure our parents that we were learning manners along with swimming and archery. The earliest of my letters had been wrapped in a rubber band, probably unread for forty-four years; letters and cards, also crammed in the packet, followed through the years from South Africa, the Soviet Union, Greece, Egypt, France, and Tunisia, many filled with the Munchausian exaggerations of exuberant tourism. Deep in the stack was a letter apologizing for some obscure and forgotten violation; I detected long-dried tears on the page, but whether hers or mine I could not tell.

Unlike Kafka, I have never written a letter of sixty pages, but I have always jammed even lengthy letters into a single expansive paragraph. I like the rambling, free-form structure that allows me to ignore logic and orderly arrangement. I once thought that an unbroken mass of words stretching for several pages announced that I was a Writer, boldly liberated from schoolmarmish conventions. When I decided not to attend law school, I imagined that a surging epistolary prose signaled my resistance to shackling, legalistic rigors, and was glad to have escaped them.

But if the organized brief that constitutes Kafka's *Letter to His Father* was either beyond me or a matter of indifference, there was one occasion when I tried to write letters with Cartesian logic. A woman had just broken up with me; an ocean away and devastated, I sought to win her back with all the rhetorical power I could command. I was convinced I could persuade her to change her mind with the right mix of longing, passion, and praise. How could I fail to convince? I expressed exactly what I felt—sorrow, apology, grief—wouldn't she bend under the weight of my language? For ten days I wrote daily letters asking her to rethink her choice, and sent them out into the world with hope and cheer, like Montaigne enthusiastically casting forth his essays. Much later, after face-to-face words brought little more response than she had offered to the missives I had launched four thousand miles across the Pacific, my therapist had me face a blank wall in her office, pose questions to the wall, relate the wall's stony replies, and finally give the wall a name. "S" or "The Dead Letter Office"? I couldn't decide, for they were one and the same.

Once, a friend had the misfortune to suffer a serious breakup in the midst of his city's worst winter storm in a century. Thirty-six inches of snow kept him housebound for a week, leading to a depressingly heroic bout of what he called "epistotherapy." One day he wrote his lost love eight letters, the next day ten, after that twelve, each letter advancing new arguments for a change of her heart. But the snow prevented him from getting through to the post office (shades indeed of Kafka), and the letters piled up on his desk. Alas, he forgot to number the envelopes, and when the letters finally arrived at their destination, the woman received thirty of them at one time, an unnerving avalanche of correspondence in no particular order. She left the bulk unread and her decision unaltered.

Despite my experience and that of my friend, I don't share Kafka's pessimism about the futility of letters—as when he predicts that the note he gives a stranger to mail to Felice will either disappear from the face of the earth or, if it does arrive at its destination, will as always effect absolutely nothing. I still write real letters, not just e-mail, because I imagine someone I care about will touch what I have touched and it will bring us closer. When my father was hospitalized with his second heart attack, from which he never recovered, I wanted to write from college, but my mother feared that anything I might say would upset him; she had informed me of his hospitalization even though he had stubbornly instructed her to say nothing. I wrote letters in my head, even visualizing his distinctively minuscule hand that I would try to imitate, becoming like him in a symbolic way. But we never touched at the end any more than Franz and Hermann.

One last story. The wife of a psychiatrist once told me her thirteen-year-old son had come to her in a quandary. "Mother," the boy asked, "I know what 'shit' means, and I know what 'fuck' means, but what does 'Kafka' mean?" Good question. I forget what the mother told her curious son, but if I were asked I'd reply that "Kafka" means "I cannot write; I must write."

8.

Figuration and Disfigurement
Herculine Barbin's *Memoirs of a*
Nineteenth-Century French Hermaphrodite

Throughout the history of the genre, more autobiographers have written about their beliefs and their emotional lives than about their physical nature. Even Rousseau, whose candor regarding his corporeal existence radically undermined existing standards of autobiographical decorum (Montaigne is the major previous exception), subordinates interest in the body to concerns with society. In those instances when the autobiographical body does come to the fore, it is commonly to provide metaphors—to connect the physical to consciousness—or because illness has disabled the subject.[1] The historical reluctance of autobiographers to focus on the body may be due less to propriety than to an assumption that physical being is neither sufficiently distinctive nor sufficiently interesting to serve as an autobiographical subject. It may also stem from a fear that emphatic concerns for the physical necessarily inhibit self-analysis or spiritual questing. Historically, the body was not considered an index of the soul, and, as Shirley Neuman has shown, confession concerning the body is usually a matter for private discourse—in church, on the couch, or in more intimate forms of life-writing such as the letter ("Autobiography, Bodies, Manhood"). But there are important exceptions, and I want to preface my discussion of Herculine Barbin's *Memoirs of a Nineteenth-Century French Hermaphrodite*, an account of the body and gender transformation, with a brief look at one of them.

In doing so I will continue to investigate the phenomenon I have characterized as an emptying out of self, where the autobiography is less a form that establishes or constructs a self than one that deliberately denies its substantiality, a form that not only exposes but even celebrates a felt emptiness in the narrating subject. The texts discussed in this chapter reject the prevalant self-validating function of life-writing. The bodies in question are not merely fragile but in fact undermine any secure identity.

I am interested here in the body as the site for inquiries into the psyche and in how two writers conceive of the body and its disfigurement as indices to anguish and openings to speech. Each of my subjects, especially Herculine Barbin, is preoccupied with dual sexuality and complex gender identifications as the basis for self-image. In each text the body becomes profoundly problematic for the writer as it dominates the life, becomes an obsessional subject, and casts his or her identity into doubt.

In *Manhood*, Michel Leiris offers a litany of his physical defects. Loathing his image in the mirror, he sees thin, hairy hands with swollen veins, inflamed eyelids, and a bald head. He lists habitual gestures such as a tendency to gnaw his thumbs and scratch his anal region, and he presents in detail an account of a terrifying tonsillectomy and another of the infection and inflammation of his penis. His self-inflicted lacerations with scissors, his dreams of losing his powers of speech, his anticipation of cancer, his penchant for self-torment (he has worn a piece of barbed wire as a badge of shame), and his general feelings of abjection all testify to an obsession with physical discomfort (what he calls "corrosion"), self-victimization, and the recollection of wounds. Leiris's masochistic fantasies include the pain of being pierced by the deadly horn of a bull which, famously, becomes his image of autobiography as a self-destructive undertaking.

An autobiography of abjection, *Manhood* reveals how thoroughly Leiris experiences his body as feminized, whether through the wounds that he is convinced will impair his masculinity; his fascination with sexually aggressive opera heroines whom he imagines will attack, victimize, and debase him; or his fantasies of self-castration. Throughout the text he luxuriates in these self-destructive tendencies because he is drawn to an image of himself as feminine, so much so that he identifies with a beheaded Holophernes whose decapitation he perceives as a figure for his own de-sexing.

Autobiography for Leiris is an open wound; self-exposure is the sole courageous act he can imagine, for though he claims he is unable to act decisively in life, he will do so in the text: "To say everything and to say it without 'doctoring,' without leaving anything to the imagination and as though obeying a necessity—such was the risk I accepted and the law I had fixed for myself. . . . It was therefore necessary that this method I had imposed upon myself—dictated by the desire to see into myself as clearly as possible—function simultaneously and effectively as a rule of composition" (*Manhood* 162–63). Leiris will see into himself, that is, through the wound, and he regards himself as a mouth speaking from that wound.

Susan Sontag has written that Leiris seeks not to understand himself but

to appall us by exposing and laying himself open to our disgust. By expressing self-loathing and confronting us with the obscene and the repulsive,
he courts his own punishment, presumably via our condemnation. Leiris's
fundamental impulse is suicidal—attacking the body and attacking himself
in the body of the text. He claims that this hostility toward the self arises
from an aggressive blending of the male and female aspects of his being:

> Examining the circumstances in which Cleopatra, Queen of Egypt,
> ended her life, I am struck by the contact of these two elements: on the
> one hand the murderous serpent, the male symbol par excellence—on
> the other the figs beneath which it was concealed, the common image
> of the female organ. . . . I cannot help noting with what exactitude
> this meeting of symbols corresponds to what for me is the profound
> meaning of suicide: to become at the same time *oneself and the other*,
> male and female, subject and object, killed and killer—the only
> possibility of communion with oneself. (*Manhood* 93)

Leiris's childhood heroine is Joan of Arc, "the hermaphrodite progeny"
of the Virgin Mary and Vercingetorix, so designated because she is both
chaste and murderous, combining in her person the two archetypal women
whose images dominate the book: Lucrece who turns coldly against herself,
and Judith who turns fiercely upon her lover Holofernes (*Manhood* 29).
Leiris's focus on the body is not simply a morbid obsession with his
own disfigurement, but an ironic and self-destructive assertion of sexual
duality. He becomes an imaginary hermaphrodite, fiercely aggressive against
himself and passively self-denying. Wounded men and wounded women
combined into a single massacred self, represent a fantasy of self-created
gender immune from any fixed identity.

Leiris flirts with the idea of androgyny as metaphor, but there is no
mere figuration about the status of this chapter's central text, where the
hermaphrodite is no longer a fiction. The question that poststructuralist
critics often ask—Who speaks here?—is profoundly relevant for the reader
of Herculine Barbin's *Memoirs*. This autobiography was written four years
before his death at age twenty-nine, and five years after Barbin (assumed
by his parents to be a girl and reared as such) was declared medically and
legally to be male and was renamed Abel Barbin. The text dramatizes the
central problem of autobiography: that of identity. If a *crisis* of identity
stands at the heart of many autobiographical texts, what could be more
fundamental than a crisis of gender identity? Who speaks here, Herculine
Barbin as woman, or Herculin Barbin as man?[2]

Adélaïde Herculine Barbin, born in 1838 in Saint-Jean-d'Angély in central France, attended a convent school and later became a school mistress. At twenty, having been discovered in bed with a woman friend, she was examined by a local doctor and, following consultations with her bishop, was designated a man by both the physician and a local magistrate. Leaving the school in anguish and trailing hints of a scandal, Herculine, renamed Abel, went to Paris where he lived alone in a wretched garret, worked for the French railroad, led an isolated life, wrote a memoir at twenty-five, and four years later in 1868 committed suicide by asphyxiating himself with the fumes of a charcoal stove.

Barbin could not truly gain a voice until she was declared male; prior to that moment, she is Lacan's infamous gap. But when "she" becomes "he," Barbin gains the power and cultural authority to write. If Barbin does not achieve representation until she is a man, it is ironic, since she wishes to remain a woman. In the convent school where she was raised and in the school where she taught for several years before her gender was questioned, Barbin seems to have avoided the self-consciousness necessary for the reflective act of bringing the self into writing. Identity formation, what Herbert Spiegelman terms the crucial "I-am-me experience" of childhood (Eakin, *Fictions in Autobiography* 218), seems not to have occurred until Barbin suffered an expulsion from an extended and largely innocent childhood and adolescence. Her life at that time, as Foucault suggests in the introduction to his edition, was essentially genderless, an androgynous sexuality before declarations had to be made. It was, according to Foucault, an almost mythic and paradisal time, devoid of the social constraints that sexual identity imposed upon her behavior and sense of self, and of the tormented self-reflexivity that dominated her life after the gender change and during the course of the legal regulation of sexuality that ensnared Barbin at a decisive moment in her life.[3]

As the text unfolds, we sense that the imposed exile from a sheltered world of girlish delight was the precipitating event that moved Barbin to self-knowledge and to speech. Autobiography permits Barbin to represent the confusion, even the self-nullification that earlier would have been too threatening for its challenges to both her sense of identity and her social role. She cannot articulate her experience while she is a child; she can only do that in the narrative, however self-destructive it may ultimately be. Paradoxically, gaining self-representation becomes an act of self-denial, and the text registers how the forced acquisition of maleness is really an emptying out of self, a terrifying absence. What autobiography normally seeks to overcome—anonymity—in this case is brought into being, for when Barbin is designated male, he gains a voice yet effectively becomes anonymous, proceeding to live without an identity. When he writes, the autobiography reiterates Barbin's perceived nothingness. However therapeutic its original intention, autobiography for Barbin is not compensatory but rather reinscribes the void that his life has become. Barbin may have "acquired" a penis, but he has lost a sense of self. The writing cannot even pretend to retrieve a sense of identity.

The assignment of a new gender identity replaces what in traditional autobiography is the epiphanic moment of self-recognition. Having been defined and designated by society (by priest, doctor, and judge), Barbin eschews self-exploration largely because he engages in a course of self-denial. Barbin is condemned to repudiate the female aspects of himself but inclined by instinct to deny the male aspects of herself. What might be misogyny in a male becomes self-hatred, masochism, and eventually suicide.

But how to speak at all? One of the most arresting aspects of the book is its early tone—prior to the account of the gender change—of a nineteenth-century sentimental, romantic novel, replete with melodramatic desire and unfulfilled longing. Many of Barbin's descriptions of her fellow students— especially of their blooming bodies, or her now-shy, now-bold advances to them, or her adventures in their beds, or the scene of parting from Sara (a kind of lover of hers)—might have been taken from Emma Bovary's typical convent reading. In speaking of her adolescence, Barbin mixes lyrical tenderness, effusive adoration, cliched sentiment, and rank hyperbole:

> Holy and noble woman! My memory of you has sustained me in the difficult hours of my life! It has appeared to me in the midst of my frenzies like a celestial vision to which I have owed strength, consolation!! (*Memoirs* 28)

> What a destiny was mine, O my God! And what judgments shall be passed upon my life by those who follow me step by step in this incredible journey, which no other living creature before me has taken! (*Memoirs* 35)

> I submitted to my destiny, I fulfilled—courageously, I believe—the painful duties of my situation. Many people will laugh. I pardon them, and I hope they shall never know the nameless sorrows that have overwhelmed me!! (*Memoirs* 85)

Such borrowings reveal the autobiography as culturally determined rather than the product of a fully autonomous self. Eakin, introducing the work of Philippe Lejeune, underscores Lejeune's belief in autobiographers' "unwitting imitation of common narrative forms that constitute the lingua franca of verisimilitude at a given moment in the life of a culture" (Lejeune, *On Autobiography* xxi). Barbin's initial faith in an autonomous individual expressing self-creating power is what makes his later realization of its impossibility so painful. Not only does the body betray itself, but cultural forces betray Barbin's belief in agency, and he then internalizes those forces. Given that Barbin's gender identity is externally determined, his problem is to ascertain exactly who is writing the script of the life and its narration.

Twice he tells us of reading Ovid's *Metamorphosis*, as if the life itself were imitating myths of gender transformation. Barbin constantly dramatizes himself: he is an Achilles out of place, a passionate lover with no proper mate, a devoted slave in a courtly love scenario. Seeing the life as markedly literary suggests that Barbin is not really in possession of it, for the narrative terms as well as the events in the life are imposed from outside. He speaks of "an unexampled fatality," and wonders if he "were not the plaything of an impossible dream" (*Memoirs* 51, 79); occasionally he imagines scenarios of authoritarian figures abusing him, and fears being tyrannized by men. Barbin is defined by others or by cultural proscriptions for which he denies responsibility.

The major defining system is that of the body, shackling her to a forced identity. The hermaphrodite has commonly been regarded as a fantasy of unity or totality, but once Barbin is made (self-)conscious about her condition, she feels fragmented, vulnerable to a destiny not of her making, and unable to achieve any identity outside what others give her.[4] Barbin dwells on a body that always seems inappropriate to her: a "hardness in her features" and her unwanted body hair mark her status as pariah. She will not swim with her fellow students, for fear of offending "those who called me . . . their sister." At times she comes close to speaking of the problem: "a gross mistake had assigned me a place in the world that should not have been mine," but pulls back from directly addressing the issue. Immediately after this passage, Barbin invokes the dreaded "confessor" (*Memoirs* 39, 54, 55), who, upon learning about Herculine's activities with Sara, is filled with horror, and begins the process leading to the gender reassignment.

In a section of *Subjectivity, Identity, and the Body* called "The Body and Its Surround," Sidonie Smith argues that an autobiographical subject may discover that the body is like that of a stranger if the cultural meanings assigned to it confound what the person feels about his or her body absent those designations (128). Not to be at home in one's body is to be in a state of exile, removed from the way the body ideally grounds the self, and ultimately to be self-less. This is Barbin's condition, and though one might wish that his growing awareness of how his body is culturally constructed would, through the writing of autobiography, restore Barbin to wholeness, that does not happen. Barbin remains homeless, so to speak.

The autobiography shows traces of both Augustine's and Rousseau's *Confessions*, the one full of shame, the other absolving a self that resists being constructed by society. At times Barbin, like Augustine, throws himself at the mercy of God; at other times, like Rousseau, he stands defiantly against convention, indifferent to the social strictures that have tormented his life. But Barbin is less comfortable with confessing than his two predecessors are. Unlike Augustine, he has no secure place from which to look back with equanimity or confidence. And unlike Rousseau, he has neither confidence nor rhetorical prowess. From Barbin's precarious perch, the reader is potentially too judgmental, so there are things he simply will not tell us.

One of the fascinating aspects of the book is its author's evasions about the body's secrets. Barbin cannot speak directly about the medical issues, saying only "reality is crushing me" (*Memoirs* 104). "Reality" can be found in the dossier that Foucault publishes with Barbin's text, which contains the medical report that led to the reclassification and to the autopsy; only in the dossier do we find the particulars about genital morphology.[5]

One of the puzzles of the *Memoirs* is that we are never sure if Sara thinks of Barbin as male or female. Is their relationship an adolescent, sisterly dalliance, or a heterosexual affair? Barbin will not tell us, for he needs to keep that issue a secret. He guards the enigma, for *he* preserves dignity only if *she* remains an embodied mystery. Barbin prefers not to reveal too much, enamored with illusions and buried truths and living in a sea of mystifications, as if protecting what he feared others would violate. The reticence about the body stems partly from Herculine's fear that she has been reduced to *mere* body, forced to see herself as an anatomical problem, not as a complicated self. When the denouement finally arrives, there are indirections, deceptions, and theatrical evasions: Sara, her mother, and Barbin all play roles and dissemble with aplomb. Leslie Fiedler notes that "the Hermaphrodite challenges the boundaries not just between male and female, but illusion and reality" (179). Barbin's narrative continually draws a veil between autobiographer and reader; the gesture provokes us to probe and turns us into voyeurs.

What we peer into is not the enigma of the anatomy, but a mystery regarding the degree of awareness and knowledge on the part of the protagonists. The textual style is one of euphemisms: "O princes of science, enlightened chemists . . . analyze then, if that is possible, all the sorrows that have burned, devoured this heart down to its last fibers; all the scalding tears

that have drowned it, squeezed it dry in their savage grasp!" (*Memoirs* 103)
Autobiography is inevitably a dialectic of what cannot be said and of the
impulse to narrate, of the *interdit* (what can only be shown *between* speech)
and of the out-spoken. Barbin's text demonstrates these commonplace
autobiographical tropes, but in it he implicitly asks a related and more
fundamental question: Should he seek life or oblivion? On one hand Barbin
desires to rescue herself and gain an identity in the face of everyone's impulse
to rename if not to obliterate her, and only the acquired male identity,
with its cultural authority, ratifies the discourse. On the other hand what is
written leads inevitably to nonbeing. Not only does Barbin's confused sense
of the body incarnate his new condition as male, but the autobiographical
mode and voice nullify her in the process. With its representation of a
passivity unable to have any effect on the world, and with its continuous
evasions, its declaration of emptiness, and its anticipation of suicide ("a few
doctors will make a little stir around my corpse" [*Memoirs* 103]), Barbin's
text confirms the subject's demise, as apprehension of emptiness gradually
leads to a desire for oblivion.

When the narration moves to what the civil court termed the "rectifi-
cation" (*Memoirs* 87), the romantic mode, with its evasions and dreamy
musings, gives way, and the tone becomes bitterly denunciatory, mocking,
and contemptuous, though with occasional traces of nostalgia, languorous
fantasy, and self-dramatic posturing. Barbin gains a male voice, but turns it
against himself as much as against those who have ridiculed and annihilated
him. Barbin as male loses all sense of the body, as if it no longer belonged to
him; though the "female" body was cause for perplexity and even disgust, it
did provide Barbin with an identity. The loss of the familiar body, however
anomalous it may have been, necessarily entails a loss of self.

Smith claims that "some kind of history of the body is always inscribed in
women's autobiographical texts—muted or loud, mimetically recapitulative
or subversive" ("Identity's Body" 271). If women in the nineteenth century
tended to silence themselves, experiencing their own gender as both a
physical inadequacy and an authorial impediment, can we regard Barbin
in these terms? Is that history inscribed in Barbin's text, and is it a woman's
history? Yes and no. Women writing autobiographically in the nineteenth
century inevitably had to suppress their bodies, representing themselves by
way of what Smith calls an out-of-body narrative. But Barbin's autobiography is almost entirely about the body. Furthermore, Barbin's predicament
makes a problem of Cixous's now-famous imperatives in "The Laugh of the
Medusa." Removed as she is from her essential femaleness, and condemned
as he is to obliterate all consciousness of his femaleness, what would it mean

for Barbin to write with and through the female body? Here is Cixous: "By writing her self, woman will return to the body which has been more than confiscated from her, which has been turned into the uncanny stranger on display. . . . Censor the body and you censor breath and speech at the same time. Write your self. Your body must be heard. . . . To write . . . will give her back her goods, her pleasures, her organs, her immense bodily territories which have been kept under seal" ("The Laugh of the Medusa" 250).

Those "bodily territories" have been denied Barbin, and he cannot get them back again in the writing, nor does his writing compensate for the loss. The argument that autobiographical practice permits women to acquire a voice from the margins of power cannot work with Barbin. In the autobiography, Barbin does not "talk back"; instead he lives in silence. But that very silence is what marks this text as quintessentially female.

And yet ultimately Barbin's identity is nullified because the subjectivity on which it depends is called into question, first by the regulatory action of authority, then as she internalizes its actions and judgments. Barbin can barely define the "I," and it is questionable whether she believes she even possesses one. The body that determines Barbin's identity is written into being by others; it has no history, in life or in autobiographical narrative practice, in which its monstrous identity might be understood. The only way for Barbin to touch the world is through that body, but the body torments because no self exists outside its inscription in that distorted body. In addition, she is deprived of identification with other social bodies.[6] Because Barbin is vulnerable to appropriation by others and by a self that is "other," no identity—individual or communal—is possible for him. As a result, he shows enormous ambivalence about self-representation.

The last section of the text expresses a desire for a dematerialized, almost ethereal existence unmoored from the reality of earthly concerns. At one moment Barbin even cultivates his suffering as a mark of superiority to the ordinary run of humankind, and toward that end he desperately attempts to celebrate his nature, as if it were an elected and defiantly willed condition. But he never stops judging himself, for he has appropriated the juridical order that cannot permit him an anomalous gender identity.

Barbin is trapped in his anatomy, double but finally nowhere. It is all a matter of perspective: from outside the hermaphrodite seems as powerful and all-knowing as Tiresias; from within, utterly impotent. For Barbin the problem is not merely a cruel physicality, but the burden of excess knowledge:

I, who am called a man, have been granted the intimate, deep understanding of all the facets, all the secrets, of a woman's character. I can read her heart like an open book. I could count every beat of it. In a word, I have the secret of her strength and the measure of her weakness, and so I would make a detestable husband for that reason. I also feel that all my joys would be poisoned in marriage and that I would cruelly abuse, perhaps, the immense advantage that would be mine, an advantage that would turn against me. (*Memoirs* 107)

Barbin wishes to be a woman again; as a man he knows too much of women, and that advantage would work against him in marriage, for he would terrify the woman with his knowledge, would become doubly powerful, not harmoniously congruent.

Barbin's continual uneasiness with his state concludes the *Memoirs*, appropriately perhaps because only feelings of disjunction could give birth to this text, the representation of a self in exile from the self. But Barbin is uneasy with his uneasiness, and the only solution seems to be death, the sole healing of the fragmentation of identity that marks the eternally divided hermaphroditic consciousness and this many-named life (at different times he calls himself Herculine, Herculin, Adélaïde, Alexina, Camille, and Abel).

At the conclusion, Barbin depicts himself walking in Père-Lachaise cemetery: "Devotion to the dead has been born in me." Graves and tombstones keep secrets best of all, and Barbin's ultimate attraction to death is that he will finally be free from the accusations and suspicions of others, which may really be his own projected guilt. This preoccupation symmetrically rounds the text, which had begun with the suspicion that "I am beyond any doubt approaching the hour of my death" (*Memoirs* 3, 109), though the suicide was not to occur until four years after the *Memoirs* were begun. But that death is prefigured in the *Memoirs* with Barbin's attack on his own body after he has "introjected society's hostility to her deviance" (Higonnet 76).

Barrett John Mandel optimistically reads autobiography as a form that immobilizes death: "One writes [autobiography] not only to affirm, but also to stave off non-being . . . turn[ing] life into art . . . fix[ing] it in a changeless form" (181). But this characterization of the genre will not work for Barbin, for the *Memoirs* is a suicide note. Barbin is always immersed in his own self-abnegation. As such, the narrative stands as a mournful testament to Barbin's lonely vigil of himself, leaving us to wonder whether for Barbin autobiography is therapy or pathology.[7]

Barbin, like conversion autobiographers generally, invokes an old life and a new life but implicitly mocks those terms, for the new life and the new self do not follow from the old ones and are not meant to be salutary corrections of them. Instead of a gain in epistemological certainty deliv-ering self-knowledge—a common trait of conversion narratives—Barbin expresses bewilderment and uncertainty, and the conventional awakening to self-understanding never takes place. And unlike with many conversion narratives, Barbin cannot discern a model for his life in some other text in the way that, for example, Augustine sees himself completed in Paul. Barbin almost sounds like Augustine: "O my God, what a fate was mine! But you willed it, no doubt" (*Memoirs* 87). But whereas conversion autobiographies purport to be exemplary, urging that we follow a certain path and insisting that we are capable of imitating the life of the autobiographer, Barbin does not wish a reader to follow his example, for he perceives his own nature as unique and grotesque, not "tropological and imitative—and imitable."[8] There is no tradition for Barbin to follow, no ready-to-hand structures that could emplot his life, let alone give him a coherent identity. As the "preconversion" part of the life comes to an end and the life crumbles into confusion, the narration begins to collapse into vituperation, invective, and despair, all coherence fading away. The text, that supposed wholeness that will repair fragmentation, becomes instead a willed act of de-composition.

What results is something very different from Jan Morris's autobiog-raphy, *Conundrum*. Morris, a transsexual who deliberately and happily chose her new female gender, characterizes her life as "thirty-five years as a male, ten in-between, and the rest of my life as me. I liked the shape of it." Her writing is an attempt at "liberated self-expression" for "a troubled soul achieving serenity" (146). In contrast with Barbin's ironically voided discourse, Morris's story of bodily transformation is nothing less than androgynous pastoral, the corpus cured.

I WROTE AN EARLIER VERSION of this chapter for an autobiography con-ference at Stanford sponsored by the Center for Research on Women. I had not done much work on women and autobiography, though over the next few years I began to teach Woolf, Stein, Kingston, Gornick, Sarraute, McCarthy, Hurston, and Beauvoir. I became interested in Barbin because (s)he rendered strikingly problematic some of the claims that feminist autobiography theorists were making about women's autobiography and subjectivity. I wondered how those theories might apply to someone trapped between genders, and I thought that the life story of a hermaphrodite would make a fascinating test case regarding women's distinct voices.

Not long after the Stanford event, I got a call from a friend who was putting together a conference on autobiography and self-representation at the University of California Humanities Research Institute at Irvine. The gathering was taking place in two weeks, and one of the speakers, Oliver Sacks, had suddenly dropped out. Did I have anything in the drawer? Well, yes, something on a hermaphrodite, but it would be presumptuous to stand in for Sacks. I could offer an introductory remark to the effect that I had written about an autobiographer who mistook something far more important than his wife for a hat; but while that irreverence might momentarily charm the audience, nothing I could say would assuage their disappointment in the pinch hitter. Untried sopranos step in for fluey divas and build their careers on such opportunities, but this is not the academic scenario. I didn't think I'd have a leg to stand on. But my friend prevailed, and I gave Barbin another go. At the conference, Paul John Eakin suggested that more autobiographies than I had acknowledged deal with the body, including Sacks's own memoir. Eakin later wrote movingly about Sacks's work, leading me to wonder if he had deliberately recuperated for autobiographical studies the great neurologist whose place I had been rash enough to usurp.

In retrospect it seems to me I was intrigued by the hermaphrodite autobiographer because the figure represents the incorporation of "the other" buried in ourselves, embodying the person who has double knowledge. Like Tiresias, the hermaphrodite knows what it is to see from both male and female perspectives, and the power accruing from this possession may represent our fantasy of knowing all sides of human experience. I am sure that my interest in Barbin's doubleness represents a desire to imagine life from both ends of the spectrum, as if Barbin embodied in his own being—however tormentingly—what novelists do when they imagine how it feels to be the other sex. The culture had been sending a message about the importance of cultivating the sympathetic imagination, the ability to see the world through another's eyes in order to open oneself to unfamiliar viewpoints. Didn't I seek to be the new sensitive male, trying to imagine, however presumptuously, what women want, contemptuous of Freud's famously exasperated question and more sympathetically enlightened because of being more responsive to difference? If so, perhaps the hermaphrodite could reveal this knowledge.

Literature and life never cease their complex dance. During the time I was working on the Barbin essay, I learned from a close friend that her former husband was undergoing surgery, having quietly and secretly prepared for transsexuality during the previous several years. Though I had seen him only twice, his story shocked me because I *did* know him. At the same time, I thought it was an extraordinarily courageous undertaking, however unimaginable the path he had chosen, and I found myself respecting his determination to embark on such a course. From all reports she is happy in her new identity, has found an appropriate mate, and has no plans to write an autobiography.

Barbin's corporeal autobiography inevitably makes me think not just of *a* body, or merely of *that* body, but of *my* body. Phillip Lopate, in the title essay of his collection *Portrait of My Body*, itemizes *his*, from his back to his neck to his fingers to his navel, in a riotously daring exploration. Reading that essay made me wonder what I might say about myself, selective item by item, and so I'll make a stab, circumspect to be sure, at anatomizing my anatomy.

Once in a Paris café a man at the next table told me I had a "tête de professeur"; I was not amused. As a professor I live a great deal in my head, but I often wish it were not so, and the stranger's remark seemed to trap my body in my profession. A sculptor once told me he'd like to do my head, but that statement too produced more chagrin than pride: I knew that my head was aesthetically interesting to the artist exactly because it was flawed. A lofty forehead—steadily balding until the recession at the back meets up with its counterpart at the front, like caisson workers joining a tunnel from each end—slopes to my eagle's beak, and I sometimes worry that the brow projects a superciliousness. I don't have William Buckley's famous arched eyebrows, but I often raise mine from scepticism or disdain, a gesture bound to alienate.

I've been told I can appear "distinguished," but I'd gladly exchange that look for something closer to "impish." Besides, I don't really believe it, for my neck frequently darts forward, and when I see photographs of myself in profile I'm reminded of a snapping turtle. A slightly rounded posture compromises my height (I'm just over 6′1″), and I often have to tell myself to stand straighter, a problem I've had ever since a counselor at Camp Robin Hood, just out of the U.S. Marines, tried to strap a board to my nine-year-old back. When I walk fast, I lope, as if I'm leaning into a wind—something like Jacques Tati in "Mr. Hulot's Holiday."

I am tall but do not always believe it, or rather, I do not always feel so. Surprised when people comment on my height, I think it obliges me to be more commanding than I desire; perhaps my slumped shoulders represent a wish not to take on the burden of authority, a bit like my desire to appear boyish. Not long ago, I was appalled when, sitting bare-chested in the sun, I glimpsed my reflection in a window and thought I looked just as my father might have if he had lived into his sixties. I saw myself as a middle-aged businessman, sitting by a pool and slathered with Bain de Soleil, the torso girthier than it ought to have been for my slender legs. I'm a hairy man generally—chest, shoulders, and back—some of the hair gone white so that I look like a snowy Esau.

When I was thirteen, I abandoned my braces before the orthodontist thought it was time, and my chin has forever remained a little on the weak side. To compensate, I occasionally monitor my image in the mirror and strike a pose, jaw thrust out, head cocked at a jaunty angle. When the mirror sends back a disappointing reflection, I have an urge to correct it. Yet there are times when I'm pleased with the image, and at such moments, when wearing a Borsalino, say, I might pass for an aging Fitzgeraldian figure.

One side of my mouth curves upward when I smile, throwing off the symmetry and producing a paradoxically anxious look. When I feel really mirthful, my belly laugh widens the grin, but more often my chuckle is ironic rather than hearty. My ears are large, but I've always thought they were one of my better features, unless it is my hands (I'm pleased when women comment on them). My skin has remained smooth except for the facial lines that seem ever more deeply incised, as if some demonic sculptor were covertly at work.

The only part of my body that looks bizarre is my hammer toes, which curl up in prehensile fashion. My arches correspondingly resemble a high-backed bridge on a Japanese scroll. Sander Gilman has a book called *The Jew's Body*, and in a chapter on the Jewish foot he shows how it was thought to resemble the devil's. My paternal grandfather Abe and his brother Sam took off in a dogsled across Canada in 1912, looking for gold in the Yukon, and when, months later, they realized it was Passover, they went searching for matzah in some rural store in the Canadian wastes. Told they were Jews, the shopkeeper was incredulous; he cast his eyes down, like Othello looking at Iago's feet, expecting to see cloven hooves. But Gilman says the Jewish foot is characteristically flat, so maybe I've escaped the stereotype after all.

I have a scar on the top of my right foot where the tip of a canoe fell on it one summer when I was eight, and another on my back from a successful surgery on a slipped disk. I don't flaunt those scars the way Evil Kneevel does his, but they don't disturb me either, probably because I can't see my back unless I'm trying on a coat in front of a three-way mirror, and who really looks down at their feet anyway? Tics? Fixations? Some people put out their tongue when they are contemplating a problem or performing a task; not for me that famous Michael Jordan compulsion, but when I'm alone I sometimes bring my lips up to my arm as if I were nibbling at a particularly tasty ear of corn, or trying to play a mute harmonica.

There is more to the dossier, but for now the rest is silence.

9.
Annulled Selves
Barbara Grizzuti Harrison's *An Accidental*
Autobiography and Michel Leiris's *Biffures*

It is difficult to imagine an odder coupling of autobiographers than the one I propose in this chapter. Barbara Grizzuti Harrison, whose *An Accidental Autobiography* appeared to considerable acclaim in 1996, is an American journalist, essayist, novelist, and travel writer; she has been characterized as a woman who has lived richly, exuberantly, and expansively. Michel Leiris, the French ethnographer, surrealist poet, and former director of the Musée de l'Homme in Paris, despite his numerous anthropological voyages and his friendship with such figures as Bataille, Sartre, Beauvoir, Picasso, and Giacometti, led a relatively private and austere existence. Harrison has written one autobiographical volume, and Leiris has written five, beginning with *L'Age d'Homme* (1939) and continuing with the four-part *Règle du jeu*, which includes *Biffures* (1948), *Fourbis* (1955), *Fibrilles* (1966), and *Frêle Bruit* (1968). In the process, Leiris made his autobiographical project nearly a life's work.

Although the organization and content of their autobiographies differ enormously, Harrison and Leiris do share important common ground and raise surprisingly similar issues concerning strategies of self-representation. No other works covered in this study are less orthodox in the ways they convey a self, especially in their resistance to chronology, temporal sequence, characterization, and causality, but especially in their depiction of the self through external phenomena: objects (often enumerated in lengthy and complex lists), books, words and their sounds, catalogues of ephemera, and aspects of physical and mental life such as scars, phobias, and illness. Both Harrison's and Leiris's autobiographies are dominated by things. The materiality of their lives is the most significant mark of their identities; things are not merely the backdrops of their lives, but are virtually synonymous with them.

Both writers turn away from conventional representations of a life by ig-

noring self-development over time, which is the most common structural element of the genre. Autobiography is necessarily constituted through memory, and Harrison and Leiris demonstrate that it may reside anywhere and be
elicited by anything. Virtually any aspect in their lives may assume symbolic
value sufficient to comprise at least provisional meanings, though whether
such tentative meanings constitute selfhood is a problem I will address.

I will treat only *Biffures*, which is the first volume of *Règle de jeu*. This
text, which stands by itself, fully exhibits Leiris's autobiographical method.
The title means not only "scratches" but also, most significantly, "gaps"
and "rubbings out." "Biffures" implicitly puns on "bifurs" (deviations or
divergences), suggesting that Leiris refuses to specify any definitive locus
of meaning in a life subject to revision, shifts, and elusive referents, and
represented by a lack of linear teleology and a resistance to coherent narrative
design. Leiris's text is constituted by a series of metonymic substitutions, and
those words and the things they point to are presumed to be equivalences
of the self.

My question about these texts is whether a self ever emerges, given the
writers' refusal to make any direct claims for an identity. Both come per-
ilously close to denying the self anything but an accidental and contingent
existence that appears to foreclose autonomy and presence. If the self is, as
these autobiographers appear to argue, a function of the objects that mark
their lives, indeed is virtually identical with that materiality, we are right to
ask if we can speak of anything like a "spiritual" or "psychological" identity
as it is represented in these works. In fact, each of these texts assiduously
effaces anything that we might wish to construe as a unified, coherent,
individualized self. While neither Harrison nor Leiris is so self-defying as
Kafka, nor so vulnerable to external construction as Barbin, neither is as
interested in inventing the self as in questioning whether it has any existence
aside from the objects that purport to define it. Both texts express a suspicion
that there may be a void at the heart of the subject, a radical emptiness that
can be compensated for only by a catalogue of the writers' "surround."
The texts are implicitly concerned with loss and emptiness, such that the
autobiographers seek to fill a void with a thick stratum of things or even of
language as material density. In the process they force us to ask whether we
can even use a term like "individuality," since external phenomena seem to
substitute for individuation. An almost concerted act of emptying out the
self characterizes these autobiographies. Harrison and Leiris, like the other
writers in this section, evince a skepticism about the viability of the self,
even questioning its ontological status and whether they possess the will or
agency to permit themselves to claim a unique subjectivity.

Though I begin with an examination of Harrison's autobiography, I want first to mention an important critical essay that did much to bring Leiris's work to English-speaking readers. In 1979, John Sturrock called for an autobiographical form that does not rely on chronology nor take its cue from biography to produce a coherent history of its subject. Exasperated by traditional autobiographies, which he saw as depending on conventions more applicable to biography, Sturrock praised Leiris for not falling back on a "bogus sense of direction" nor imitating the imperatives of psychoanalysis with its mandate for coherent and purposive storytelling. "If the object of autobiography is to take possession of our past in as original and coherent a way as possible, then chronology works against that object by extending that past merely conventionally and claiming itself to be the source of life's meanings." As Sturrock sees it, chronology misleads by attempting to appear faithful to the sequence of events in the life. Sturrock does not call for discontinuity, but for "a continuity which is not chronological," an "associative" account. Far from advocating that autobiographers randomly assemble events, he urges "a revaluation less of the past than of the present, of the moment of writing." Thoughtful readers of autobiography are aware that such a moment, when a writer implicitly or explicitly tells the story of the story, is often inscribed in the writing. Sturrock champions Leiris because the latter foregrounds the act of composition and emphasizes the making of the *story* of the life as much as of the life itself ("The New Model Autobiographer" 54, 55).[1]

But an absence of chronology is not the only nontraditional feature of autobiography that Sturrock advocates. He implies that *anything* in the life can stand for the "mentalité" of the writer. Thus an autobiographer who accents material phenomena in the life may, by invoking them in a certain way, tell us more about the self than mere sequential history will yield. In Sturrock's "new model autobiography," a text can be as free, associational, and unregulated as the writer wishes. Accordingly, Harrison and Leiris in their different ways argue implicitly for what we might call a gestalt theory of the genre, in which virtually any aspect of the life may become a metonym for the self who has experienced and for the self who writes. The question I want to address here, however, is whether in either case we can speak of a distinct self or whether the autobiographers' narrative procedures implicitly subvert what Shirley Neuman terms "a humanist" conception of the genre in which "the autobiographer is seen as discovering meaningful pattern in the flux of past experience in order to arrive at an understanding of himself as unique and unified" ("Autobiography" 214). The very nature of Harrison and Leiris's self-narrations not only confound traditional tropes of autobiography (the models of compensation and self-invention), but may suggest that each writer willfully undermines the self, whether it is conceived in experience or in textuality.

Although Harrison's *An Accidental Autobiography* is far from an arbitrarily constructed narrative, no single aspect of her life counts more than any other, nor does the work build to a climax of revelation. She disclaims that memory is linear or hierarchical, and asserts that she neither remembers with historical sequence nor privileges certain memories over others. "Synchronicity and caprice, improvisation and intransigence are the engine by which memory drives and is driven." Harrison maintains the imperative "not to corrupt the way my thoughts came to me by seeking to impose upon them a pattern" (*Accidental* ix). She remembers in circular, disconnected ways, though such seemingly disorganized recall is hardly chaotic; in fact, she *wants* things "to cohere." The question is whether she will make them do so despite her claims for spontaneity and for the equivalence of all experience.

The sequence of nine chapters arranged alphabetically by title (another gesture that denies progressive narration) covers her bouts with emphysema and severe breathing problems; her dislike of her overweight body; her constrained and somewhat isolated childhood as a Jehovah's Witness; lists of the objects she has collected throughout her lifetime; the significant men in her life and those whom she wishes had been; her travels in North Africa, India, and Latin America; rooms and houses in her past; scars on her body; and the swimming she took up late in life. Is there coherence in this seemingly arbitrary dispersal? Yes and no. No, because she moves from topic to topic without any sense of teleology, in either the life or the text. The accretion of topics is analogous to a batch of silk swatches she once purchased that represent diverse historical periods and artistic styles. Occasionally she itemizes memories only by their free associational links. These enumerations are prefaced with such randomizing remarks as: "I remember these things" and "for the purpose of establishing . . . order . . . a list will do as well as a collection. In fact, some lists are themselves worthy of collection" (*Accidental* 113, 163, 168).

But yes, there is coherence because everything she writes about *is* the life and becomes a sign of that life, and, more important, there *is* an organizing hand at work. She decides to make a collage of the collected silks, which ultimately "organized themselves into the configuration of a design" (*Accidental* xi), the reflexive verb belying her own job of ordering. In addition, there are important connections among her chapters. The first is called "Breathing

Lessons" (an account of how she made her damaged lungs function again), and her final one is called "Swimming Lessons" (an account of her attempt to be weightless in water in order to regain the weightlessness and freedom she felt as a child, and to compensate for being overweight). Her auto-biography embodies the central vision that everything counts, and while the narrative might appear to be randomly inclusive, there is surprising unity when the life is perceived in retrospect. Learning to regain her breath implies that voicing her life in autobiography is a perilous though necessary endeavor. In "Breathing Lessons," she feels as if she is coming to the end of her breath, and this awareness leads into a lengthy valedictory recitation of things she has done in her life, along with a desire to continue living— largely to undertake her autobiography. The next chapter, "Food, Flesh, and Fashion," centers on the pleasures and dangers of the senses. It is followed by "Home Economics," which traces her puritanical upbringing and her need to break into an uninhibited sensuality. Harrison's text is like her image of the mind: an "ordered labyrinth of the unconscious" (*Accidental* x), seemingly without formal purpose, yet built upon certain patterns of desire.

Because her adult life has been unplanned, even willfully disorganized, Harrison writes a horizontally structured autobiography, which treats her experiences—swimming, love, books, food, work—as all equally impor-tant. The important men in her life seem no more or less significant than the objects in her house that she exhaustively catalogues. She refuses distinctions others might take for granted. For example, two men loom large in her life: an English teacher from high school in New York with whom she began a quasi-erotic relation, and "Jazzman," her first lover who resurfaced in her life thirty-five years after an initial breakup, only to leave once again. Yet three other men occupy equally important places, one a mere voice from her childhood (Red Barber, the Brooklyn Dodger announcer in the 1940s and '50s), the second a fictional character (Peter Wimsey, Dorothy Sayers's detective), and the third a historical figure (Frederico Secundo, the thirteenth-century king of Sicily). Life and art, the personal and the public, coalesce in her narrative.

In what sense is this autobiography "accidental"? Nowhere does Harrison explain her use of the term. I suspect that in a life haunted frequently by death ("I am a walking *memento mori*. I remind people that someday they too will cease to breathe" [*Accidental* 13]), her survival may feel accidental, a gift. If Harrison is a *memento mori* for others, a reminder of *their* mortality, her own mementos ultimately remind her of the end *she* cannot stave off despite her accumulations. Harrison's body begins to fail her, and when she learns to swim in order to regain a freedom remembered from childhood, the disparity of the two conditions is yet another *memento mori*. Finally, the writing itself is "accidental," that is, fortuitous, since she had not expected to live long enough to produce it, and it is thus a negotiation with death.

An Accidental Autobiography is mostly a collection of memories and associations, just as the life has been dedicated to collecting objects and experiences. Indeed, her collecting impulse dominates much of the account, whether the goal is to accumulate experiences, lovers, books, *objets d'art*, clothes, or even inventories and lists. One of her chapters is titled "Loot and Lists and Lusts (and Things)."

> We collect to survive; our survival depends in part on our ability to classify and codify and catalogue: we hunt and choose in order to tame chaos, to bring order to a world too full of being, too full of things. We hunt and gather and collect and accrete for the reason we do everything else: we die. . . . Over our possessions, we allow ourselves to believe, we have control. With our possessions we weave our shrouds. Everything we collect is a *memento mori*. (*Accidental* 138)

After citing a list of artifacts owned by a sixteenth-century noblewoman, Harrison exclaims, "The lady's catalogue was a kind of autobiography" (*Accidental* 168). Collecting unites Harrison's past and present, and she lives in part to amass materials for the act of retrospection.

But the catalogues of things in her life suggest a fragmentation of the self (the catalogues are as eclectic, diverse, and deliberately uncentered as she and her text appear to be). These lists become "a meditative metaphor for an impossible organization of the self." After enumerating the objects in her bedroom—an inventory of such miscellaneous abundance there scarcely seems room for Harrison—she uncovers swatches of fabrics from a shopping bag: "I will not die until I have made a tapestry of them" (*Accidental* 85, 372). In the midst of the material overflow, Harrison's fantasies of order and control represent her desire to tame excess, to place objects in a narrative design that justifies their importance in her life and gives shape to what otherwise might seem like an indulgence of supplementarity. And yet the autobiography is not unlike the collage of silks or the tapestry of swatches, for even as she seeks to harness the spillage, a subversive instinct to resist design counteracts the more conventional narrational aesthetic. To be sure, she is often conflicted on this issue, and the autobiography reveals her constant ambivalence: thus her fleshly amplitude (a continuous refrain), something like the way things in the text overflow its bounds, is both cause for embarrassment and unapologetic evidence of a life lived with plenitude. "I [am] caught in a web of conflicting impulses and desires. Exposure, and defense. Hiding, and revelation." But finally she will not lament: "To indulge one's appetite . . . is to create space, the space in which to assert one's abandon and desire" (*Accidental* 62, 57). Is she talking about eating, or writing autobiography? The issues are identical: the overflowing lists stand for a life of indulgent desire, and the autobiography is as copious as the life it describes.

In a work that brims with data and particularity, Harrison says "detail increases an object's stature" (*Accidental* 166). Naomi Schor associates the feminine with the surface (she intends nothing pejorative), employing Barthes's notion in "The Reality Effect" that details participate in an economy of excess, are a luxury beyond necessity. Barthes and Schor are both talking about fictional plots, but Harrison's textual amplitude functions much the same way, insisting on desire that cannot be confined or restrained.

But there is a more compelling reason why this autobiography is swollen, especially with sensual delight. Harrison's text is an archive of pleasures, unrecapturable and tauntingly out of reach except through memory and re-creation. She writes, "I want everything—candlelight and music, soft fabric and strong hands caressing me, perfume and wine, love, sex, food, joy, the dance of the blood. . . . I want *always*. . . . In the meantime I pursue a catalogue from my favorite gourmet food store," and "I want, I want, I want" (*Accidental* 61, 335). Harrison the Rain Queen.

She calls her mind "a curio cabinet" (*Accidental* 167), and she is like a curator, exhibiting the objects whose value inheres in the way they embody her consciousness. Furthermore, the collecting enterprise becomes the ideal preparation for writing autobiography. James Clifford, in his essay "On Collecting Art and Culture," quotes Baudrillard on collected artifacts: "The environment of private objects and their possession—of which collections are an extreme manifestation—is a dimension of our life that is both essential and imaginary. As essential as dreams." Clifford asserts that "collecting has long been a strategy for the deployment of a possessive self . . . and authenticity," and we might see Harrison's passion for accumulation as an attempt to give shape and solidity to her life (220, 218). Harrison announces, "We hunt and treasure so as to feel a sense of continuity . . . with the past," and again, "I feel united to history when I touch the Indian things I possess—my own history, and that of the subcontinent" (*Accidental* 138, 151). Her collecting represents an impulse to bestow identity and control the past by aestheticizing it. "I am contained in my past (and my past is contained in me)" (*Accidental* 76). Just as she cannot imagine *not* living in the past, so in the autobiography she continually inhabits a nostalgic mode.

But does she finally achieve identity? As a child, she impersonates other people in order to create herself, and as a result always feels fraudulent, without a sense of self. A version of this phenomenon reoccurs when she is grown: she aspires to become like an idealized high school teacher, even to re-create his apartment. Her collecting instinct resumes when she attempts to replicate the objects in his world, and she wonders if her lust to collect originates in her love of him or in her desire to *be* him. Her identity is imbricated in the obsession for imitation. That teacher, whom she calls her "creator," spurs her first attempt at autobiography—a school writing exercise called "Portrait in a Mirror": "I invented a self made of wishes." (*Accidental* 212). Her present self is similarly questionable. In a text that forgoes a single narrative line because such unity would falsify herself, Harrison proposes multiple avenues to self-understanding: travels, bodily functions and blemishes, lovers, artifacts, and clothing. Reunited with Jazzman, she finds his body familiar as she reads it like Braille. Something like that happens in her writing. She reads her possessions and sees the self largely through others: "We tempt people to read us, we invite them to consider our objects so we see ourselves reflected in their eyes" (*Accidental* 153). She "reads" the material objects of her world. But is there in fact a self not reflected through others' eyes or through "things"?

I detect an uneasy self-effacement in Harrison's autobiographical procedure, an implicit contradiction to her assertion of desire and will. She expresses an urge to reclaim the self, in writing if not in actuality, yet the question remains: does Harrison discover an identity or conceal it, perhaps even suppress it? Her autobiographical method makes us wonder if a self really emerges or if it disappears into the appropriation of other people and the materiality that appear to stand in for the life.

In *Scratches (Biffures)*, Leiris calls attention to the process by which he composes the work. He gathers together scraps of paper, miscellaneous documents, index cards, letters, journals, and other bits of ephemera with which to structure his collage-like autobiography. He is obsessed with his method of assemblage because for Leiris, no less than for Harrison, autobiography consists of randomly collected memories rather than a chronologically structured account of the life. Indeed, the process of collecting and assembling is an integral aspect of the life. Avoiding consistency or any defining center of his life, Leiris seeks a narrative equivalent to the surprises and inchoateness of his experience. Normally a discussion of how one decides what to include in an autobiography is a supplement to the autobiographer's narrative, but for Leiris such a discussion becomes the very stuff of his existence; the act of investigating the life *is* the life. "I formed a file for my own use in which I noted down on loose sheets of paper . . . the memories of my childhood or youth I didn't want to forget—brief fragments, hardly more than memory ticklers." (*Scratches* 237). Nothing is lost on him, however elusive the experiences and the filaments binding them together. Leiris cultivates uncertainty because all markers of the self are as fragile, ephemeral, and self-contradictory as the self to which they point.

Throughout the five volumes of autobiography, Leiris's self-portrayal is fragmentary, and he never attempts a coherent portrait of himself. "All my inkblots, my hesitations, my stumbling over words, all the crossouts or interlineations that accumulate in each of my sentences and that I am so likely to attribute to the clumsiness of expression in fact betray indecisiveness in my thought and . . . the deep fear that prevents me from advancing except by sudden leaps, detours, and backtrackings, as though each time I had to affirm something or myself" (*Scratches* 248). Each time Leiris says "I" he flinches, preferring gaps, inconsistencies, even an erasure of the self rather than the "literariness" that would falsify.

The principal constituents of Leiris's representation include "numbing effluvia," objects, scraps of things, curiosities; through the writer's recollection (literally a re-collecting), any given object may metamorphose into other things due to what he regards as the mercurial nature of objects and language alike. Although Leiris feels dismay at the vast and proliferating assemblage of objects that enter the text via "my gloomy little routine of collecting," he cannot cease writing until at some point he arbitrarily stops, "however mortifying it may be to conclude a book without having reached any real point of arrival (the disclosure of some truth that was not there at the beginning)" (*Scratches* 242, 245, 258). Several critics have pointed out that Leiris is by (professional) nature an ethnographer of the self, assembling data and information more from outside than inside; he is also a seemingly random observer who avoids summary judgments or definitive conclusions, committed to incompletion if not incoherence.[2] Leiris's relation to the world of sounds, objects, and other phenomena constitutes the basis of whatever questionable self-understanding he achieves, and the words he uses to name things in his world become, collectively, all the "I" he will acknowledge. Objects, in their tactile and tangible materiality, constitute his destiny, and *Biffures* investigates the uncertain meanings he attributes to them. Refusing to establish a continuous account of the life, he narrates a seemingly haphazard set of incidents replete with objects that characterize his interests.[3] John Sturrock remarks, "the question the free-range auto-biographer [one freed from a chronological organizing principle] puts to himself in writing, is not 'What came next?' but 'What is coming next, as I write?'" And again, "seldom in literature are we able to share so directly in the equivocal pleasures of going nowhere" ("Autobiographer Astray" 220, 213). Leiris himself, much like the reader, seems never to know what may show up in the narrative.

The title of the work is the key to Leiris's autobiographical strategy. The word "biffures" is not explained until late in the text, and only then does Leiris's theorizing intention come into play. The pun in *bifur* and *biffure* encompasses the complexity of his autobiographical method. *Bifur* suggests bifurcation (at railway junctions, for example, when tracks diverge and reconverge); a *bifur* connotes a rapid switching of subject matter, or as Leiris puts it, "somersaults, trippings or slippings of thought occurring as a result of a fracture, a dazzling flash . . . manifesting itself in speech; losses of footing or leaps from one level to another . . . eddies, wrinkles . . . or other alterations" of language (*Scratches* 238). This catalogue shows Leiris's mind at work as it enacts the slipperiness of his subject: the bifurcation of sense. These switches and changes of direction in thought characterize both subject matter and method. The term *bifur* converges and colludes with the term *biffure*, meaning "scratch or erasure," indicating the way we relive, delete, and amend aspects of our life in the act of contemplating it. Leiris implies both that his life and writing are like a palimpsest, and that he scratches beneath surfaces, scratches things out, deleting or replacing them in the act of writing about these processes. The procedure of continual narrative erasure may be extended to Leiris's conception of self, which is also under threat of erasure from within.

Leiris cultivates the *bifurs* ("bifurcations, meanderings, different digres-sions"), for they "make the mind step outside of its rut, indulge it to seek its fortune off the beaten paths or to derail it." But we must recognize conver-gencies as well, surprising associations and linkages that also underlie subject matter and method. Following associations, pursuing unexpected paths, and diverging from any momentary insight all correspond to corrections he might have imposed on his life at various junctures. He worries that such corrections could imply he imposes a destiny or formula on his life, but the procedure of *biffures* (erasures that prevent any grand revelation) preclude any obvious and coherent direction in the account. The result is "to group together in a single picture all sorts of heteroclite facts relating to my person in order to obtain a book that would finally be an abridged encyclopedia of myself" (*Scratches* 242, 243, 244). An encyclopedia: again a collection of details without a necessary grand design, an assemblage that describes both the writing and the self. In establishing "the rules of the game" and "the rules of the I" (*jeu* and *Je* are pronounced almost identically), he will not claim coherence nor deny the incomplete and fragmentary nature of the self.

Why does Leiris insist that his work lack "finish" (in the sense of both completion and polish)? Leiris's deepest fear is of time and death, and since completion implies that one exists in time, the fear precipitates his compulsion for the interminable. Direction and purpose, in the life and in the writing of it, come too close to a teleology which, in its pure biological sense, portends extinction, the ultimate "rule of the game." Leiris's refusal to go "somewhere" represents an evasion of finality, for he asserts that an autobiographical discourse that resists the subject's progressive development gains an immunity from time. So long as he emphasizes the present moment of writing, whose subject matter is Leiris thinking and not the Leiris who has achieved something in a completed past, he can imagine a suspended state of time. Ironically, the fear of demise leads Leiris to represent the self as lacking any coherent center or essence.

Autobiographers frequently regard their work as constituting an illusory postponement of death—the Beckettian notion of speech as a deferral of the endgame. Leiris's deferral consists of endlessly changing direction, scratching or crossing out, digressing, and "keep[ing] alive conflicting hypotheses" (Brée 201). By writing five volumes of autobiography, Leiris employs the genre to create the illusion of new beginnings. By deferring the conclusion of the autobiographical project, he doubtless fantasizes that he may put off his own death. But unlike Barbara Harrison, who amasses possessions in order to surround herself with illusions of immortality,[4] Leiris accumulates objects and discovers that his collections are composed of "the most ephemeral of inanimate things, whose fragility proves to be fashioned after my own," and stands in contrast with acquisitions in museums and libraries "whose stability can only remind me . . . how temporary I am" (*Scratches* 224). Leiris's autobiographical text is an elegy for the inevitable failure to write himself into permanence.

Each section of the text appears disconcertingly unrelated to the previous one. In "Songs," Leiris speaks of words that attain a "special luster" when set to music, a process he associates with memories of his first communion, when words written in gold in his Bible attained magical power. Leiris often recaptures the past through objects and words that for him have achieved an aura of wonder. From the start, he gives us fragmentary, almost impressionistic glimpses of his early life, and we must put them together if we are to read his past from these disjunctive traces. In a completely different vein, the next section, "In Court Dress," focuses on "barriers, borders, or limits, openworks of curving iron or scallops of arcades and houses" (*Scratches* 12, 30). Remembering a balcony railing at his parents' house, Leiris speaks of his attraction to the feel and taste of the metal, then dwells on the railing as a barrier separating the house from the space beyond. Through the balcony he sees a red glow from the signage at the ZIGZAG cigarette paper factory, a name that describes Leiris's autobiographical mind. The child associates the glow of the sign with fire, and when a paint factory burns down, he further associates the firemen's costume, whose name in French means "in court dress," with a similar sound that is the name of a nearby town. The narrative sequence is dictated in part by free association, just as the child could never predict where associations would carry him. Leiris's feelings of vertigo, and his bifurcations, forkings, and accumulated associations all indicate his resistance to a coherent network of filiations.

In "Alphabet," Leiris focuses on letters as objects that not only constitute words, but themselves have distinctive characteristics: "Letters do not remain 'dead letters,' but are washed by the sap of a precious kabbala, which jars them from their dogmatic immobility and fills them with life, to the very tips of their branches. Quite naturally the *A* changes into a Jacob's ladder . . . the *I* (the soldier standing at attention) into a column of fire or clouds" (*Scratches* 35–36). This excursus reveals how Leiris early on staked his claim to be a writer; the child learned to create by endowing letters with improbable attributes and associating those letters with particular sounds, tastes, and sights. Eventually, he constructs a whole system of mythology from the resonance of certain names, becoming his own creator. Even as a child he believed that language could be playfully transformed by an imagination rivaling that of God. When Leiris writes the autobiography, he reenacts the earliest pleasure of making syllables and words collide by juxtaposing incongruous memories, words, and experiences. The autobiography forces us to stretch our horizon of expectation and to regard the discussions of writing as no less important than the events which that writing portrays. Leiris defines himself as a writer as he transforms experience through a subjective process by which data and reference become language: "It was necessary that the fascination exerted on me by language lead me to study its arcana once again by attaching myself, this time, to certain facts that stood out in my eyes against the mass of other facts for the very reason that they were *facts of language* whose primary stimuli were words" (*Scratches* 237). Leiris's notion of language is hermetic and private, and one of the difficulties in reading *Biffures* as autobiography results from its insistence on the feel of words in the mouth and on the ear rather than on their discursive meaning or on the way language might signify character.

In "Persephone," Leiris undertakes his most complex discussion of writing. He begins by denying the external world's influence on him, for "it appears beyond question that everything happens in my head and it alone is responsible . . . for what I have the illusion of taking from the outside." (*Scratches* 67). He admits that he and things, the outside, might be joined in a system of inspiration, which he relates to "a mechanism of the body that is itself an exchange." Inspiration is a breathing in and out, an exchange of inside and outside; not surprisingly, the section enumerates various reciprocal movements between the inside and the outside, all of them standing for the process of remembering and writing.

But Leiris's autobiographical procedure, especially its resistance to self-revelation, creates a crisis for him: he wonders whether his fixation on the pleasures of words and on "rejecting a healthy, virile plunge in favor of aesthetic daydreaming" (*Scratches* 89) effectively keeps him from delineating a self. Were he simply to dredge up scenes from the past, he fears he would write nothing but "dead abstractions." Narcissus, reluctant to take the plunge into the lake of memories, is Leiris's figure for the writer. Leiris feels he should pierce the watery membrane that leads to the past, but "tottering between present and past, between imagination and memory, between poetry and reality, I hesitate, I waver, I stagger, I oscillate" (106). He alternates between a desire to conduct research into his past and a fear that such an investigation is irrelevant and will falsify by constructing a self whom he regards as questionable. For Leiris there *is* no self in the past, only one who writes, now, and this self is also tenuous. Leiris seems much like the Kafka who declares, "I am made of literature, I am nothing else" (*Letters to Felice* 304).

As Leiris moves toward the conclusion of *Biffures*, he becomes increasingly anxious that he has substituted a collage of autobiographical epiphenomena for an account of the self. Preoccupied with his method of recall and recording, he explains how he has gathered together effluvia and ephemera—scraps of paper, letters, publicity leaflets, photographs, souvenirs—anything that might stand in for himself. He has fetischized objects that substitute for him. His text is the perfect vehicle to inscribe a self that seems at every turn to deny its own essence. Text and self resemble the body he described in *L'Age d'Homme:* temporary, unstable, fragmented, approaching a state of mutilation. Leiris's procedure makes him "an embalmer of dead things," and he fears that he has bound himself "to ancient toys and dusty fetishes that I ought rather to put up for auction" (*Scratches* 233). He questions how authentic a portrayal, if any, he has achieved.

The self remains elusive, just as his project remains tentative. His strategy both acknowledges the difficulty of attaining self-knowledge and dramatizes that difficulty. For Leiris, not only can there be no single true self, but in keeping with his notions of divergence and erasure, there can be only a multitude of incomplete and ghostly selves, and by the end of the work he seems almost to have disappeared. But though his writing emphasizes externals rather than psychological material, and though he often frustrates our expectations for a consistent self-analysis, Leiris does show how he became the writer he is, and perhaps that is "self" enough. It is this mix of self-effacement and self-questioning reconstruction that makes his text so compelling.

BECAUSE I HAVE LIVED BY MYSELF off and on for many years, the objects in my house have become companions as well as signposts that constitute an eclectic history. Many of them come from travels, and like a provincial museum without much of a plan, my house contains a brimming pot-pourri: a faded leather saddlebag from Timbuktu; a Turkish shoeshine box containing vials of wicked unctions from the Grand Bazaar in Istanbul; a bulging copper cauldron from Greece that resembles a headless Buddha; a three-legged, one-earred wooden camel from Tunisia; and a pair of French posters from the 1890s that conduct a sort of spirituous dialogue—a pro-Absinthe advertisement depicting a woman with flowing hair who rides witch-style on a bottle of *La Fée Verte*, and an anti-Absinthe one depicting two sallow-faced decadents with a prostitute at a café sipping the lurid drink while at the next table a healthy bourgeois family gaily smiles at their bottle of Quinquina. Other art confirms my Francophilia: photographs of the Eiffel Tower under construction, the Statue of Liberty looming over the fourteenth arrondissement foundry where it was fabricated, advertisements for eaux-de-vie and fin-de-siècle shoe polish, lithographs from the 1890s showing foxy Parisian *grisettes* in sepia hues.

On the landing there's a Balinese painting on cloth portraying a battle of demigods and devils so cluttered with figures it seems less about the triumph of good over evil than about the fear of empty space. Like Barbara Harrison, I am suspicious of void and seek to fill up spaces. If I lived in a traditional Japanese house, I would need to resist hanging pictures on the shoji. Though I abhor clutter, I'm an accumulator, and no sooner do

I jettison than I restock. There's not much room for additions: when a friend gave me a mirror on a recent birthday, acknowledging my interest in autobiography, I could hardly find a nook where it might sit, just beyond meaningful reflection.

Let's take a turn around my study. In one corner, photographs of three Beckett plays I directed. There, in *Happy Days*, against a black sky, Winnie peers from her mound, umbrella uplifted against the heat; there, in *Play*, three dead figures stare blankly from their urns, faces turned to stone; and there, in *Not I*, a set of menacing teeth, which is all that appears of an anonymous woman's shattered life, stands out against the void. On another wall an engraving from the 1790s of Rydal Water, discovered after a day of rambling in the fells of the Lake Country. A couple of carved wooden boxes from Indonesia and Iran sit across from a tarnished Russian samovar and a polished flat copper menorah from Israel holding glass containers for oil; every year I plan to fill them for Hanukkah but never do. A 1930 *Fortune* cover depicts a vintage typewriter, each key flat and round with a black rim raised just above the striking surface making the urge to punch it irresistible. Beside it a poster from another play I directed, *Volpone*, a richly robed skeletal hand clutching a diamond in its bony fingers. Then a magazine cover announcing a story on restaurant reviewers in Portland; I'm featured inside, and a friend and I, both food writers, appear on the cover dressed like a couple of swells, gripping black masks that cover our eyes as if we were at a Venetian carnival.

Books form the heart of the room, probably three or four thousand of them. I lack the maniacal impulse to shelve them alphabetically, but I do have a general system, and in my cozy redoubt the groupings are mostly by subject—Fiction, Shakespeare, Autobiography, Classical Antiquity, Poetry, Cultural History, Art, Psychology. There was a time when the books resembled a phalanx of obedient soldiers, but they have long since strewn themselves about, lying every which way like the tumbled tombstones nestling against one another in the Jewish cemetery of Prague (the Kafkas seem especially unruly).

I tend to think about my books archaeologically, the history and order of their acquisition representing layers of a life. Walter Benjamin, unpacking his library, writes that "the collector's passion borders on the chaos of memories," and I think of my entire house that way, from a stained glass window designed by an ex-girlfriend to a cedar fence constructed by a different one (like Krapp's tapes, the house exfoliates an archeology of romance). The books have become what Doris Grumbach calls the "detrital reminder of times and places": I spy a five volume late eighteenth-century set of English poetry bought for a quarter apiece at town auction in Amherst during my senior year in college, when I hoped the purchase would validate me as a worthy student of literature; and scattered here and there are the earliest ninety-five-cent Anchors, the heralds of the paperback revolution that now seem like incunabula—Lawrence's *Studies in Classic American Literature*, Fergusson's *The Idea of a Theater*, and Stendhal's *Charterhouse of Parma*. Some of my books date from the days when publishers generously sent out free examination copies, when I used to cook up courses just to persuade the reps to stock my shelves. One shelf sags with leather-bound volumes of Jacobean plays, their covers dessicated and brittle as the Timbuktu saddlebag (I ordered them long ago from Blackwell's, and nothing could match the thrill when they arrived by ship from England). There are the many volumes in navy blue of the Oxford History of English Literature, embossed with the gold Oxford seal, but now they seem as dated as Fanny Farmer cookbooks. There are many volumes bearing on their spines a large "R," whose vertical line spells out "Routledge"; these are the Borzoi of contemporary criticism, and their titles—*Nationalisms and Sexualities*, *Gendering Orientalism*, and *Textual Intervention*—are the wanton progeny of the Trillings and the Tates with whom they keep uneasy and warring company. Periodically I prune the library like a conscientious gardener, for fear that I might live the nightmare I once had: I dreamt I was climbing a towering bookcase, footing upward a shelf at a time to reach *Anatomy of Criticism*, only to slip and bring books and shelves crashing down on me, burying me alive like poor Leonard Bast in *Howard's End*.

I recently tallied the number of critical studies on autobiography in my library, and the seventy or so works range from Anna Robeson Burr's 1909 leaden-titled monograph *The Autobiography: A Critical and Comparative Study* to Sidonie Smith and Julia Watson's hip-sounding collection, *Getting a Life: Everyday Uses of Autobiography*. Burr writes about Caesar's *Commentaries* and Cardan's *De Vita Propria Liber*, and Smith and Watson's contributors analyze "The Mediated Talking Cure: Therapeutic Framing of Autobiography in TV Talk Shows" and "Performing Teen Motherhood on Video: Autoethnography as Counterdiscourse." For a time, I wondered whether criticism that couldn't keep up with a theory of personal ads or recovery narratives could make its mark. But while the sheer accumulation gives me momentary pause about adding another item to the mass, I convince myself of an obligation to carry on the line, a son inheriting from often younger mothers and fathers.

AUTOBIOGRAPHICAL POSTURING

10.

Romantic Posing
The Life and Death Writing
of Benjamin Robert Haydon

In this section, I turn my focus to two visual artists—Benjamin Robert Haydon and Eugène Delacroix—who made their autobiographical writing a refuge from public disappointment and a means for self-exploration that their painting could not entirely satisfy. One might expect that these artists would subordinate their writing to their principal creative work, and critics have traditionally considered Haydon's *Autobiography* and *Diary* and Delacroix's *Journal* much as they have looked on Van Gogh's Letters—as mere adjuncts to the painting, sources for biographical information reflecting on the more serious activity. Yet for the artists themselves, writing rivaled their painting, and they often regarded the paintings as incomplete unless written about. Each artist's body of autobiographical writing reveals the unfolding of a mind and a personality so as to constitute a history of a developing consciousness. The autobiographical writing so complements the body of artistic work that the latter seems incomplete without the writing. As such, the writing is not merely an addendum to an identity established by the visual material, but is itself constitutive of that identity. When these artists turn to life-writing, they enact a conception of self not unlike what they do with their art. One of my concerns is how autobiographical writing achieved such a status for these men and a parity with their painting.

I shall also emphasize a strategy enacted in these texts—the author's tactic of staging himself as someone else. I am concerned with the way the self assumes the mask or role of others, the writer appropriating another's being to enhance his own. The figures in this section constitute their narratives through a process of identification with others, as if the self were not, so to speak, quite self-sufficient. They borrow and absorb another's identity in order to assert their own. There are times when the posturing voice appears contentious and challenging, and when the self acts out diverse identities with a range of quasi-theatrical stances. These narratives express the writers' desire for self-affirmation, but despite their drive for aggrandizement, as we shall see the writing ultimately undermines their claims.

Why do they pose? Is there something about the act of painting models that encourages these artists similarly to stage themselves in written self-portraiture? Is the visual representation of reality necessarily so constructed that writing a self partakes of a related anti-copying impulse in which authenticity involves blurring the line between oneself and another? To be sure, an appropriation of others' identities may be understandable given these painters' defiantly competitive instincts. It may also be that an artist so put-upon as Haydon felt even more insecure as a writer than as a painter and hence invoked literary figures as support for an embattled ego.

Before turning to Haydon, I want to say a few words about an argument Van Gogh makes in his letters, a position not radically different from that of the other two figures. There are many instances in the letters where Van Gogh acknowledges writing and painting as equally important activities. He often asserts that there is a compatibility between a particular writer and a painter: "There is something of Rembrandt in Shakespeare . . . and of Delacroix in Victor Hugo" (*Letters* 1: 196). He claims that love of literature and love of painting complement one another, and that "to draw in *words* is also an art" (*Letters* 1: 395). Van Gogh's letters convey the richness of an inner life virtually compensatory for one who continually suffered difficult material circumstances, a lack of critical notice, and continual loneliness, and writing the letters seems to have convinced him that his life had purpose, direction, and meaning. One critic claims that the letters gave Van Gogh "a necessary conviction that a shape and scheme existed in a life which otherwise appeared troubled and lacking in design. It was a shape and scheme which, by its very continuity, implied the possibility of resistance to . . . forces of psychic disturbance" (Roskill 24).

The letters to Theo, which represent the bulk of Van Gogh's correspondence, are addressed to a beloved and compassionate younger brother and are gestures toward a closeness denied at every other turn of his life. They are also meditations that allow him to try out a variety of moods, positions, and identifications. In his dealings with the world Van Gogh never hesitated to express emotions forthrightly, and he often suffered for it; as a result, the letter became a vehicle in which he could speak out to the one listener who would instinctively understand and withhold judgment. Van Gogh's communication with Theo expressed a need as pressing as that of painting, and the letters are the way Van Gogh creates a community of two, a bridge to the only person who might relieve him of an abiding fear of being a pariah. Theo's epistolary presence makes it easier for Van Gogh to confront the questions "Where am I? What am I doing? Where am I going?" (*Letters* 1: 155). He seeks Theo's love and respect, and especially his sympathy for the life Van Gogh has chosen. Evoking Theo's presence *in the letters* is one of the few abatements for his loneliness.

Van Gogh's stance is characteristically that of an embattled man waging a struggle with his art, his peers, and even his sanity. He acknowledges that creative people have always worked against the grain and that his own work arises through the need to give expression—through painting and through language—to that adversarial position. For Van Gogh, battling despair is a prerequisite for creativity. He absorbs other artists into his self so as to better combat them. Even in his self-portraits Van Gogh experiments and wrestles with contending aspects of himself: at various times he is self-assured, challenging, uncertain, and agonized. Letters and self-portraits are battlegrounds in which Van Gogh wages a struggle between his fiery nature and a more controlled, even submissive or victimized one. One aspect of his self forever challenges the other to acknowledge what it might be inclined to resist. Van Gogh queries himself in the letters, and in many of the self-portraits his eyes are searchingly interrogative, the visual equivalent of a self-questioning stance in his letters.

Van Gogh lives in these letters, inhabiting them as if convinced that his insights and emotions can be validated only when expressed and responded to. In his readiness to enter into Theo's mind with empathic imagination, Van Gogh reaches for the reciprocity that might otherwise arise only from a face-to-face encounter. Occasionally he poses questions about the mystery of the inner self: "There is something inside of me; what can it be?" (*Letters* 1: 198–99). This and similar inquiries addressed to Theo are less introspective questions than attempts to connect with the brother he has internalized. Robert Hughes sees the letters as "the product of a mind literally obsessed with the need to explain itself . . . and make its most intimate crises known" (Hughes 269). In the process of autobiographical scrutiny Van Gogh forges a series of selves that reflects his changing moods: proud outsider, helpless victim, misunderstood pariah, and stranger in his own family.

For Van Gogh, self-representation involves not merely a kaleidoscope of shifting aspects of the self, but often the appropriation of other men's identities. Especially when struggling to define the self, he identifies with a host of others: Shakespeare, Hugo, a miner, the prostitute with whom he lived for a time, and such painters as Gauguin, Delacroix, and Rembrandt. Van Gogh celebrates Shakespeare's compassionate identification with a range of figures; he consciously imitates the clergyman in George Eliot's

Scenes of Clerical Life—a clergyman who rescued a prostitute and was in turn cared for by her. The most powerful of the identifications in the letters is with Dr. Gachet, who tended Van Gogh during his last illness at Auvers and whose image was one of the last Van Gogh painted before his suicide. He likens the portrait of Gachet to a *self*-portrait executed a month earlier; for Van Gogh, Gachet was "something like another brother, so much do we resemble each other physically and mentally" (*Letters* 3: 496). Indeed, Van Gogh had expressed a desire to be a doctor and told Gachet he would like to exchange professions with him. This identification seems like a transformative gesture to bestow health on himself. Throughout the letters, Van Gogh exhilarates in taking on another's selfhood, asserting freedom and obliterating emptiness by constituting himself as a fluid identity.

A famous example of this impulse appears in Norman Rockwell's *Triple Self-Portrait*, in which the artist paints himself from behind, seated at his easel and staring into a mirror he has set up next to the canvass on which he is working, and on which appears a half-finished self-portrait; around the edges of that inner canvass are reproductions of self-portraits by Dürer, Rembrandt, and Van Gogh. Rockwell is not merely inspired by the other self-portraits, he competes with them and takes on their power.[1] When they undertook self-portraiture, Rembrandt and Van Gogh represented themselves in the guises of others. As we shall see, Haydon and Delacroix indulge in a similar impulse in their autobiographical writings.

On June 22, 1846, moments before he committed a kind of double suicide by shooting himself and slashing his throat in front of an unfinished picture in his studio, Benjamin Robert Haydon, historical painter, would-be savior of British art, and friend to both generations of English romantic poets, wrote (with understandable misquotation) the final words in the diary he had kept for thirty-eight of his sixty years: "'Stretch me no longer on this rough World'—Lear" (*Diary* 5: 553).[2] With a symmetrical gesture he could hardly have been conscious of creating, Haydon was inserting the closing parenthesis of allusion around his life. In 1808, at the beginning of what he envisioned as an illustrious calling, Haydon noted in the first entry of his diary that he stood upon the cliffs of Dover where "Lear defied the storm" (*Diary* 1: 3); when a storm actually broke over the coast, Haydon fancied himself as the tormented king. He was moved to reread the play and thus began a series of identifications with Lear that would linger through thousands of diary pages and hundreds of autobiographical ones.[3] Haydon's purpose at the start was to attack France's domination of romantic art and to assert his self-proclaimed role in Britain's challenge to that domination.

We can take the defiant posturing at the start of his career and the self-dramatizing pathos at the end as coordinates in the life and as the signs and motives for his writing, which in both its magnitude and its obsessive self-aggrandizements became the rival of, if not the substitute for, his painting. With the exception of Van Gogh, there may be no other visual artist whose need to write—out of self-justification and compensation—was so great as Haydon's, and who produced so extended a literary self-portrait, in part through constant identification with figures both historical and fictional, in order to create an alternative life to the one that brought him such grief.

Haydon began serious sketching in 1792, at the age of six, and although an inflammation of his eyes permanently dimmed his sight, he pursued his profession as if possessed. From the beginning, he read biographies of ambitious men and prophesied his own fame, drawing up a list of painterly subjects that would bring about this result. He was the first English artist to see the importance of the Elgin Marbles, and they influenced him for life. He soon entered into embattled relations with the Royal Academy, especially chagrined at not being elected to membership. His disputatious life led to numerous fights with patrons over financial matters, alienated friendships, and a conviction that the entire art establishment was bent on opposing him. In between several stays in debtors' prison, he set up a school to rival the Academy, fought rancorous battles with everyone, and continued to rail against portraiture as insufficiently heroic. He finally received substantial requests for work, but five of his children died, and the loss of commissions to decorate the houses of Parliament rendered him particularly bitter. Haydon committed suicide not long after Tom Thumb greatly outdrew an exhibit of his work held in the same building where the midget appeared.

I want to raise three related questions: Why was Haydon so committed to some form of life-writing? What function did it serve for him? And what is its relation to his art?

Haydon believed that history painting, by which he meant biblical and mythological, as well as historical, subject matter, was the only art worth pursuing. He scorned portrait and landscape painting, believing they required no grand talent or intellectual power. His natural inclination was to paint ideas and concepts, by which he meant subjects that lent themselves to philosophical disputation. Graham Perry, in "The Grand Delusions of Benjamin Haydon," claims that the artist "was disposed to place much greater emphasis on the painted expression of ideas (preferably sublime ideas) than on the transcription of natural effects" and that Haydon's "written accounts of his paintings are always infinitely more exciting than the finished works, because his imagination was essentially verbal" (10, 21). This impulse, as well as the urge to glorify himself without relying on outside affirmation, always in short supply for Haydon, may suggest why writing had such value for him. Writing is his compensation for loss, and the arena in which he could try out—exhibit, if you will—alternate versions of a self too vulnerable in public life. Ironically, writing is also the instrument he ultimately wields against himself.

Haydon declares he is fonder of books than anything else on earth. Incapable of the greatness to which he aspired, he insures that writing represents himself as well as if not better than the grandiose but scorned paintings. Virginia Woolf says of Haydon: "We catch ourselves thinking, as some felicity of phrase flashes out or some pose or arrangement makes its effect, that his genius is a writer's. He should have held a pen." (191). If the painted portrait appeared to Haydon as an inferior genre, the literary self-portrait did not. Writing meant as much to him as painting, which seemed to have significance only insofar as it might grant fame; when it did not, he tried to make writing serve first for self-aggrandizement, then for consolation. His ambition and his self-image occupied most of his thought, and when the ambition betrayed him, he attempted to make writing a reliable refuge.

Haydon's applications for exhibitions were constantly rejected; we might regard his turn to autobiography as a gesture toward (self-) exhibition. The figure that emerges from both the *Autobiography* and the *Diary* is indeed that of an exhibitionist, fluctuating between histrionic self-inflation, hyperbolical defiance, and excruciating self-laceration. Unable to accomplish what he intended, and consistently unrecognized, Haydon tends to live largely in his imagination, and the autobiographical writings are the space where that imagination resides, temporarily safe from the reality of his external life.

Within the *Diary*, Haydon plays out a range of roles, allowing him to justify himself and to appear as oppressed scapegoat. These strategies find a place in the privacy of the book, where we witness at once a heroic will asserting itself against all opposition and a humbling self-effacement. For Haydon, vacillating between euphoria and despair, autobiography simultaneously permits a therapeutic assertion and a diminution of self. He is free within the writing to vindicate his actions without public consequence and to relive his experiences without having to be accountable. Sheltered from consequence (he apparently did not intend publication during his lifetime of either the *Diary* or the *Autobiography*), Haydon takes a secret pleasure in his attacks upon painters, critics, and patrons, and tries out in writing what he could not easily do in the world.

There is an amplitude to his journals that corresponds to the grandiose scale of his historical paintings and to the heroism of their subjects, both those he actually painted and those he only desired to paint: Achilles, Christ, Napoleon, Samson, Adam, Solomon, Antigone, Orpheus, Lear, Andromache, Macbeth, Caesar, Hercules. Many of these figures occur in his writing as persons or characters with whom he strongly identifies. His writing similarly refuses to be narrowly focused; a partial list of topics includes meditations on the Bible; literary criticism of Homer, Dante, and Milton; discussions of human and animal anatomy; treatises on the Elgin Marbles; character analyses of Wordsworth, Keats, and Napoleon; technical discussions of oil painting; attacks on debtors' laws; stories of betrayal by those whose patronage he had expected; gossip about other artists and critics; detailed descriptions of his progress on a given painting; critiques of English and continental politics; attacks on the art establishment and its institutions; and lengthy self-analysis. But Haydon's *Diary* and his *Autobiography*, despite their sprawl and catch-all nature, have what we might call an autobiographical plot. I mean this not merely in the sense of a theme or cluster of related themes that we can trace through the life. Rather I mean "plot" in the sense of its author's motive for writing, as De Quincey in *Confessions of an English Opium-Eater* urges us to understand a motif as a motive "in the sense attached by artists and connoisseurs to the technical word *motivo*, applied to pictures." (3: 233). Haydon makes his need to write and the purpose for that writing a dominant theme of his *Autobiography* and his *Diaries*.

At twenty-two, Haydon started the diary that he would continue throughout his life, and he made almost daily entries in twenty-four volumes. When he was fifty-three, he began writing his autobiography and labored several years on that work, which covered his life only to 1820, twenty-six years before his death at sixty. It is likely that writing about the succeeding years would have caused too much pain; to describe the difference between youthful aspirations and early promise of fame, and later neglect and a lifetime of failed hopes and oppression from an unappreciative public might have frayed an already delicate psyche. It was difficult enough for Haydon to record on a daily basis his defeats and embattled status; to place the events in a retrospectively structured account of impending disaster might have been too anguishing.

The *Autobiography* and the early diaries are filled with assertions of greatness and immortality, and a devotion to the calling of art as if it were a God-given mission. Even his prayers for divine blessing have the self-assured tone of a man who, if he cannot cajole God to shower talent upon him, at least is on intimate and easy terms with the deity. Some of the autobiographical writing is a trying out of such attitudes, and even toward the end Haydon's confidence persists as he summons his old bravado: "My position still is solitary and glorious. In *me* the solitary sublimity of High Art is not gone" (*Diary* 5: 407). Walter Jackson Bate, in his biography of Keats, described Haydon's "vivid, simple-hearted energy" and his "endless, booming confidence" (98, 101). These traits do occasionally emerge in Haydon's writing, especially in the early diary entries and in the autobiography's account of his youth. One of the dominant voices is that of the young man outdoing the greats of the past and staking his place in history: "People say to me: 'You can't be expected in your second picture to paint like Titian and draw like Michel Angelo; but I will try'. . . . 'Oh yes, but you ought not to do what Michel Angelo alone might try.' Yes, but I will venture—I will dare anything to accomplish my purpose" (*Autobiography* 94).

When the eye disease he suffered from as an adolescent left him temporarily blind, Haydon proclaimed he would be the first great sightless painter. In the *Autobiography* a heroic Haydon combats and overcomes disease, official resistance to his youthful bravado, and the Academy's timidity toward historical painting along with its elevation of the portraiture he detests. There is a description of an archetypal moment of stocktaking as he begins his first painting: he alludes to the close of *Paradise Lost* as the world of promise opens before him, prophesies that he will bring honor to England with his art, and argues that difficulties are stimulants that discourage only the indolent. His writing is full of Julien Sorrel-like posturing: "I was so elevated at . . . the visit of crowds of beauties putting up their pretty glasses and lisping admiration of my efforts, that I rose into the heaven of heavens, and believed my fortune made. I walked about my room, looked into the glass, anticipated what the foreign ambassadors would say, studied my French for a good accent, believed that all the sovereigns of Europe would hail an English youth with delight who could paint a heroic picture" (*Autobiography* 104). Every encounter is a test, every creative act a competition with past greatness; he uses the *Autobiography* to convince himself that he is correct in his defiance, heroic in his convictions. His life often gave the lie to such self-evaluation but in the writing he could create an image for himself that would provide reassurance, even solace.[4] There is an ebullience and daring in his self-congratulation: "I had proved the power of inherent talent, and I had shown one characteristic of my dear country—bottom. I had been tried and not found wanting. I held out when feeble, and faint, and blind, and now I reaped the reward" (*Autobiography* 199).

When Haydon wrote this passage, which describes the reception of his work *The Judgment of Solomon*, the painting was gathering dust in a warehouse. Haydon sees its ignominy as a metaphor for his own decline in popular and official esteem, but he once more prophesies: "Shame on those who have the power without the taste to avert such a fall; who let a work which was hailed as a national victory rot into decay and dirt and oblivion! But it will rise again; it will shine forth hereafter, and reanimate the energy of a new generation" (*Autobiography* 236). This challenge corresponds to Haydon's motives for autobiography: self-vindication in the Rousseauean mode, and a nostalgic reliving of a self-deluded greatness. Autobiography sanctions his struggles not by merely recording them but by elevating them to a heroic status in spite, or perhaps because of, the difficulties. Haydon greatly overestimated the power and originality of his work, and this misjudgment makes his condemnation of his critics suspect, unlike the way Van Gogh's self-justification inevitably gains our assent. Although Haydon's most recent biographer argues that the "myth of ill-usage was one he cultivated assiduously throughout his life," the autobiography reveals how Haydon refused to "bear affliction and disappointment" (George 92). At the same time, Haydon's tone suggests he occasionally relishes his self-destructive actions, turning grief to a compensatory use.

Haydon grants both characteristics—heroic assertion and anguish from ill-usage—their due, and seems almost to luxuriate in long passages documenting persecution and official neglect, as if oppression were itself a sign of genius. Each mode produces its characteristic rhetoric of hyperbole, whether in the high Romantic sublime or in the Rousseauean complaint. Throughout the *Diary* and the *Autobiography*, Haydon's view of himself alternates between that of a misunderstood, martyred man and that of a successful, dominating one. His identification with satanic energy—"give me the sublimity of chaos, give me the terror of Hell, give 'Hail, horrors, hail . . . and thou profoundest hell receive thy new possessor' " (*Diary* 1: 309)—is a Romantic strategy to achieve power as it recoils against orthodox Christian beliefs. The impulse is to equate greatness with suffering wherever it can be found, and the seminal figure behind both the *Autobiography* and the *Diary* is Rousseau.

In a trope that becomes commonplace in Romantic confession, Hayden asserts his sincerity. Characteristically, he will not be outranked on this or any other score; referring not to painting but to honesty and confessional integrity, he announces "I will defy any man . . . to beat me" (*Autobiography* 90). The "Author's Introduction" to the *Autobiography* bears a striking resemblance to the famous opening of Rousseau's *Confessions:* Haydon claims that his writing originates from a sense of unjust persecution and that although he has made occasional mistakes, and has even been sinful, his sincerity and decent intentions will exonerate him in the eyes of his readers. But Haydon's deepest instinct is for Rousseau-like suffering, the cultivation of which he hopes will testify to misunderstood genius. Indeed, he is self-congratulatory about his willingness to endure pain: "I am one of those beings born to bring about a great object through the medium of suffering" (*Diary* 3: 334).

As he writes the *Autobiography*, his own life is crumbling about him— several children have died, he has spent months in debtors' prison, he fears his creative juices may be drying up, his work has been attacked in the press, and even former supporters have deserted him. Composing autobiography both risks further pain and cultivates that pain as a sign of stoical resignation and courage. He discovers an energizing resolve by confronting his enemies in writing, a power conferred by contentiousness itself. In an argument with Leigh Hunt, Haydon determines to get the better in print; Hunt is a dangerous opponent because he is editor of the *Examiner*, in whose pages they will do battle. In the *Autobiography*, Haydon's punning metaphor draws the fight with Hunt into Haydon's own painterly domain: "Though this is not the first time Leigh Hunt is mentioned it is the first opportunity I have had of bringing him fairly *on the canvas.* . . . This controversy consolidated my power of verbal expression and did me great good. . . . I resolved to show I could use the pen against the very man who might be supposed to be my literary instructor" (*Autobiography* 142–44, my emphasis).

Painting becomes Maileresque combat "because [in the eyes of a mis-guided public] Reynolds beat West in force, depth & color, Portrait Painters beat Historical Painters" (*Diary* 3: 118). Losing the game is inevitable, because "the Historical Painter, whatever be his talent . . . is considered half cracked or completely mad" (*Diary* 311), so Haydon, always stimulated by failure, intensifies these struggles in the autobiographical writing and goes from victim to scourge. Completing a painting under trying circumstances is analogous to his undertaking autobiographical writing, and he seems to welcome difficulty, arguing in the *Diary* that too luxurious a climate encourages indolence, too uncomplicated a romance undermines its value, and too charmed a life dulls its vigor.

Haydon parallels a refusal to submit to contingencies with a commit-ment to canvasses heroic in size and in subject matter. The *Autobiography* concludes with a description of him starting a new work, determined to make it his largest ever. "I always filled my painting-room to its full extent; and had I possessed a room 400 feet long, and 200 feet high, and 400 feet wide, I would have ordered a canvas 399–6 long by 199–6 high, and so have been encumbered for want of room, as if it had been my pleasure to be so" (*Autobiography* 346). By transcending limits he projects his hopes into the two principal figures of the painting—Christ and Lazarus. From the perspective of the *Autobiography*, written two decades after this depicted scene, Haydon saw himself as both the miracle-performing Christ and the resurrected Lazarus, symbol of his own hoped-for rebirth after twenty years of futile effort.

Haydon tries to avoid excessive difficulty, arguing that his painting keeps him from madness and pain, and yet he cultivates difficulty as a catalyst for creativity, linking this strategy with the trope of heroic identification. Napoleon and Nelson are only two of many figures whom Haydon views as different from the run of ordinary men because insurmountable difficulties stimulate them to great action. "Nelson is an illustrious example of what persevering, undivided attention to one Art will do . . . to what a length never resting in indolent enjoyment after exertion will go. He began the war unknown . . . and concluded it famous throughout the World" (*Diary* 1: 284).

Throughout his writing, Haydon wavers between the egotistical sublime of heroic self-assertion and the negative capability of self-effacement or identification with other men, most frequently with Napoleon, Wellington, and Michelangelo. It might appear that the impulse to associate with greatness is no less self-projecting, since Haydon takes on the identities of triumphant figures. But ironically this strategy can also represent a form of self-denigration, in that the identification implicitly asserts the failure of, and undermines the claims for, the originality he purports to prize. Unlike, say, Keats in his *Letters* playfully trying out a series of roles by inventing spider-like from within, Haydon defines himself by taking on the personae of other artists or historical figures. His autobiographical writing meets the problem of unavailable originality by allowing him to assert a range of identifications, as though mimicry could substitute for or validate genius. Such identifications look like mere allusions but are really desperate attempts to appropriate others' power.

Haydon aspires to the achievements of Raphael and Michelangelo. He reports a dream in which Michelangelo appeared to him; in a Wordsworthian echo he muses: "I certainly think something grand in my destiny is coming on, for all the spirits of the illustrious dead are hovering about me" (*Diary* 3: 510). And in a letter to Keats, Haydon portrays himself as an amalgam of Prospero, Lear, and Hotspur: "I have no doubt you will be remunerated by my ultimate triumph. . . . [B]y Heaven I'll plunge into the bottom of the sea, where plummets have now never sounded, & never will be able to sound, with such impetus that the antipodes shall see my head drive through on their side of the Earth to their dismay & terror."[5] Haydon's compulsion to identify with other beings is disturbing, though one might admire his Tamburlaine-like desire to seize upon elements outside the self and incorporate them in order to vitalize himself. The irony is that while Haydon desired to claim greatness by projecting himself into others' roles or by subsuming other selves, he never could make his influence felt.

Wherever on the curve of his life he locates himself, the exemplary figure is always Napoleon, advancing on Moscow, retreating, escaping from Elba, defeated once again. Haydon is of two minds regarding Napoleon: he reveres the Emperor's titanic power yet is comforted by his ordinariness and vulnerability. In 1844, Haydon had painted some twenty-five portraits of Napoleon, and while there was an economic motive for this obsession, it also reflects Haydon's penchant for finding infinite variations in an emulated figure and a desire to be many different persons—a version of Rembrandt's life-long series of self-portraits. Just so, Haydon's *Diary* fights against the tendency of autobiography to freeze the self into a fixed image; the *Diary* expresses not merely the inevitable fragmentation of all journal writing, but a pleasure in creating multiple personae and perspectives: "This book is a picture of human life, now full of arguments for religion, now advocating virtue, then drawn from chaste piety, & then melting from a bed of pleasure, idle & active, dissipated & temperate, voluptuous & holy! burning to be a martyr when I read the Gospel! ready to blaze in a battalion when I read Homer! weeping at Rimini and at Othello. Laughing & without sixpence, in boisterous spirits when I ought to be sad & melancholy when I have every reason to be happy!" (*Diary* 2: 273). Haydon's fascination with the swings of fortune appears everywhere. He receives a commendatory sonnet from Wordsworth that cheers him but soon relapses into melancholy; he walks the streets filled with grief, but within moments enters a drawing room "like a comic hero in a farce." Whether we call him a manic-depressive or a doubt-ridden genius, he both constructs and undermines the foundations of a putative self-confidence.

Haydon's life-writing contrasts with the polished surfaces of classical certitude in Gibbon's autobiography, whose author perceives his existence as a work of art given compositional grace and symmetrical order. Lacking Gibbon's assurance, Haydon consequently fragments his self, his text exemplifying what William Howarth calls "autobiography as drama," where the writer stages his life for his readers. Sidonie Smith's conception of performativity, analogous to Howarth's position, argues that the "injunction to be a deep, unified, coherent, autonomous 'self' produces necessary failure, for the autobiographical subject is . . . incoherent, heterogeneous, interactive. In that very failure lies the fascination of autobiographical storytelling as performativity" ("Performativity" 18, 20). One might argue that Haydon's self-dramatizations defy essentialist and proscriptive norms of subjectivity and that his staging of himself in a range of heroic roles questions any fixed identity or unified self, making his self-representation problematic because always so self-consciously theatricalized.

The origins of this fragmentation may reside in Haydon's preoccupation with loss. At the end of a calendar year, Haydon, in the *Diary,* frequently represents the year's passing as an irresistible tide sweeping away everything in its path. Time, for him, is also a devouring reptile or a conqueror who exceeds Napoleon in power. At such moments Haydon's voice is that of Leonardo da Vinci in the *Notebooks,* foreseeing universal ruin in the swirling and anarchic waters of our helpless condition. In a world that presents so many images of frustrated ambition, diminished power, and unexpected suffering, it is not surprising that the self appears unstable.

Haydon knew, as the Romantics generally did, the impossibility of fulfillment, and his autobiographical writing testified to that recognition. When he is most critical of his drift, the prose itself becomes fragmented as Haydon anatomizes the disconnected moments of his life. Here he tries out his Hamlet persona:

> My mind fatuous, impotent—drewling over Petrarch—dawdling over Pausanias—dipping into Plutarch. Voyages and Travels no longer exciting—all dull, dreary, flat, weary, & disgusting. I seem as if I should never paint again. I look at my own Xenophon, & wonder how I did it—read the Bible—gloat over Job—doubt Religion to rouse my faculties, and wonder if the wind be East or S.S. West— look out of the window and gape at the streets—shut up the shutters, & lean my hand on my cheek—get irritable for dinner, two hours before it can be ready—eat too much, drink too much—and go to bed at nine to forget existence! I dream horrors, start up, & lie down, & toss & tumble, listen to caterwauling of cats, & just doze away as light is dawning. . . . With my Ambition! my talents! my energy! Shameful. (*Diary* 3: 549)

The *Diary* expresses the gradual recognition that all desire leads to disappointment. Haydon eventually understands hope is an enchantment: the nearer we think we get to fulfillment, the less desirable, let alone attainable, it becomes. There are moments when Haydon endows the painters who preceded him, his friends, a beloved, and his work with the potential to redeem his despair. And he declares bravely (ironic in retrospect) that wretched men "shoot themselves—but not me" (*Diary* 5: 412). But he also knows that all "grand conceptions" and "elevated sensations of an ambitious and glorious soul" are unreliable (*Autobiography* 165).

Aggrieved outrage and vituperation against the world mark one pole of Haydon's sensibility, reckless self-destruction the another. Harold Bloom has noted how, according to Freud, though one part of the ego's self-love may be projected onto an external object, another part invariably remains in the ego (*Romanticism and Consciousness* 12). One could say the same thing about self-hatred, and such a description fits Haydon's situation. "I am not yet 40 and can tell of a Destiny melancholy and rapturous, severe, trying, & afflicting, bitter beyond all bitterness, afflicting beyond all affliction, cursed, heart burning! heart breaking! maddening, not to be dwelt on lest its thought scathe my blasted heart and blighted brain" (*Diary* 2: 499). There is as much self-loathing as scorn of the world in this entry, as Haydon turns against both the world and his self-delusions.

Autobiography granted Haydon a certain freedom to experiment with his life by trying out and anticipating, within the security of the writing, all possible consequences of his action. As he lost commissions and suffered official neglect, he turned to the autobiographical project for solace, the privacy of the writing compensating for neglect and justifying his worth. But even his occasional triumph turns bitter, and the writing unfolds this design as if Haydon were both compelled actor and composing author of his tragedy. For all his posturing, Haydon ineluctably gives way to despair, aware of a tragic arc to his life yet unable to accept it. The autobiographical writing, vacillating between hope and despair, expresses the instability of its author as he attempts both to write himself into transcendence and to lament the failures he can no longer deny. Though the writing may occasionally bring peace, more often it intensifies the anguish as he relives it and self-consciously explores every detail, unable to escape a fascination with his own psyche. "I do not think any man on Earth ever suffered more agony of mind than I have done, & so would the World think if it knew why, and yet I always had an abstracting power, & that saved my mind and made me look down & meditate, as it were, on my own sufferings. They became a curious speculation" (*Diary* 3: 38). Some autobiographers trust readers will benefit from their wisdom, but Haydon writes to console *himself.* But even that goal is not easily attainable. Autobiography purports to be Haydon's escape from sorrow, but it is really the net that enmeshes him in his grief. Self-absorption becomes a tragic game, the writing both the vantage point from which to perceive his life's slow dying and a virtual instrument of that end.

MY IDEA TO WRITE ON visual artists as autobiographers originated when I moonlighted for several years at the Portland Museum Art School. The students, in addition to their studio work, took a course or two in what was loosely termed "humanities." While students at Reed tend to see the world in verbal metaphors, my students at the Art School saw it in visual terms, and their perspective challenged me to design a literature course for them. Rebellious against analysis, they believed that a need to explain one's art constituted a sign of failure; good work was self-justifying. So I thought they might benefit from reading what various painters, sculptors, and architects had to say about their work. I offered a class called "Autobiography and the Artist," drawing on Ben Shahn's "The Biography of a Painting," Van Gogh's *Letters, The Diaries of Paul Klee*, Gauguin's *Intimate Journals*, Louis Sullivan's *The Autobiography of an Idea*, Jacques Lipschitz's *My Life in Sculpture*, and Judy Chicago's *Through the Flower*. I urged the students to heed Shahn's self-imposed obligation to explain "the whole stream of events and of . . . changing thinking . . . the childhood influences, . . . all my views and notions on life and politics . . . which must constitute the substance of whatever person I was"; and then to inquire with Shahn "what sort of person I really was, and what kind of art could truly coincide with that person." I had the students keep journals about the origins—psychological or otherwise—of their art, and gradually they relinquished their skepticism.

I came across Haydon's *Diary* and *Autobiography* in a used book shop, and remembered that Wordsworth had written two sonnets to him, and Keats one. Keats's, on the Elgin Marbles, was the more memorable because it is probably the only poem on so lofty a subject that uses as a rhyme word "phlegm." What interested me in Haydon was how, when his expectations failed to materialize, he resisted surrendering to reality; that stubborn refusal to submit to the world, however unavoidable his frustrations, seemed curiously noble, and I was drawn to Haydon's courage and endless attempts at self-renewal, however futile and self-destructive they appeared to be.

I am attracted by the boldness in Haydon, a boldness I have known in others when, with less calamity, they have experimented with their lives and reinvented themselves, in some cases every few years. People who change careers seem especially heroic to me. I also admire some former students who have followed quirky paths: one delivered mail while he read Spinoza, another pumped gas and studied Plato between cars. Despite its commitment to searching out unorthodox ideas, the academic life institutionalizes stability (my institution is a veritable Platonic Form). In college I felt it would be dangerous to get off the speeding career train and sidetrack myself even for a moment, and part of me persists in that behavior, though not always in the theory.

As a child of the 1950s I expected my life to follow well-grooved patterns and certifiable blueprints. Even at twenty-one I thought about a life the way we were taught to regard texts: among the best things you could say about both books and lives was that they had unity, coherence, and architectonic structure. It is not surprising that the assaults literary theory made on the unified, essentialist self began in the mid '60s, around the time an antiauthoritarian culture questioned structures of all kinds, especially political and social ones. Just as literary critics discovered contradictions of language in texts, which called their assumptions into question, so many of us were beginning to realize that our own lives might not be so stable and "organic" as we once supposed. The counterculture undermined our comfortable assumption that our lives would have the structure of the well-ordered novel so admired by New Critics. Disunity and fragmentation seemed the order of the day, but it was not always easy for me to embrace that condition. Once, when I felt the erasure of continuity at the end of a love affair and lamented the loss of "a through line," the woman replied, "*You* are your own through line." Fair enough, but that seemed improbable to me, as though the order and plot of a life arise from circumstances, and at that moment the circumstances felt too chaotic and unmanageable. I wasn't sure I even had a clear sense of self I could name, define, and act upon.

And yet, for all my ambivalence about continuity, the fact that I proceeded directly from college to graduate school to the position I have occupied all my adult life—a marathon engagement with a single institution that has lasted beyond what I ever thought imaginable when I started out to teach—has permitted me, in a paradoxically fortunate way, to experiment with my life, as if the stability granted and encouraged the prospect of other lives I could not have anticipated and am glad not to have missed.

Like Haydon, I seek out incongruities and am better at "contrast" then "compare." An ideal day, one I cull from memory, began at a camel auction in the western desert of Egypt; moved to a princely lunch at a Cairo hotel where pashas once sipped sherbets on silk divans; led to the rehearsal of a play I was directing at Cairo's English-speaking theatre; followed with a discussion in the apartment of Hassan Fathy, Egypt's foremost indigenous architect; slipped into the twilight serenity of a felucca sailing down the Nile; and finished with a fire dance of Nubian women on the edge of Al Jizah where it meets the sands of Qattara.

When I was learning the alphabet in kindergarten, the teacher sent me to the blackboard to draw the letter "A." Poised to chalk the crossbar, I started several feet to the left of the diagonals and continued an equal distance far across to the right, intending to erase back to the intersections. I was worried that if I simply drew the line within the diagonals of the "A," I might not meet them precisely, and wanted to be sure. This image has defined me: fearful that I might not have enough, I run to excess. At a dinner party I will serve four people enough food for eight, afraid I will run out. I sympathize with Haydon's unhampered sensibility, the maximalist who must have been monstrously chagrined to lose out to Tom Thumb of all people.

Haydon's need to incorporate others' voices into his own involves the pleasure of trying out roles and theatricalizing his life as a continuous experiment in self-transformation. Such an absorptive instinct, which I remember possessing from an early age, not only provoked my interest in every historical figure I could learn about, but has much to do with my interest in theatre and in autobiography. My attraction to certain autobiographers stems from the fact that I can imagine trying on their personae, curious as to what it might feel like to be them. But whether this desire satisfies mere curiosity, attempts an imaginative playfulness, or indulges a craving for capaciousness to make up for a felt insufficiency, I'm not sure I can say.

11.

"A Serpent in the Coils of a Pythoness"
Self-Dramatization in Eugène Delacroix's *Journal*

On September 3, 1822, Eugène Delacroix began the journal he would keep, punctuated by several long interruptions, for the next forty-one years. At the very outset, he declared, "I am writing only for myself," and this disclaimer of any wish to publicize his inner life is largely true (*Journal* 1). Much of the *Journal* consists of intensely private meditations on his habits of mind and work, accounts of fears and anxieties, analyses of his struggles in his work and his longings for greatness, and assurances that his art has adequately compensated for the deprivations of family and sustained love. One of Delacroix's leading American critics notes that "the focus of his life was inward, its drama loaded inside his own consciousness . . . he was essentially an isolated . . . figure" (Trapp xvii–xviii). The *Journal* is not only a record of Delacroix's attitudes and ideas—it is also a place for him to explore his shifting emotional grounds, its pages offering a sanctuary free of internal and external censorship and providing an opportunity to investigate his complex, often self-contradictory sensibility. Inside the *Journal*, Delacroix could experiment with his life without any obligation to structure behavior and feelings into coherent order. Journals are by nature fragmentary productions, their form dictated by time considerations, not necessarily by psychological rhythms. The journal (or diary) as a discontinuous form lends itself to the possibility, perhaps the inevitability, of self-contradiction and continual reformulation. It does not presuppose a development between an earlier self and the writing self, and is free to resist psychological unity or continuous narrative perspective.[1]

Suzanne Bunkers sensibly argues that a journal "is not written as a retrospective narration and interpretation of a life already lived but as a commentary on life as it *is* lived, that is, on life as process rather than as product" (191). Such a description fits Delacroix, who refused to regard his life as having achieved a definitive form. To record his life, he not only turned to the autobiographical mode most resistant to resolution, he took pleasure in recording incongruous, often contradictory responses to the world around him, as well as the daily fluctuations of his mind. The *Journal* allows Delacroix to represent himself as a series of multiple, diverse, and inconsistent selves. Delacroix seems to have chosen the journal form in order to undermine any impulse he might have to revise, feeling no responsibility to establish a coherent and unified self.[2]

Though Delacroix often wrote every day, there are gaps and hiatuses in the *Journal*, including one of twenty-three years. H. Porter Abbott, discussing diary fiction, notes that the diarist writes irregularly and inconsistently, in a style "marked by false starts and abrupt stops, by blanks, and by logorrhea." This creates "the effect of immediacy: that is, the illusion of being there, of no gap in time between the event and the rendering of it." Such an agenda suits Delacroix's interest in spontaneous and momentary expression. As Abbott helpfully suggests, diary production "return[s] us to the moment of composition and in so doing returns us to that point of temporary withdrawal, outside the action, necessary for putting down the words on paper." Such moments also "return us to new beginnings in the present," and this procedure fits with Delacroix's insistence on the immediate, nonretrospective function of the writing to convey the mind's vacillating nature (16, 28, 25).

Delacroix's voice is continually engaged in the process of discovering itself, and the *Journal* is marked by rapid changes in mood and belief. Both horrified by and delighted in such alternations, Delacroix's judgment on himself is inevitably ambivalent. Here he berates himself, yet with undisguised fascination: "Vain mortal, can nothing restrain you, neither your bad memory and feeble strength, nor your unstable mind that fights against ideas as soon as you receive them?" (*Journal* 32)

Delacroix knows that the self he tracks in the *Journal* is elusive, unable to be structured into unity. At times this is cause for distress, at others for wonder at the sheer unpredictability of his own moods. In the fullest study to date of Delacroix's writings, Michele Hannoosh claims that "the *Journal* seems to recognize the ungraspability of the self it allegedly seeks to capture, the mobility of a self it wishes to stabilize, and which escapes at every moment the words that try to contain it" (4). I would qualify this judgment slightly: though at moments Delacroix is indeed baffled by himself, he often finds the incoherence of his self cause for intrigue, delight, and even creative energy. Sometimes the discovery itself is as much a jolt as the inconsistent actions, yet he expresses a pleasurable surprise at his inconsistency: "How changeable I am! A new idea can confuse my mind in a moment, and upset my firmest resolutions" (*Journal* 8). This revelation comes in 1822 from a young man of twenty-four; at age fifty-nine he is still enticed by the process: "What contradictions there are in one man's mind! The variety of opinions held by different men is astonishing enough, but a man with a sound intellect can conceive every possibility" (*Journal* 379). The emphasis on fluidity fits Delacroix's insistence that the *Journal* is a private affair; he is his own audience and does not need to justify his incongruous positions to any other reader or critic: "A man of talent . . . should not be afraid of contradicting himself" (*Journal* 165). There are times, to be sure, when change is not so benign. Throughout the *Journal*, Delacroix acknowledges that the human subject stands in danger of disintegration, a matter for personal concern, even anxiety. Memory fades, thoughts elude him, fragmentation torments him. But still he addresses even this prospect with a mixture of dread and intrigue, and in the *Journal* he can try out diverse points of view and meditate upon the problem of unstable identity.[3]

The disjunctive moments occur throughout Delacroix's life, not just at some pivotal point that, in a more conventional autobiography, might signal a crisis leading to a resolution, if not to a conversion. Because of the immediate, nonretrospective nature of a journal, it is bound to be repetitious, and the repetition of critical moments (of which there are numerous instances) suggests that resolution is not easily attained. Because a journal lacks conventional autobiography's beginning, middle, and (approach to an) end, it is paradoxically a daily record and an open-ended form. We might speculate that Delacroix chose a discontinuous form of life-writing because it was appropriate for his needs and self-recognition, but it may be rather that keeping a journal made him aware of, indeed helped to instill and promote, his inconsistent nature.

Delacroix was a great reader of autobiographies, memoirs, and diaries, but before Rousseau, Saint-Simon, and Casanova, all of whose life-writing he invokes in the text, his model was Montaigne: "Is it absolutely necessary for a book to follow all the rules? After all Montaigne wrote by fits and starts—such works are often the most interesting" (*Journal* 118). Those digressions and meanderings that follow no preconceived plan, what James Cox calls Montaigne's "wayward freedom of the mind" (7), strongly influenced Delacroix's conception of self-representation. Montaigne's curiosity about everything, as well as the way he makes any and all subjects reflect upon and symbolize his self, had a decided impact on Delacroix's *Journal*. Nor is it surprising that early in his career he painted himself as Hamlet and later did a series of lithographs of the Danish prince; Delacroix often identified himself as a Hamlet-like figure of doubt, self-questioning, and improvisation.

Several times he expresses his desire to be a writer, especially a poet. Delacroix's ideal writer would not bother overmuch with careful design: "It is always right and appropriate to set down ideas as they come to you, even if you have no consecutive work on hand into which they can immediately be incorporated. But all such notes take on the form of the moment" (*Journal* 401). His major writing project was to be the *Philosophical Dictionary of the Fine Arts;* its attraction for him lay in the work's absence of sequence or transitional passages, since he viewed calculation and architectonic structures as anathema, a rein on spontaneity and immediacy as much as conventional autobiography would have been. But the *Dictionary* was left incomplete; even this fragmentary form was beyond him as a separate, discrete work. Delacroix did incorporate sporadic passages of the *Dictionary* into the *Journal*, making the latter work even less expository than otherwise, the *Dictionary* entries now a part of the random observations of an ever-changing sensibility.

Delacroix's writing complements his painting insofar as the latter relies on analogous principles. "A painter's execution will be beautiful only if he reserves the right to be carried away by his inspiration, to a certain extent, and to make new discoveries as his work proceeds" (*Journal* 61). Much of his painting has the quality of improvised performance, the dash and spontaneity of the technique the appropriate instrument to capture the headlong rush and volatile energy of the subject matter. Not unlike his beloved Leonardo da Vinci, dismayed and fascinated by the power of natural process and the destructive ravages of time, Delacroix is affected by change and chaos; passing moments can sweep away our pleasure, "a vivid imagination" can obliterate our thoughts, and lapses of memory destroy attempts at continuity and coherence.

Delacroix feels vulnerable in the face of external forces, especially the force of time. A conventional autobiographer following the course of the life from a retrospective viewpoint might regard time as a shaping medium of that life, one that makes possible a discernible pattern in experience and the development of a coherent identity. A journal writer, however, might regard time as a succession of reminders that the individual is up against a pitiless, corrosive force. The sheer act of keeping the *Journal* reminds Delacroix that time is inexorable and that writing is never more than a substitute for experience: "These trifles, written down at random, seem all that remain to me of my daily life as it slips away" (*Journal* 219). Hamlet's self-revulsion figures here. "I caught sight of myself in the looking-glass when I arrived home and felt almost frightened at the wickedness of my face." An imagination of horror and failure in the face of time runs through the *Journal*, a dark view emphasizing the loss of physical powers and memory, "an unbearable sense of emptiness," and a fear of losing his reason altogether (*Journal* 44, 43, 97). Delacroix's need to take on others' identities constitutes a desire to borrow their energy in the face of waning power and a sense of gradual evanescence.

Whenever Delacroix discusses aesthetics, his own creative process, or such technical issues as pigment and line, there's a continuity between painter and anxious autobiographer. Just as he affirms an inconsistent and contradictory self, opposed to generalizing and universalizing, so we have Delacroix's famous insistence on quick sketches, restless improvisations, and impulsive brush strokes, all of which express work that is in process rather than completed, a phenomenon analogous to the generic procedures of the journal. Numerous passages argue for unfinished works of art that retain the "rough sketch of an idea" (*Journal* 222), sustain its original feeling, and do not "enclose the imagination within a circle [which] prevents it from straying beyond its limits" (*Journal* 173). Baudelaire stresses Delacroix's kinetic self-assertion when he writes in his eulogy of the painter: "He was all energy, but energy which sprang from the nerves and from the will" (323). Just so, the *Journal* posits a self as much in girational movement as his paintings, which emphasize swirling energy, unstable balance points, and propulsive forces. In both Delacroix's resistance to imposing a finished look upon his work and the loosening of form in the *Journal*, he fears obliterating the marks of the creative process and of momentariness.

The *Journal* jumps from topic to topic, reworks earlier material to amend or contradict, and self-reflexively comments upon his activity as a writer whose prose style represents freedom from absolute self-definition. Delacroix's self neither unfolds nor evolves; against the regular and quotidian beat of time he stresses the momentary states of being and the fleeting impressions that mark his existence, the journal writing always dramatizing his wrestling with an irresolute mind. Boswell's protest against autobiographical completeness could apply to Delacroix: "I find it is impossible to put upon paper an exact Journal of the life of Man. External circumstances may be marked. But the variations within, the workings of reason and passion, and what perhaps influence happiness most, the colourings of fancy, are too fleeting to be recorded" (qtd. in Bruss, *Autobiographical Acts* 61). These flashes of subjectivity challenge a reader to create a whole figure from the disparate images. The *Journal*, devoid of "links and transitions" (*Journal* 259), is seductive because we are drawn into the mind of the writer much as we are pulled into the vortex of the paintings, challenged to puzzle out the enigmatic and self-contradictory figure.

A large measure of Delacroix's fascination is that he has staged himself as a variety of characters, and in this regard we may link him with Haydon. This is not surprising for so theatrical a painter who was also a great reader of texts (in the *Journal* he writes about Byron, Voltaire, Goethe, Fenimore Cooper, Scott, Shakespeare, Dante, Cervantes, George Sand, and Homer, as well as the numerous literary subjects he painted). Baudelaire, among others, called Delacroix a literary painter, and critics have long noted that Delacroix projected himself into many of the characters (and even the animals) he painted or sketched: Hamlet, Faust, Sardanapalus, the Giaour, Jacob, lions, tigers. Despite Delacroix's assertions of uniqueness— he admiringly cites Molière's eventual refusal to be further influenced by his early models Plautus and Terence—he often identifies himself with poets (Dante, Shakespeare, Byron, and Scott), painters (Michelangelo and Titian), and musicians (Paganini). He looks to these artists for inspiration, and, though preoccupied with his own sense of destiny, associates his fate with theirs. Thus the more he absorbs power and energy from others, the more difficult it is to locate Delacroix's core identity. This "staging" occurs throughout the *Journal*, not just in the paintings; over and over he asserts his wish to be like Byron, or like a jungle cat.

Delacroix's desire to identify with other creators, despite his protestations to the contrary, suggests he needs them for validation. He also seems to recognize a competitive impulse. The perceived danger in utilizing others' self-image for his own is that the gesture implies dependence as well as appropriation. In one *Journal* passage, when he is torn between urging imitation of predecessors and resistance to authority, he writes a sentence that curiously contradicts itself and that both endorses and opposes imita-tion: "Artists should learn not to despise everything that does not come from their own inspiration, but to strip themselves of the almost blind fanaticism which prompts us all to imitate the great masters" (*Journal* 300–01). At an-other time, when speaking about the inspiration of Byron, Delacroix claims that "living in the minds of others is what is so intoxicating" (*Journal* 41). The common image of Delacroix—reinforced by Baudelaire's extravagant assertions of the painter's volcanic energy, his passionate love of passion, and the "Molochism" of the work—is that of the possessed and demonic genius whose solipsistic art is without precedent. But in the *Journal*, personality and tradition are partners, and claims for originality are tempered by an awareness that his inspiration is partly owed to others. Although Delacroix seeks a heroic and original greatness in keeping with Romantic striving and the affirmation of individual power, he achieves that goal by internalizing others' visions. "Some artistic temperaments are strong enough to absorb and take advantage of everything. In spite of being brought up in ways that would not have come naturally to them, they find their own path through the mazes of other men's precepts and examples" (*Journal* 300). Originality and "deference to tradition," which Frank Trapp calls the twin hallmarks of Delacroix's creativity (26), manifest themselves in his concern on the one hand to display a forceful personality and assert a greatness unmediated by the pressures of traditional form, subject matter, or convention; and on the other hand to combat accusations of imperiousness by acknowledging his debt to, even his absorption of, earlier artists. Delacroix's identity is constituted through an attraction to otherness along with a concomitant resistance to that attraction.

Delacroix's stress on models qualifies commonplace notions of Romantic subjectivity. In fact, his search for exemplars and avatars is consistent with his sense of destiny and daring; the process of identification—with Byron when Delacroix is young, with Titian when he is old—endows him with power. A common trope in autobiography is the struggle against ostensible models in the writer's life (including other autobiographers), adversaries who force the writer to achieve an autonomous identity as person or as autobiographer. In the former vein, one thinks of those famous fathers, James Mill and Hermann Kafka; in the later, of Rousseau "against" St. Augustine, Henry Adams "against" Henry James. Delacroix, perhaps because he resists coherent self-representation, locates his identity through, and sometimes even grafts it onto, that of others. He admonishes himself: "Concentrate deeply when you are at your painting and think only of Dante" (*Journal* 38). I have noted that Delacroix identified with the big cats who, in his paintings of hunts, seem less the prey than the aggressors. Whenever he was recovering from some illness, he would draw and paint those animals at menageries, as though to draw strength from the beasts and miraculously absorb their power and beauty.

Delacroix's preoccupation with mutability and multiplicity enforces the need for discernible patterns in his life, however tentative they may be. Woven into Delacroix's discussions of art, music, literature, salon culture, philosophy, and daily life is a continuous pledge to self-examination. But Delacroix's impulse is hardly a guarantee of coherence. Often he is an enigma to himself: "I am a man. What is this *I*? What is this thing *a man*?" (*Journal* 24) The questions sound the knell of a tolling theme in the *Journal*: How can the self be known, even to itself, when it is so various and based partly on the identities of others? There is a constant interrogative mood throughout the *Journal*, elicited by the imponderable nature of the observing self. "I have two or three, perhaps four friends, but I am forced to be a different man with each of them, or rather, to show to each the side of my nature that he understands. It is one of the saddest things in life that we can never be completely known and understood by any one man. Now I come to think of it, this is the worst evil in life, this inevitable loneliness to which our hearts are condemned" (*Journal* 15–16). The inability to discern either a transparent self or a pattern in the life may be a function of his incorporation of others. Ironically, Delacroix's fear of self-contradiction as a danger-sign that one may be derivative does not address the problem of derivativeness in his insistence on imitating other figures.

Delacroix conveys the image of a combative and aggressive figure, especially when he refers to both writing and painting as a "battle": "Unless I am writhing like a serpent in the coils of a pythoness I am cold" (*Journal* 38). The sheer physicality of the image suggests the visceral struggle in which the battle against a confining force demonstrates his power and his determination. He likens the struggle to "the terror of rousing the sleeping lion whose roarings move us to the very depth of our being" (*Journal* 45). But he is as much the lion as the one who rouses the beast, just as he seeks to be the civilized man of talent as well as "the savage, [who] is in tune with nature as she really is." Delacroix is always on both sides of the equation. Fierce combat naturally marks such paintings as *The Lion Hunt*, *The Tiger Hunt*, *Jacob Wrestling with the Angel*, and *Giaour and the Pasha*, where Delacroix gives concrete form to his journal meditations on energy threatened by conventions and civilization, as well as on the other way around.

The great painting *The Death of Sardanapalus* (1827) powerfully exhibits Delacroix's combative impulse and his identification with others. It is tempting to link Delacroix with Sardanapalus as the archetype of the misunderstood, Romantic isolato, the man who, as Delacroix says about himself, lives utterly in his own mind, projecting his interior scenarios into reality or into art. Sardanapalus is also, like Delacroix, a believer in the transitoriness of all things and the hopelessness of any sustaining vision. In the painting, the king reposes on his bed with bored detachment and fatalistic resignation, watching as his commands to have his favorite concubines raped and slaughtered, his treasures destroyed, and the entire bed chamber consumed in a funeral pyre are being carried out. While terrible violence is enacted in front of him, the king looks on wearily, dreaming of peace and disengagement after having commanded the violent splendor and frenzy that surrounds him. Contemptuous of morality, disillusioned with vanity, and yet the instigator of savage deeds, he embodies the spirit of contradic-toriness.[4] The internal contradictions of the work—its coupling of despair and calm, eroticism and death, worldliness and transcendence—links it to Delacroix's tendency to embrace multiple points of view. Sardanapalus expresses resignation to fatality as well as a transcendence of it through an act of heroic will, much as Delacroix believed he owed his creative power to the struggle to overcome weakness or inertia, and attributed his identity to the ceaseless conflict *within himself*. Sardanapalus's posing is not unlike Delacroix's own.

In a crucial *Journal* entry, Delacroix affirms that painting, however difficult and enervating, lends him vitality: "Painting, it's true, like the most exacting of mistresses, harasses and torments me in a hundred ways. . . . What seemed so easy at a distance, has now become dreadfully and unceas-ingly difficult. But how is it that this unending struggle revives instead of destroying me, and far from discouraging, comforts me and occupies my mind when I leave it?" (*Journal* 408) The struggle between resignation and resistance to natural process characterizes much of the *Journal*, resistance usually triumphing over a temptation to lapse into despair. The *Journal* continues to affirm a beneficial strife, out of which imaginative power constitutes itself. The conflict that permeates the *Journal* involves such issues as Delacroix's love of women versus his need to remain ascetic and undistracted from creative intensity, and his desire to behave as an erudite social man versus an impulse to be more private and work-centered. Goethe caught the spirit of Delacroix's ambivalence when, regarding the plates for *Faust*, he commented: "Delacroix seems to have felt at home here and roamed freely, as though on familiar ground, in a strange fusion of heaven and earth, the possible and the impossible, between the coarsest and the most delicate" (qtd. in Prideaux 81). Delacroix did not so much choose one mode or another, but mined the dialectic for the subject matter of the paintings, though his allegiances were usually with "the possible" as a way to energize the self.

Many of the paintings focus either on a moment of choice (the subject deliberates on a drastic course of action and struggles within herself, like *Medea* contemplating the murder of her children) or on the perilous decision whose resolution will precipitate an action. Delacroix finds in that choice the generating impulse of the work. In the *Journal*, Delacroix similarly dramatizes the act of uncertainty and indecision that precedes an action, keeping a close watch on his shifting impulses and recording the way autobiographical writing reflects his vacillations. The emphasis on process characterizes self-analysis as well as painting, just as in the writing he tries to catch his thought at the emotional cresting point, analogous to the way it is "performed" by figures like Medea, Faust, and Hamlet. Delacroix's identification with such models usually occurs at a dramatic, gestural moment when he represents the conflict as a staged pose before the action is released.

When Delacroix took up the *Journal* again in January 1847, after a lapse of twenty-three years (not counting the brief Notebooks he kept during his Moroccan journey in 1832), it was after a day at the Natural History Museum among the exotic animals. "I felt my whole being rise above commonplaces and trivialities. . . . Tigers, panthers, jaguars, lions, etc. Why is it that these things have stirred me so much? Can it be because I have gone outside the everyday thoughts that are my world; away from the street that is my entire universe?" (*Journal* 55–56) Then he remarks on his renewed occupation as journal writer: "I am writing this by my fireside, feeling very glad that I stopped to buy this notebook on my way home. I am beginning it on an auspicious day. I hope that I shall long continue to keep a record of my impressions. I shall often realize the advantage of noting down my impressions in this way; they grow deeper as one recalls them" (*Journal* 56). The energy of the animals and the power he appropriates from them get expressed in the renewed act of writing about himself. Identifying with the animals gives rebirth to the writing and announces a revolt against limitations even while recognizing that they cannot be ignored. For Delacroix, writing no less than painting dramatizes a sense of life and energy as well as of death and destruction. In the same week that he began the new *Journal*, Delacroix entered a long description of Rubens's *Lion Hunt*. On one hand he emphasizes the fierce energy, movement, and expressive power of the work, and on the other he stresses the death throes of the hunter even as he plunges his dagger into the lion's body. Delacroix points to the conflict and the confusion—"the eye does not know where to rest" (*Journal* 57)—and we can take this duality for his own ambiguous identity.

Now willful and powerful, now severely self-judging; now a practitioner of apocalyptic longings, now one reconciled to work as the sole balm for disappointments and losses, Delacroix makes authenticity a matter of restless impulse in the face of mortality, as well as a willingness to shift grounds about both external matters and his own mind: "I see now that my turbulent mind needs activity, that it must break out and try a hundred different ways before reaching the goal towards which I am always straining" (*Journal* 38). His fear of inertia may be linked to a sense of destiny—he will triumph only if he is never still, torn between defiance and surrender.

The violence of the clashes between horse and lion, horse and tiger, or lion and armed rider all express the double-natured aspect of Delacroix's romanticism: unleashed will and agonizing defeat. Delacroix refers to his era as an "unbridled century" (*Journal* 161), identifying abuse of power with a horse freed from restraint. Delacroix knew that unchecked, limitless energy was both an illusion and a dangerous dream, but only through contention and struggle—in short, through work (which includes autobiographical writing)—could he reach fulfillment.

This commitment to work comes close to sublimation and, if any proof is needed, it is provided by a letter to George Sand on January 12, 1861: "Nothing delights me more than painting and moreover it makes me feel as fit as a man of 30; painting is my sole preoccupation, and I beguile others only for its sake. Which is to say I am buried in my work" (*Ecrits* 2: 76, my translation). Here is Delacroix's insistence on mind and will over death, but just barely.

Writing, not just painting, thus provides some consolation, a way to combat time and decay. If it takes the imaginary absorption of others into the self to enlarge his identity, so be it. The act of keeping a journal, both the recording and the later reflection and rereading, allowed Delacroix to prevent the past from disappearing altogether: "A long interruption of my poor Journal [about one month]; I feel very sad about it. These trifles, written down at random, seem all that remain to me of my daily life as it slips away" (*Journal* 219). Hannoosh argues that because of Delacroix's method of constant reincorporation of previous material, "the past preserved in [the *Journal*] is . . . ever alive, always at hand to enrich and qualify the present" (18). This implies, rightly I think, that in the *Journal*, Delacroix emphasizes the inexorable effects of time and attempts to combat them by eschewing both a fatal linearity and a deluded solipsism.

I BECAME INTERESTED in Delacroix's *Journal* during a year when I lived in Paris and taught at the American University of Paris. My apartment was not far from the Delacroix museum, which was formerly his house and studio on the Place Furstemberg, one of the prettiest Parisian squares. I like to read books in the places where their authors wrote, so I spent many autumn afternoons studying the *Journal* in the leafy garden behind the museum. I was frequently the only visitor.

A few streets beyond, in a chapel of Saint Sulpice, there are three large works by Delacroix, and I often took the short walk between museum and church to look at them when my reading was done. In one mural, Delacroix painted Heliodorus, who tries to rob the treasure of the temple at Jerusalem and is driven out by a divine horseman and two avenging angels; in another mural, Satan is cast from Heaven by the archangel Michael; in a third, Jacob wrestles with the angel, the two opponents locked in fierce combat. The chapel focused my interest in Delacroix's theme of combat. Critics have read the Saint Sulpice murals as the painter's allegory of the Romantic artist's struggle with his materials, or with authority, or with art itself. I saw the contest of Jacob and the angel as an emblem of Delacroix's wrestling with his own self in the *Journal;* Jacob extracting a victory on the verge of being crushed parallels the autobiographical writing that proclaims an expressive power even as its author records his fears and his defeats.

I admired Delacroix's bravado in rendering Satan, Heliodorus, and Jacob as boldly assertive as himself, never submissive or humble. Turning loss into triumph is a common motif in the *Journal,* and when in advanced age he painted the chapel, Delacroix proudly declared that "this unending struggle revives me instead of destroying me" (408), the painter like Jacob besieged yet blessed. At the time he was painting in Saint Sulpice people referred to "the Chapel of Monsieur Delacroix," as if the artist had appropriated the sacred place for his own. Stamping his mark on the church is like affirming himself in the *Journal,* as he turns a story of vulnerability into one of defiant will.

When I was working on Delacroix, my friend Howard Waskow visited me in Paris; he was writing a book with his brother Arthur about their contentious relation as siblings, stretching back to their earliest days in the family, and I will have more to say about this memoir in the last chapter. Arthur Waskow in turn had written a book titled *Godwrestling,* which used the story of Jacob and the angel as a metaphor for political and personal struggles in his own life, including that with his brother. Howard and I, classmates at Yale Graduate School and former colleagues at Reed, have engaged in our own disputation over the years, our "wrestling" usually about politics or relationships, and it occurred to me that I was drawn to amicable contentiousness with him as one way to resist a temptation to identify with a strong and persuasive personality.

During the same year, I made pilgrimages to another church, which provided me with a more unexpected discovery than that in Saint Sulpice. I liked to wander among the few remaining kitchen supply vendors, *foie gras* shops, and fin-de-siècle cafés of Les Halles, where the neighborhood butchers in their bloody aprons knocked back their early morning cognac. I often went from Saint Sulpice to Saint Eustache, the late-Gothic parish church of Les Halles that was ringed by the nineteenth-century food pavilions that constituted Paris's great central food market until it was demolished in 1969. The two divine spaces, oddly enough divided up for me the sacred and the secular, Saint Eustache especially celebrating a world that was becoming important in my life.

On my first visit to Saint Eustache, I was hardly prepared for a startling sight midway down the left nave: a sculptural group depicting the wholesale produce merchants on a forced march out of Les Halles on the eve of its destruction. Tucked between a chapel containing the bones of the martyred Saint Eustache and another displaying Mary with the dead Christ in her arms, stands a massive, vividly painted polychrome-and-resin sculptural ensemble by the British artist Raymond Mason. A dozen or so figures walk across the stage set of the chapel, hauling their fruits and vegetables away from the darkened food halls, the somber buildings looming in the background of the piece. What other city would consecrate a cathedral chapel to the men and women who once supplied food to every restaurant and kitchen in the French nation? Paris does not have a museum dedicated to cuisine, but perhaps no secular institution could bestow the appropriate piety upon France's most hallowed cultural practice.

The solemn processional is a theatre of noble pain, the figures grief-stricken, stunned, and mute. One merchant, wearing his ascot with grave dignity, carries a huge cabbage leaf; a stone-faced man, clad in strawberry red, holds an upright cauliflower plant; a stoically proud woman, her jacket green as the vegetables surrounding her, cradles a box of apples as if they were precious jewels rescued from the ruins; and a sorrowful vendor lugs a cart laden with potatoes, asparagus, chard, and a single pineapple. Most movingly, a stern old woman in a black dress, her head wrapped in a brightly colored scarf, clutches a stalk of broccoli as if she were bearing an offering, however futile. Boxes of produce are piled about, and on the pavement, crushed beneath the wheels of the cart, lies a single tomato, its pulp about to run gore.

Here is an expulsion from Paradise, as surely as any showing Adam and Eve forced to leave the Garden. There has been no primal disobedience by the vendors, only a distant and inexorable executive order demanding that they evacuate the market and that the place be razed. The expulsion may be from a secular Eden, but Mason has given it mythic and sacred dimensions, and in the process glorified food and its devotees. I kept returning to this gastronomical chapel and its haunting tableau, whose title is "The Departure of Fruits and Vegetables from the Heart of Paris," but which is less a departure than an exodus, the cortège a memorial to the products of the soil, the market, and the people who sold them, but also to what has become a lost paradise, a forlorn Proustian memory. When Mason installed his secular sculpture, it caused a minor scandal among some of the pious, but he prevailed, for in his work, Les Halles seems more like the Notre Dame of Paris than its belly. The Saint Eustache food handlers became my patron saints, just as St. André, whose image appears alongside a brace of sausages and a pig in one of the stained glass windows of the church, serves as the patron of the Society of Charcuterie that has long worshipped there.

By the late 1980s, when I lived in Paris, I had been reviewing restaurants for a few years (my night job, as I called it), was planning a food book about Portland that came out several years later, and eating seriously to store Paris food memories against my return to American culinary indifference. I continually went back to Saint Eustache as a sort of spiritual home. I had just taken a trip to the Vaucluse, where the vineyards are planted with cherry trees so that the taste of the fruit comes through the wine; and to an artisanal cheese maker deep in the Herault, whose *chèvre* tastes of the thyme and rosemary on which his goats graze. After my gastronomic picaresque, I understood why the French regard food and the holy as one.

Paris was my literary and culinary research center. I taught at The American University of Paris and wrote during the day, but the anticipation and contemplation of food always took over from the afternoon's ruminations. I looked forward to the twilight hour, what the French call the "blue hour" or the "cinq-à-sept," and though "five to seven" designates the hours of assignation with one's mistress, a rendezvous before dinner with the neighborhood fish-monger and his briny sea-urchins, or with the woman in the boulangerie who shows off her *pain à l'oignon*, or with the charcuterie owner who makes and sells a truffled rabbit terrine, proved reward enough. Respect for tradition and passionate expertise among growers, producers, and merchants taught me much I would use when I came to write about food and restaurants. What you learn in Paris comes down to one thing: How the French transform nature into culture, turning raw stuff into civilized pleasure. The *affineur* showed me the way he rotates his cave-stored cheeses to finish them perfectly and how he knows the exact ripeness of a *chaource* so he can sell it at the perfect moment depending on whether a customer is serving it that night or the next. The fish man gave me a course on the Brittany oyster beds that grow his *fines de claires,* discoursing on the salinity of the estuary where they are raised near the island of Noirmoutier, then ceremoniously placing the oysters on a bed of seaweed and gently handing me the box as if it contained the Maltese Falcon, even insisting on a particular wine to go with them. I remember buying a duck in the market from a woman who commanded me as I left, "Cook it well"; she knew what had gone into the nurturing of that bird and she wanted me to hold up my end of the bargain. I had thrown myself into "la grande bouffe" and, as Adam Gopnik says, was "living the same participles day after day, planning, shopping, chopping, roasting, eating"—building a repertoire and going to school to the ordinary neighborhood merchants, each of whom seemed as if he or she could contribute a learned treatise to the *Larousse Gastronomique*.

It all stood me in good stead when, a couple of years ago, I was chosen as one of the three best restaurant reviewers in the country by the James Beard Foundation, and though I lost to Ruth Reichl of the *New York Times*, I was more pleased to be nominated than disappointed not to win, which is more or less what Katherine Hepburn said after getting a nomination but not the Oscar.

Over a recent dinner with Reichl, I mentioned we had gone head-to-head for the award several years earlier. "Did I win?" she cooed. I could not tell if her question meant she was superbly self-assured, charmingly modest, or so used to prizes that she simply could not remember. It may be my own fault, but I'm still both amused and chagrined when, no matter what I might say to my Reed colleagues about Shakespeare or Conrad, they seem more eager to talk to me about food than about literature.

Once, when I called on a winegrower near Bordeaux, he told me he produced two reds: a lighter, spicier one with the taste of cherries and nuts and a richer one with "a noble attack" and fuller range of sensations. "The first one," he said proudly, "is my Van Gogh; it strikes you right away with its passion and finesse, and while you will be astonished by it, you know everything you will ever know at the moment you experience it. Nothing is hidden. But the other is my Rembrandt, with its shades and nuances of dark and light; you cannot easily plumb its depths or its secrets." "And could you," I ventured, "make a Delacroix?" He thought intently for a moment, pacing around his cellar. "Ah," he replied at last, "that would be a struggle, and then you'd never know what you had; a Delacroix would yield up too many conflicting sensations."

SELF AS OTHER, THE OTHER AS SELF

12.

Conflict and Incorporation

Edmund Gosse's *Father and Son*

In this section I turn to a number of autobiographers who define themselves through their connection to others—father, mother, siblings, servants, even a psychiatrist. Such figures are not subsidiary nor merely incidental, but integral to the way the autobiographers establish and represent the self. Not only are other people portrayed as crucial to the life of the writer, the self in the text becomes understandable only *through* the life of the other. In several cases the writer attempts to achieve an identity by writing *against* an other. But even when the autobiographer acknowledges the necessity for the opposition, alterity constitutes the ground of self-formation, and we perceive how writer and adversary are ineluctably joined. In these autobiographies the line between autonomy and the relational, or between self and other—the boundary that might seem necessary for a discrete identity—is never easy to establish, even for the writers themselves.

Critics of autobiography from Stephen Spender to Mary Mason to Paul John Eakin have insisted on the relational nature of life-writing. Eakin argues that the private self is always part of a larger public whole, whether it's family, community, or culture, and further, that the self depends to a considerable extent on the encompassing world for its behavior, understanding, and definition. For Eakin, autobiography as a genre is no less relational than selfhood, and in his later work he has turned to "autobiographies that offer not only the autobiography of the self but the biography *and* the autobiography of the other," where "the stress is on the performance of the collaboration and therefore on the relation between the two individuals involved" (*How Our Lives Become Stories* 58–59). In the cases of Edmund Gosse and Edward Dahlberg, who write respectively about a father and a mother, each of their autobiographies might appear to be indistinguishable from a biography of the other figure, yet each autobiographer reveals how entwined the self is with the parent even as the

protagonist struggles to break free into individuality. In the final chapter, I
show how a group of autobiographers question a myth of individuality by
writing life-stories that, in both content and representational form, express
how others become part of the self through a mode of autobiographical
writing I call "double-voicing."

Eakin has declared that "we never really know why writers write what
they write, and this very unknowability can make any inquiry into an
author's intentions seem fruitless if not impertinent" (*How Our Lives Become
Stories* 149). In an even more definitive assertion, Philip Roth writes: "What
we know is that . . . nobody knows anything. You *can't* know anything. The
things you *know* you don't know. Intention? Motive? Consequence? Meaning? All that we don't know is astonishing" (209). What *can* we know—or
say—about these writers' intentions in constructing autobiographies with
such an emphasis on another figure? Probably nothing that will satisfactorily
encompass all of them; nevertheless, my intention in this section is to try to
show why certain writers have incorporated other figures so centrally, and
what happens when those autobiographers wrestle with the problem of their
distinctness, especially when the attention they give to others may appear to
threaten their freedom. I am less concerned about theorizing the universality
of what Susanna Egan has termed the "dialogic" nature of the genre than
I am to understand how certain autobiographers negotiate selfhood by
striving to achieve one through a contested relation. That achievement
is complex and interesting exactly because in attempting to distinguish
oneself from another, they reveal the process by which the self struggles
for its identity. A range of diverse impulses gets played out in the works I
consider here: a temptation to reject the other; an acknowledgment that
without the other, one might be entirely different; a desire to become like
the other; and a realization that the other is a necessary lens through which
self-understanding comes into focus.

"Father and Son": the title of Edmund Gosse's autobiography of 1907
scarcely implies an opposition between the two figures. Gosse's text, which
takes him to age seventeen and a decisive break from his father as he embarks
on a literary career in London, is an account of the author's complex view
toward the man who shaped his early life with so much stern control. Gosse's
autobiography is a model of tonal complication in its attempt to be fair and
judicious to the older man where he might have chosen to be bitter and ac-
cusatory. Though his autobiography is a portrait of irreconcilable conflict in
which the boy gradually realizes that his father is not God let alone infallible
or always reasonable, Gosse avoids the extremes of either accommodation
or antagonism. His text is an exercise in complication and ambivalence.

Born in 1849 into a household of Plymouth Brethren, a small, narrowly Calvinistic sect, Gosse struggled against the inflexible orthodoxy and soul-stiffening rigidity of his father's way of life. Gosse writes the autobiography as an exercise in impartiality despite the tyrannical education and his father's authoritarian theology and intolerance for others' opinions. Only an escape from his father's joyless severity enabled Gosse to take "a human being's privilege to fashion his inner life for himself," and yet in *Father and Son* he regards Philip Gosse as a "noble figure," a man of integrity and conviction, devoid of any hypocrisy, and without a trace of self-interest. In the autobiography, Gosse employs the very detachment that allowed him to survive his childhood: his descriptions of his narrative as "a *document* . . . a *record* of educational and religious conditions," a "*diagnosis* of a dying Puritanism," and an "*unbiased*" examination all suggest a restraint that the child developed as a defense against his father's aggression and as an instrument to forge his character (*Father and Son* 277, 213, 3; my emphasis).

Gosse even shows sympathy for his own upbringing, not unlike John Stuart Mill's strategy in his autobiography. Indeed, much of *Father and Son* depicts Gosse as a child trying to create harmony with his father, even to be like the older man. Gosse internalizes the conflict, as if he harbored a "father side" and a "son side." We can read the opening words of the text—"this book is the record of a struggle between two temperaments, two consciences" (*Father and Son* 5)—as implying a conflict both between Philip and Edmund and within Gosse himself. Much of the autobiography is a defense against too forceful a condemnation of the father; his critique is not a direct attack but one made via scenes that dramatize his father's narrowness. I want to examine Gosse's representation of his childhood and adolescence, especially the way his style controls the subterranean resentment and the way he delineates the gradual achievement of identity without any repudiation of the father, indeed adjusting his ambivalence to the requirements of an emergent self.[1]

Gosse structures the autobiography of his struggle for survival around a trope of evolution and its themes and its language. Early in the text, Gosse describes his father's attempt to reconcile the scientific and theological conflicts centering around Darwinism. This historical incident is crucial for understanding the son, for it warns him away from the reductive thinking he avoided in his childhood as much as he skirts it in his narrative. Gosse's father was a noted marine biologist, but in the great Darwinian controversy he was incapable of scientific detachment.

[T]hrough my Father's brain, in that year of scientific crisis, 1857, there rushed two kinds of thought, each absorbing, each convincing, yet totally irreconcilable. There is a peculiar agony in the paradox that truth has two forms, each of them indisputable, yet each antagonistic to the other. It was this discovery, that there were two theories of physical life, each of which was true, but the truth of each incompatible with the truth of the other, which shook the spirit of my Father with perturbation. It was not, really, a paradox, it was a fallacy, if he could only have known it, but he allowed the turbid volume of superstition to drown the delicate stream of reason. He took one step in the service of truth, and then drew back in agony, and accepted the servitude of error. (*Father and Son* 75)

The result was *Omphalos: An Attempt to Untie the Geological Knot* (1857), in which Philip Gosse argued that God created phenomena, including living creatures, full-blown, but that all things bore the "stigmata of a pre-existent existence" (Gosse, *The Life of Philip Henry Gosse* 278). At first glance Philip Gosse's theory seemed a model of adaptation to the claims of both sides, but the father's emphasis was really opposed to the scientific analysis of his historical moment, and readers mockingly interpreted the theory to mean that "God hid the fossils in the rocks in order to tempt geologists into infidelity" (*Father and Son* 77–78). But Gosse can be sympathetic to his father's inability to live with ambiguity even as he is critical; in his biography of Philip, written almost two decades before *Father and Son*, he suggests the nature of the father's limitation in a way that is indulgent rather than caustic. For scientific philosophy, "he was fitted neither by native aptitude, nor by the possession of a mind clear from prejudice. Thoroughly sincere as he was, and devoted to truth as he believed himself to be, he lacked that deeper modesty, that nobler candour, which inspired the genius of Darwin. The current interpretation of the Bible lay upon his judgment with a weight that he could never throw off, and his scientific work was of value only in those matters of detail which remained beyond the jurisdiction of the canon" (*The Life of Philip Henry Gosse* 276).

In viewing this episode as symptomatic of temperamental deficiencies he must avoid, Gosse employs the language of evolution not only to describe ensuing conflicts with his father, but to suggest that the son has the better mode of adaptation and can function in a superior fashion because he perceives more. Gosse spends much of his childhood as a detached observer, seeking perspective on his experience. Throughout the autobiography, there are images of Gosse's father "absolutely motionless, with his eye glued to the microscope." His father "saw everything through a lens, nothing in the immensity of nature." At age ten, the baptism sanctifying him for membership as an adult Brother places him on the "stage" of a microscope, under the scrutiny of the older man. The father's mind is myopic, "acute," and "narrow"; he is "a collector of facts" incapable of "forming broad generalisations and of escaping in a vast survey from the troublesome pettiness of detail" (*Father and Son* II, 97, 86–87). When Gosse begins to read fiction and feels his mind liberated, he describes a significant book as "a powerful telescope." One way to characterize the conflict between father and son is the difference between microscopic and telescopic vision. The figure of Gosse at the telescope determines his point of view in the autobiography as he coolly observes both his and his father's mind. Ironically, in the closing days of Philip's life, he gazed through a telescope by an open window "with something more than an astronomer's curiosity. His letters show that the expectation of the personal coming of the Lord was embedded in his mind, not understood in a symbolic or metaphysical sense, but anticipated as the fulfillment of a divine promise which at its destined moment would become a visible reality. With such expectations the heavens were inevitably associated" (Charteris 217). When the father finally uses a telescope, it is to witness the second coming in the heavens.

Evolution is also the conceptual model for Gosse's shaping of his individualism. Early on, he declares that the autobiography is about "struggle," not only between two temperaments, but also "two epochs"; one of the characters "was born to fly backward," the other "could not help being carried forward." Gosse speaks of "mutation," "inheritance," and "adaptation" using the language of social evolutionary theory to define his quest for a separate identity. Life for the child is a form of adaptation, and he is ultimately a "survivor" (*Father and Son* 5). Only when he breaks from his father, concluding a process of gradual separation, does Gosse view him as regressive, mired in an ultrafundamentalist system of belief. Gosse's terms invoke the common currency of Victorian progress, as he leaves his anachronistic father behind. Cynthia Malone notes that in Gosse's assessment of their relation, "the empirically based reasoning of nineteenth-century geology . . . counters [Philip's] faith with the fossil evidence of continual change" (23).[2] Gosse implicitly dedicates his autobiography to progress and to the future. He refers to his father as a seventeenth-century man, while Gosse himself anticipates an enlightened self-development, concluding the narrative with an adolescence in which the son has been "carried forward" to the future. The *Omphalos* theory is bad evolution, and Edmund is tied to the umbilical cord of his father's archaic preconceptions. Mill's essay "The Spirit of the Age" provides the terms of contention that characterize Gosse's relation to his father. Mill views the history of the intellect as evolutionary in character, but progress occurs only when men pass through a "transitional" stage in which earlier doctrines are questioned by an open mind, put to proof, and discarded when proved invalid. Gosse maintains just such flexibility, but the father is like one of "those men who carry their eyes in the back of their heads and can see no other portion of the destined track of humanity than that which it has already traveled" (29).

At an early age, Edmund pledges to become a child-saint; he describes how, at his mother's death bed, he made the half-understood dedication to the Brotherhood, recognizing only later that it determined everything in his childhood and early adolescence. The vow itself is a kind of omphalos connecting him to his father through "my Mother's will," which held him "to the unswerving purpose which she had formed and defined" (*Father and Son* 12). Against the inherited obligation, Gosse poses the fact of his developing individuality, which from the start intensifies his isolation and solitude. At first he forges a self in private, where he can nourish the tender beginnings of self-consciousness. In an image of the child growing like a flower planted on a narrow and precarious ledge of a cliff, Gosse implies that he survives only by cunningly adapting within the narrow constraints.

Father and Son functions in part to reclaim childhood and the years Gosse lost when he was initiated too rapidly into an adult world. Deprived of childhood stories—romance, fairy tale, and legend—Gosse becomes what Wordsworth calls "a dwarf Man" (*The Prelude* [1805] V, 295).[3] His parents forbid him to read fiction, regarding storytelling as a sin. But their emphasis on hard truth naturally provokes the child's curiosity. Denied access to fantasy, his faculty for questioning and doubt increases. Gosse's isolation from society allows him to cultivate silence and to practice observation and skepticism. The autobiography shows him employing his father's analytic faculty against him, in the form of challenging trials conducted by the son, counterparts to the father's prayers and rational inquiries that substitute for achieved faith.

Gosse describes three occasions on which he unfrocks his father and diminishes the older man's claims to authority; each incident produces a corresponding increase in the child's self-consciousness. On the first occasion, his father states something as true that Edmund knows is false. On the second, Gosse mischievously ruins his father's small garden, but the father blames some workers. On the third, after hearing his father warn against idolatry, Gosse tests the limits of sacrilege by praying to a chair, an episode that ironically anticipates and parallels the father's venture with the telescope at his window, and satirizes the father's fundamentalist theology. In each episode, Gosse's identity develops as a function of how he judges his father. In the second one, the child's refusal to admit responsibility or to show guilt results from a conscious testing of the father's knowledge and power, and his language suggests a calculated strategy: he arrives at "the awful *proof* that he was not . . . omniscient"; "I cross-examined my Father . . . and pinned him down to the categorical statement that idolatry consisted in praying to any one or anything but God himself. . . . I pressed my Father further on this subject" (*Father and Son* 27, 28, 37). Gosse writes what amounts to a recasting of the famous comb and ribbon thefts in Rousseau's *Confessions*, representing himself as neither the victim of injustice nor the victimizer of another, but one who scrutinizes the dominant figure's claims for authority and epistemological certainty.

The expected pang of conscience after Gosse's destructive act in the garden, his lies, and the exposing of the father, does not occur; instead, he exchanges a superego for an alter ego or a secret second self. In the key passage, Gosse describes an act of individuation, the first glimmerings of genuine selfhood. "[O]f all the thoughts which rushed upon my savage and undeveloped little brain at this crisis, the most curious was that I had found a companion and a confidant in myself. There was a secret in this world and it belonged to me and to somebody who lived in the same body with me. There were two of us, and we could talk with one another. It is difficult to define impressions so rudimentary, but it is certain that it was in this dual form that the sense of my individuality now suddenly descended upon me" (*Father and Son* 28). Gosse's emphasis is less on triumph over the father than on the acquisition of a self. The displacement of the father does occur, but he mutes the attack by fantasizing a kind of brother and surrogate for the father, in effect a self-enlargement. This procedure allows Gosse to experiment with a new inner voice, one that he will express uninhibitedly at the end of the autobiography, when he anticipates a literary vocation and a full sense of self-realization. Throughout the remainder of his childhood, he preserves this secret self, sign of his newly achieved individuation. "Through thick and thin I clung to a hard nut of individuality, deep down in my childish nature. To the pressure from without, I resigned everything else, my thoughts, my words, my anticipations, my assurances, but there was something which I never resigned, my innate and persistent self" (*Father and Son* 142). Creating a second self is an act of self-invention, a giving birth to himself.[4]

In gaining a self, Gosse affirms his right to exist; he needs confirmation from someone other than his father, and this internal voice is at once his own and that of authorizing agent. The new self exercises creative and performative power, by which I mean that the child feels impelled to tell his story to the internalized self much as the autobiographer feels narratively empowered to tell the story to the reader. I would claim, in fact, that the creative activity in childhood ultimately makes possible the autobiography. As the child gains confidence in his worth, we can imagine the second self as a kind of early audience, listening to Gosse and urging him to further acts of imagination, even of transgression. Those acts in childhood prepare for the ultimate transgressive act (however muted) of autobiography itself. It is not that the young Gosse has no language and suddenly acquires it, but that for a while he speaks only the language of his father. As Gosse moves from The Word to words—from divine and paternal authority, and spiritual vocation, ultimately to his vocation as a man of letters—the two acts that both dramatize and validate this shift are the acquisition of a self through speaking and the writing of autobiography.[5] The second self begins the gradual process of repairing alienation, guiding the child's first steps away from aloneness. Gosse moves toward identity as he achieves a voice and begins to own it, aware of his self-formative capability. When in the last line of the autobiography he speaks of "fashion[ing] his inner life for himself" (*Father and Son* 227), he virtually links the two acts, the earlier self-*discovery* analogous to the later self-*creation*.[6] The twin roles of this subversive and companionate second self—analytical and aggressive— suggest Gosse's desire both to imitate his father and to displace him. The second self is not only an expression of fantasy long denied, but a sign of future possibility.

Gosse explores the subversive potential of this gradually unrepressed self. He persuades himself he can induce the birds and butterflies in his father's illustrated books to fly out of the pages leaving holes behind, and imagines that the second self can look down on his father and take his measure. Philip Gosse's warnings against pleasure might account for the son's dream about stealing a rare pigment (carmine) from his father's paint box, a dream that suggests his desire to be like his father (he would prefer to call him "beloved brother," but is forbidden to do so), to sit at the paternal desk and make the same drawings, yet also to usurp the father's place. The dream, a central episode in the autobiography, has its origin in a curious episode in which Gosse is carried off from church one evening by a harmless eccentric woman from the congregation. Gosse's description of his dream emphasizes the child's terror during the kidnapping, and yet its emotive energies suggest the excitement and reckless abandon of the escape from the church.

It seemed to me I was taking part in a mad gallop through space. Some force, which had tight hold of me, so that I felt myself an atom in its grasp, was hurrying me on, over an endless slender bridge, under which on either side a loud torrent rushed at a vertiginous depth below. . . . It seemed as if we,—I, that is, and the undefined force which carried me,—were pushing feverishly on towards a goal which our whole concentrated energies were bent on reaching, but which a frenzied despair in my heart told me we could never reach, yet the attainment of which alone could save us from destruction. Far away, in the pulsation of the great luminous whorls, I could just see that goal, a ruby colored point waxing and waning, and it bore, or to be exact it consisted of, the letters of the word CARMINE. (*Father and Son* 106–07)

The ravaging forces may represent the guilt of his forbidden quest, but they also imply a surge of unrepressed desire. In the face of threatened engulfment, Gosse avoids destruction by seizing his father's most precious possession; "carmine" is the father's "shibboleth of self-indulgence . . . a symbol of all that taste and art and wealth could combine to produce" (*Father and Son* 110). Gosse wants to be like his father, but with a passion and self-expressive daring the older man could never achieve. The dream emphasizes the divided nature of Gosse's self.

As if to compensate for the guilt-provoking usurpation in the dream, Gosse attempts to prove his doctrinal rigor by becoming even stricter than his father and surpassing the older man in piety. He investigates the theological qualifications of his stepmother with a severity that makes even his father cringe. "Our positions were now curiously changed. It seemed as if it were I who was the jealous monitor, and my Father the deprecating penitent" (*Father and Son* 155).

A child's identification with an aggressor allows him to deal with fearful external forces; becoming like the threatening person, the child plays a game "in which through the metamorphosis of the subject . . . anxiety is converted into pleasurable security," the exorcising of the threat accomplished through the impersonation. In this way "the child transforms himself from the person threatened into the person who makes the threat" (A. Freud 111, 113). Gosse's imitations of his father's piety and his baiting of a neighbor whose devoutness he questioned were ways both to absorb and deflect the father's power. By becoming as rigorous as the father, Gosse could soften the attacks whenever Philip suspected his son's lack of zeal, but could ultimately defend himself against the father by using the older man's own weapons.

This identification gets into the tone of the autobiography itself, where the sympathy and respect constitute a rhetorical equivalent for the child's psychology of accommodation. Anna Freud characterizes identification with the aggressor as the internalizing of other people's criticism of one's behavior and hence a step toward self-criticism. Gosse's deference toward the father in the autobiography represents both a strategy and a kind of internalized criticism, as if the childhood subversions, whether fantasized or expressed, had to be partly atoned for.

But gesturing toward restitution is not where the textual center of gravity lies. The autobiography alternates between aggression and accommodation. When, toward the end of the book, Gosse depicts how at his moment of greatest doubt "the artificial edifice of extravagant faith began to totter and crumble," he notes that for a long time he concealed the break with the father "even from myself" (*Father and Son* 210). Gosse adds an epilogue calling his father a misguided yet "unique and noble figure"; to turn completely against his father in the autobiography would ironically destroy too much of his own self, and Gosse never fully discredits the father. His ambivalence is also a function of an attraction to both religion and art. "I was at one moment devoutly pious, at the next haunted by visions of material beauty and longing for sensuous impressions. In my hot and silly brain, Jesus and Pan held sway together." He stresses the duality of the theological and the aesthetic via a series of conflicting pressures: "I returned with a brain full of strange discords, in a huddled mixture of 'Endymion' and the Book of Revelation, John Wesley's hymns and *Midsummer Night's Dream*" (*Father and Son* 109, 209). Gosse sums up his ambiguity in an image that looks back to the struggle of evolution and anticipates uncertainty and spiritual homelessness.

> Of the world outside, of the dim whirlpool of London, I was much afraid, but I was now ready to be willing to leave the narrow Devonshire circle, to see the last of the red mud, of the dreary village street, of the plethoric elders, to hear the last of the drawling voices of the "Saints." Yet I had a great difficulty in persuading myself that I could ever be happy away from home, and again I compared my lot with that of one of the speckled soldier-crabs that roamed about in my Father's aquarium, dragging after them great whorlshells. They, if by chance they were turned out of their whelk-habitations, trailed about a pale soft body in search of another house, visibly broken-hearted and the victims of every ignominious accident. (*Father and Son* 204–05)

In the climactic episode of Gosse's adolescence and of the autobiography, he tests for the last time the strength of those beliefs so long imposed upon him. Gosse challenges God as he had earlier challenged his father; he invokes Jesus to take him to Paradise before he is ruined by the temptations of London, but the "glorious apparition" does not materialize.

> This was the highest moment of my religious life, the apex of my striving after holiness. I waited awhile, watching; and then I had a little shame at the theatrical attitude I had adopted, although I was alone. Still I gazed and still I hoped. Then a little breeze sprang up, and the branches danced. Sounds began to rise from the road beneath me. Presently the colour deepened, the evening came on. From far below there rose to me the chatter of the boys returning home. The tea-bell rang,—the last word of prose to spoil my mystical poetry. "The Lord has not come, the Lord will never come," I muttered, and in my heart the artificial edifice of extravagant faith began to totter and crumble. From that moment forth my Father and I, though the fact was successfully concealed from him and even from myself, walked in opposite hemispheres of the soul, with "the thick o' the world between us." (*Father and Son* 210)

The trial convinces Gosse he has been fair to his father, while the theatrical scene overwhelms him with its beckoning loveliness. Mostly he emphasizes the way art (the theatrical posturing), romance (the "gardens sloping to the sea, which twinkled faintly beyond the towers of the town"), nature (the twilight hour), and society (sounds of chattering boys and the tea-bells) combine to replace doctrinaire theology.[7]

Gosse implicitly counterposes this scene to the epiphany of Augustine's *Confessions*, where the Christian autobiographer also leans from a window overlooking a garden and anticipates a vision of God's grace that will lead to conversion. In Augustine's revelation, his life has its analogue in scripture and its affinities with the entire Christian community. By contrast, Gosse repudiates the imitative and imitable nature of his experience, for his "conversion" affirms a unique, particular nature, not one that exists in a spirit of replication as Augustine's conversion implies and demands. Geoffrey Galt Harpham has argued that Augustine "is 'converted' when [he] discovers that [his] life can be made to conform to certain culturally validated narrative forms" (44), and Augustine insists as well on his place in a chain leading from Saint Paul to the readers of his text. Gosse's autobiography testifies to what is peculiar and distinct, and his "conversion" to aesthetics sanctions the writing of autobiography as an account of a unique identity.

But in London, where his father reaches him through an obsessive and badgering correspondence regarding Edmund's faith, Gosse remains conflicted, his soul "undulating and shapeless." In the face of his father's long-distance commands to study scripture and doctrine, Gosse feels "despair at my own feebleness" and "pity for my Father's manifest and pathetic distress." His father's religion "divides heart from heart," but it also divides the son's own heart within itself. At the conclusion of *Father and Son*, as if desperately justifying his break, Gosse includes a long carping letter from his father expressing the older man's piety. "The solitary letter, in its threatening whiteness" that lies hauntingly on Gosse's table, bursts upon us (*Father and Son* 212, 213, 233). Only at the end of the text, after showing how the grim letter permits no compromise, does Gosse finally write without qualification or apology, somewhat reminiscent of the conclusion to Joyce's *Portrait*. As I mentioned earlier, Gosse's inclusion of the father's letter is directly contradictory to Kafka's fabricating *his* father's reply, Gosse's self-assurance reversing Kafka's self-effacement.

And yet Gosse shared many traits with his father, especially his own tendency later in life to be as authoritarian and prudish in society as the older man in his theocratic community. In a memoir of the autobiographer, Evan Charteris claims that for Gosse society was the "sphere in which he was inclined to pedantry, seeing a certain sanctity in etiquette and rules of procedure. These things mattered; they were part of the machinery by which an institution of which he delighted to be a member was kept together. There was something almost transcendental about them, and it was not for profane hands to put them on one side" (240). Gosse's rigid adherence to form also allies him with his father. William Irvine, the editor of *Father and Son*, hints at the similarity: "Perhaps his childhood was the only real and serious part of his life. Perhaps, in spite of his hatred of puritanism, he found when he really came to know Pan, that he didn't like him at all" (xli).

Gosse's resemblance to his father emerges as well in the *Journals* of André Gide, whom Gosse championed in England and who encountered Gosse in Paris. Gide recorded their meeting on October 3, 1916: "As in the past, his movements seemed to me prompted perhaps a bit more by his mind than by his heart, or at least by a sort of self-respect. Intelligence, which with him always has a weather-eye, intervenes and checks him on the slope of surrender. He begins to catch himself at the moment when I was beginning to like him. Moreover, it is perhaps not so much me as himself that he distrusts" (2: 148). Despite his admiration for Gide, Gosse was shocked by the narrative honesty of *Si le grain ne meurt*; the facts of Gide's sexuality did not trouble him so much as their revelation in print: "I cannot help asking myself, in the face of this narrative—Was it wise? Was it necessary? Is it useful?" "*why* have you done it, and what advantages to any one can accrue from it?" Gide's reply touches on matters that Gosse had to set aside. "Why did I write this book? because I *had* to write it. . . . I expect nothing but consequence painful to me. . . . It would have seemed to me cowardly to let myself be stopped by contemplation of the distress, or of the risk."[8] Gide, also reared in a puritanical home, retained none of Gosse's circumspection; in his *Journal* he announces the more radical step: "I am not writing these Memoirs to defend myself. I am not called on to defend myself since I am writing them in order to be accused" (2: 194). But *Father and Son* is written to *resist* accusation, whether from the public or from the father whose values he had internalized after all.

Gosse's tendency to withdraw into rigid forms is also cited by Virginia Woolf, who claims that because childhood ill-prepared Gosse for the world, he "observed formalities punctiliously which are taken as a matter of course by those who have never lived in dread of the instant coming of the Lord." Woolf's analysis firmly links Philip and Edmund: "How much better Gosse would have been as a writer, how much more important he would have been as a man, if only he had given freer rein to his impulses, if only his pagan and sensual joy had not been dashed by perpetual caution. . . . He hints, he qualifies, he insinuates, he suggests, but he never speaks out, for all the world as if some austere Plymouth Brother were lying in wait to make him do penance for his audacity" (Woolf 86–87). These comments remind us that Gosse could never fully escape from Philip's influence, that his second self remained ideal or potential rather than actual, and that the autobiography represents not only father *versus* son, but also the father *within* the son.[9]

Gosse's life and his autobiography are defensive acts intending to avoid conflict. *Father and Son* gestures toward its author's self-creation, but never at the expense of his father, for that would endanger the public image of Philip Gosse, question the son's admiration, and leave Gosse himself open to attack. Such a position might also claim more for himself than Gosse wishes. Even in the autobiography, he can never break completely with the father, as if self-determination were too dangerous. Though the autobiography attempts to justify and to give himself an understandable motivation for a break with which he continues to feel uncomfortable, the text is less the representation of rupture than an artfully cautious attempt to say only what needs to be said. We might imagine there were greater reserves of antagonism, but Gosse will not say, for that notion would stir up more discomfort than he could bear.

I CANNOT READ Gosse's autobiography without thinking about my father's role in my transition from childhood to maturity, as well as about my decision to spend my life differently from his, not defending clients in court but reading, teaching, and writing about books. Gosse had to separate himself from his father in order to survive, while in so many ways I wanted to be like mine—I especially envied Joe's easy way in the world. Still, I regarded Gosse's autobiography as a mirror to reflect my very dissimilar life and was perhaps drawn to the work because Gosse seeks to minimize the differences between father and son.

While writing about Gosse, I've been reflecting on two emblematic scenes with my father. When I was about eight, the path I took to grade school cut through a vacant lot, and I invariably arrived there at the same time as a group of older boys, who sometimes taunted me and, on a couple of occasions, pushed me to the ground. Because he knew I was frightened, my father one day followed at a distance, and when the inevitable encounter with the gang took place, he rushed forward to scatter them, threatening to hunt them down if they repeated their bullying. I was gratified to have the protection but ashamed not to have waged my own battle, both wanting and resenting my father's interference. Ten years later he was once again my guardian, stirring up even greater ambivalence.

During my freshman year at college, my parents visited me and brought along my girlfriend from our New Jersey town. I had booked them adjoining ground floor rooms at The Lord Jeffrey Amherst Inn, with a terrace opening onto a small garden. In the 1950s, Amherst students were forbidden to visit their dates' rooms, so Judy and I arranged that I would conspicuously kiss her good night in the lobby, walk to the side of the Inn, climb a fence, negotiate a hedge, and make my way to her room through the French doors that gave onto the terrace. On a late November night, a light snow fell as I carried out the plan.

A month later I came home to Elizabeth for winter break. During a long conversation with my father in which I told him about my life at college, I felt more grown-up than ever; for the first time, perhaps, we spoke to each other as men. Suddenly he asked me about the night with Judy at the Inn, and as my poise gave way to perturbation, he told me the following story. He and my mother had gone to sleep when he heard noises from the garden outside their room. Arising from his bed and peering out of the window, naked except for the drapes wrapped around him like a winding sheet, he watched me furtively cross the lawn, clear the hedge, and make my way to the appointed rendezvous. Fearing a security officer might intercept me, he stood guard at the window—ready to tell the "House Dick" that his son was searching in the snow for lost keys—until he saw I was safely in Judy's room.

My initiation into manhood, Gosse's theme, came not from the night with Judy, but from that conversation with my father. I had no desire to share my sexuality with him, and although this latest instance of protection recalled to mind, with considerable unease, the earlier episode, I was proud he saw me as a mature young man.

Years later I told my mother's sister Harriet this story, and she, whom I knew to have been in love with my father and whom I darkly suspected had had an affair with him, recounted a tale of my father's early sexuality. When he was at college in West Virginia in the mid-1920s, he began to date my mother, who was hundreds of miles away at school in eastern Pennsylvania. He could not afford the nightly long distance calls, but the local telephone operator in Morgantown, who was also in love with him, allowed Joe to make free calls as long as he continued to sleep with her, and they maintained their lubricious bargain for several years. When I heard this story about my roguish father I was more intrigued than upset. By this time I was ready to talk about our intimate lives, and I wished I could have spoken with him about both episodes, however unthinkable *that* exchange. At any rate it could not be, for four months after our talk about the Inn, he was dead at forty-eight from a heart attack.

He had had an earlier attack when I was thirteen, and during the intervening years I was continually cautioned not to talk too loudly, not to contradict, not to upset him in any way. I could not argue or even debate with my father without worrying I might jeopardize his health, even kill him; nor could I stand up for my ideas and values if they conflicted too much with his. I felt rage, but the enforced repression kept me silent. Deprivation kindled anger, and anger aroused guilt. Unable to battle him, it was easier to take on his ways, and they were certainly attractive enough so that I didn't especially feel a loss of independence. But I was holding myself back. Once I spotted him smoking a cigarette I knew the doctors had forbidden, and desperately wanted to warn him to stop, but so guarded had I become I feared that even a sign of concern would violate the family prohibition.

He was not the kind of man who teaches his son how to extract a hook from a mountain trout or to repair a carburetor, but I tried to emulate his urbane manner, and I admired the way people recognized him on the streets of Elizabeth and slapped him on the back. I don't remember ever consciously wishing to go "beyond" him. But many years later when he was long since dead, I was in a Morocco souk bargaining for a carpet, and the young rug dealer refused to budge from his price, insisting that his father, the owner of the shop, would never accept my low offer. I foolishly flaunted Islamic respect for authority and told him the laws of nature dictate that sons *must* disobey, even kill off their fathers. It goes without saying I got neither the rug nor the usual cup of ceremonial tea, lucky to escape unscathed from the medina of Marrakesh. Does this incident speak less to cultural insensitivity than to belated Oedipal struggles?

My father was a lawyer, and I had always assumed I would follow in his footsteps. I was a compulsive reader as a child and knew I wanted to make a large place in my life for books, but I had no thought of a career aside from one in the law. My only gesture of self-assertion in this matter was to imagine a law firm whose title was "Roger Porter and Father, Attorneys." In my junior year at college, Alfred Kazin, my professor of American literature, asked about my plans. I told him I wanted to be a lawyer. "Why?" "Because," I replied, rehearsing the fatuous cant I had always heard at home, "I want to work with people." Kazin was stunned by the idiocy of the remark. "Young man," he sneered with understandable contempt, "one becomes a lawyer because one loves 'The Law.'" I realized I had no idea what Kazin meant by the term, but saw the words "The Law" like "S.P.Q.R." carved in marble on a Roman Senate building, or perhaps semiotically pulsating like CARMINE in Gosse's dream.

As an only child I sought mentors (the "men" contained in that sturdy word) for protection and guidance. I found one in a family friend, Henry Waldman, the youngest judge in New Jersey history, on the bench at twenty-nine but whose heart was in poetry. Henry often abandoned his law office in mid-afternoon to roam Greenwich Village, a poet-manqué who adored the renegade bohemian writer Maxwell Bodenheim, and haunted Greenwich Village coffee houses before the place became a playground for tourists. He took me to secondhand bookstores and introduced me to ethnic food and opera. We went to Asti's restaurant in New York, where we heard the waiters sing "La donna mobile" and ate *osso buco*. Henry wrote letters to me without using capital letters, which made me feel I was part of a circle of initiates, and of course he steered me to e.e. cummings, an adolescent's dream poet.

One Christmas Eve my father and I had the worst argument of my life, despite the injunction against stirring up the waters. I had wanted to watch a television production of *A Christmas Carol* with Laurence Olivier, he wanted to see *What's My Line*. Two stubborn wills collided, my father clinging to seniority, I contending for "culture." When I called him a philistine he stormed off to bed. The next morning, after a sullen exchange of presents, I walked the streets of Elizabeth for five hours in a blizzard, more than long enough to cool my heels and worry my parents sick. That incident pushed me a step or two away from his profession: how could my father uphold the law and yet be so unjust?

At Amherst, the father was Armour Craig. Craig was a crafty thinker who delighted in being elliptical enough to convince you there were convolutions, evasions, and mysteries in every text. Watching him turn a poem like a jeweler examining the facets of a diamond, I learned that reading was hard but rewarding work, and felt that not just serious books but the good, examined life itself was given over to ambiguity, paradox, and complexity, those critical shibboleths of the day. During one of our weekly thesis discussions, Craig praised my insight about some poem and at the same time pulled his long black socks over his calf in a way I took to be the epitome of casual grace. I saw in the gesture a greater elegance than the battered tweeds and chinos of the other professors, and I knew I wanted Craig's combination of style and erudition.

When one of my senior-year roommates and I talked about our plans to go to graduate school and to teach, we thought of our lives in evolutionary terms not unlike Gosse's, though we put it in ways that spoke to our status as third-generation Jews in America and to a specific model of Jewish-American history. My grandfather had been a small shopkeeper, my father a professional, and I was going to be an academic. In seeing a pattern in which I would be "carried forward," I could not imagine how our children could progress any further on the evolutionary curve.

My father died when I was old enough—nineteen—to have developed plenty of superego but not so old that I had the chance to understand him fully or contend with him meaningfully. Friends tell me I can be both deferential and adversarial. Of course: I still want mentors, and I'm too old ever to need them again.

Years after my father's death Allen Ginsberg came to Reed for a poetry reading. He had become as respectable-looking as a well-fed banker, his navy blue blazer, white shirt, and rep tie suggesting nothing of the earlier bad boy of American letters. Among the poems he intoned (he was still chanting like a Tibetan monk) was one describing his father's burial in an ill-maintained graveyard along an industrial zone on the Newark-Elizabeth boundary. The poem's images depicted a railroad track bordering the grave site, which stood next to a scrap yard and the Penn Central power station—the enormous Anheuser-Busch brewery with its flying eagle sign luridly lighting up the cemetery on even the gloomiest winter day—and the fumes from the Bayway refineries just beyond Newark Airport and Exit 14 of the Jersey Turnpike. I knew instantly from his picture that our fathers shared a common resting place. The first great Ginsberg poem I had loved—"Kaddish"—was suddenly no mere abstraction but a premonition of the death of our fathers, lying now just a few feet from each other in B'nai Israel Cemetery. After the reading I told Ginsberg of my realization, and for a moment he became the older brother I never had as we mournfully and joyfully celebrated our common filial fate.

13.
My Mother and Myself
Edward Dahlberg's *Because I Was Flesh*

Edward Dahlberg is one of the great exiles and isolatos of modern American letters. His fiction and criticism, much of it written from the late 1920s through the '40s, was generally met with contempt or indifference, driving its author alternately into silence, literary polemics, or scorn for his readers and for other writers. Only with *Because I Was Flesh*, Dahlberg's 1964 autobiography, does he turn his vitriolic humor against himself. The result is his great book. It is an oddly "collaborative" autobiography in that his identity unfolds through his conflicted identification with his parents, both of whom brought him great misery. Dahlberg's major intention in his autobiography is to give textual birth to his mother; in this verbal act he also becomes the double of the grand inseminator, his elusive father, who, in the book's frequent pun, is seedy Saul. As he writes his mother into renewed existence, Dahlberg too becomes a procreator, identifying with Saul, the progenitor of the story. The autobiography both expresses and results from a generative impulse.

Early in *Because I Was Flesh*, Dahlberg announces that "whatever I imagine I know is taken from my mother's body, and this is the memoir of her body." While the book appears to be as much a biography of Lizzie, a lady barber in Kansas City during the early decades of this century, as it is an autobiography, Dahlberg's text is an account of his gradual realization that his mother's body is "sepulchred" *in him*. His other dominant self-image is of a "sack of woe" to be filled by the elusive father, a "baleful seminal drop of a depraved rotting forefather [who] lived solely to discharge his sperm" (*Flesh* 88, 44). What also fills the emptiness that haunts this melancholy narrator is the presence of other bodies, the generations who inhabit his corpus and generate his sorrow. Only when Dahlberg acknowledges without shame the similarity of his flesh to theirs does he gain his subject: the sufferings and the pleasures of his physical being and his connection with others via the flesh.

Dahlberg's work raises a question I have examined earlier: does the writing of autobiography compensate for previous pain and deprivation, or may it, on the contrary, intensify the anguish? Dahlberg writes not merely from a desire for confession but to assuage his pain, as if by identifying his woe with that of others he could find a community of sufferers to erase his solitary anguish. But at the same time, he argues for affliction and adversity as crucial autobiographical subject matter, and at the outset he states his credo: "It is just as important to be unfortunate as it is to be happy." Like Bernhard's *Gathering Evidence* and Kafka's *Letter to His Father*, *Because I Was Flesh* does not give easy assurance that either remembering or writing one's misery will transcend grief or eradicate the difficulty of the present. "We caress and stroke our rotten, starved years" (*Flesh* 2, 4). While his final reconciliation with his mother, the cause of so much of Dahlberg's misfortune, suggests he has made some peace with his past, the autobiography is a litany of despair, his narrative voice full of self-laceration. It is hard to endorse the views of those critics who claim that Dahlberg's purpose is "to remember the past, to reanimate it, and through the transformation of misfortune, to mitigate the pain" (Shloss 584); or that his language "seems a calculated form of literary reparations for the emotional penury of his upbringing," enabling him "to overcome the vehement, coercive ideology he nursed from childhood" (Leibowitz 14, 328).

What I would call with oxymoronic intent "heroic diminishment" is a constant feature as well. Dahlberg's early years were marked by deprivation, loneliness, and humiliation; all his life he fought back, emerging "a combative, peevish man" able to play "a repertoire of roles with self-delighting or nasty bravura: the huffy philosopher as clown, denying all our received opinions; Job, scratching his sores, railing at the injustice of his plight and excoriating the comforters" (*Flesh* 4). But his heroics and inflated rhetoric cannot fully transcend the anguish brought on by the writing of his troubled past. Retrospection brings pain, as the autobiography dwells relentlessly and remorselessly on his mother's destructive ways as well as on his own inherited weakness. The autobiography is a lament for home and love, and no facile claims for the transcendent value of art can mask the fact that when Dahlberg relives experience in autobiography he re-creates the shame of his early anonymity, deprivations, and lingering self-hatred. In a letter written to Allen Tate shortly after completing *Because I Was Flesh*, Dahlberg noted: "I am done with that slut, my autobiography. . . . To write about one's mother is too harrowing, and to follow her Ghost month in and month out . . . is too great a pressure upon my mildewed and becrazed brain" (*Epitaphs* 243 [letter of October 8, 1962]). Writing with a "diseased imagination," he creates a "song against myself," in thrall to the past, which only increases his present suffering. The text represents an attempt to poise consciousness against the anguish of the life, yet the more he struggles to free himself from the past (i.e., his mother) through writing, the more powerful the hold of the past becomes as he discovers the determinate forces that produce his lament.

The text—what Dahlberg calls "the song of the fungus" and a "lazar house of literature"—is obsessed with bodily decay. But he contends that the preoccupation with physical corruption and sexual nausea affirms his humanity, the "flesh" of the title. He clings to even the vilest memories of rot, shame, and sexual degradation because they remind him of his ordinariness. To deny or transcend his base nature would place him above the gods, who no less than he are in constant sensual agony. "The Kosmos is the seminal cornucopia, and the Kabbalists speak of the massive genitals of Jahweh" (*Flesh* 75, 141, 105). All wisdom for Dahlberg comes from his body and from those of his mother and father, and while physical afflictions torment his existence they provide the ground for his self-understanding.

The dominant figure of the book is the body as verbally incontinent—it must always speak its needs; in neither the life nor the text will the body be silenced. Dahlberg's autobiography is a vast outpouring of speech about the corpus—words from antiquity, from the Kabbala, from both Testaments, from the horde of literature remembered and fabricated, from friends, from family, and from prophets. "As soon as the Word was made flesh, man was unable to be quiet, or work, or think, until he had dropped his seed" (*Flesh* 105). The book is full of long, careering speeches, a piling up of vituperation and scorn and lamentation, as if words alone could relieve his anguish. In the autobiography, Dahlberg gains a voice, but the voice is a cry of despair and carnal lust.

Dahlberg describes his outcast state as a child and young man: sent by his mother to an orphanage when her lover refuses to have anything to do with the boy, and denied by her any knowledge of his father's identity, Dahlberg eventually begins an odyssey across America to search for himself and the father, in the process intensifying his solitariness and feeling of worthlessness. He writes autobiography hoping to reconcile himself with the parents whose actions he has so long condemned, trusting that writing will compensate for his suffering, ease his exile, and repair the severed connections to his past. But whether the autobiography accomplishes that goal is questionable. What is not in doubt, however, is that Dahlberg sees himself only through a mother who was all too present and a father who was all too absent.

Dahlberg begins *Because I Was Flesh* as if he were the exiled Odysseus reflecting upon a distant Ithaca. He invokes a lofty, inflated image of his childhood home of Kansas City, celebrating its feverish frontier and sexual energies, elevating what he later will describe in grimy, realistic detail:

> Kansas City is a vast inland city, and its marvelous river, the Missouri, heats the senses; the maple, alder, elm and cherry trees with which the town abounds are songs of desire, and only the almonds of ancient Palestine can awaken the hungry pores more deeply. It is a wild, concupiscent city. . . . Kansas City was my Tarsus; the Kaw and the Missouri Rivers were the washpots of joyous Dianas from St. Joseph and Joplin. It was a young, seminal town and the seed of its men was strong. Homer sang of many sacred towns in Hellas which were no better than Kansas City, as hilly as Eteonus and as stony as Aulis. . . . Let the bard from Smyrna catalogue Harma, the ledges and caves of Ithaca, the milk-fed damsels of Achaia, pigeon-flocked Thisbe or the woods of Onchestus, I sing of Oak, Walnut, Chestnut, Maple and Elm Streets. Phthia was a bin of corn, Kansas City a buxom grange of wheat. Could the strumpets from the stews of Corinth, Ephesus or Tarsus fetch a groan or sigh more quickly than the dimpled thighs of lasses from St. Joseph or Topeka? (*Flesh* 1–2)

This style of glorification with its slide into mundanity is consistent throughout the text. But the mundane is not always eulogized. Dahlberg alternately extols and reviles his mother, just as he views himself as heroic and degraded. The generating principle of the book is that of the writer's power of magnification; the startling opening is not simply a commemoration of Dahlberg's origins but a celebration of his ability to give mythic status to ordinary experience, including eventually his mother, the "mater dolorosa of rags" (4). Dahlberg's autobiography, though it reads like a jeremiad against human vanity, hymns the author's town and the woman who reared him, but above all his own bardic vitality. Despite his complaints about misfortune, Dahlberg asserts the primal, imaginative energies that he hopes will raise him from despair and redeem his self-image. In the process, he acknowledges his mother as an inseparable part of him, and though he writes to assert his own identity, that identity cannot be considered apart from hers.

From the beginning of *Because I Was Flesh*, the child reveals his estrangement by refusing to use the first person: he is simply "the boy," and later, when he describes his years in the forced exile of the Jewish Orphan Asylum in Cleveland, he calls himself by his institutional identification— number 92. The illegitimate son of Saul Gottdank, a small-town Lothario and salesman, and Lizzie Dalberg [*sic*], Edward was born in Boston Charity Hospital in 1900. Saul soon deserted Lizzie, and mother and son traveled to London, Dallas, Memphis, New Orleans, Louisville, Denver, and finally Kansas City, where she opened the Star Lady Barbershop. The child experiences loneliness and isolation while Lizzie spends her time at the shop or with a succession of sleazy men who exploit and eventually leave her. Dahlberg's characteristic situations in the autobiography are those of exclusion, solitariness, and flight, and he commonly portrays himself as Ishmael or the Wandering Jew. As a boy, he cowers in the adjoining room while Lizzie entertains her men; often he haunts the shop only to be sent into the street. During an early illness, he is "graved in his bed," alone with his fearful imagination. Lizzie has scant time for the child as he grows up, and she complies with the wishes of a suitor, banishing Edward to the orphanage so he will be out of the way and thus initiating him into the Ishmael archetype. Her neglect generates Dahlberg's greatest indictment. Throughout his years in the orphanage, he feels exiled from his mother and expects to be exiled from his new home. Later he takes to the road, imitating his restless father—"going somewhere is a lust." Catching a series of freight trains heading west, he is a "houseless beggar," a "castaway," a "pariah." Whether riding the rails or roaming in the California deserts, Dahlberg is continually deracinated: "He who is not pursued by the Erinyes has no love or justice or sorrow for the house of flesh" (*Flesh* 114, 90). He drives himself into obscurity and sadness, and cultivates martyrdom.

Lizzie's seductive manner causes him grief. Her sexuality, intensified in the child's mind by the loss of his father, turns his bond with her into bondage. Mute witness to his mother's sensuous rubbings after her bath, and lookout while she urinates in dark doorways, the child alternates between a Hamlet-like shame of her "privy sheets and illicit pillowcases" (*Flesh* 155) and a romantic dream of being close to her. Oedipal longings and disgust collide; sensual temptations are everywhere (he hears Lizzie's sexual moans in the adjoining room), and even the flushings of toilets arouse him. He feels his mother's lust as the origin of his own pain: the more she tries to lighten the burden of her life with romance, the seamier she appears to the son. Much of the book is a plaint for his captivity to "the sensual itch," tormented by a feverish imagination and exiled from his own childhood.

At times Dahlberg celebrates Lizzie's vigorous sexuality as healthy and unrepressed instinct, but he often turns his frequent scorn for the flesh

against her and himself, vilifying his own carnality: "This is the autobiography of my faults" (140). He cannot escape the legacy of either parent:
"At the age of forty my face was dominated by my mother's, as well as
the thousand devils that I had come by from Saul." He berates Lizzie for
making him prey to unslaked desire: "If I saw a milkwhite rump, my body
became a seminal song. My flesh cried: let me smell her sandals or clap my
nose upon her navel, for I hunger, itch, piss, eat and die." Dahlberg feels
compassion for his mother's broken hopes and empty life but is angered for
inheriting a troubling sexuality: "Her sadness . . . was to be mine." He calls
his text "the memoir of [my mother's] body," but of course it is also the
memoir of his own, for the son finds himself in the mother and the mother
in him, his life tracing an arc of unhappiness parallel to hers: "Whatever I
imagine I know is taken from my mother's body" (*Flesh* 227, 155, 115, 4).

But despite his anger over her self-absorption and neglect, Dahlberg's
comic tone expresses compassion for Lizzie. It is a mordant humor, both
a savaging and a salvaging. Dahlberg ridicules Lizzie's desperate artifice
in hiding her age, yet he reveals sympathy for her endurance in the face
of feckless suitors. Dahlberg's acceptance arises out of kinship with her;
mother and son are the vulnerable of the earth, a pair of losers. "I was born
to sorrow, but as a boy I did not know that my desolation was to be not
much different from my mother's" (*Flesh* 113). Seeking the origins of his
own unhappiness, Dahlberg obliterates distinctions between himself and
her, saying in effect: "Because I was flesh also, I am not different from you,
my mother."

Dahlberg's need to reconstruct the past derives from his original deprivation and replicates earlier attempts to construct a familiar world.
In the orphanage he tries to piece together the features of his absent
mother's face, and this effort is repeated in the narrative as a gesture of
autobiographical reconstruction, a renewed attempt at identity-formation
through the mother: "On various occasions the boy endeavored to gather
together the face of his mother; he had not seen her for so long, and
though he willed to perceive her he could not. At unexpected moments,
she appeared to him, on a sudden, and when afterwards he did his utmost
to grasp her image he was unable to identify her, and he wept, and his heart
sat down by the River Dan. He knew her eyes, nose, chin and mouth, but
each time he tried to put them together, instead of seeing a whole face, he
saw nothing" (*Flesh* 87). Dahlberg's embarrassment and vexation fade in
the desire to set her face before him once again as he writes. Each effort
to compose her face into significance corresponds to the autobiographical
undertaking. The displaced boy and the adult narrator seek to memorialize

the mother but also to see themselves graven into her image. Dahlberg discovers how she is "sepulchred" in him and how they share a common and reconcilable fate. Lizzie lives again when Dahlberg accepts his own pain through her life.

His mother's solitary death rouses him to the memorial that *is* the autobiography. Dahlberg's fear of his own decay moves him to raise Lizzie's life in prose: he becomes Christ to her Lazarus. Her "bones still have sentience . . . she is and she is not." At the conclusion of the autobiography, he grants her an apotheosis, seeing her as "glorious" even in her rags, "for a moment wearing nothing but her ecstasy" (*Flesh* 229). Lizzie is the seedbed of Dahlberg's art, a generative force that turns him back to his past, permitting him to celebrate as well as to mourn.

As autobiographer, Dahlberg forges connections through history and across time, but as a child he felt disconnected from his own past. He has his mother's Swedish name, but Lizzie's family is from Warsaw; the child even believed the name was apocryphal. More significant, Saul's absence intensifies his alienation: "In what city are my father's footprints? Does he walk, does he breathe, and is he suckled by the winds? See, I am a shade emptied of ancestors." Saul haunts the work, a ghostly presence drifting in and out of Lizzie's life, but in his absence we sense something deeper than the son's mere lack of a support or a model: he expresses a primal terror of having no "progenitor": "Even a worm has a parent, but nobody begat me. I am nothing, and I came out of nowhere." Like Oedipus, he is a stranger and a riddle to himself. Dahlberg haunts graveyards, reading the tombstones for clues of his father and attempting to join his flesh with Saul's, much as he had attempted to do with his mother's image: "I tried to piece together the image I had had when I was six years old of the man I believed to be my father and I collected his separate features" (*Flesh* 168, 69, 216). His memories of Saul are "sepulchral," as if Dahlberg himself were dead or unborn until Saul can be revived in his consciousness. To rediscover Saul is to resurrect himself. The question beats insistently through the autobiography: "Who is my father?" But while the autobiographer views his father with a tolerance born of his own cynical views of human nature, Saul's obsessive carnality disturbs him. If Saul is the drop of sperm from *his* father, Dahlberg fears that he himself is nothing more—the line of vile inheritance stretches out.

Dahlberg's abhorrence of his father's lust is greater for his own reenactment of Saul's driven state, and it generates the self-hating tone of the work. As a young man, Dahlberg is a failed seducer whose frustrations echo in every comic self-laceration in the text. Terrified that he may be like Saul, he later accepts the similarities though he qualifies the relation by portraying himself as a buffoon version of his father, a would-be seducer as schlemiel: "After I discovered that Goethe, Heine, Beethoven and Nietzsche had all had syphilis, I thought I could not be a genius unless I found a woman who would be lenient enough to share this disease with me. I began to look about for a whore who might help me become a man of letters. . . . I pined for erudition, a half hour with a prostitute and a magnificent infectious disease. But nothing came of my aspirations; I was so helpless that I could not even get the pox" (*Flesh* 131). This partial identification with the father, combined with an alienation from him, becomes an autobiographical trope: an identification with the past through an internalizing of its values, combined with a struggle against such accommodation. Because Dahlberg's autobiography is about the incorporation of as well as his separation from his father, the text dramatizes the ambivalence of the Oedipal struggle, as Dahlberg preserves a continuity with Saul even while repudiating too close a link.

When Dahlberg acknowledges his connection and similarity to "Ver-dammter Saul," he frees himself to write autobiography. The link to the father is also made via Dahlberg's notion of writing as a sexual begetting. He is obsessed with generation in every form—"As soon as the Word was made flesh man was unable to . . . work . . . until he had dropped his seed"—but Dahlberg makes flesh, his life, into the Word. For Dahlberg, writing is a kind of erotic act, his text a seminal effort he can no more suppress than could Saul, "who lived solely to discharge his sperm" (*Flesh* 44). Saul must be acknowledged for Dahlberg to release the energy by which he becomes his own father, an act that Harold Bloom calls the characteristic American sublime trope of self-rebegetting (*Poetry and Repression* 244). For Dahlberg, autobiography fills a textual space with the evidence of his own procreative energy, and as he creates himself in the text he asserts his own paternity. His principal myth is that of the writer nurturing the self and overcoming earlier losses through the cultivation of a self-aggrandizing power. The autobiography, as it were, is parthenogenetic.

Alternately drawn to and repelled by the assembling of his mother's face and his father's body (both in memory and in narrative), Dahlberg is similarly ambivalent about the past and the writing of autobiography, as he opens psychic wounds in the act of narrating. "It is a great pain to divulge the life of a mother, and wicked to betray her faults. Why then do I do it? I have nothing better to do with my life than write a book and perhaps nothing worse" (*Flesh* 4). In a letter to Robert Hutchins, Dahlberg speaks of his helpless captivity to the past, however painful the process of unearthing it: "I have the sort of homesickness for Kansas City which Odysseus had for Ithaca, I for my past wretchedness and Odysseus for his porkers and Penelope" (*Epitaphs* 21 [letter of September 17, 1958]). Autobiography cannot be wholly curative for Dahlberg since each probing of his origins and each attempt to draw closer to his parents provokes *self-loathing*. Dahlberg's commitment to self-discovery, however, almost offsets the near-disabling act of his narration. Autobiography is a narcissistic genre, though it need not be self-glorifying. Norman Mailer once claimed that "it is too simple to think of the narcissist as someone in love with himself. One can detest oneself intimately and still be a narcissist. What characterizes narcissism is the fundamental relation. It is with oneself. The same dialectic of love and hate that mates feel for one another is experienced within the self" (31). Dahlberg's narcissism correspondingly expresses a divided attitude toward the self of the past and toward the narrative act.

In writing about himself through the mother, joining himself to her in body, mind, and text, Dahlberg shows he is aware of narcissism's dangers. Of course the "memoir of my mother's body" is ultimately that of his own; his mother "had two miserable afflictions, neither of which she was ever to overcome," and one of these is "her flesh—which is my own" (*Flesh* 3). Hence Dahlberg's text—whether we regard it as covert biography or a form of layered life-writing—embeds their identities and becomes a quasi-incestuous gesture in which Dahlberg takes his absent father's place, much as the child had once wooed the mother's affections in hopes of ending his displacement by surrogate fathers. We normally think of autobiography as depicting one's self-generation, but Dahlberg claims that achievement in the process of giving renewed life to his mother.

Any therapeutic yield is in doubt as he compulsively replays scenes of boyhood unhappiness. Nevertheless, Dahlberg cannot cease writing autobiography; his logorrhea, his unstoppable ransacking of history and myth, and his vast Whitmanian catalogues fill an inner void with an avalanche of words and allusions. The hyperbolic and allusive style allows him to search for meaning wherever he can—in Old Testament prophecy, in classical rhetoric, in Renaissance mysticism. Dahlberg seeks his spiritual home anywhere, by enlarging the shabby realities of his life and joining with the humanistic past. His echoes of the Bible, of church fathers, and of seventeenth-century religious prose render him part of a story of fallen, natural man; they also convey Dahlberg's dream of escaping isolation by incorporating all history into himself. He finds or creates fathers everywhere—in ancient authorities, gnomic philosophers, mythographers, and fabulists. His incantatory language has an almost magic capacity to recreate and endow himself with power. Herbert Leibowitz notes that

"The Word is Dahlberg's redeemer. . . . Words become his loving, nurturing parents" (Leibowitz 317). "Redemption" may be questionable, but while as a boy Dahlberg was silent, intimidated by the glib womanizers who surrounded his mother, in his adult role he becomes a match for givers of the word from Moses to Whitman, writing in aphorisms or maxims to lend himself authority.

I assume there are as many kinds of discourse, or "languages," of self-representation as there are selves. Still, Dahlberg's frenzied allusion-making, his compulsion to write himself into history and myth, and his desperate-sounding attempts to endow the self with grandeur in the face of abjection may strike us as an inflation of discursive practice, exceeding what Jauss has termed a "horizon of expectation." And yet Dahlberg's style reminds us that there is no exclusively "true" or "appropriate" language for a particular life. Mark Freeman, a psychologist writing about the process by which individuals reconstruct their pasts into narrative, suggests that if an autobiography is embellished, or "worked," it may be more honest not only to the writer's complexity but to the way we inevitably represent ourselves through metaphor and rhetoric.[1] Dahlberg accordingly dramatizes himself to try to make the tawdry aspects of his life vivid and compelling, if not bearable; joining sleaze to high culture is his way of romanticizing dereliction. The inflated style does express Dahlberg's identity; it is an attempt to remake himself by demonstrating the power of a rhapsodic narrative imagination to transcend the conditions of his earlier life.

At the conclusion of the work, his mother, in response to the question "What is truth?" says simply, "My life." The directness of Lizzie's phrase is telling: when all the hyperboles, the dense allusions, and the sententia are stripped away, there remains *a life*, in its nakedness; when all else is gone, this remains. What Dahlberg finally comes to is the desire to remember Lizzie and to honor her life despite—or rather because of—its flesh, flaws, and follies. We might conjecture that he cannot begin to grieve—for her and for himself—until he has propagated her life by giving it a story.

Narrative for Dahlberg is a form of gratitude. Heidegger, in a philological tour de force, shows that in Old English the verbs "to think" and "to thank" were closely related, and he conjectures that "thought" implies "the thanks" felt for its inspiration. "Both memory and thanks move and have their being in the *thanc* [the Old English word for thought]" (140). That is, the heart gives thanks for what it is and what it has: thought. "Original thanking is the thanks owed for being." Heidegger means that the most fundamental gift we have is our essential nature as a thinking being, for which we give thanks, and that memory is the "gathering of thinking back into what must be thought," that is, our gratitude (141, 143). These terms resonate with what Dahlberg has done for his mother at the text's conclusion. Regardless of his early and sustained grief, he owes thanks to Lizzie for her bestowing on him a way of being (a form of thinking), and the memory of that endowment becomes the thanks embodied in the narration of her life.

Dahlberg has finally pieced together her face, indeed her entire being. Through his mother's story, he claims his own; through the story of his own life, he has given Lizzie breath. And through the story of Saul, he has given himself breath as author. Dahlberg shows that even if we wish to believe that our identity is autonomous, it is inescapably a part of our parents, however estranged from them we may be. *Because I Was Flesh* is autobiography as *memento mori*, both his parents "sepulchred" in him.

I DON'T REMEMBER EXACTLY WHY or when I started calling my mother "Anita." Of course it was my way of not remaining a child, a fear rekindled whenever I returned home for a holiday visit to her New Jersey apartment, especially after I was divorced and wished to fight off the feeling I had become a child again back in my old room. No doubt I wanted to be on equal terms with my mother, but I wasn't just taking my dead father's place since in fact I started using her first name well before his death. Anita always did her best not to infantilize me, but there were times when she couldn't help herself: my earliest memories are of her trying to shield me from difficult situations ("tell them your mother said so" was her refrain applied to many circumstances in my childhood). But mostly she gave me room to maneuver, urging me to spend a college summer in Africa, defending my decision to choose teaching over law, and encouraging my move to Oregon to take a job at Reed. She didn't expect me to remain in the Northwest, but she never asked me to return to the East, nor nagged me to provide her with grandchildren, though there were many pointed stories about the fecundity of her friends' children.

I often complained that Anita was passive, a woman without grand ideas or an evident philosophy of life, and I became impatient with her lack of specificity and detail, her tendency to dismiss things I deemed important, and her desire for simplicity when I sought complexity. I badgered her too long and too often, trying even her Griselda-like patience. But she supported me despite her disapproval of my divorce and what she perceived as an aimless round of subsequent relationships. Even when she frowned on some foolish thing I had done, she let me find my way, however much I suspected she was looking over my shoulder. Once when I was home on vacation and had spent most nights visiting friends in New York, my stepfather Leo chastised me for not giving my mother sufficient attention. Anita may have felt the same way, but she could seldom declare outright what she wanted, and I probably took advantage of her reticence.

I sensed that Anita had a repository of private thoughts stored up not as evasions but as lifelong gleanings she gave out only on special occasions. There is a passage in *To the Lighthouse* that seems appropriate to her; Woolf likens Mrs. Ramsey to the treasures that had recently come to light when the tombs of Egypt's Valley of the Kings were opened and explored. "[Lily Briscoe] imagined how in the chambers of the mind and heart of the woman who was touching her were stood, like the treasures in the tombs of kings, tablets bearing sacred inscriptions which if one could spell them out, would teach one everything, but they would never be offered openly, never made public. What art was there, known to love or cunning, by which one pressed through into those secret chambers?" Anita was present for me, but I often sensed that the deepest reaches of her being were perplexingly inaccessible. Whenever I returned home for visits and stepped off the elevator, she would greet me in the hallway but hold me at arms length, unwilling to embrace. Her guarded gesture seemed a sign of deeper withholdings.

Unlike with Leo, whom I respected in part because we could fight out our disagreements like a couple of sparing partners in a ring, my mother seemed unwilling to take on a scrappy, feisty role with me. But occasionally she would rise up and criticize some position I had just upheld, especially because she was shocked by the freedoms of the 1960s, which were alien to her. I wondered where that toughness hid itself under her frail shell; it showed up late in her life, during her second marriage, when she unexpectedly achieved a new autonomy and self-assertion, perhaps because she had grown in self-confidence, perhaps because she loved but never adored Leo as she had my father and for the first time felt the equal of a man.

There's a story about my mother that would probably surprise her friends because it contradicts the image of the sweet, self-effacing, somewhat fragile woman. Two weeks after my father's death, I returned home from college for the summer. Shortly after my arrival, I was in my bedroom on a sweltering June afternoon when Anita came in. Her marriage had been idyllic, and at forty-eight she was devastated by my father's sudden death, weeping constantly and unable to contain her enormous grief and the terror of impending loneliness. She wedged in beside me on the loveseat and told me a surprising tale. My father was a lawyer in a two-man firm (the partner was Phidias Polis, a name amusing to me now, having taught both the sculptor and the Greek city-state). The partnership was based on an even split of fees, but because my father brought in well over 75 percent of the income, he covertly held back some fees for himself, believing his work and reputation warranted the practice. This activity was unknown to my mother, but when the estate was settled, the deception was discovered, and reparations had to be made. My mother was staggered, for my father's integrity was suddenly in question, and she feared a scandal. In the hallway outside my bedroom stood a file cabinet, where my father stored inactive cases brought home from his crowded office. Anita was terrified the police would appear at our door and locate unreported fees going back decades, starting a process that would decimate the estate and hurl us into bankruptcy.

As she spun out the saga and her dread, she threw her arms around my neck, her tears drenching my cheeks. I was frozen and helpless. My mother had depended completely on my father's guidance, but now, to my astonishment, she proposed a startling plan. We would turn on the furnace, take the old files to the basement, and cast them into the flames. As she detailed this scheme she clung ever tighter to me, rocking back and forth, heaving and convulsing. The stifling afternoon heat and her choking embrace made the thought of starting up the furnace seem insane, and my mind flashed with images of Auschwitz.

I do not remember how I extricated myself from her grip, nor whether I dissuaded her from the enterprise. But we did nothing, and though my mother and I spoke easily to one another, we never mentioned the episode again. (Was her reluctance to embrace me in later years the result of a wish to expiate the darkly Oedipal clasp and to annul whatever disapproval I might still be harboring from the bedroom scene?) It was as if my father's deed and the incident itself were aberrations in our lives, and we simply allowed time to cover them over as flesh grows around an intruding splinter.

I came to feel especially tender toward her in the last years, after Leo's death. That event did not bring the sharp romantic anguish that came when my father died, but it did make her lonely and vulnerable, locked into a final widowhood accompanied by the beginnings of her gradual physical decline.

When Anita was eighty-two, she had a heart valve replacement and a quadruple bypass, but because her lungs, heart, and kidneys were so weak, she never got free of the respirator. She had continuous dialysis as well as a tracheotomy and surgery to control internal bleeding, remaining for seven terrible weeks in intensive care. During the whole time, she was unable to speak, and the mother who had always listened intently was now unable to respond, if indeed my words even got through to her. I grimly joked that she received every service except obstetrics, but because my birth had occurred in the very same hospital where she now lay dying, she had once had that care in the building as well.

Anita had made a living will, and I knew of her desire not to be incapacitated in a nursing home. And so, when her doctors declared unequivocally that she could not make a good recovery and would be forever unable to breathe without the respirator, I held a meeting with the stepfamily and close friends. We decided, after long and agonized discussions, to carry out her wishes (she was unable to talk, too weak to write, even to nod), and agreed to ask that the machine be disconnected. The next day, in a blurry daze, I wrote out the request to the appropriate hospital committee.

On the morning when I planned to submit the fateful petition, I went to her room for a visit, the matricidal document scorching my jacket. In seven weeks Anita had never been out of bed, but now she was sitting up in a chair. The respirator was breathing for her, to be sure, but sitting up she was, and I felt dizzy, filled with the misery of my mission. When I left I could not deliver what seemed more than ever a death warrant.

The next day I returned to the hospital to find her in a coma. The nurse told me she might last in such a state for weeks. After sitting in silence for an hour, I kissed Anita goodbye and took a taxi to the airport. When I arrived back in Portland, I called the hospital for an update. My mother had died ten minutes after I left her room, as I was on the way to my flight. Within hours I was heading east once again, more than ever an only child.

14.

Self and Other Is One Flesh

Double Voicing in Nathalie Sarraute's *Childhood*,
Ronald Fraser's *In Search of a Past*, and Howard
and Arthur Waskow's *Becoming Brothers*

Autobiographers, though not necessarily their critics, usually insist that their narratives express a core conception of "self," the hard nugget of identity defining an essential and irreducible "I." By these notoriously controversial terms, I do not mean to imply a self separate from influences of history, family, or society, let alone one untroubled by uncertainty, fragmentation, internal contradiction, nor the difficulty (if not the impossibility) of capturing a "real" self in language. Rather, I mean a "self" that, in the narrative, appears *to the writer* to represent what he or she believes to be irreducible and at least provisionally authentic. If the self appears to the writer to lack wholeness or completeness, the narrative may attempt to resolve the fractures into some version of unity. For some autobiographers the act of writing constitutes a search for that core conception that the writer enshrines in the text: I write, therefore I am. Postmodern autobiography theory argues against the notion of a self that has a unified essence prior to its expressive constitution in text. Here is Sidonie Smith's succinct formulation of this now-familar, even canonical (though not uncontested) position:

> There is no essential, original, coherent autobiographical self before the moment of self-narrating. Nor is the autobiographical self expressive in the sense that it is the manifestation of an interiority that is somehow ontologically whole, seamless and "true." For the self is not a documentary repository of all experiential history running uninterruptedly from infancy to the contemporary moment, capacious, current, and accessible. . . . Benedict Anderson suggests that [an] "estrangement" from our experiential history necessitates "a conception of personhood, *identity*. . . . which, because it cannot be 'remembered,' must be narrated." ("Performativity, Autobiographical Practice, Resistance" 17–18)[1]

But Smith and others who hold this position do not address whether, even if the self is constituted only in textual representation, it remains a single, discrete entity. We generally assume that autobiographers write out of a deep-seated belief in the integrity of a singular self. We presume that an *auto*-biography is written by a single person; joint authorship seems incongruous to the genre. Even theorists who hold that the autobiographer is not necessarily the most reliable witness of the life concede that autobiography usually results from an act of solitary composition, whatever the forces (social, political, sexual, racial, economic) that might determine and shape the textual outcome.[2]

But there are autobiographies that defy such assumptions. In this chapter I want to look at three texts that, in very different ways, propose that the self may be multiple, or at least cannot be defined by a single authoritative voice. Two of the works maintain in their narrative procedures that a complex self must be represented by oppositional or contradictory voices. The other is jointly authored, the writers claiming that neither one alone can see the whole picture or assert the definitive truth about the other or about himself for that matter. These texts imply that an autobiographical narrative that argues for a conclusive identity may be less convincing than one that maintains indefiniteness due to what I will term its "double" or "multiple" voicing. In these texts, not just the conclusions about the self, but just as important, the *mode* of investigating, becomes a problem. These texts undermine claims of singularity, and the narratives are structured to reflect the conflict within, or the complementarity among, the narrating selves.[3]

Such double voicing has little to do with postmodernist conceptions of the disappearance or the death of the author. The writers I will examine here may doubt that truth is represented by the mere assertion of memory, or that the past can be recovered without continuous qualification; but far from denying that autobiography can tell us something truthful about the self, let alone calling the self or even the genre into question, these strategies of double voicing reveal that their writers are committed to a *more* encompassing truth, as they experiment with forms appropriate to the integrity of that search. These four autobiographers especially refuse to make absolute distinctions between what is *self* and what appears to be "other."

Indeed, they complicate conceptions of individualism and subjective knowledge, which we think of as integral to autobiography. Identity, Howard and Arthur Waskow imply, is not generated solely from within the subject but results from an amalgam of diverse voices and competing, often contradictory, assertions. And knowledge, Ronald Fraser argues, cannot be guaranteed by one person's memory even of those incidents and people closest to him. But agency is not completely relinquished in these new forms. The Waskows remind us that it is through the two brothers' interaction and each one's willingness to yield up his claims to speak with exclusive authority that each self gains power.

By the term "double voicing" I am not alluding to the phenomenon of "double-voiced discourse" first noted by W. E. B. DuBois, where the black man (and writer) has to play conflicting roles in both his and the white world; rather I am employing the term to embrace authors who may not necessarily be conscious of any cultural role they are playing (though one could claim that Fraser's strategy, as we shall see, critiques a class bias that would regard his former servants' views of his boyhood as less important than those of his own). Double voicing, as I use the term, refers to a strategy for representing the self in language and form. In all three cases, the "other" voice(s)—Sarraute's "You," Fraser's servants and therapist, each Waskow brother—serve to validate, qualify, or correct the principal voice.

Such interventions in traditional strategies for self-definition and self-representation test our familiar notions of subjectivity. In these texts, subjectivity expands to encompass and incorporate into the self what Robert Frost calls the "not-me." The presence of another voice or other voices, rather than eradicating the notion of the self, may broaden it, for subjectivity in these works is constituted and constructed from multiple sources. As Leigh Gilmore puts it, "Selves proliferate in autobiography" ("Policing Truth" 59).

Feminist critics have long theorized that such a move characterizes women's autobiography, and that women's texts exemplify a more collective and relational quality than men's autobiographies.[4] "The Other" has usually been construed as a racial or ethnic Other, or a female Other to the central male figure. But in the three texts I consider, the autobiographers identify their Others as inescapably part of themselves, at once welcome and difficult to accept, at once familiar and strange. In such texts, where multiple voices prevent the writer from asserting a fixed or definitive self, autobiography becomes a continuous process of renewal and an oscillation among points of view and voices that address different aspects and stages of experience. To borrow the paradox that Gertrude Stein often mentions in *The Autobiography of Alice B. Toklas*, in double-voiced autobiographies the outside becomes the inside, for what appears external (to the self) becomes internal, although never quite identical.

Finally, I want to raise the question of authority in these autobiographies. We have generally assumed that in autobiography, authority resides in the autonomy of the "I"—if not that of the narrator, then that of the author. This issue becomes problematic when multiple voices or competing claims for evidence and insight contest for a privileged point of view or the truthful interpretation of the past, especially when more than one person authors a text. In *Altered Egos: Authority in American Autobiography*, G. Thomas Couser asks of a number of texts: What is it that allows us to read autobiography with a surety that the author is justified in presenting the life in a certain way? Couser establishes a "dialogic view" of autobiography, where discourse becomes a battleground in which the self struggles to establish its presence. Couser claims that autobiographers adduce a "provisional" or "negotiated" view of the self, but one that is not anti-individualistic nor "inconsistent with the idea of individual autonomy" (250). He argues that as a genre, autobiography inevitably contains a multiplicity of authorial voices and agencies. In the words of Joseph Harris, "The self is seen not *merely* as a single, simple essence, but as an incredibly rich and layered tapestry of languages we constantly weave and reweave" (162).

I too am concerned with such Bakhtinian discursiveness, the way several autobiographers negotiate among competing voices or divergent claims for authority in arriving at autobiographical authenticity. In my examples, when no single voice dominates, the autobiographer surrenders claims for absolute certainty regarding the self, the tensions within the text remaining unresolved. In fact, I would argue that the reason these autobiographers write is precisely to challenge such traditional notions, exploring without necessarily resolving the contradictions that enrich the self. And that furthermore, the strategies for providing evidence about the self are congruent with the complex nature of the self that emerges from the investigation.

In Nathalie Sarraute's *Childhood*, we hear two distinct voices that battle for supremacy, and the autobiography is largely concerned with that struggle, much of the text revolving around a debate between an "I" and a "You" that offers conflicting readings of the past. Sarraute proposes discordant interpretations of the childhood rather than any single truth; small but defining incidents become sites for disagreement by the two distinct narrative voices. Sarraute's refusal to reconcile these voices and her insistence on maintaining a dialogic tension in the narrative characterize her childhood as an unresolved conflict—between desire and conscience.

These voices pointedly challenge one another, the "You" judgmentally and accusatorily responding to the "I's" justifications and defense. Sarraute employs the "You" voice for two important functions. One is to chastise the "I" when she oversimplifies or falsifies her motives or her reactions to difficulties within the family, especially when she characterizes herself as the nice and obedient child and when she denies aggressive feelings toward both the mother who abandoned her and the stepmother who ignored her. The other function is to question and complicate the reductive, overdetermined patterns the "I" contends were present in the childhood. In effect, the "You" serves as her conscience. Though the two voices seem like comfortable companions, even sisters, they are really two aspects of the self engaged in a sometimes fierce internal debate.[5] Sarraute's intention in structuring the autobiography as a dialogue between two sides of the person is not to resolve internal conflict but to underscore that the conflict constitutes a more complex identity.

In the interrogational opening of *Childhood*, the "You" becomes an inquisitor or cross-examining prosecutor. From the outset, issues regarding the reliability of the "I's" memory come to the fore. The autobiography begins abruptly with the "You's" surprise that the "I" is even bothering to write her memories. She then warns her not to impose a false pattern and make things too "fixed once and for all," too much "'a sure thing,' decided in advance." The "You" accuses the "I" of resorting to distorting eloquence whenever she feels threatened by "inchoate[ness]," and she warns the "I" against giving simplistic explanations for behavior, forcing the latter to admit that she inclines toward reductivism. At stake is the difficulty of finding the correct words to express barely understood feelings, a difficulty that addresses and exemplifies the problem of self-knowledge autobiographers often confront but do not generally make the subject of their texts.[6] Sometimes the "I" feels shaky about the accuracy of emotional recall: "Even now . . . when [a scene] comes back to me, faded and partially obliterated, I feel . . . but what?" (*Childhood* 3, 2, 56) Early in the autobiography, we scarcely know what the precise subject matter is until we gradually understand that the unverifiability of claims regarding the past and the painful process of validating those claims *are* the substance of the work. How can anything Sarraute says be reliable if she questions propositions regarding herself and if neither of the two voices has ultimate authority? If the language representing her past is inevitably unreliable, casting suspicion on the accuracy of her responses to experience, then Sarraute's identity is a problem for herself: can she ever know who she is?

The child's desire long ago to please her parents parallels the autobiographer's temptation to please the reader by offering unambiguous interpretations of her past. But the "You" will not let her counterself escape from scrutiny, and she accuses the "I" of evasion: "You really believe that?" "Come on, make an effort . . . good, go on . . . *that's* what you felt then." She nudges her to reconsideration: "It could be . . . mightn't it be . . . ? We sometimes don't realize . . ." "Is that true? Have you really not forgotten what it was like there?" Sometimes the "I" fights back: "Now you're going too far" (*Childhood* 63–64, 1–2, 65). At other times she assures the "You" that she will strive for greater precision. When her stepmother Vera tells Nathalie that where they currently reside is not Nathalie's real home, the little girl is devastated. The "You," resisting the "I's" feeling that Vera is the evil stepmother of folklore, hypothesizes that the stepmother may simply have been trying to spare Nathalie the heartache of leaving the house she would soon vacate to rejoin her mother. The "You," ever the realist, accuses the "I" of "taking off into fiction" (*Childhood* 115). The dialogic form insists on the disruptive necessity of plural readings of the past, and because the potential revision of every claim constitutes the method of the work, once Sarraute establishes the presence of the other voice she is free to hypothesize and elaborate. Although the second voice urges the "I" to avoid the enticements of unqualified assertions, and mocks the "I's" claims to exact truth, the "I" nonetheless enjoys her copiousness of language: "I can't resist it, I want to touch, to caress this immutable image, to cover it with words, but not too thickly, I'm so afraid of spoiling it" (*Childhood* 33).

Sander Gilman addresses an aspect of "Otherness" that bears on Sarraute's double narrative construction: "There is always an Other for us, no matter how we define ourselves. The ultimate Other is the doppelganger, the Other which is our self, but a self projected into the world. This Other becomes the ideal reader, becomes the intended audience for the work of art" ("Inscribing the Other" 14). Sarraute's "You," the Other that is also herself, is like an ideally critical reader of autobiography, listening hard, skeptical of truth claims about certain narrative statements, and on the lookout for rhetoric that conceals, falsifies, or lacks conviction. A reader of an autobiographical text who now affirms, now questions, and now challenges, performs the same task that each of Sarraute's voices attempts: while we can judge only the representation, not the past itself, we too may be impelled to question unqualified statements and to evaluate conflicting hypotheses. Through the formal procedures of her text, Sarraute turns us into collaborators of interpretation along with the questioning voice. One appeal of her autobiography, with its continual narrative interventions, probings, and testings, lies in the debates and alternative readings of the past proposed by each interpreter, as well as in their mutual scrutiny and even resistance. The procedure forces perspective against counterperspective, demanding that the primary narrator ("the I") listen to, if not necessarily endorse, an inner voice that may be discomfiting, even embarrassing.[7] *Childhood* is a confessional narrative that demands rigorous assessment, whatever its ultimate conclusions about the self or selves who stake their particular claims.

Like Sartre's *The Words*, much of Sarraute's autobiography is about her inclination, even as a child, to gratify others through her writing. When a teacher demands an essay on the topic of her first sorrow, she does not write about her anguished loss of her mother's affection—the subject she feels she ought to treat—but instead writes a more acceptable piece about the death of her dog, sheer make-believe and as formulaic as the kind of autobiography the mature Sarraute declines to write. Falsifying language and emotion, the young girl deploys words "beautifully dressed in their best clothes," which "acquire a respectable air, good manners." One of Sarraute's childhood fears is that the words she uses are really someone else's, that even her most personal phrases will turn out to be, say, Balzac's—a particularly distressing anxiety since even at the time she realizes that "I am nothing other than what I have written" (*Childhood* 187, 148). Seldom has an autobiographer scrutinized and expressed with such self-consciousness her own language and its adequacy to convey who she is. As the mature writer struggles to find the words to say it, she employs autobiography to refamiliarize herself with herself by rendering the "I" unstrange to the "You." Because each voice is a twin aspect of a single composite self, the "You" has profound impact on the "I." By the end of *Childhood*, the principal narrator has internalized the objections of her interrogator, as she begins to question the "reconstitution of what I must have felt" (*Childhood* 154). The two voices begin to work together to establish whatever truth can be gleaned from their mutual investigations, less antagonists than partners assisting one another in an enterprise in which both have an interest.

James Olney proposes that "to accept a *You/I* split . . . is one of many ways . . . of seeking the unified *I* that seems to have become—to put it in the most optimistic terms—so elusive in our time" (*Memory and Narrative* 248). Such unity, if it is ever achieved in Sarraute's narrative, must recognize the inevitable tensions in the autobiographical project: the "I's" desire to write a psychologically and narrationally coherent story, one that is well-structured and artistically controlled; the "You's" desire for unadorned truth attributable more to accurate recall and honesty than to art. The autobiography is a drama in which Sarraute expresses both her compliance *and* her transgression, her controlled narrative and her unruly dissent. Only when the "I" is prodded by her alter ego can her words convey an authority unavailable to either repressed accommodations or to conventional "souvenirs d'enfance."

In a different way, Ronald Fraser's *In Search of a Past: The Manor House, Amnersfield, 1933–1945* also contends that interpretations of the past and of the self necessarily involve others in the process. In the absence of definitive evidence about his history, Fraser distrusts his memory, appealing to others' often contradictory versions of the past not only to spur his own recall but to reveal how insufficient he is as a sole witness of his life. Fraser, who grew up on an English estate between the wars, interviews surviving family servants who remember him as a child; later he recounts his psychoanalyst's understanding of his patient, including the latter's attitude regarding Fraser's reliance on other people's memories of himself. Fraser's narrative, a continuous commentary upon commentary in which he plays others' interpretations against his own intuitive understanding, questions whether any single view of himself, or even a composite of multiple external views, can be final.

Fraser divides his autobiography into sections titled "We," "They," "She/He/She," "You," "Us," and "I." These pronouns designate the figures who populate his text: the father, a once vigorous Scots Lord, who, as the autobiography opens, is an Alzheimers patient about to enter a rest home; Fraser's American mother; his younger brother; servants from his childhood at The Manor House; his psychiatrist; and of course himself at various stages of his life, including the time when he writes the autobiography. Each of the other persons mirrors back to Fraser a partial image of his self, and each portrays a different view of Fraser's past. Until the final section, titled "I," every chapter title is, with one possible exception, plural, suggesting that Fraser regards his life as ineluctably embedded in others' lives and that his view of himself cannot be fully distinguished from their view of him. The ambiguous exception, "You," may allude to Fraser himself (the second person singular viewed by the family's former servants), or to those servants who remember the child as passive, vulnerable, and a bit lost.

The text is structured around oral history—a series of interviews with the retired servants, several of whom served as paternal and maternal figures for "Master Ronnie" when he was growing up in the absence of caring parents—and psychoanalysis, the sessions reported verbatim. To complicate matters both narrationally and epistemologically, during much of Fraser's psychoanalysis he relates how the servants' memories of his early life have contributed to his own self-interpretation, though the therapist doubts the efficacy of this mode of investigation: "Reality for [the therapist] is not out there but inside me." "How," the therapist inquires, "can one write about one's past without an 'I' as the focus?" (*Search* 90) But for Fraser "the past is a collective experience"; his innovation for autobiography is to insist that his text, as well as his life, is a "making" of others' making, "a perspective in which each stood equally witness to a past you had in your different ways shared" (*Search* 109, 6, 10).

Fraser has difficulty claiming an "I" because "the house was divided and so was I." On one hand he was born to privilege and expected to maintain an impersonal relation with the servants who raised him; on the other hand he felt inadequate for the role foisted on him by his father and resisted its stringent demands. "For [Ilse, his nanny] I was only valid if I was a good little boy. Passive, I have to confirm her—her confidence and love—by being what she needed me to be. Not what I was" (*Search* 89, 95). Not until the final section does Fraser title a chapter "I." The first person pronoun is difficult for him to achieve and even more difficult for him to use: "*You* is the pronoun I most often use about myself. I never had a clearly defined 'I.'" Admittedly, he prefers *watching* an experience to *living* it. As an adolescent his favorite author was Christopher Isherwood, and for a long while he defined himself as a "camera I," observing rather than participating. This early and continuing lack of self-consciousness provokes his search for a self among so many diverse and questionable witnesses of his life.

The book begins with Fraser's driving his aged father, whose memory is completely shattered, to a rest home. Ironically, Fraser's own memory of the past is dim: father and son pass the manor house that, barely glimpsed behind walls and hedges, "remained impenetrable," and his past life at Amnersfield appears in his mind's eye as if seen "through the wrong end of the telescope" (*Search* 4, 6). Corresponding to this hazy recognition, Fraser's version of the past is vulnerable to self-deluding fictions, even to lying, but especially to others' impressions. We barely notice that the opening scene is told to his psychiatrist, in a session that occurs much later in the narrative. The autobiography begins as a series of flashbacks and memories within memories. Fraser remembers the psychiatrist examining his patient's memories of the servants' memories of the boy who is now the patient. But the psychiatrist is a cautionary voice, skeptical whether "the evidence I had gathered ten years ago" (the interviews with the servants) will enable rather than obstruct revelation.

Fraser's investigative procedure is thus complex: his "voyage of inner discovery" strives to bring the past into focus, but because he inflects his reading of the past through the former servants' interpretations, additionally subjecting their version to his revisions, his self-interpretation can never stand fully apart from the construction of others. As Eakin notes, "Fraser's identity is circumscribed and defined by a carefully structured network of social relations" (*Touching the World* 105). In turning to these witnesses, Fraser tries to rescue the past from oblivion, but the question remains, "What past, and whose?"

Fraser conducted the interviews in the 1960s but packed away his notes and transcripts until, in the late 1970s, he felt a growing sense of personal malaise, "nullity" and "passivity," and decided to begin psychoanalysis. The set-aside materials, a record of "memories, fears, desires, hatreds which cried out for order, meaning" (*Search* 107), returned to light when he entered analysis, distilled the transcripts of the interviews, and introduced this evidence to his therapist. Fraser's evaluation of the servants' views of himself became part of the analysis, one mode of investigation interweaving with the other. As he declares at the end of the autobiography, he chooses to be both the object and the subject of his history, writing about it from outside (gathering others' views) and inside (evaluating those views). This procedure represents two modes of inquiry and imbricates various sides of Fraser. His life is a medley of different voices: the gardener Bert and his words of proletarian rebellion, his American mother's expressions of democracy, his father's old world speeches, and voices of other writers. Fraser acknowledges that even his own words may be borrowed: "I would be a writer, I told myself. 'What could be more exhilarating than to start from one's lived experience and, by the art of writing, recreate it for the reader as a general experience, without for all that losing its bitter taste of singularity?' I said to P [his psychiatrist] last Thursday, omitting to add that I'd found the words in Sartre's book on Flaubert" (*Search* 107). Just as he cannot *understand* the self without probing the influence of the diverse figures in his life, so he cannot *narrate* the self until he integrates the interviews and his responses to them with the revelations that emerge from his psychoanalysis.

As a child, Fraser wrote to gain an early identity, an act he hoped would free him from the domination of his father and grant him autonomy. But the attempt to "elude the destiny they had in store for me by [authoring] a self-assigned destiny" (*Search* 110), to become an authentic "I" and not a secondhand "you," failed to make him feel whole and independent. The autobiography thus represents a renewed claim for self-assertion. But because Fraser's chosen form privileges the views others have of him, it is not clear that there *is* an integral self; indeed, the text presents many Frasers: the boy perceived by his former servants, the mature man who evaluates those perceptions, the older man who has edited the transcriptions of the interviews, the yet older man who has edited the notebook journals written during the years of his psychoanalysis, and the writer who decides which of *these* "texts" will make it into the composite autobiography and how they will reflect on one another. "Fraser," the object and subject of his story, is a series of selves composed of disparate views, views that are then reconfigured by the autobiographer as he accounts for the therapist's evaluation of his patient's response to the servants' views. "Fraser" and his book result from such multiple strands of evidence as well as from his continuous adjudications of that evidence. At the end he is still split: "I had a different 'I' for each of them" (*Search* 185).

The question raised by the autobiography is whether its employment of the interviews and of the psychoanalytic proceedings moves Fraser closer to self-knowledge or inhibits his quest. Though the final section is titled "I," it is not apparent that Fraser, either in the analysis or in the writing, has achieved a clear sense of identity, and it is difficult to assert that this fragmented, multilayered autobiography conduces to definitive self-knowledge, in part because his autobiographical form replicates the inconclusiveness of the life. Any final sense of self must be endlessly deferred in this text of telescoping perspectives; the self is very much in process, and the writer remains obsessed with an ongoing, presumably unending, search.

The work's title, *In Search of a Past*, implies that Fraser's "I" is always in suspension, always inconclusive. His therapist's final recorded words may stand for this sense of deferral: he says, as therapists always do, "Well, we'll have to leave it there for today." And Fraser, as if to acknowledge the open-endedness of his search, of his method, and even of his very identity, concludes the book by replying as patients always do, "I'll see you next Monday" (*Search* 187).

Fraser makes us understand how a self is constituted more by relationships than by autonomy, just as the autobiographical narrative is constituted more by collaboration than by introspection. While Fraser's method may ultimately undermine any certain comprehension of the life, there is a compensatory enrichment in his acknowledgment that mutuality is necessary in order for him to possess his past. The self is inevitably composed of many lives and other selves. While Fraser celebrates an "I" in the final chapter, the first person singular pronoun trumping all the "he's" and "she's" and "we's" and "you's" of the earlier chapters, he never surrenders the awareness that the "I" cannot and does not exist without the community of others who make up the totality of his identity: "I feel them gathering, coming together, until they fill the emptiness around me, and in their eyes, unimaginably, I see an indestructible love, in their bodies touching each other, an unsurpassable assurance, and I stand there, my hands by my side, like a child overwhelmed with wonder" (*Search* 186).

In *Becoming Brothers*, Howard and Arthur Waskow write an account of their childhood, adulthood, and family, contributing separate as well as cowritten chapters describing the same events, each from his own point of view, and maintaining a discussion throughout the text about their relationship to one another, including their ongoing participation in the writing project itself. Their autobiography dramatizes how the process of the "double writing" shaped the form that in turn constitutes the authors' identities, both common and separate. The distinct selfhood of each brother is never called into question, but the book's unusual structure suggests how each one becomes known through his relationship to the other and, just as crucially, through the act of corporate authorship. Each coauthor becomes who he is by *becoming* a brother, and each gains a fuller self in the act of cowriting the autobiography.

The text incorporates the double voices of Sarraute and the play between the "I" and the "not I" of Fraser, and the line between autobiography and biography is deliberately vague. Each brother's life is inextricably connected with that of his sibling, but neither one can fully understand himself until he understands his brother, and neither can speak truthfully until he honors the other's voice, so like and yet so strangely different from his own.

The intertwined narrative had its origin in a need to heal a long-unspoken rift between the men that emerged when they were in their fifties. The progress of the writing—over some eight years—enacted the gradual, tentative restoration of openness and closeness, the act of composition catalyzing the opportunity for each brother to hear the other's voice, something each claimed the other had been unable to do throughout most of their lives. The anguish of acknowledging their estrangement hurt them into writing. Arthur: "The book has made us brothers." Howard: "What is happening in this writing that we do? . . . We are creating a relationship. . . . Call it the making of meaning; call it play; call it . . . transformation" (*Brothers* 109, 214). Thus the title, *Becoming Brothers*, has a dynamic, educative quality in that the work is not merely an account of something that happened but an active process, a *becoming* that moves through the time of writing, and a *making*, not just a portrayal, of closeness.

Howard, who earlier wrote a study of Whitman, sees their book as a Whitmanian joining of hands along a traveled road. Often in the jointly composed chapters, each brother responds to what the other has just written, agreeing, qualifying, disputing, nudging the other along. They also include letters to one another that address the writing of the book and their conflicting and conflicted ways of remembering and analyzing childhood events. Occasionally they dispute who has the correct word or the accurate voice concerning some past incident. In the memoir itself and in the act of authoring it, they necessarily replay old childhood refrains about domination and anger, or their different roles as insider and outsider, teacher and listener, disgruntled intellectual loner and buoyant social accommodator. There are chapters on their neighborhood, family home, and life in the Baltimore Jewish community in the 1940s and 1950s; their alliances and allegiances within the family; their attitudes toward their parents (especially toward a strong-willed mother who was bedridden for years with tuberculosis); and their very different ways of interpreting family stories and quarrels. The concluding chapters discuss how the two men have moved closer to one another through their collaboration, narrating a harmony of which the writing itself is the most visible evidence.

In the first half of *Becoming Brothers*, most of the writing is by Howard, but by the end of the work their portions divide evenly, paralleling the way Arthur becomes more actively involved in the project as it progresses. At first he is ready to cede most of it to Howard, but Howard invites his older brother to be a more active contributor, reversing their childhood pattern in which Arthur's voice was dominant. In complementary fashion, Howard's voice during the course of the writing becomes more and more freed from having to take Arthur's response into account, a reversal of earlier instances when Howard tried to assimilate Arthur's political values. The text raises several questions fundamental to double-voiced autobiographical narrative: how do you develop your own voice while at the same time allowing room for that other voice in your life?

This is indeed a book about voices and speaking. Not only in the ways the two brothers distinctly perceive and narrate the world—Howard the more personal, Arthur the more spiritual; Howard the literary critic-cum-psychologist, Arthur the political theorist-cum-leader of the Jewish renewal movement—but more interesting, the way the book is written as a complex intertwining of voices, a book in which each one speaks who he is by acknowledging and celebrating his difference from and his connection with the other. Each brother tells a story that includes the other, but the combined stories are self-conscious explorations of each one's struggle ("wrestling" is the frequent term), first to differentiate himself from the other, then to comprehend that difference, and finally to pay tribute to it. *Becoming Brothers* is also a play of languages: Howard's more psychologically based and literary, Arthur's more political and theological. The brothers fought with words throughout their childhood, and in the writing they each recount those earlier scenes, often arguing interpretations. Howard imagines them as Quentin and Shreve in *Absalom, Absalom*, trying to piece together the family history; we see the brothers as detectives with language, painstakingly recreating and disputing interpretations of family narratives. As the book weaves in and out of the brothers' systole-diastole relation, each one acknowledges how his voice responds to the other's.

The center of the text is a description of their mother's death and of the brothers' conflict about who will speak at her funeral. Arthur wants both of them to recount her significance to them, but Howard, feeling emotionally unable to do so, does not want Arthur's voice to interpret for him. In this emblematic sense, the autobiography emphasizes the need to acknowledge interpretive differences. The brothers decided that Howard would describe their mother's death from tuberculosis, and that Arthur would write the chapter about the funeral as compensation for his not having free rein to conduct the service as he had initially wanted. The intertwining stories incorporate one another's positions and make room for one another's voices, and in turn the storytelling elicits a reciprocal letting go, analogous to the mother's letting go of her breath. The autobiography is a mutual breathing, a to-and-fro of composition that corresponds to what is being achieved in their relation. Just as each of them comes to self-knowledge through the drama of a sustained interaction, so the double autobiography is produced through a movement "in and out [of] each other's words," each one teaching the other and forming the relationship anew even as they revise, with the implications of that term for re-seeing.

As Arthur acknowledges a debt to Howard's detective work on the family, he places that family history in a tradition of what he calls "God-Wrestling," the title in fact of an earlier book he wrote and later expanded after the collaboration on *Becoming Brothers*, to show how his new grasp of personal and family history illuminates his understanding of Jewish history. *Becoming Brothers* thus becomes a kind of second edition of *Godwrestling*, and the latter, in its second edition, becomes in turn a sequel to the autobiography, something analogous to the way *within* the autobiographical text each writer seconds and edits his brother's version of the life. "It has been a strange kind of wrestle, since each of us was groping toward ending the very split that made for wrestling in the first place. Howard reached beyond it when he asked me to write a book with him about the two of us. I reached beyond it when, in telling the story of [our mother's] life and death, I realized I needed him to join with me in telling it" (*Brothers* 169).

Like Sarraute's and Fraser's texts, *Becoming Brothers* is both autobiography and meta-autobiography, for we perceive how the book came to be written and the decisions that necessarily precede most self-writing but that normally get suppressed in the telling. In all three double-voiced texts, self-analysis is dialogic, a process of disputation and confirmation, of memory, perception, judgment, knowledge, experience, and adjustment conducted within a self that exists in the center of a narrative network of relationships— family, lovers, friends, associates, witnesses, and commentators.

I WROTE AN EARLIER VERSION of this chapter for a conference on auto-biography held at the University of Groningen, in The Netherlands, a meeting titled "All by Myself: The Representation of Individual Identity in Autobiographical Writings." I was not alone in presenting a paper that subverted the conference title; by the end of the session most participants agreed that "All by Myself" was a disputable concept, having more to do with Sinatra's signature song than with the "relational" approaches many of us had taken toward subjectivity.

The notion of double voicing interests me because we cannot be under-stood apart from the others who make up our lives. On a more personal note, I attribute my concern as well to an only child's loneliness. I had always longed for siblings, and as a boy I created a whole cast of them in my imagination. As Hamm says in Beckett's *Endgame*, a play I once directed, "the solitary child . . . turns himself into children, two, three, so as to be together, and whisper together, in the dark." Informed by my parents that as an only child I was in danger of being spoiled (they did not say whether "being" implied an inescapable condition or something they could not help doing to me), I thought that only a sibling could spare me that fate. I also wanted a confidant to share and confirm my view of my parents. At seven or eight, I was so desperate for a brother I pretended to have a miniature radio in my right leg that I could turn on with a button in my thigh and from which a companionate voice would emerge. We had many conversations, this auditory other and I; he urged me to take risks and he reassured me at moments of anxiety. I had procured an instant twin and imaginary playfellow. From an early age I felt incomplete, truncated; as a result I've always been attracted to Aristophanes's myth of the lover who searches for the beloved—the body that has been severed from his own—that, when found, restores him to a state of wholeness.

When I was a child my favorite performers were Edgar Bergin and Charlie McCarthy. Ventriloquism seemed hauntingly magical, and at times I identified with the multivoiced human who could throw his words into another's mouth, but at other times I imagined myself filled with the words of a master. Charlie won the audience's applause for his sassy and ironically wise comebacks, so he was not just a doltish piece of wood. But the problem of power seemed complex, because even though Bergin played the straight man, turning on himself via Charlie's sarcasm, his virtuosity expressed a formidable verbal control. At the same time the thought of becoming someone else, or at least taking on his traits, was both thrilling and frightening. I think this is why, though I relished directing in the theatre, acting invariably unsettled me. Whenever I acted I was never certain who I really was, which is not quite the point of the art. To this day the teasing curtain calls of Shakespeare's comedies affect me with a kind of ontological vertigo. It may be that autobiography is at the core a ventriloquial genre, for the writing "I" puts a voice into that other "I," the surrogate whom the author has created to speak for her.

Once on Sicily, alone and having spoken to no one for three days, I struck up an imaginary conversation with a close friend. I heard his voice in my head as clear as the waters off Siracusa, where I was traipsing about the badly preserved remains of an ancient Greek stadium. I knew exactly what my friend would say ("even the ruins are ruined"), and for an hour I constructed a consoling dialogue faithful to one we might have had on that scorched August afternoon. Hearing his voice, rhythms, and tone as precisely as if he were walking with me among the crumbled stones was a comfort that rescued me from lingering solitude.

At times I am multivoiced. In an old and recurrent dream, I am giving a party where a group of friends from various stages of my life—summer camp, high school, college, graduate school—have gathered; none of them knows the others, but they all have been close with me. I am speechless, because I have been a different person with each one, even having adopted his way of thinking and talking. How can I possibly speak now, with all of them surrounding me? Every time I open my mouth, only the imitated friend recognizes me, the others staring at me, a sudden stranger. More important, how can I recognize myself? I am each friend, but who am I? Do I have a voice I can call my own? I understand what André Aciman means when he asks in *False Papers*, "How could I tell the difference between identity and mimicry?"

I enjoy taking up others' positions and temporarily trying on others' roles, persuading myself that the gesture represents an expansive, empathetic engagement with another being. Is this why I wrote my senior thesis on Ezra Pound's *Personae*? Sometimes I seek a Laurentian merging (the only child's desire for an alter ego), but at other times I fear I would have to give up too much (the only child's reluctance to make space for an Other). A therapist once urged me to consider a woman very different from me much as an anthropologist might regard with sympathetic fascination a creature from another culture, but I could never be comfortable with this idea. And yet even in a love relationship, I have frequently adopted the characteristics of the woman, mistakenly assuming that the way to get affirmation was by taking on the other's being. A retreating girlfriend once said to me, "You and I are so alike that I don't feel I'm missing anything by not being with you; I have myself and that's like having you!" Cold comfort farm.

Though I loathe astrology, I have always thought that my being a Gemini was cosmically correct. As "a twin," at least in zodiaical terms, I became an English major because in the 1950s, "ambiguity" was the critical password, and I perceived an official sanctioning of my own ambivalence about nearly everything, my penchant for seeing around corners and doubling every option. "Double voicing" might have been my mantra.

I tend to second-guess myself (like Sarraute)—often hesitant to act because I anticipate disappointment, but fretful if I do act because I fear mistaken choices. Perhaps especially for these reasons I'm attracted to autobiography, the genre that represents a second chance and revision. Fitzgerald famously said there are no second acts in American life, but autobiography is the defiant second and third act, allowing the writer to try out a variety of new identities that compensate for disappointment, even that make over the life. Double-voiced autobiographies may especially embody authorial strength, as the writer perceives himself mirrored in or identified with others, inventing new selves and expanding the range of particularity. But if I were writing a work in which I split myself into several selves, I might wonder about my core identity: how can I be this, when I'm also that? Or if, like Fraser, I made another person in the work as paramount as myself, as capable as I of producing evidence of my selfhood, I'd worry that we might become conflated and I'd lose whatever particularity was mine.

Among the autobiographers I treat in this book, Howard Waskow is the only one I have known personally. It's not easy writing about a friend's autobiography—you keep judging his self-revelation by how you think you know the person, pleased by the statements that affirm your perceptions, taken aback by the surprises. If there were ever competition between the critic and the writer, it was here. But then I had had a competitively admiring relation with Howard all along, despite or perhaps because we were members of a small men's group that met for many years to discuss our marriages and love relationships, our work, families, friendships, childhoods, sexuality—everything. Howard is a strong presence, earthy and girthy, and there's no getting around him; I occasionally made him into a conscience, but Janus-faced, I rebelled. If I think I've given someone too much authority, I draw back, resisting the counsel I may have sought. Still, the friendship has stood over the years, and I think of it like a gnarled, long-buffeted but enduring tree.

Not long ago I invited him to my class in autobiography, on the evening when we were discussing *Becoming Brothers*. For Howard, who had resigned from Reed many years before, it was a kind of homecoming. And the students were exhilarated, after reading Augustine, Rousseau, and Yeats, to have a live autobiographer on hand. Of course I knew too much—or thought I did—about the life in that book, to be a totally disinterested reader, but for a moment I tried to think of Howard as, say, Saul Friedlander or Georges Perec or any other respected autobiographer who would have been simply a spectral presence in the classroom, a shade lurking behind the printed words. But of course Howard was too present for that, and I surrendered to the fact that he was simply and insistently *there;* any attempt to turn that breathing body into mere text was absurd. In the class that evening, Howard was an earnestly jovial reader of his own life, and my including his brotherly autobiography in this book, beyond its appropriateness for the chapter, is a gesture of affection and a remembrance of that occasion.

Epilogue
Unearthing the Father

In the early fall of 1998, I presented a portion of the Nabokov chapter at
a conference on autobiography sponsored by West Virginia University. I
participated in the conference in part because my father had gone to college
at West Virginia, and I thought it would be instructive to stroll the lawns
and the walks where seventy years earlier he had been an undergraduate.
When I was nine I had visited the campus with him, but this new occasion
would allow me to see the place through adult eyes and, more important, to
reaffirm a bond with my father, who had died when I was just eighteen and a
college freshman. A week before the conference I wrote the autobiographical
coda to the Nabokov chapter, and as I flew by commuter plane from
Pittsburgh to Morgantown, my meditation on childlessness was very much
on my mind.

Midway through the conference sessions, I took a break and wandered
about in the crisp autumn air, coming upon a cluster of gray stone buildings,
prairie Gothic in style, that formed an open quadrangle. Though they had
been renovated about a decade earlier, they retained a nineteenth-century
aura, and as I sat in front of them on a stone bench, I tried to imagine my
father in the same spot, when he was a student in the late 1920s. The campus
was undeniably attractive, but I could not imagine why he had come to
this place, far from his native Newark. West Virginia did not appear a likely
destination for a poor but ambitious Jewish boy, the son of a butcher, his
eyes set on either a medical or a legal career. Did he experience isolation
and loneliness? Did he get along with the farm boys and the coal miners'
children? How alien did the hills of Appalachia that surrounded the town
appear to him in his first long separation from home?

My mother had come from Uniontown, a scant thirty miles up the road
across the line in Pennsylvania. My father met her on a blind date. As the
family lore had it, he was up on a ladder decorating his fraternity house for

a party, and when she walked into the room he instantly told himself he would one day marry that girl. It took him seven years. As I stared at the venerable buildings, wondering why he had chosen this remote place for his education, I suddenly realized that if he had not come here I would not exist. It was a simple and obvious truth, but the revelation struck me with brute force.

The next day, I decided to explore the town, eventually discovering a musty bookstore. I noticed a shelf filled with old university yearbooks. As it happened, the last volume in a row of *The Monticola: The Annual of West Virginia University and the Class Book of the Junior Class* was dated 1927. I recalled that my father graduated in 1929, so he would not be among the seniors in the volume. But each fraternity was featured separately, and knowing that he had been in Pi Lambda Phi, I began to search for that fraternity's page. And all at once there he was, my twenty-year-old father, looking out from an oval photograph with the caption "Joe Porter, Pledge." I stood in the aisle of the bookstore, transfixed and shaking. Who could say how long the yearbook had lain on the shelf, but for a moment I imagined that the volume—and my father himself—had waited for years to be ransomed from oblivion, and I even fantasized it was his own copy, sold years ago perhaps to purchase train fare home to Jersey. I felt as if I were rescuing my father from exile.

On the page there were pictures of other young men whose names I dimly remembered from childhood dinner conversations: Robert Wallach, Erwin Nelowet, Mose Boiarsky. And there was a photograph of the fraternity house, a stately, stone residence with a wraparound and columned porch, the very site of the conception of my conception.

Then another image caught my eye: the photograph of a man whose name was legend in the family, but who I never realized had been a fraternity brother of my father: Sonny Schlossberg. Years before I was born, my mother's sister, on a night when both she and Schlossberg were roaring drunk, decided on a dare to elope. Aunt Harriet's marriage to the sloshed Schlossberg lasted but four months, and she never married again. Suddenly I understood how my parents must have met. Schlossberg, no doubt dating Harriet at the time, likely told my father that his girlfriend up in Uniontown had a kid sister, and that sometime he should fix him up for a double date.

I bought the yearbook for $7.50.

Walking up the street with my treasure in hand, returning to the autobiography conference, I felt as if I had drawn a circle of commemoration, or rather as if a circle had been drawn for me, enclosing memory, speculation, and dream. I had plucked a piece of my past from that unlikely shelf, a tangible memorial that seemed to complete the previous day's reverie on the stone bench. I had looked out over the West Virginia hills, and from the fragile page my father had gazed back at me—I who had already lived fourteen years longer than he had—and I imagined not so much his astonishment at my great find as a father's pride and praise. He could no more have dreamed that one day I would speak at his alma mater, and inadvertently stumble upon his innocent and fresh face in that bookstore where perhaps he had once bought his textbooks, than I could have dreamed that I would never have a child, someone who might memorialize me much as I had celebrated my father in an unforeseen act of observance.

Face to face with my past, in a place crackling with discovery, I remembered that in *Speak, Memory*, Nabokov discovers in a European library a book written by *his* father, long since dead, a book the child had never seen. That afternoon, in the unlikely soil of Morgantown, criticism and autobiography melded into one flesh.

In effect, two meldings occurred, and they both speak to the book I now bring to a close. As I faced the picture of my youthful father in that bookstore, I could at last regard him as an equal. I had seen photos of him from the flapper era, but I was a young child when I had gazed on those photos pasted into my "baby book" with its light blue quilted cover, photos meant to chart the beginnings of our small family. A little boy, I thought of the man in those pictures, though only in his mid-twenties, as large, wise, definitive. Now I looked at my young father, his lost youth meeting my aging face, and I felt as if he were a beloved subject, but one unfamiliarly shy, even fawnlike, not quite certain of himself, a haunting and somewhat haunted figure that I, detective of missing persons, had brought to light. It was as if I could see him forming before me, even as I could see myself being formed in and through him. How often as a child I had heard the phrase "when you were just a gleam in your father's eye." Now, in his West Virginia photograph, I saw that gleam in the big gray-green cat's eyes I remembered, the unmistakable charm, the glint. And I saw myself, deep within those eyes, and reflected back.

Then an uncanny thing happened. I suddenly recalled the *last* photograph ever taken of him, when he returned home from an overindulgent party one day in 1955, just moments before he collapsed with the heart attack that, at forty-eight, proved fatal. In that final image, which sat on my mother's dresser for years even after she remarried, he always looked ancient to me, no less so as over the years I gained ground on his terminal age. Although he was fourteen years my junior on that day in Morgantown, I felt younger than the figure I summoned to mind from that last photograph.

And yet I felt older and riper than the face that looked out at me from the timeworn page of the yearbook. Call us equal, then, two men meeting in the middle. It's my fantasy that we stared at one another with mutual wonder.

The other melding describes a kind of coming of age, belated to be sure, but, as the traditional age for writing autobiography is hardly much beyond my own, not so late after all. Having served as "critic-son" to the established authors in this study, I have now come to write my own sporadic version of autobiography, in some sense joining my work to theirs. I think of this act, however fragmentary, disjunctive, and partial, as a gesture toward twinship with the subjects of my study, and a way of achieving some autonomy. It would be preposterous, of course, to assert that I feel the equal of the autobiographers I discuss, and that is not what I wish to claim. Rather, it is that while the face-to-face encounter with my father helped me to acknowledge who I now am, so as I place these codas next to my discussions of others' autobiography, I feel free to authorize myself and to stake out the role of brother-in-writing.

Notes

INTRODUCTION

1. In an essay on intentionality, Annabel Patterson remarks that Wimsatt and Beardsley defined the problem of intention as one "in aesthetics, not in hermeneutics" (142). Quentin Skinner distinguishes between the "motive" for writing, something outside the text, what he calls an antecedent of the writing, and the "intention," a feature of the work itself, something expressed *in* the writing (210–21).

2. See William Howarth's seminal essay, "Some Principles of Autobiography."

3. See Judith M. Melton's recent study, *The Face of Exile: Autobiographical Journeys*.

4. Much of the "personal criticism" of the past decade has allied critical subjectivity with the concerns of women's writing and feminist theory, sometimes encouraging dialogue between the critic and her readers. For a discussion of these and related issues, see Miller, *Getting Personal*, esp. 1–30; Freedman, Frey, and Zauhar; Kadar; and Veeser.

5. Gates is quoted in Heller A9.

1. THE SINGER IN THE SONG

1. See also Seidel; Melton.

2. Olson 44. Olson's study focuses on the way Odysseus's storytelling overcomes incoherence and chaos; he argues that stories or songs—expansions of reports, news, gossip, and rumor—are the foundation of Odysseus's "poetic glory." See also Segal.

3. See Benardete.

4. Paul Zweig claims that "For Homer, the memorable life was modeled on a story, and had as its goal to become story" (*The Adventurer* 93).

5. See Cavarero, chapters 2 and 3, for a discussion of the "narratable self" in *The Odyssey*.

6. For discussions of Odysseus as poet, see Thalmann; Stewart; and Murnaghan.

2. THE PLEASURES OF NOSTOS

1. Svetlana Boym distinguishes between two types of nostalgia. The first she calls "utopian nostalgia," which emphasizes a "return to that mythical place"; such nostalgia "sees exile . . . as a definite fall from grace that should be corrected" and is "reconstructive." The second, which she calls "ironic nostalgia," is "enamoured of distance, not of the referent itself" and "accepts (if it does not enjoy) the paradoxes of exile and displacement" (241). Nabokov comes closer to Boym's second category.

2. See Sarup.

3. Robert Newman expresses a similar proposition: "We might view memory as a narrative of homecoming just as we see narrative as an act of memory" (3).

4. For further discussion of the importance of the butterfly as a trope in Nabokov's writing, see Foster; Nabokov, *Butterflies*.

3. FILLING UP THE SILENT VACANCY

1. See Benveniste 224–26 and Lejeune, *Le Moi autobiographique* 8–10.

2. At his death, Gibbon's autobiography consisted of six manuscript drafts plus a fragment of a seventh, written between 1788 and 1793 and covering different periods of his life, though with considerable overlap. Shortly after Gibbon's death in 1794, his friend and literary executor, John Holroyd, Lord Sheffield, edited the drafts into a single volume. Despite a fully annotated edition of the *Memoirs of My Life*, compiled in 1966 by Georges A. Bonnard, John Murray's edition remains the only complete text of all the drafts. The Saunders edition of Gibbon's *Autobiography*, the source of most of my citations, employs the Sheffield compilations and reinstates the passages Sheffield deleted. Saunders's introduction and Bonnard's preface should be consulted for fuller accounts of the bibliographical problem. For an interpretive account of the various versions, see the chapter on Gibbon in Spacks; Epstein.

3. William Howarth regards Gibbon's work in the "exemplary" mode of autobiography: assured, didactic, and "oratorical." But while Gibbon begins with unshakable faith in himself, he comes to question the absolutes that mark his earlier self-conception as a public monument.

4. John N. Morris asserts that the "informing principle of the autobiography of an historian" is a conception of "a man interested in the *fortunes* of things, and *how they turn out*. It is a principle in harmony with the historian's professional assumptions that the true nature of events can only be understood in retrospect" (85).

5. Robert Folkenflik comments perceptively on the way Gibbon's narrative self confronts his younger, more naive, self ("Child and Adult"). I would disagree only with the extent to which Folkenflik believes that Gibbon has transcended the

emotional turbulence of those earlier years and escaped the consequences of what seems to me to be repression.

6. Patricia Meyer Spacks claims that Gibbon's "passion operates through his reason," and that his memoir-writing shows him "constructing his defenses while refusing to acknowledge what he is defending against" (113). Martin Price shows that Gibbon prefers to stand outside himself, ironic and skeptical; in order to realize such detachment, Gibbon must acknowledge the danger that passion and interest pose to his freedom. Price concludes that Gibbon "insist[s] upon a double vision: the life of the mind and its physical substrate; the intuitive sureness of rational judgment and the probability of the accidental" ("The Inquisition of Truth" 402).

7. In a particularly bitter passage, Gibbon decries his father's reckless habits and unsettled accounts. Financial disorder becomes an image for a perilous world; and the father's gaming table is "a dark and slippery precipice," an image anticipating one at the end of the autobiography, when life is envisaged as a mountain from which everyone "aspire[s] to descend or expect[s] to fall" (207).

8. See the reproduction of the first page of Memoir E in *Autobiography* 26. Gibbon in the first sentence had written only "lab," but it seems clear he intended "laborious."

9. See Low, *Gibbon's Journal* xxix.

4. UNSPEAKABLE PRACTICES, WRITABLE ACTS

1. For a discussion of these issues, I am indebted to Thomas C. Bailey.

2. For a discussion of Franklin as a master player of roles, see Sayre.

6. REDEMPTIVE EVASIONS

1. See Coe 104–38. For a study of autobiographical archetypes and myths, including those of paradise and paradise lost, see Egan, *Patterns of Experience* 68–103.

2. See Raine 234.

3. The term and the definition are from Leo Marx.

4. For a discussion of dreams in Muir, see Finney 197–206.

5. At several junctures in both texts, Muir returns from the story to the fable, as if he were an exile unable to live in the ordinary fallen world. One of these moments occurs when he and his family literally return to the Orkney Islands so that their son, who had been struck by a car, could recuperate. In going back to Orkney, Muir reexperiences his childhood, and this renewed possession of his past corresponds to the repetition in the narrative of the fable, itself a reminder of the desire for regeneration and an end to the repeated cycles of loss and renewal. For a fuller discussion of Muir's expulsion from paradise and his strategies—both psychological and rhetorical—for regaining it, see Fleishman 379–87.

7. AUTOBIOGRAPHICAL WRITING AS DEATH WEAPON

1. The five works are *A Child, An Indication of the Cause, The Cellar: An Escape, Breath: A Decision,* and *In the Cold.*

2. Alfred Hornung's statement that Bernhard "re-emerges [from the sanatorium] with an indefatigable will to live" overlooks the death-driven conclusion to the autobiography (185).

3. Gerald A. Fetz, incorrectly I believe, denies Bernhard's obsessive attacks on his own character, though granting occasional self-laceration: "Even though [Bernhard] is not without his self-critical moments, [he] projects most of his anger and criticism outward" (220). Fetz sees similarities in the two writers' attitudes toward horror, sickness, and death, and in their sense of victimization by their respective societies and in their outsider status.

4. For a discussion of the disintegration of the unified self as a commonplace of late-nineteenth- and early-twentieth-century German writing and cultural production, see Kurz.

5. Peter Schwenger maintains that marriage would not so much keep Kafka from writing generally but, by breaking his dependence on the father, would eliminate Kafka's great subject and the fountainhead of his art (60).

6. The case superficially resembles, but is very different from, Gertrude Stein's *Autobiography of Alice B. Toklas,* where Toklas's continual praise of Stein is meant to be taken as Stein's own self-adulation.

7. Galen Longstreth, in a thesis written partly about Kafka's letters to Milena and to Felice, notes perceptively about a particular letter to Milena: "The written selves echo each other. . . . Kafka sees himself as the *you* to whom he writes and the *I* from whom he receives letters" (*Letters as Literature: Epistolary Identity, Convention, and Performance,* Reed College, 1998: 18).

8. Karl later seems to reverse himself when he says "Kafka's accusation is that he is precisely what Hermann attempted to make of him. . . . [T]he son whom Hermann cannot bear is an exact product of the father's fashioning" (608). But even here Karl sees Kafka placing the blame more on the father than on himself.

9. For an interesting discussion of this phenomenon, see Gunn 1–34.

8. FIGURATION AND DISFIGUREMENT

1. G. Thomas Couser's *Recovering Bodies* is the major study to date of the autobiography of illness and physical dysfunction. In *Subjectivity, Identity, and the Body,* Sidonie Smith makes the case for the body as crucial to any consideration of selfhood. Paul John Eakin has written about the autobiographical bodies of Oliver Sacks and John Updike in *Touching the World.* While relatively few autobiographies focus on the body, there are some especially worth mentioning: Eleanor Clark, *Eyes, etc.: A Memoir*; Marie Cardinal, *The Words to Say It*; Oliver Sacks, *A Leg to Stand*

On; Reynolds Price, *A Whole New Life*; and Audre Lorde, *The Cancer Journals*. Memoirs of people with cancer and AIDS have especially proliferated in recent years.

2. The *Memoirs*, originally published in the medical literature in the early 1870s, were rediscovered by Michel Foucault in the Paris archives of abnormal sexuality. They were published anew in 1978. In this volume, Foucault included detailed medical reports written at the time of Barbin's gender reassignment and at the time of the autopsy, as well as a short story based on the case titled "A Scandal in the Convent" and written a quarter century after Barbin's death by the German psychiatrist Oscar Panizza.

3. Judith Butler argues that Barbin's ambivalence about her body resulted from a prohibitive law, one that, because of its regulations about what constituted normative sexuality, made her believe that her body, not juridical law, was the cause of her gender confusion (96–106).

4. See Suleiman.

5. Shirley Neuman analyzes the results of the two medical reports, especially the claims by both doctors that Barbin should be considered male despite the fact that what might have been a penis appeared more like an enlarged clitoris, and that the urethra was clearly feminine. Neuman argues that the doctors designated her as male on the evidence that Barbin was capable of orgasm, and that to regard her as female would have disrupted cultural sanctions against "an impassioned woman." The doctors were unwilling to allow Herculine to decide how she experienced her body; ultimately they "could see the ambiguously sexed hermaphroditic body only as tending toward and needing to be assimilated into the canonical male body" ("Autobiography, Bodies, Manhood" 144–46).

6. Judith Butler states the case succinctly: "Inasmuch as 'identity' is assured through the stabilizing concepts of sex, gender and sexuality, the very notion of 'the person' is called into question by the cultural emergence of those 'incoherent' or 'discontinuous' gendered beings who . . . fail to conform to the gendered norms of cultural intelligibility by which persons are defined. . . . Herculine is not an 'identity,' but the sexual impossibility of an identity" (17, 21).

7. In a discussion of the narratological issues in Barbin's text, Vincent Crapanzano shows how the radical break in the life cannot, despite Barbin's best intentions, be repaired or even explained by its author. Crapanzano calls the text "a failed attempt to discover therapeutically, as it were, a narrative that could account for that break" (63–64).

8. The terms are from Geoffrey Galt Harpham (45).

9. ANNULLED SELVES

1. Paul John Eakin, though relatively sympathetic to Sturrock's position, is

reluctant to uphold him completely, since Eakin argues that chronology is "deeply implicated in the motivation to cast life history into narrative form," and he assumes the autobiographer's unavoidable "temporal consciousness" (*Fictions in Autobiography*). See also Eakin, "Narrative and Chronology."

2. See Brée; Blanchard, "Between Autobiography and Ethnography" and "'N stuff . . ."; and Bailly.

3. According to Michael Sheringham, the autobiographer's materials in *La Règle de jeu* are "minor incidents, memories, objects, snippets of information [which] take on the properties of words—to be exploited, interrogated, forced to surrender their secrets" (252).

4. See the discussion of this phenomenon in Norman O. Brown, *Life against Death* (Middletown: Wesleyan UP, 1959).

10. ROMANTIC POSING

1. See Lejeune, "Looking at a Self-Portrait," *On Autobiography*, 109–18. In Rockwell's triple self-portrait, he paints himself painting himself, the artist's image on the depicted canvass charmingly made to look more attractive than his reflected image in the studio mirror.

2. In an essay on romantic portraiture, "The Romantic Circle," Richard Holmes observes that this quotation from *King Lear* "realizes a tragic pun which only a painter could have made—as if his whole life had been a 'stretched' canvas over a frame of agony" (35).

3. Haydon described the birth of his first son like Lear pronouncing on the inevitable doom in store for the child: he heard "a puling, peaked cry, as of a little helpless living being, who felt the air, & anticipated the anxieties, & bewailed the destiny of his irrevocable humanity" (*Diary* 2: 392). Heroic defiance, prophetic doom, and exhaustion are characteristics Haydon continually attributes to his own Lear-like being.

4. In a study of literary diaries, Robert A. Fothergill claims that Haydon reveals a "capacity to be ravished by the intensity of his own conception" and portrays a character who "intoxicates himself with the most monstrous self-perceptions." Fothergill's overheated rhetoric captures an aspect of Haydon's self-representation but hardly does justice to its complexity (157, 31).

5. Haydon to Keats, January 23, 1819 (in Keats 278).

11. "A SERPENT IN THE COILS OF A PYTHONESS"

1. For a discussion of diaries as the autobiographical form most consonant with postmodern theories of the self, see Nussbaum 128–40.

2. Elizabeth Bruss states the case for discontinuity in life-writing when she argues that "the 'story' . . . autobiography tells is never seamless, and often it is not

a story at all but a string of meditations and vignettes—fractional events that may be painful or joyous in their partial disinterment, irrepressible or simply casual in their transient spontaneity" (*Autobiographical Acts* 164).

3. "The *Journal*. . . allows within the temporal duration of discourse the instantaneity of the visual image, and within the domain of fleeting time the simultaneity otherwise denied the human mind" (Hannoosh 10).

4. See Spector.

12. CONFLICT AND INCORPORATION

1. For a harsher account of Gosse's resistance to viewing things from the father's perspective, see Mandel, "Full of Life Now" 58–62. In "Sir Edmund Gosse and His Modern Readers," Peter Allen describes Gosse's father as "a tragic hero" rather than a "merely villainous figure," one whose "good and even noble qualities" have been "sacrificed to dogmatic faith" (492). In an essay on childhood rebellion in nineteenth-century literature, Howard R. Wolf remarks that Gosse describes his revolt against the father in a "tone of partial reconciliation and atonement (207).

2. Malone observes that in the nineteenth century the word "epoch" referred not to a historical period but to a geological one; thus when Gosse frames the familial conflict as epochal, he "refutes the creationist model of history" and "positions Philip Gosse in an older, archaic world" (27).

3. Several books that Gosse lists as missing from his childhood are those Wordsworth praises for preventing a premature plunge into adulthood: *Jack the Giant Killer* and *Robin Hood*. Wordsworth speaks of the books that "have overbridged / The froward chaos of futurity," impelling the child into the world before Nature can slowly wean him from too much dependence upon what is outside himself (*The Prelude* [1805] V, 371–72).

4. Gosse's fight for recognition begins at the moment of birth. His father laconically records the event in his journal: "E. delivered of a son. Received green swallow from Jamaica" (*Father and Son* 8).

5. See Folkenflik and Folkenflik.

6. For a discussion of "self-fashioning" in Gosse as it relates to the problem of truth versus lying, see Helsinger.

7. For a discussion of *Father and Son* as a parody of spiritual autobiography and a comic version of traditional religious texts, see Fleishman 300–09. Linda H. Peterson contends that "the primary literary genre that gives shape to *Father and Son* is the spiritual autobiography, even when Gosse works against it" (171).

8. Gosse to Gide, January 7, 1927 (in Gide and Gosse 189); Gide to Gosse, January 16, 1927 (in Gide and Gosse 190–91).

9. Ira Bruce Nadel, in an essay about Victorian resistance to Rousseauean confession, argues that many mid-nineteenth-century English autobiographers

avoided the representation of embarrassing candor and "a fatal pride in one's individual glory," substituting for these romantic tendencies a more impersonal and rational defense of ideas and values, and replacing a "troubling engagement with . . . feelings" with a modest, self-protective account of deeds, "confession" with "apology" (190, 193). Nadel sees Gosse divided between self-disclosure and self-disguise. Gosse is also torn between his own desire to reveal long-buried impulses and his father's resistance to the inner life, manifested in the son's reluctance to explore troubling feelings. Hence there is more identification with the father than we might expect in a narrative of a break and of the acquisition of independence.

13. MY MOTHER AND MYSELF

1. Freeman, esp. chapter 5, "Fact and Fiction."

14. SELF AND OTHER IS ONE FLESH

1. For other versions of this position, see de Man; Lang, "Autobiography in the Aftermath of Romanticism"; Sprinker; P. Smith; and Gilmore, *Autobiographics*.

2. For a discussion of "the moment in autobiography in which the subject perceives himself, or less frequently herself, as another self," see R. Folkenflik, "The Self as Other" 215.

3. Paul John Eakin makes a convincing case for thinking about autobiographies as more than solo performances. He notes that "autobiography promotes an illusion of self-determination: *I* write my story; *I* say who I am; *I* create myself. The myth of autonomy dies hard, and autobiography criticism has not yet fully addressed the extent to which the self is defined by—and lives in terms of—its relations with others" ("Relational Selves" 63). Eakin addresses the ways autobiographies manifest the relational aspect of lives, especially how family members are incorporated into autobiographical narratives; I am interested as well in a narrative strategy in which the self is represented by more than one voice and employs those voices to complicate the narrator's identity. I presented an early version of this chapter before Eakin's recent work on relationality appeared.

4. Mary Mason famously argues that one of the distinguishing marks of women's autobiography is that the heroine achieves identity not as an act of solitary individuality, but through relation to others, representing the self *by* representing others. See also *Life/Lines*, where Brodzki and Schenck assert, regarding Gertrude Stein's narration of her life via the narration of another's, "Being *between two covers* with somebody else ultimately replaces singularity with alterity in a way that is dramatically female" (11).

5. Valerie Minogue, in "Fragments of a Childhood: Nathalie Sarraute's *Enfance*," characterizes the two voices as "that of the burrower, who delves into and tries to merge with the recollected sensation [and] that of the critical sifter who challenges,

warns of self-indulgence, exaggeration, falsification, and points to the gap between the sensation of *then* and the words and images of *now*" (72). Bella Brodzki, in "Mothers, Displacement, and Language," sees the two narrative voices as split by gender: the "I," which she calls "expressive," is feminine; the "You," which she calls "analytic," is masculine. In the French text, the pronouns and adjectives associated with the second voice are indeed masculine, with the other voice feminine; this distinction does not exist in the English translation. Eakin, who calls the "You" "an older, wiser, and warier sister," is more concerned with the relation of Sarraute's present self of writing to her earlier self of experience than with the relation of the "I" and the "You" (*Touching the World* 33). See also Hewitt 53–91.

6. For Sarraute's discussion of the difficulty of capturing interior states in language, see *Tropisms* and *The Age of Suspicion*.

7. In a discussion of *Childhood*, Michael Sheringham suggests the analogy of an analysand confronting an analyst who alternately speaks, listens, intervenes, or remains silent (163).

Bibliography

Abbott, H. P. *Diary Fiction: Writing as Action*. Ithaca: Cornell UP, 1984.

Aciman, André. *False Papers: Essays on Exile and Memory*. New York: Farrar, 2000.

Adorno, Theodor. *Minima Moralia: Reflections from a Damaged Life*. Trans. E. F. N. Jephcott. London: Schocken, 1974.

Allen, Peter. "Sir Edmund Gosse and his Modern Readers: The Continued Appeal of *Father and Son*." *E.L.H.* 55 (1988): 487–503.

Altieri, Charles. "What Is at Stake in Confessional Criticism." Veeser 55–67.

Altman, Janet Gurkin. *Epistolarity: Approaches to a Form*. Columbus: Ohio State UP, 1982.

Anderson, Mark. "Notes on Thomas Bernhard." *Raritan* 7 (1987): 81–96.

Ashley, Kathleen, Leigh Gilmore, and Gerald Peters, eds. *Autobiography and Postmodernism*. Amherst: U of Massachusetts P, 1994.

Augustine, Saint. *Confessions*. Trans. R. S. Pine-Coffin. New York: Penguin, 1961.

Austin, J. L. *How to Do Things with Words*. Cambridge: Harvard UP, 1962.

Bailey, Thomas C. "The Rhetoric of Self: Benjamin Franklin at the Edge." Unpublished paper.

Bailly, Jean-Christophe. "A River with No Novel." *Yale French Studies* 81 (1992): 35–45.

Bakhtin, Mikhail. *The Dialogic Imagination*. Trans. Caryl Emerson and Michael Holquist. Austin: U of Texas P, 1981.

Barbin, Herculine. *Being the Recently Discovered Memoirs of a Nineteenth-Century French Hermaphrodite*. Ed. Michel Foucault. Trans. Richard McDougal. New York: Pantheon, 1980.

Bate, W. Jackson. *John Keats*. New York: Oxford UP, 1963.

Baudelaire, Charles. "The Life and Work of Eugène Delacroix." *The Mirror of Art*. Trans. Jonathan Mayne. New York: Phaidon, 1955.

Benardete, Seth. *The Bow and the Lyre: A Platonic Reading of The Odyssey*. Boulder: Rowman, 1997.

Benjamin, Walter. "The Storyteller: Reflections on the Works of Nikolai Leskov." *Illuminations*. Ed. Hannah Arendt. Trans. Harry Zohn. New York: Schocken, 1969. 83–109.

Benveniste, Emile. *Problems in General Linguistics*. Trans. Mary Elizabeth Meek. Coral Gables: U of Miami P, 1971.

Bergland, Betty. "Postmodernism and the Autobiographical Subject: Reconstructing the 'Other.'" Ashley, Gilmore, and Peters 130–66.

Bernhard, Thomas. *Gathering Evidence: A Memoir*. Trans. David McLintock. New York: Knopf, 1985.

Blanchard, Marc. "Between Autobiography and Ethnography: The Journalist as Anthropologist." *Diacritics* 23 (1993): 72–81.

———. "'N stuff . . . : Practices, Equipment, Protocols in Twentieth-Century Ethnography." *Yale French Studies* 81 (1992): 111–27.

Bloom, Harold. *How to Read and Why*. New York: Scribner, 2000.

———. *Poetry and Repression: Revisionism from Blake to Stevens*. New Haven: Yale UP, 1976.

———. *The Visionary Company: A Reading of English Romantic Poetry*. New York: Doubleday, 1961.

———. *The Western Canon: The Books and Schools of the Ages*. New York: Harcourt Brace, 1994.

———, ed. *Romanticism and Consciousness*. New York: Norton, 1970.

Boyd, Brian. *Vladimir Nabokov: The American Years*. Princeton: Princeton UP, 1991.

Boym, Svetlana. "Estrangement as a Lifestyle: Shklovsky and Brodsky." *Exile and Creativity: Signposts, Travelers, Outsiders, Backward Glances*. Ed. Susan Rubin Suleiman. Durham: Duke UP, 1998. 241–62.

Brée, Germaine. "Michel Leiris: Mazemaker." Olney, *Autobiography* 194–206.

Brodzki, Bella. "Mothers, Displacement, and Language in the Autobiographies of Nathalie Sarraute and Christa Wolf." Brodzki and Schenck 243–59.

Brodzki, Bella, and Celeste Schenck, eds. *Life/Lines: Theorizing Women's Autobiography*. Ithaca: Cornell UP, 1988.

Brooks, Peter. *Troubling Confessions: Speaking Guilt in Law and Literature*. Chicago: U of Chicago P, 2000.

Bruner, Jerome. "The Invention of Self: Autobiography and Its Forms." Autobiography and Self-Representation. University of California–Irvine, March 3–4, 1990.

Bruss, Elizabeth. *Autobiographical Acts: The Changing Situation of a Literary Genre*. Baltimore: Johns Hopkins UP, 1976.

———. "Eye for Eye: Making and Unmaking Autobiography in Film." Olney, *Autobiography* 296–320.

Bunkers, Suzanne. "Midwestern Diaries and Journals: What Women Were (Not) Saying in the Late 1800's." Olney, *Studies in Autobiography* 190–210.

Butler, Judith. *Gender Trouble: Feminism and the Subversion of Identity.* New York: Routledge, 1990.

Calder, Robert. *Willie: The Life of W. Somerset Maugham.* New York: St. Martin's, 1989.

Cavarero, Adriana. *Relating Narratives: Storytelling and Selfhood.* Trans. Paul A. Kottman. New York: Routledge, 2000.

Chandler, Marilyn R. "A Healing Art: Therapeutic Dimensions of Autobiography." *a/b: Auto/Biography Studies* 5 (1989): 4–14.

Charteris, Evan. *The Life and Letters of Sir Edmund Gosse.* London: Heinemann, 1931.

Cixous, Hélène. "The Laugh of the Medusa." Trans. Keith Cohen and Paula Cohen. *New French Feminisms: An Anthology.* Ed. Elaine Marks and Isabelle de Courtivron. New York: Schocken, 1981. 245–64.

Clifford, James. *The Predicament of Culture: Twentieth-Century Ethnography, Literature, and Art.* Cambridge: Harvard UP, 1988.

Coe, Richard N. *When the Grass Was Taller: Autobiography and the Experience of Childhood.* New Haven: Yale UP, 1984.

Cohen, Anthony P. *Self-Consciousness: An Alternative Anthropology of Identity.* New York: Routledge, 1994.

Corngold, Stanley. *Franz Kafka: The Necessity of Form.* Ithaca: Cornell UP, 1988.

Couser, G. Thomas. *Altered Egos: Authority in American Autobiography.* New York: Oxford UP, 1989.

———. *Recovering Bodies: Illness, Disability, and Life Writing.* Madison: U of Wisconsin P, 1997.

Cox, James. *Recovering Literature's Lost Ground: Essays in American Autobiography.* Baton Rouge: Louisiana State UP, 1989.

Crapanzano, Vincent. " 'Self'-Centering Narratives." *The Yale Journal of Criticism* 5 (1992): 61–79.

Dahlberg, Edward. *Because I Was Flesh: The Autobiography of Edward Dahlberg.* New York: New Directions, 1964.

———. *Epitaphs of Our Times: The Letters of Edward Dahlberg.* Ed. Edwin Seaver. New York: Braziller, 1967.

de Man, Paul. "Autobiography as De-Facement." *M.L.N.* 94 (1979): 919–30.

De Quincey, Thomas. *The Collected Writings of Thomas De Quincey.* Ed. David Masson. 14 vols. London: Black, 1897.

Delacroix, Eugène. *Ecrits d'Eugène Delacroix.* Tome 2. Paris: Plon, 1942.

———. *The Journal of Eugène Delacroix.* Ed. Hubert Wellington. Trans. Lucy Norton. Ithaca: Cornell UP, 1980.

Eakin, Paul John. *Fictions in Autobiography: Studies in the Art of Self-Invention.* Princeton: Princeton UP, 1985.

———. *How Our Lives Become Stories: Making Selves.* Ithaca: Cornell UP, 1999.

———. "Narrative and Chronology as Structures of Reference and the New Model Autobiography." Olney, *Studies in Autobiography* 32–41.

———. "Relational Selves: The Story of the Story." *True Relations: Essays on Autobiography and the Postmodern.* Ed. G. Thomas Couser and Joseph Fichtelberg. Westport, Conn.: Greenwood, 1998. 63–81.

———. *Touching the World: Reference in Autobiography.* Princeton: Princeton UP, 1992.

———, ed. *American Autobiography: Retrospect and Prospect.* Madison: U of Wisconsin P, 1991.

Egan, Susanna. *Mirror Talk: Genres of Crisis in Contemporary Autobiography.* Chapel Hill: U of North Carolina P, 1999.

———. *Patterns of Experience in Autobiography.* Chapel Hill: U of North Carolina P, 1984.

Emerson, Ralph Waldo. *Ralph Waldo Emerson.* Ed. Richard Poirier. New York: Oxford UP, 1990.

Epstein, William H. "Professing Gibbon: The Autobiographical Profession of Literary Study." *Eighteenth Century* 27 (1986): 115–40.

Felski, Rita. *Beyond Feminist Aesthetics: Feminist Literature and Social Change.* Cambridge: Harvard UP, 1989.

Fetz, Gerald A. "Kafka and Bernhard: Reflections on Affinity and Influence." *Modern Austrian Literature* 21 (1988): 217–41.

Fiedler, Leslie. *Freaks: Myths and Images of the Secret Self.* New York: Simon, 1978.

Finney, Brian. *The Inner I: British Literary Autobiography of the Twentieth Century.* New York: Oxford UP, 1985.

Fish, Stanley. "Biography and Intention." *Contesting the Subject: Essays in the Postmodern Theory and Practice of Biography and Biographical Criticism.* Ed. William H. Epstein. West Lafayette, Ind.: Purdue UP, 1991. 9–16.

Fleishman, Avrom. *Figures of Autobiography: The Language of Self-Writing in Victorian and Modern England.* Berkeley: U of California P, 1983.

Folkenflik, Robert. "Child and Adult: Historical Perspective in Gibbon's Memoirs." *Studies in Burke and His Time* 15 (1973): 31–43.

———. "The Self as Other." *The Culture of Autobiography: Constructions of Self-Representation.* Ed. Robert Folkenflik. Stanford: Stanford UP, 1993. 215–34.

Folkenflik, Vivian, and Robert Folkenflik. "Words and Language in *Father and Son.*" *Biography* 2 (1979): 157–74.

Foster, John Burt, Jr. *Nabokov's Art of Memory and European Modernism.* Princeton: Princeton UP, 1993.

Fothergill, Robert A. *Private Chronicles: A Study of English Diaries*. London: Oxford UP, 1974.

Foucault, Michel. "An Interview with Michel Foucault." *Death and the Labyrinth: The Works of Raymond Roussel*. Trans. Charles Ruas. London: Athlone, 1986. 169–86.

Fox-Genovese, Elizabeth. "Confession versus Criticism, or What's the Critic Got to Do with It?" Veeser 68–75.

Franklin, Benjamin. *The Autobiography of Benjamin Franklin*. Ed. Leonard W. Labaree, Ralph K. Ketcham, Helen C. Boatfield, and Helene H. Fineman. New Haven: Yale UP, 1964.

Fraser, Ronald. *In Search of a Past: The Manor House, Amnersfield, 1933–1945*. London: Verso, 1984.

Frecerro, John. "Autobiography and Narrative." *Reconstructing Individualism: Autonomy, Individuality, and the Self in Western Thought*. Ed. Thomas C. Heller, Morton Sosna, and David Wellbery. Stanford: Stanford UP, 1986. 16–29.

Freedman, Diane P., Olivia Frey, and Frances Murphy Zauhar, eds. *The Intimate Critique: Autobiographical Literary Criticism*. Durham: Duke UP, 1993.

Freeman, Mark. *Rewriting the Self: History, Memory, Narrative*. New York: Routledge, 1993.

Freud, Anna. *The Ego and the Mechanism of Defense*. Trans. Cecil Baines. New York: International Universities, 1966.

Gadamer, H. G. "The Problem of Historical Consciousness." Trans. Jeff L. Close. *Interpretative Science: A Reader*. Ed. P. Rabinow and William M. Sullivan. Berkeley: U of California P, 1979. 103–60.

George, Eric. *The Life and Death of Benjamin Robert Haydon*. Oxford: Oxford UP, 1967.

Gibbon, Edward. *The Autobiographies of Edward Gibbon*. Ed. John Murray. London, 1896.

——. *The Autobiography of Edward Gibbon*. Ed. Dero A. Saunders. New York: Meridian, 1961.

——. *The History of the Decline and Fall of the Roman Empire*. Ed. J. B. Bury. 7 vols. London: Methuen, 1896–1902.

——. *The Letters of Edward Gibbon*. 3 vols. Ed. J. E. Norton. London: Cassell, 1956.

——. *Memoirs of My Life*. Ed. Georges A. Bonnard. London: Nelson, 1966.

Gide, André. *The Journals of Andre Gide*. Vol. II. Trans. Justin O'Brien. New York: Knopf, 1948.

Gide, André, and Edmund Gosse. *The Correspondence of André Gide and Edmund Gosse, 1904–1928*. Ed. and trans. Linnette F. Brugmans. New York: New York UP, 1959.

Gilman, Sander. *Franz Kafka, the Jewish Patient*. New York: Routledge, 1995.

———. *Inscribing the Other*. Lincoln: U of Nebraska P, 1991.

Gilmore, Leigh. *Autobiographics: A Feminist Theory of Women's Self-Representation*. Ithaca: Cornell UP, 1994.

———. "Policing Truth: Confession, Gender, and Autobiographical Authority." Ashley, Gilmore, and Peters 54–78.

Glassman, Peter. "Acts of Enclosure." *The Hudson Review*. 30 (1977): 138–46.

Gosse, Edmund. *Father and Son: A Study of Two Temperaments*. 1907. Ed. William Irvine. Boston: Houghton Mifflin, 1965.

———. *The Life of Philip Henry Gosse, F.R.S.* London: Kegan Paul, 1890.

Grumbach, Doris. *Fifty Days of Solitude*. Boston: Beacon, 1994.

Gunn, Daniel. *Psychoanalysis and Fiction: An Exploration of Literary and Psychoanalytic Borders*. Cambridge: Cambridge UP, 1988.

Hannoosh, Michele. *Painting and the Journal of Eugène Delacroix*. Princeton: Princeton UP, 1995.

Harpham, Geoffrey Galt. "Conversion and the Language of Autobiography." Olney, *Studies in Autobiography* 42–50.

Harris, Joseph. "The Plural Text/The Plural Self: Roland Barthes and William Cole." *College English* 49 (1987): 158–70.

Harrison, Barbara Grizzuti. *An Accidental Autobiography*. New York: Houghton Mifflin, 1996.

Haydon, Benjamin Robert. *The Autobiography and Journals of Benjamin Robert Haydon*. Ed. Malcolm Elwin. London: Macdonald, 1950.

———. *The Diary of Benjamin Robert Haydon*. Ed. Willard Bissell Pope. 5 vols. Cambridge: Harvard UP, 1963.

Heidegger, Martin. *What Is Called Thinking?* Trans. J. Glenn Gray. New York: Harper, 1968.

Heller, Scott. "New Brand of Scholarship Mixes Experience, Expertise." *The Chronicle of Higher Education*, May 6, 1992: A9.

Helsinger, Howard. "Credence and Credibility: The Concern for Honesty in Victorian Autobiography." *Approaches to Victorian Autobiography*. Ed. George P. Landow. Athens, Ohio: Ohio UP, 1979. 56–63.

Hewitt, Leah D. *Autobiographical Tightropes*. Lincoln: U of Nebraska P, 1990.

Higonnet, Margaret. "Speaking Silences: Woman's Suicide." *The Female Body in Western Culture*. Ed. Susan Rubin Suleiman. Cambridge: Harvard UP, 1986. 68–83.

Hoffman, Daniel. "Edwin Muir: The Story and the Fable." *Yale Review* 55 (1966): 403–26.

Holmes, Richard. "The Romantic Circle." *The New York Review of Books* XLIV (April 10, 1997): 34–35.

Homer. *The Odyssey*. Trans. Richmond Lattimore. New York: Harper, 1968.

Hornung, Alfred. "Reading One/Self: Samuel Beckett, Thomas Bernhard, Peter Handke, John Barth, Alain Robbe-Grillet." *Exploring Postmodernism*. Ed. Matei Calinescu and Douwe Fokkema. Amsterdam: John Benjamins, 1987. 175–98.

Howarth, William. "Some Principles of Autobiography." Olney, *Autobiography* 84–114.

Howe, Irving. *Literary Modernism*. Greenwich, Conn.: Fawcett , 1967.

Hughes, Robert. *The Shock of the New*. New York: Knopf, 1981.

Jay, Paul. *Being in the Text: Self-Representation from Wordsworth to Roland Barthes*. Ithaca: Cornell UP, 1984.

Johnson, Samuel. *The Yale Edition of the Works of Samuel Johnson*. Ed. W. J. Bate, John Bullitt, and L. F. Powell. Vol. II. New Haven: Yale UP, 1958.

Jung, Carl. *Memories, Dreams, Reflections*. Trans. Richard and Clara Winston. New York: Pantheon, 1963.

Kadar, Marlene, ed. *Essays on Life Writing: From Genre to Critical Practice*. Toronto: U of Toronto P, 1992.

Kafka, Franz. *The Diaries 1910–1923*. Trans. Martin Greenberg. New York: Schocken, 1976.

———. *Letter to His Father*. Trans. Ernest Kaiser and Eithene Wilkins. New York: Schocken, 1966.

———. *Letters to Felice*. Trans. James Stern and Elisabeth Duckworth. New York: Schocken, 1973.

———. *Letters to Friends, Family, and Editors*. Trans. Richard and Clara Winston. New York: Schocken, 1977.

———. *Letters to Milena*. Trans. Philip Boehm. New York: Schocken, 1990.

Kaplan, Caren. *Questions of Travel: Postmodern Discourses of Displacement*. Durham: Duke UP, 1996.

Karl, Frederick. *Franz Kafka: Representative Man*. New York: Fromm International, 1993.

Keats, John. *The Letters of John Keats*. Ed. Maurice Buxton Forman. London: Oxford UP, 1952.

Kristeva, Julia. *Powers of Horror*. Trans. Leon S. Roudiez. New York: Columbia UP, 1982.

Kundera, Milan. "Afterward: A Talk with the Author." *The Book of Laughter and Forgetting*. Trans. Michael Henry Heim. New York: Viking Penguin, 1981.

Kurz, Gerhard. "Nietzsche, Freud, and Kafka." *Reading Kafka: Prague, Politics, and the Fin de Siècle*. Ed. Mark Anderson. New York: Schocken, 1989. 128–48.

Lang, Candace. "Autobiography in the Aftermath of Romanticism." *Diacritics* 12 (1982). 2–16.

———. "Autocritique." Veeser 40–54.

Leibowitz, Herbert. *Fabricating Lives: Explorations in American Autobiography*. New York: Knopf, 1989.

Leiris, Michel. *Manhood: A Journey from Childhood into the Fierce Order of Virility*. Trans. Richard Howard. San Francisco: North Point, 1963.

——. *Scratches* (Biffures). Vol. 1 of *Rules of the Game* (*La Règle de jeu*). Trans. Lydia Davis. Baltimore: Johns Hopkins UP, 1991.

Lejeune, Philippe. *On Autobiography*. Ed. Paul John Eakin. Trans. Katherine Leary. Minneapolis: U of Minnesota P, 1989.

——. *Le Moi autobiographique* (The autobiographical pact). Paris: Seuil, 1986.

Low, D. M. *Edward Gibbon, 1737–1794*. New York: Random House, 1937.

——, ed. *Gibbon's Journal to January 28, 1763*. New York: Norton, 1929.

Mailer, Norman. "Henry Miller: Genius and Lust, Narcissism." *American Review* 24 (1976): 1–40.

Malone, Cynthia. "The Struggle of *Father and Son*: Edmund Gosse's Polemical Autobiography." *a/b: Auto/Biography Studies* 8 (1993): 16–32.

Mandel, Barrett J. " 'Basting the Image with a Certain Liquor': Death in Autobiography." *Soundings* 57 (1974): 175–88.

——. "Full of Life Now." Olney, *Autobiography* 49–72.

Marcus, Laura. *Auto/biographical Discourses: Theory, Criticism, Practice*. Manchester: Manchester UP, 1994.

Marx, Leo. *The Machine in the Garden: Technology and the Pastoral Ideal in America*. New York: Oxford UP, 1964.

Mason, Mary. "The Other Voice: Autobiographies of Women Writers." Olney, *Autobiography* 207–35.

Maugham, Somerset. "On His Ninetieth Birthday." *A Writer's Notebook*. Garden City, New York: Doubleday, 1949.

——. *The Summing Up*. New York: Doubleday, 1938.

——. *A Traveller in Romance: Uncollected Writings 1901–1964*. Ed. John Whitehead. New York: Potter, 1984. 263–66.

Melton, Judith M. *The Face of Exile: Autobiographical Journeys*. Iowa City: U of Iowa P, 1998.

Mill, John Stuart. *Mill's Essays on Literature and Society*. Ed. J. B. Schneewind. New York, 1965.

Miller, Nancy K. *Bequest and Betrayal: Memoirs of a Parent's Death*. New York and Oxford: Oxford UP, 1996.

——. *Getting Personal: Feminist Occasions and Other Autobiographical Acts*. New York: Routledge, 1991.

Minogue, Valerie. "Fragments of a Childhood: Nathalie Sarraute's *Enfance*." *Romance Studies* 9 (1986): 71–83.

Morris, Jan. *Conundrum*. London: Faber, 1974.

Morris, John N. *Versions of the Self: Studies in English Autobiography from John Bunyan to John Stuart Mill*. New York: Basic, 1966.

Muir, Edwin. *An Autobiography*. London: Hogarth, 1954.

——. *The Story and the Fable*. London: Harrap, 1940.

Murnaghan, Sheila. *Disguise and Recognition in The Odyssey*. Princeton: Princeton UP, 1987.

Nabokov, Vladimir. *Nabokov's Butterflies*. Ed. Brian Boyd and Robert Michael Pyle. Boston: Beacon, 2000.

——. *Selected Letters, 1940–1977*. Ed. Dmitri Nabokov and Matthew J. Bruccoli. New York: Harcourt, 1989.

——. *Speak, Memory: An Autobiography Revisited*. New York: Putnam's Sons, 1966.

——. *Strong Opinions*. New York: McGraw-Hill, 1970.

Nadel, Ira Bruce. "Apologize or Confess! The Dilemma of Victorian Autobiography." *Biography* 5 (1982): 189–204.

Neuman, Shirley, ed. *Autobiography and Questions of Gender*. London: Frank Cass, 1991.

——. "Autobiography, Bodies, Manhood." Neuman, *Autobiography and Questions of Gender* 137–65.

——. "Autobiography: From Different Poetics to a Poetics of Differences." Kadar 213–30.

Newman, Robert D. *Transgressions of Reading: Narrative Engagement as Exile and Return*. Durham: Duke UP, 1993.

Nussbaum, Felicity A. "Toward Conceptualizing Diary." Olney, *Studies in Autobiography* 128–40.

Olney, James. *Memory & Narrative: The Weave of Life-Writing*. Chicago: U of Chicago P, 1998.

——, ed. *Autobiography: Essays Theoretical and Critical*. Princeton: Princeton UP, 1980.

——, ed. *Studies in Autobiography*. New York: Oxford UP, 1988.

Olson, S. Douglas. *Blood and Iron: Stories and Storytelling in Homer's* Odyssey. Leiden, New York, and Koln: Brill, 1995.

Parke, Catherine N. "Edward Gibbon by Edward Gibbon." *Modern Language Quarterly* 50 (1989): 23–37.

Parker, Andrew, and Eve Kosofsky Sedgwick, eds. *Performativity and Performance*. New York and London: Routledge, 1995.

Pater, Walter. *The Renaissance*. New York: Random House, n.d.

Patterson, Annabel. "Intention." *Critical Terms for Literary Study*. Ed. Frank Lentricchia and Thomas McLaughlin. Chicago: U of Chicago P, 1990. 135–46.

Paul, Sherman. *Repossessing and Renewing: Essays in the Green American Tradition*. Baton Rouge: Louisiana State UP, 1976.

Pawel, Ernst. *The Nightmare of Reason: A Life of Franz Kafka*. New York: Random House, 1984.

Perry, Graham. "The Grand Delusions of Benjamin Haydon." *Keats Shelley Memorial Bulletin* 31 (1980): 10–21.

Peterson, Linda H. *Victorian Autobiography: The Tradition of Self-Interpretation*. New Haven: Yale UP, 1986.

Poirier, Richard. *The Performing Self: Compositions and Decompositions in the Languages of Contemporary Life*. New York: Oxford UP, 1971.

———. *The Renewal of Literature: Emersonian Reflections*. New Haven: Yale UP, 1987.

Porter, Roger J., and H. R. Wolf. *The Voice Within: Reading and Writing Autobiography*. New York: Knopf, 1973.

Price, Martin. "The Inquisition of Truth: Memory and Freedom in Gibbon's Memoirs." *Philological Quarterly* 54 (1975): 391–408.

———. *To the Palace of Wisdom: Studies in Order and Energy from Dryden to Blake*. New York: Doubleday, 1964.

Prideaux, Tom. *The World of Delacroix: 1798–1863*. New York: Time, Inc., 1966.

Raine, Kathleen. "Edwin Muir: An Appreciation." *Texas Quarterly* 4 (1961): 233–45.

Roth, Phillip. *The Human Stain*. London: Jonathan Cape, 2000.

Said, Edward. "Reflections on Exile." *Granta* 13 (1984): 159–72.

Sarraute, Nathalie. *Childhood*. Trans. Barbara Wright. New York: George Braziller, 1984.

———. *Tropisms* and *The Age of Suspicion*. Trans. Maria Jolas. London: Calder, 1964.

Sartre, Jean-Paul. *The Words*. Trans. Bernard Frechtman. New York: Random House, 1981.

Sarup, Madan. "Home and Identity." *Travellers' Tales: Narratives of Home and Displacement*. Ed. George Robertson, Melinda Mash, Lisa Tickner, Jon Bird, Barry Curtis, and Tim Putnam. London: Routledge, 1994. 93–104.

Sayre, Robert F. *The Examined Self: Franklin, Adams, James*. Princeton: Princeton UP, 1964.

Schor, Naomi. *Reading in Detail: Aesthetics and the Feminine*. New York: Methuen, 1987.

Schwenger, Peter. "Barthelme, Freud, and the Killing of Kafka's Father." *Fictions of Masculinity: Crossing Cultures, Crossing Sexualities*. Ed. Peter F. Murphy. New York: New York UP, 1994. 57–73.

Segal, Charles P. "*Kleos* and Its Ironies in *The Odyssey*." *L'Antiquité Classique* 52 (1983): 22–47.

Seidel, Michael. *Exile and the Narrative Imagination*. New Haven: Yale UP, 1986.

Shea, Daniel B. "The Prehistory of American Autobiography." *American Autobiography: Retrospect and Prospect*. Ed. Paul John Eakin. Madison: U of Wisconsin P, 1991. 25–46.

Sheringham, Michael. *French Autobiography: Devices and Desires*. Oxford: Clarendon, 1993.

Shloss, Carol. "*Because I Was Flesh:* Edward Dahlberg and the Rhetoric of American Identity." *The Massachusetts Review* 22 (1981): 576–84.

Skinner, Quentin. "Motives, Intentions, and the Interpretation of Texts." *On Literary Intention*. Ed. David Newton-De Molina. Edinburgh: Edinburgh UP, 1976. 210–21.

Smith, Paul. *Discerning the Subject*. Minneapolis: U of Minnesota P, 1988.

Smith, Sidonie. "Identity's Body." Ashley, Gilmore, and Peters 266–92.

———. "Performativity, Autobiographical Practice, Resistance." *a/b: Auto/Biography Studies* 10 (1995): 17–34.

———. *Subjectivity, Identity, and the Body: Women's Autobiographical Practice in the Twentieth Century*. Bloomington: Indiana UP, 1993.

Smith, Sidonie, and Julia Watson. *Getting a Life: Everyday Uses of Autobiography*. Minneapolis: U of Minnesota P, 1996.

Sontag, Susan. *Against Interpretation and Other Essays*. New York: Farrar, 1964.

Spacks, Patricia Meyer. *Imagining a Self: Autobiography and Novel in Eighteenth-Century England*. Cambridge: Harvard UP, 1976.

Spector, Jack J. *Delacroix: The Death of Sardanapalus*. New York: Viking, 1974.

Spender, Stephen. *World Within World: The Autobiography of Stephen Spender*. Berkeley: U of California P, 1966.

Sprinker, Michael. "Fictions of the Self: The End of Autobiography." Olney, *Autobiography* 321–42.

Stewart, Douglas J. *The Disguised Guest: Rank, Role, and Identity in the Odyssey*. Lewisburg, Pa.: Bucknell UP, 1976.

Sturrock, John. "The Autobiographer Astray: Leiris and *La Règle du jeu.*" *Moy Qui Me Voy: The Writer and the Self from Montaigne to Leiris*. Ed. George Craig and Margaret McGowan. Oxford: Clarendon, 1989. 206–20.

———. "The New Model Autobiographer." *New Literary History* 9 (1977–78): 51–63.

Suleiman, Susan Rubin. "(Re)Writing the Body: The Politics and Poetics of Female Eroticism." *The Female Body in Western Culture*. Ed. Susan Rubin Suleiman. Cambridge: Harvard UP, 1986. 7–29.

Tambling, Jeremy. *Confession: Sexuality, Sin, the Subject*. Manchester: Manchester UP, 1990.

Thalmann, William G. *Conventions of Form and Thought in Early Greek Epic Poetry*. Baltimore: Johns Hopkins UP, 1984.

Trapp, Frank Anderson. *The Attainment of Delacroix*. Baltimore: Johns Hopkins UP, 1971.

Van Gogh, Vincent. *The Complete Letters of Vincent Van Gogh*. 3 vols. Boston: New York Graphic Society, 1958.

———. *The Letters of Vincent Van Gogh*. Ed. Mark Roskill. New York: Athenaeum, 1963.

Veeser, H. Aram, ed. *Confessions of the Critics*. New York: Routledge, 1996.

Vidal, Gore. "Maugham's Half & Half." *United States: Essays 1952–1992*. New York: Random House, 1993. 228–50.

Waskow, Howard, and Arthur Waskow. *Becoming Brothers*. New York: Free Press, 1993.

Wimsatt, William K. (with Monroe C. Beardsley). "The Intentional Fallacy." *The Verbal Icon: Studies in the Meaning of Poetry*. Lexington: U of Kentucky P, 1954. 2–18.

Wolf, Howard R. "British Fathers and Sons, 1773–1913: From Filial Submissiveness to Creativity." *The Psychoanalytic Review* 52 (1965): 53–70.

Wood, Michael. Introduction to *Mrs. Craddock*, by Somerset Maugham. New York: Arno, 1977.

———. *The Magician's Doubts: Nabokov and the Risks of Fiction*. Princeton: Princeton UP, 1994.

Woolf, Virginia Woolf. "Edmund Gosse." "Genius: R. B. Haydon." *The Moment and Other Essays*. New York: Harcourt, 1948. 84–92, 186–92.

Wordsworth, William. *The Prelude or Growth of a Poet's Mind*. Ed. Ernest de Selincourt. London: Oxford UP, 1933.

Zweig, Paul. *The Adventurer*. New York: Basic, 1974.

Index

Abbott, H. Porter, 167

Absalom, Absalom (Faulkner), 228

An Accidental Autobiography (Harrison), 131–38; catalogues of objects in, 136–38, 144; compared with Leiris's autobiography, xvi, 131–34, 141; formal peculiarities of, 134–35; unexplained title of, 135–36

Aciman, André, 15, 20; *False Papers*, 230

Adorno, Theodor, 4

The Adventurer (Zweig), 237 n.4

Aeschylus, 66; *Agamemnon*, 64

Agamemnon (Aeschylus), 64

L'Age d'Homme (Leiris), 131, 143

The Age of Suspicion (Sarraute), 245 n.6

Allen, Peter: "Sir Edmund Gosse and His Modern Readers," 243 n.1

Altered Egos (Couser), 54–55, 218

Altieri, Charles, xx

Altman, Janet Gurkin, 111–12

American University of Paris, 176, 179

Amherst College, 16, 236; Porter's undergraduate years at, 50, 62, 146, 196–97, 199

Anderson, Benedict, 215

Anderson, Mark, 102

Aristophanes, 229

Augustine, Saint, 32, 92, 127, 172, 232; *Confessions*, 91, 123, 193

Austen, Jane, 13

Austin, J. L., 110

"The Autobiographer Astray" (Sturrock), 140

Autobiographical Acts (Bruss), xii, 63, 170, 242 n.2

autobiographical narrative: conversion in, xiv, 55, 89, 102, 126–27, 192–94, 241 n.7; cultural influences on, 121–22, 193; dialogic, 215–16, 220–22, 225, 226–27, 229, 244 n.3 n.5; exilic, xv, 3–13, 17–22, 28–29, 238 n.1 n.3; fragmentation of, xviii, 134–35, 136, 138–39, 140, 142; importance of, xii, 6–11, 14, 133–34, 210, 241 n.1; present vs. historical "I" in, xiii–xv, 4–5, 10, 13, 14, 37–38, 238 n.5; "story" vs. "fable" in, xiv, 55–56, 82–85, 89–91, 239 n.5. *See also* performance; rhetoric

autobiography: anticipation in, 10, 22, 24, 47, 100–101, 124, 162, 189, 192–93; authority in, 54–55, 120, 124, 188–89, 217–18, 219–22; the body in, 117–30, 135–36, 143, 201, 203, 205–9, 240 n.1, 241 n.2 n.3 n.5 n.6; chronology in, 104, 114, 131–32, 133, 138, 140, 241 n.1; compensatory qualities of, xiv–xvi, 3–4, 18, 19, 23, 55–56, 81, 231; compensatory qualities of, in question, 121, 125, 132, 133–34, 202, 203; as defense, xv–xvi, 37–39, 54–57, 62, 67–70, 76, 81, 91–92, 239 n.6; eighteenth-

autobiography (*cont.*)
century, 43, 45, 49, 50; formal structures
of, xiv–xv, 9, 25, 68–70, 121–22, 133–34,
241 n.1; gender in, 117–27, 241 n.2 n.3
n.5 n.6 n.7, 245 n.5; generational continuity in, 11, 18, 22, 25–26, 30–33, 199,
201, 207–9; intention in, xi–xv, 49–50,
55, 92, 121, 155, 184, 237 n.1; intersection
of, with biography, xvi, 50, 183–84, 201,
209, 226; journal writing as, 149, 152–
63, 166–76, 177, 243 n.3; letter writing
as, 103–16, 149–52, 159, 194, 226–27,
240 n.7; linguistic self-consciousness in,
xi–xii, 7, 25, 28, 68–69, 120, 221, 223;
myth of paradise in, 29, 81–85, 87, 92,
120, 178–79, 239 n.1 n.5; myth of self-
creation in, 183–84, 208, 209–10, 229,
244 n.3; nineteenth-century, 121, 124,
187–88, 240 n.4, 243 n.1 n.9; paradoxes
of, xiii, 11, 23, 37, 93–94, 120–21, 217;
plot of, 31, 82, 83, 89, 155, 164; spiritual,
54–55, 88–93, 190, 192–94, 209–10, 243
n.7; theatrical posturing in, xvi, 61, 65,
70, 123, 124, 149–63, 168–69, 171–75; as
therapy, 67, 89, 91–92, 126, 146, 209,
222–25, 241 n.7, 245 n.7; visual artists
and, xvi, 149–52, 153–60, 163, 168–69,
173–76, 242 n.1 n.2, 243 n.3; women's,
124–25, 127, 217, 237 n.4, 244 n.4 n.5.
See also autobiographical narrative; autobiography criticism; confession; performance; the self in autobiography;
truth in autobiography
The Autobiography (Burr), 146
Autobiography (Haydon), 149, 154, 155–59,
162, 163
An Autobiography (Muir), 82–84, 86–88,
89, 90, 91–92
"Autobiography, Bodies, Manhood" (Neuman), 117, 241 n.5
autobiography criticism, xvii–xx, 49–51,
54–55, 121–22, 133–34, 183–84, 241 n.1,
244 n.3; impact of feminist criticism on,

106–7, 124–25, 127, 217, 237 n.4, 244 n.4
n.5; impact of modern theory on, xi–xv,
xix–xx, 4, 29, 37–38, 50, 99, 146, 164,
215–16, 242 n.1
The Autobiography of Alice B. Toklas
(Stein), 217, 240 n.6, 244 n.4
The Autobiography of an Idea (Sullivan),
163
The Autobiography of Benjamin Franklin,
54–66; accretive structure of, 59–61;
compared with Gibbon's autobiography,
xv–xvi, 37–38, 54, 62, 63, 81; compared
with Maugham's autobiography, 76;
Porter's interest in, 62–66; printer's
conception of self in, 55, 56, 57; project
of moral perfection in, 57–59; resistance
to introspection in, 54–57, 58–59, 61–62
The Autobiography of Edward Gibbon, 37–
53; compared with Franklin's *Autobiography*, xv–xvi, 37–38, 54, 62, 63, 81; as
historian's autobiography, 38–39, 42, 46,
47, 48–49, 238 n.4; relationship of, to
The Decline and Fall, 40, 44, 45, 46–49;
repression of emotion in, 40–42, 43–45,
71, 238 n.5, 239 n.6; rhetorical equipoise
in, 37, 39–42, 43, 44–45, 49–50, 160;
shift from confidence to uncertainty in,
37–39, 42–43, 45–49, 238 n.3, 239 n.7;
significance of, for Porter, 49–53; textual
changes in manuscripts of, 39, 45, 238
n.2, 239 n.8
"Autocritique" (Lang), xx
"The Awkward Bow of John Keats"
(Bagg), 113

Bagg, Robert: "The Awkward Bow of John
Keats," 113; *Nostia*, 16
Bakhtin, Mikhail, 218
Barber, C. L., 95
Barber, Red, 135
Barbin, Herculine: suicide of, 120, 121. See
also *Memoirs of a Nineteenth-Century
French Hermaphrodite*

Barthes, Roland: "The Reality Effect," 137

Bataille, Georges, 131

Bate, Walter Jackson, 156

Baudelaire, Charles-Pierre, 170, 171

Baudrillard, Jean, 137

Baylor University, 77

Beardsley, Monroe C.: "The Intentional Fallacy," xiii, 237 n.1

Beauvoir, Simone de, 127, 131

Because I Was Flesh (Dahlberg), 201–14; compared with Gosse's Father and Son, xvi, 183–84; generative impulse in, 201, 206–7, 208, 209, 210–11; inflated style of, 202–3, 204, 209–10; scorn for body in, 203, 205–6, 207–8; trope of exile in, 203–5, 208–9

Beckett, Samuel, 100, 102, 114, 141; Endgame, 65, 229; Happy Days, 65, 145; Not I, 65, 145; Play, 65, 145

Becoming Brothers (Waskow and Waskow), xvi, 177, 216, 217, 226–29, 232; letters in, 226–27

Being in the Text (Jay), 87

Benjamin, Walter, 9, 104, 145

Bequest and Betrayal (Miller), xviii–xix

Bergin, Edgar, 229–30

Bernhard, Thomas. See Gathering Evidence

Beyond Feminist Aesthetics (Felski), 106–7

Beyond the Pleasure Principle (Freud), 90

the Bible, 141, 155, 161, 186, 209

Biffures (Leiris), 131, 132, 138–44

biography, 7, 49, 133; importance of, in autobiography, xvi, 50, 183, 201, 209, 226

"The Biography of a Painting" (Shahn), 163

"The Blood of the Walsungs" (Mann), 80

Bloom, Harold, 49; Poetry and Repression, 208; Romanticism and Consciousness, 162; The Visionary Company, 84; The Western Canon, xi

Bodenheim, Maxwell, 198

Boiarsky, Mose, 234

Bonnard, Georges A., 238 n.2

Boston MA, 52

Boswell, James, 65, 170

Boyd, Brian, 22

Boym, Svetlana, 238 n.1

Brecht, Bertholt: Mother Courage, 65

Brod, Max, 108, 113

Brodzki, Bella: Life/Lines, 244 n.4; "Mothers, Displacement, and Language," 245 n.5

Brooks, Peter: Troubling Confessions, 67–68, 110

Bruner, Jerome, xiv–xv

Bruss, Elizabeth: Autobiographical Acts, xii, 63, 170, 242 n.2

Bunkers, Suzanne, 166

Bunyan, John, 60; Pilgrim's Progress, 55

Burke, Kenneth, xi

Burr, Anna Robeson: The Autobiography, 146

Butler, Judith, 241 n.6

Byron, Lord, 171, 172; Manfred, 80

Caesar, Julius, 40; Commentaries, 146

Cairo, 15, 65–66, 164–65

Cairo American College, 15, 65

Calder, Robert, 71, 73, 76

The Cancer Journals (Lorde), 241 n.1

Cantos (Pound), 51

Cardan, Jerome: De Vita Propria Liber, 146

Cardinal, Marie: The Words to Say It, 240 n.1

Casanova, Giovanni Giacomo, 168

Cavafy, Constantine, 15

Cavarero, Adriana, 237 n.5

Cellini, Benvenuto, 65

Cervantes, Miguel de, 171

The Charterhouse of Parma (Stendhal), 146

Charteris, Evan, 187, 194

Chicago, Judy: Through the Flower, 163

"Child and Adult" (Folkenflik), 238 n.5

childhood: aesthetic return to, in autobiography, 20–29, 201–11; beliefs about

childhood (*cont.*)
  language in, 141–42; conflict and rebellion in, 43–46, 185–96, 238 n.5, 243 n.1 n.3 n.4; discordant interpretations of, 218–29, 244 n.5, 245 n.7; as idyll, 81–90, 92, 120–21, 239 n.5; nullification of, in autobiography, 100–101, 103; Porter's memories of, 29–33, 79–80, 196–99, 229–30, 235
Childhood (Sarraute), 218–22, 228, 244 n.5, 245 n.7
Cixous, Hélène: "The Laugh of the Medusa," 124–25
Clark, Eleanor: *Eyes, etc.*, 240 n.1
Classics and Commercials (Wilson), 72
Clifford, James: "On Collecting Art and Culture," 137
Colby College, 52
Commager, Henry Steele, 16
Commager, Lisa, 16
Commentaries (Caesar), 146
confession: Augustinian mode of, 91, 123, 172, 193; autobiography as, xiv, 55, 110, 202, 221; criticism as, xvii–xix, 78–80; resistance to, in autobiography, 67–71; Rousseauean mode of, 117, 123, 157–58, 168, 189, 243 n.9
Confessions (Augustine), 91, 123, 193
Confessions (Rousseau), 69, 70, 168, 172, 232, 243 n.9; influence of, on Barbin, 117, 123; influence of, on Gosse, 189; influence of, on Haydon, 157–58
Confessions of an English Opium-Eater (De Quincey), 155
Conroy, Frank, 14
Conundrum (Morris), 127
Cooper, James Fenimore, 171
Corngold, Stanley, 108
Couser, G. Thomas: *Altered Egos*, 54–55, 218; *Recovering Bodies*, 240 n.1
Cox, James, 54, 56, 60, 62, 63, 168
Craig, Armour, 199
Crapanzano, Vincent, 241 n.7

The Crucible (Miller), 65, 66
cummings, e.e., 198
Curchod, Suzanne, 40–41, 44

Dahlberg, Edward: *Epitaphs*, 202–3, 208–9; letters of, 202–3, 208–9. See also *Because I Was Flesh*
Dante, 155, 171, 172
Dartmouth College, 62
death: as aesthetic challenge, 23–26; as energy and self-enlargement, 173–74, 175, 176; fear of, 42, 43–44, 45–49; memorializing of, 135–36, 206–7, 211; as opportunity for interpersonal growth, 228; Porter's experience with, 31, 115–16, 199–200, 212–14; postponement of, 6, 10, 11, 12, 141; wish for, xvi, 99–113, 124, 126–27, 240 n.2 n.3
The Death of Sardanapalus (Delacroix), 173–74
The Decline and Fall of the Roman Empire (Gibbon), 40, 44, 45, 46–49
Defoe, Daniel, 60
Delacroix, Eugène, 166–80; Porter's interest in, 176–77, 180; preoccupation of, with autobiography, 166–71, 172–73, 176; preoccupation of, with struggle, 172, 173–74, 176, 177, 180; staging in works of, xvi, 149–50, 152, 171–75; Van Gogh's interest in, 150, 151. Works: *The Death of Sardanapalus*, 173–74; *Journal*, 149, 166–80; *Medea*, 174; *Philosophical Dictionary of the Fine Arts*, 169; plates for Goethe's *Faust*, 174, 175; Saint Sulpice murals, 176–77
"The Departure of Fruits and Vegetables from the Heart of Paris" (Mason), 178–79
De Quincey, Thomas: *Confessions of an English Opium-Eater*, 155
De Vita Propria Liber (Cardan), 146
Deyverdun, Georges, 42, 46
diaries. *See* journal writing

Diaries (Kafka), 104, 106, 107, 109, 113
The Diaries of Paul Klee, 163
Diary (Haydon), 149, 152, 154–56, 157–58, 159–60, 161–62, 163, 242 n.2 n.3 n.4
double-voicing, 215–32; concept of, in autobiography, xvi, 50–51, 183–84, 215–18, 229–32, 231, 244 n.3 n.4; in Fraser's *In Search of a Past*, 222–26; in Sarraute's *Childhood*, 218–22, 244 n.5; in Waskow and Waskow's *Becoming Brothers*, 226–29
"The dream of reason produces monsters" (Goya), 64
DuBois, W. E. B., 217
Dürer, Albrecht, 152
Durrell, Lawrence, 15

Eakin, Paul John: on autobiography as textual performance, xiii, xv, 37, 38, 54; on the body in autobiography, 128; on chronology in autobiography, 241 n.1; on intention in autobiography, 184; on the myth of autonomy in autobiography, 121–22, 183, 244 n.3. Works: *Fictions in Autobiography*, xiii, 54, 120, 241 n.1; *How Our Lives Become Stories*, 183, 184; "Relational Selves," 244 n.3; *Touching the World*, 37, 38, 54, 224, 240 n.1, 245 n.5
Egan, Susanna, 184; *Mirror Talk*, xii; *Patterns of Experience*, 239 n.1
Egypt: Porter's experiences in, 15, 65–66, 164–65; in Woolf's *To the Lighthouse*, 212
Elgin Marbles, 153, 155, 163
Eliot, George: *Scenes of Clerical Life*, 151–52
Eliot, T. S., 13
Elizabeth NJ, 196, 198, 199
Emerson, Ralph Waldo: "Experience," xvii
Endgame (Beckett), 65, 229
Epitaphs (Dahlberg): 202–3; 208–9
Epstein, William H., 238 n.2
Erikson, Erik, 50
Examiner, 158

exile: from the body, 122–26; from childhood, 90–91, 120, 201, 203–5, 208–9, 239 n.5; Gibbon's experience of, 39–40; Nabokov's experience of, 17–22, 28–29, 238 n.1 n.3; Odysseus's experience of, 3–13; Porter's experience of, 14–15, 29–30, 234; significance of, in autobiography, xv
Exley, Frederick, 14
"Experience" (Emerson), xvii
Eyes, etc. (Clark), 240 n.1

False Papers (Aciman), 230
Father and Son (Gosse), 183–200; biographical form of, xvi, 183–84; evolutionary language of, 185–88, 192, 243 n.2; as exercise in impartiality, 184–85, 192–93, 195–96, 243 n.9; father's letter at end of, 111, 194; identification with father in, 191–92, 194–96, 244 n.9; letters in, 111, 187, 194; and nineteenth-century literature on childhood, 188–92, 243 n.1 n.3; as parody of spiritual autobiography, 192–94, 243 n.7; Porter's reflections on, 196–200; "self-fashioning" in, 187–94, 243 n.4 n.6
Faulkner, William: *Absalom, Absalom*, 228
Faust (Delacroix), 174, 175
Faust (Goethe), 174
Felski, Rita: *Beyond Feminist Aesthetics*, 106–7
feminist criticism, 106–7, 237 n.4; and women's autobiography, 124–25, 127, 217, 244 n.4 n.5
Fergusson, Francis: *The Idea of a Theater*, 146
Fetz, Gerald A., 240 n.3
Fictions in Autobiography (Eakin), xiii, 54, 120, 241 n.1
Fiedler, Leslie, 123
Fifty Days of Solitude (Grumbach), 32
Fish, Stanley, xii
Fitzgerald, F. Scott, 231

Fleishman, Avrom, 91, 239 n.5, 243 n.7

Folkenflik, Robert: "Child and Adult," 238 n.5; "The Self as Other," 244 n.2

Ford, John: *'Tis Pity She's a Whore*, 80

Foster, John Burt, Jr., 238 n.4

Fothergill, Robert A., 242 n.4

Foucault, Michel, 25, 120, 123, 241 n.2

Fox-Genovese, Elizabeth, xix

"Fragments of a Childhood: Nathalie Sarraute's *Enfance*" (Minogue), 244 n.5

Franklin, Benjamin. See *The Autobiography of Benjamin Franklin*

Franz Kafka, the Jewish Patient (Gilman), 109–10

Fraser, Ronald. See *In Search of a Past*

Freccero, John, 102

Frederico Secundo, king of Sicily, 135

Freedman, Diane P., 237 n.4

Freeman, Mark, 210

Freud, Anna, 191, 192

Freud, Sigmund, 128, 162; *Beyond the Pleasure Principle*, 90

Frey, Olivia, 237 n.4

Friedlander, Saul, 232

Frost, Robert, 15, 62, 95–96, 217

"Full of Life Now" (Mandel), 243 n.1

Gachet, Dr. (Van Gogh's physician), 152

Gadamer, Hans-Georg, xix

Gates, Henry Louis, Jr., xix

Gathering Evidence (Bernhard), 99–103, 240 n.1; compared with Kafka's *Letter to His Father*, 99–100, 104, 202, 240 n.3; death wish in, xvi, 100–103, 240 n.2 n.3

Gauguin, Paul, 151; *Intimate Journals*, 163

gender, xvii, 117–29, 241 n.5 n.6 n.7, 245 n.5

George, Eric, 157

Getting a Life (Smith and Watson), 80, 146

Getting Personal (Miller), 237 n.4

Giacometti, Alberto, 131

Gibbon, Edward, 51; *The Decline and Fall of the Roman Empire*, 40, 44, 45, 46–49;

letters of, 41–42. See also *The Autobiography of Edward Gibbon*

Gide, André: *Journals*, 194–95; *Si le grain ne meurt*, 195

Gilman, Sander: *Franz Kafka, the Jewish Patient*, 109–10; *Inscribing the Other*, 220; *The Jew's Body*, 130

Gilmore, Leigh: "Policing Truth," 217

Ginsberg, Allen: "Kaddish," 199–200

Glassman, Peter, 56

Godwrestling (A. Waskow), 177, 228

Goethe, Johann Wolfgang von, 171; *Faust*, 174

Gopnik, Adam, 180

Gornick, Vivian, 127

Gosse, Edmund. See *Father and Son*

Gosse, Philip, 183–96; ambivalent portrait of, in *Father and Son*, 184–85, 192–94, 243 n.1 n.9; archaic science of, 185–88, 243 n.2; *Omphalos*, 186, 187; son's challenge to, 111, 188–92, 243 n.4; son's resemblance to, 194–96

Gottdank, Saul, 205

Goya y Lucientes, Francisco José de: "The dream of reason produces monsters," 64

"The Grand Delusions of Benjamin Haydon" (Perry), 153–54

Grumbach, Doris, 145; *Fifty Days of Solitude*, 32

Hamlet (Shakespeare), 66, 161, 168–69, 171, 175

Hannoosh, Michele, 167, 176, 243 n.3

Happy Days (Beckett), 65, 145

Harpham, Geoffrey Galt, 193

Harris, Joseph, 218

Harrison, Barbara Grizzuti. See *An Accidental Autobiography*

Harrison, Kathryn: *The Kiss*, 80

Haxton, Gerald, 69

Haydon, Benjamin Robert, 149–65; contrasted with Gibbon, 160–61; Porter's interest in, 163–65; preoccupation of,

with heroic figures, 158–61; preoccupa-
tion of, with loss, 161–62; reasons of, for
writing autobiography, 153–57, 162–63;
Rousseau's influence on, 157–58; suicide
of, 152, 153; theatrical posturing by, xvi,
149–50, 152–53, 171, 242 n.2 n.3 n.4.
Works: *Autobiography*, 149, 154, 155–59,
162, 163; *Diary*, 149, 152, 154–56, 157–58,
159–60, 161–62, 163, 242 n.2 n.3 n.4; *The
Judgment of Solomon*, 157
Hazlitt, William: "On Going a Journey,"
71
Heidegger, Martin, 12, 210
Heliodorus, 177
Helsinger, Howard, 243 n.6
Higonnet, Margaret, 126
Hoffman, Daniel, 85
Holmes, Richard: "The Romantic Circle,"
242 n.2
Holroyd, John, 238 n.2
Homer, 155, 171; *The Iliad*, 5, 13. See also
The Odyssey
Hornung, Alfred, 240 n.2
Howarth, William, 161, 238 n.3
Howe, Irving, 92
How Our Lives Become Stories (Eakin), 183,
184
Hughes, Robert, 151
"Hugh Selwyn Mauberley" (Pound), 51
Hugo, Victor, 150, 151
Hunt, Leigh, 158
Hurston, Zora Neale, 127
Hutchins, Robert, 208

The Idea of a Theater (Fergusson), 146
identity. *See* the self in autobiography
"Identity's Body" (Smith), 124
The Iliad (Homer), 5, 13
"The Inquisition of Truth" (Price), 239 n.6
Inscribing the Other (Gilman), 220
In Search of a Past (Fraser), 222–26, 228;
plural notion of identity in, xvi, 216–17,
223–26, 231; structure of, 222–23

intention, xi–xv, 49–50, 55, 92, 121, 155,
184, 237 n.1
"The Intentional Fallacy" (Wimsatt and
Beardsley), xiii, 237 n.1
Intimate Journals (Gauguin), 163
Irvine, William, 194
Isherwood, Christopher, 223

James, Henry, 13, 172
James Beard Foundation, 180
Jauss, Hans Robert, 210
Jay, Paul, 27, 90; *Being in the Text*, 87
Jesenska, Milena, 104
Jewish autobiography: Dahlberg's, 205;
Kafka's, 109–10; Porter's, 31, 77–78, 94,
130, 199–200; Waskow brothers', 227,
228
The Jew's Body (Gilman), 130
Jonson, Ben: *Volpone*, 66, 145
The Journal of Eugène Delacroix, 149, 166–
80
The Journals of André Gide, 194–95
journal writing: characteristics of, 160,
166–67, 168, 170–71, 243 n.3; by Dela-
croix, 149, 166–76, 177; by Haydon, 149,
152–63, 242 n.2 n.3 n.4; by Kafka, 106,
107, 109, 113
Joyce, James, 95; *Portrait of the Artist*, 194
The Judgment of Solomon (Haydon), 157
Jung, Carl Gustav: *Memories, Dreams,
Reflections*, 89

Kadar, Marlene, 237 n.4
"Kaddish" (Ginsberg), 199–200
Kafka, Franz, 103–16; compared with
Bernhard, 99–100, 104, 240 n.3; compared with Gosse, 111, 194; internalizing
of father's judgment by, 103–13; letters
of 103–13, 143, 194, 240 n.6 n.7 n.8;
Muir's interest in, 93; Porter's interest
in, 52, 113–16; self-erasure by, xvi, 103–
4, 106–8, 109, 111–13, 132, 143; views
of, on marriage, 105–6, 108–9, 240 n.5.

Kafka, Franz (*cont.*)
Works: *Diaries*, 104, 106, 107, 109, 113; *Letters to Felice*, 104, 105–6, 107, 108–9, 112, 113, 115, 143, 240 n.7; *Letters to Friends, Family, and Editors*, 108; *Letters to Milena*, 104, 105–6, 109, 112, 113, 240 n.7; *Letter to His Father*, 103–13, 114–15, 194, 202, 240 n.6 n.8; "The Penal Colony," 105
Kafka, Hermann, 105, 172, 240 n.8. See also *Letter to His Father*
Kansas City MO, 201, 204, 205, 208–9
Kaplan, Caren: *Questions of Travel*, 4, 18
Karl, Frederick, 112, 240 n.8
Kazin, Alfred, 198
Keats, John, 155, 156, 160, 163; letters of 113, 159; *Letters*, 113, 159
King Lear (Shakespeare), 51, 152, 160, 242 n.2 n.3
Kingston, Maxine Hong, 127
The Kiss (Harrison), 80
Klee, Paul: *Diaries*, 163
Kristeva, Julia, 17–18
Kundera, Milan, 6
Kurz, Gerhard, 240 n.4

Lacan, Jacques, 120
Lang, Candace: "Autocritique," xx
Larousse Gastronomique, 180
"The Laugh of the Medusa" (Cixous), 124–25
Lawrence, D. H., 56, 61, 62; *Studies in Classic American Literature*, 146
A Leg to Stand On (Sacks), 240 n.1
Leibowitz, Herbert, 202, 209–10
Leiris, Michel, 138–44; compared with Harrison, xvi, 131–34, 141; emphasis of, on process, 138–39, 143–44; as "free-range" autobiographer, 139–42; reflections of, on language, 141–44. Works: *L'Age d'Homme*, 131, 143; *Biffures*, 131, 132, 138–44; *Manhood*, 118–19; *La Règle du jeu*, 131, 242 n.3

Lejeune, Philippe: *Le Moi autobiographique*, xv, xviii; *On Autobiography*, 121–22, 242 n.1
Leonardo da Vinci, 169; *Notebooks*, 161
letters, 103–16, 149–52; as autobiography, 104, 111–12; Dahlberg's, 202–3, 208–9; Gibbon's, 41–42; in Gosse's *Father and Son*, 111, 187, 194; Kafka's, 103–13, 143, 194, 240 n.6 n.7 n.8; Keats's, 113, 159; Porter's, 113–16; Van Gogh's, xvi, 149, 150–52, 153, 157, 163; in Waskow and Waskow's *Becoming Brothers*, 226–27
"Letters as Literature" (Longstreth), 240 n.7
The Letters of John Keats, 113, 159
The Letters of Vincent Van Gogh, xvi, 149, 150–52, 153, 157, 163
Letters to Felice (Kafka), 104, 105–6, 107, 108–9, 112, 113, 115, 143, 240 n.7
Letters to Friends, Family, and Editors (Kafka), 108
Letter to His Father (Kafka), 103–13, 114–15, 194, 202, 240 n.6 n.8
Letters to Milena (Kafka), 104, 105–6, 109, 112, 113, 240 n.7
Life/Lines (Brodzki and Schenck), 244 n.4
life-writing. *See* autobiography
Lion Hunt (Rubens), 175
Lipschitz, Jacques: *My Life in Sculpture*, 163
Longstreth, Galen: *Letters as Literature*, 240 n.7
Lopate, Phillip: *Portrait of My Body*, 129
Lorde, Audre: *The Cancer Journals*, 241 n.1

The Magician's Doubts (Wood), 23, 26
Mailer, Norman, 209
Malone, Cynthia Northcutt, 111, 187, 243 n.2
Mandel, Barrett John, 126; "Full of Life Now," 243 n.1
Manfred (Byron), 80
Manhood (Leiris), 118–19

Mann, Thomas: "The Blood of the Wal-
  sungs," 80
Mason, Mary, 183, 244 n.4
Mason, Raymond: "The Departure of
  Fruits and Vegetables from the Heart
  of Paris," 178–79
Maugham, Somerset, 67–80; archives of,
  at Baylor University, 77; desire of, for
  critical approval, 72–74; elitist incli-
  nations of, 74–75; masked sexuality
  of, 69, 70, 72, 75–76; popularity of, in
  Japan, 76–77. Works: *Mrs. Craddock*,
  70; *A Writer's Notebook*, 72. See also *The
  Summing Up*
McCarthy, Charlie, 229–30
McCarthy, Eugene, 52
McCarthy, Joseph, 64, 79
McCarthy, Mary, 127
Medea (Delacroix), 174
*Memoirs of a Nineteenth-Century French
  Hermaphrodite* (Barbin), 119–27; crisis of
  gender-identity in, 117, 119–27, 241 n.3
  n.5 n.6; crisis of self-representation in,
  xvi, 120–21, 123–24, 126–27, 132, 241 n.7;
  Foucault's edition of, 241 n.2; Porter's
  reaction to, 128–30; textual style of, 121,
  123–24
Memories, Dreams, Reflections (Jung), 89
memory: aesthetic framing of, in autobiography, xv, 17–29, 238 n.3; importance
  of, in autobiography, 4, 6, 9–12, 210–
  11; lapses of, 169–70; paradisal quality
  of, 81, 85, 87, 88, 90–91, 92; randomness
  of, in contemporary autobiography, 132,
  134, 135–36, 138–39, 141–42, 143, 242 n.3;
  relational quality of, 216–17, 219, 222–
  23, 229; sepulchral quality of, 203, 206–
  7, 210–11; significance of, for Porter, 15,
  29–30, 32–33, 51, 145–46, 164–65, 234–35
Memory and Narrative (Olney), xx, 221
meta-autobiography, 28, 92, 229
Metamorphosis (Ovid), 122
Michelangelo, 38, 156, 159, 171

A Midsummer Night's Dream (Shakes-
  peare), 65
Mill, James, 172
Mill, John Stuart, xiii, 185; "The Spirit of
  the Age," 187–88
Miller, Arthur: *The Crucible*, 65, 66
Miller, Nancy K.: *Bequest and Betrayal*,
  xviii–xix; *Getting Personal*, 237 n.4
Milton, John, 155; *Paradise Lost*, 156
Minogue, Valerie: "Fragments of a Child-
  hood: Nathalie Sarraute's *Enfance*," 244
  n.5
Mirror Talk (Egan), xii
modernism, 14, 17–18, 26, 72–73, 92
Le Moi autobiographique (Lejeune), xv,
  xviii
Molière, 171
Montaigne, Michel de, 115, 117, 168
The Monticola, 234
Morgantown wv, 197, 233, 235
Morris, Jan: *Conundrum*, 127
Morris, John N., 238 n.4
Morris, Willie, 14
Mother Courage (Brecht), 65
"Mothers, Displacement, and Language"
  (Brodzki), 245 n.5
Muir, Edwin, 81–96; collectivist leanings
  of, 84, 89, 93–94; interest of, in Kafka,
  93; paradisal myth of, 81–85, 87, 92,
  239 n.1 n.5; "pilgrimage" of, through
  Europe, 90–91; Porter's interest in, 93–
  96; representation of childhood by, 81–
  83, 85–88, 90, 92, 239 n.5; representation
  of modernity by, 88; rhetorical defenses
  of, xv–xvi, 37, 91–92; on "story" vs.
  "fable," xiv, 55–56, 82–85, 89–91, 239 n.5.
  Works: *An Autobiography*, 82–84, 86–88,
  89, 90, 91–92; *The Story and the Fable*,
  55, 82, 85, 89, 91, 92, 93
Murray, John, 238 n.2
My Life in Sculpture (Lipschitz), 163

Nabokov, Vladimir. See *Speak, Memory*

Nadel, Ira Bruce, 243 n.9
Napoleon Bonaparte, 155, 159, 160, 161
Necker, Jacques, 41
Nelowet, Erwin, 234
Nelson, Horatio, viscount, 159
Neuman, Shirley, 133; "Autobiography, Bodies, Manhood," 117, 241 n.5
New Age, 89
Newark NJ, 199–200, 233
New Criticism, xi, xii–xiii, 13, 49–50, 164
New Jersey, 29, 52, 79, 198. *See also* Elizabeth NJ; Newark NJ
Newman, Robert D., 90, 238 n.3
"The New Model Autobiographer" (Sturrock), 133, 241 n.1
New York NY, 198
New York Times, 180
Nostia (Bagg), 16
Notebooks (Leonardo), 161
Not I (Beckett), 65, 145
Nussbaum, Felicity A., 242 n.1

The Odyssey (Homer), 3–16; memory in, 4, 6–7, 9–10, 12; narrative self-consciousness in, xii, xiii, 4–11, 13, 237 n.2 n.4 n.5; Porter's interest in, 13–16, 33; reunion scene in, 11–13; trope of exile in, xv, 3–13, 17, 204, 209; truth vs. lying in, 4–8, 9–10
Olney, James: *Memory and Narrative*, xx, 221
Olson, S. Douglas, 237 n.2
Omphalos (Gosse), 186, 187
On Autobiography (Lejeune), 121–22, 242 n.1
"On Collecting Art and Culture" (Clifford), 137
"On Going a Journey" (Hazlitt), 71
Orientalism (Said), 15
Orkney Islands, 84, 85, 86–87, 239 n.5
Out of Place (Said), 4, 15
Ovid: *Metamorphosis*, 122

Paganini, Niccolò, 171
Panizza, Oscar: "A Scandal in the Convent," 241 n.2
Paradise Lost (Milton), 156
Paris, 129, 144, 176–80
Parke, Catherine N., 40
Parker, Andrew, xi
Pater, Walter: *The Renaissance*, 93
Patterns of Experience (Egan), 239 n.1
Patterson, Annabel, 237 n.1
Paul, Sherman: *Repossessing and Renewing*, xvii
Pawel, Ernst, 113
"The Penal Colony" (Kafka), 105
Perec, Georges, 232
performance: concept of, in autobiography, xi–xiv, 63, 103, 161, 183, 215–16; concept of, in criticism, xix, xx; in Franklin's *Autobiography*, 61–62, 65; in Gibbon's *Autobiography*, 38; in Gosse's *Father and Son*, 190; in Homer's *Odyssey*, 4–5, 13; in Kafka's *Letter to His Father*, 103–4, 110; in Muir's *Autobiography*, 92; in Nabokov's *Speak, Memory*, 26. *See also* rhetoric; the self in autobiography: narrated vs. historical forms of
"Performativity, Autobiographical Practice, Resistance" (Smith), 68, 161, 215–16
The Performing Self (Poirier), xi
Perry, Graham: "The Grand Delusions of Benjamin Haydon," 153–54
Personae (Pound), 230
Peterson, Linda H., 243 n.7
Philosophical Dictionary of the Fine Arts (Delacroix), 169
Picasso, Pablo, 131
Pilgrim's Progress (Bunyan), 55
Plautus, 171
Play (Beckett), 65, 145
Poetry and Repression (Bloom), 208
Poirier, Richard: *The Performing Self*, xi; *The Renewal of Literature*, 103

"Policing Truth" (Gilmore), 217

Polis, Phidias, 212–13

Porter, Anita (author's mother): 114, 116, 197, 211–14, 233–34

Porter, Joseph (author's father): early death of, 95, 115–16, 212–13; political views of, 79; Porter's relationship with, 196–200; senatorial bid of, 52; undergraduate photograph of, unexpectedly discovered, 233–36

Porter, Roger J.: academic career of, 13–14, 29, 52, 62–64, 65, 79, 94, 163, 164; authorial "codas" by, xvii–xx, 236; books and objects collected by, 144–46; child-hood of, 32–33, 229–30; childlessness of, 29–33, 233, 235; confessions of, 78–80; corporeal autobiography of, 129–30; "double voiced" qualities of, 51, 165, 229–32; experiences of, in Egypt, 15, 65–66, 164–65; experiences of, in Greece, 15–16; experiences of, in South Africa, 94–96; food writing of, 52, 145, 177–80; friendship of, with Howard Waskow, 177, 231–32; interest of, in autobiogra-phy, 29–33, 49–51, 62–63, 78, 146, 165, 231; interest of, in letter writing, 113–16; interest of, in literature, 51, 52, 95–96; interest of, in theatre, 16, 64–66, 145, 230; Jewish background of, 31, 77–78, 94, 130, 199–200; letters of 113–16; marriage of, 16; political beliefs of, 52–53, 94–95; religious beliefs of, 77–78, 94–95; romantic history of, 14, 115, 164, 196–97, 231; travels of, 14–16, 114, 144–45; visit of, to Paris, 176–80; visit of, to Tokyo, 76–77. See also Porter, Anita; Porter, Joseph

Portland OR: food writing in, 145, 179; Museum Art School in, 163; Porter's opinion of, 29–30, 51; theatre in, 65, 66. See also Reed College

Portrait of My Body (Lopate), 129

Portrait of the Artist (Joyce), 194

postmodernism, 4, 18, 80; theories of the self in, 50, 215–16, 242 n.1

poststructuralism, xi, xx, 119

Pound, Ezra, 96; Cantos, 51; "Hugh Selwyn Mauberley," 51; Personae, 230

The Prelude (Wordsworth), 188, 243 n.3

Price, Martin: "The Inquisition of Truth," 239 n.6; To the Palace of Wisdom, 45

Price, Reynolds: A Whole New Life, 241 n.1

Prideaux, Tom, 174

Proust, Marcel, 27, 53

psychoanalysis, 67, 89, 91–92, 133, 222–25, 245 n.7

Questions of Travel (Kaplan), 4, 18

Ralph, James, 57

"The Reality Effect" (Barthes), 137

Recovering Bodies (Couser), 240 n.1

Reed College: charged atmosphere at, in 1960s, 63–64, 79; Ginsberg's visit to, 199–200; Howard Waskow's career at, 177, 232; "The Learning Community" at, 94; Porter's career at, 16, 29, 65, 95, 164, 180, 211; seriousness of students at, 13–14, 77–78, 163

La Règle du jeu (Leiris), 131, 242 n.3

Reichl, Ruth, 180

"Relational Selves" (Eakin), 244 n.3

Rembrandt, 150, 151, 152, 160, 180

The Renaissance (Pater), 93

The Renewal of Literature (Poirier), 103

Repossessing and Renewing (Paul), xvii

rhetoric: as defense, xv–xvi, 37–38, 54–57, 62, 76, 81, 239 n.6; importance of, in autobiography, xi–xii, 49, 63, 69, 99; as model of rational selfhood, 39–40, 43–44, 54–55, 56–57; use of, by Dahlberg, 202–3, 209–10; use of, by Porter, xx, 115. See also performance

Rockwell, Norman: Triple Self-Portrait, 152, 242 n.1

Rogers, Carl, 50

"The Romantic Circle" (Holmes), 242 n.2
Romanticism and Consciousness (Bloom), 162
Roskill, Mark W., 150
Roth, Philip, 184
Rousseau, Jean-Jacques. See *Confessions*
Rubens, Peter Paul: *Lion Hunt*, 175

Sacks, Oliver, 128; *A Leg to Stand On*, 240 n.1
Said, Edward: *Orientalism*, 15; *Out of Place*, 4, 15
Saint-Simon, comte de, 168
Saint Sulpice murals (Delacroix): 176–77
Sand, George, 171, 176
Sarraute, Nathalie: "double-voicing" by, xvi, 217, 218–22, 226; Porter's interest in, 127, 231. Works: *The Age of Suspicion*, 245 n.6; *Childhood*, 218–22, 228, 244 n.5, 245 n.7; *Tropisms*, 245 n.6
Sartre, Jean-Paul, xv, 131, 224; *The Words*, 221
Saunders, Dero A., 238 n.2
Sayers, Dorothy, 135
Sayre, Robert, 65
"A Scandal in the Convent" (Panizza), 241 n.2
Scenes of Clerical Life (Eliot), 151–52
Schenck, Celeste: *Life/Lines*, 244 n.4
Schlossberg, Sonny, 234
Schor, Naomi, 137
Schubert, Franz, 53
Schwenger, Peter, 240 n.5
Scott, Sir Walter, 171
Sedgwick, Eve Kosofsky, xi
Seidel, Michael, 19
"The Self as Other" (Folkenflik), 244 n.2
the self in autobiography: acceptance of, 12; consciousness of, xi–xv, xvii, 7–9, 25, 68–69, 120, 162–63, 188–94, 221, 223; erasure of, xvi, 99–113, 117–19, 120–21, 124–27, 132–34, 138–44, 240 n.2 n.3 n.4 n.7 n.8; essentialist models of, 38,
67–68, 141, 143–44, 161, 164, 215–16, 218; gendered consciousness of, 119–27, 241 n.6, 245 n.5; identification of, with parental identity, 103–13, 201–11, 240 n.8; liberation of, from parental identity, 183–96, 243 n.1 n.4 n.9; materiality of, 131–44; narrated vs. historical forms of, xii–xv, 4–5, 9–11, 13, 14, 37–38, 49, 62, 102, 166–68, 238 n.5, 245 n.5; as other, xvi–xvii, 149–52, 159–61, 171–76, 183–84, 215–32, 242 n.1, 244 n.2 n.3 n.4; postmodern theories of, 50, 215–16, 242 n.1; rational framing of, xiv, 37–49, 54–63, 239 n.6; rhetorical framing of, 39–40, 43–44, 54–55, 56–57, 61–62; suppression of, 67–76, 85, 88–89, 91–92, 138; temporal consciousness of, 6, 8–9, 10–11, 17–18, 32, 50–51, 131–32, 141, 169–70; transcendence of, 84–85, 88–89, 92. *See also* exile; memory
sexuality: Dahlberg's disgust at, 203, 205–6, 208; Kafka's disgust at, 108–9; Leiris's disgust at, 118–19; sublimated, 41–42; unveiled, 137, 195, 196–97; veiled, 67, 69, 70–71, 72, 75–76. *See also* gender
Shahn, Ben: "The Biography of a Painting," 163
Shakespeare, William, 150, 151, 171, 230; *Hamlet*, 66, 161, 168–69, 171, 175; *King Lear*, 51, 152, 160, 242 n.2 n.3; *A Midsummer Night's Dream*, 65; *The Tempest*, 65
Shea, Daniel B., 54
Sheffield, Lord, 46, 238 n.2
Sheringham, Michael, xiv, 242 n.3, 245 n.7
Shloss, Carol, 202
Si le grain ne meurt (Gide), 195
"Sir Edmund Gosse and His Modern Readers" (Allen), 243 n.1
Skinner, Quentin, 237 n.1
Smith, Sidonie: *Getting a Life*, 80, 146; "Identity's Body," 124; "Performativity, Autobiographical Practice, Resistance,"

Smith, Sidonie (*cont.*)
   68, 161, 215–16; *Subjectivity, Identity, and the Body*, 122, 240 n.1
Sontag, Susan, 118–19
South China Morning Post, 52
Spacks, Patricia Meyer, 238 n.2, 239 n.6
Speak, Memory (Nabokov), 17–33, 69; butterfly trope in, 22–23, 24, 25, 27, 28, 238 n.4; compensatory aestheticism in, 20–22, 23–27, 29; deepening meaning of, for Porter, 29–33, 233, 235; as meditation on writing, 27–28; trope of exile in, xv, 17–22, 28–29, 238 n.1 n.3
Spectator, 60
Spender, Stephen, 183; *World Within World*, 90
Spiegelman, Herbert, 120
"The Spirit of the Age" (Mill), 187–88
Spock, Benjamin McLane, 52
Stanford University, 127
Stein, Gertrude, 127; *The Autobiography of Alice B. Toklas*, 217, 240 n.6, 244 n.4
Stendhal: *The Charterhouse of Parma*, 146
The Story and the Fable (Muir), 55, 82, 85, 89, 91, 92, 93
Studies in Classic American Literature (Lawrence), 146
Sturrock, John: "The Autobiographer Astray," 140; "The New Model Autobiographer," 133, 241 n.1
subjectivity. *See* the self in autobiography
Subjectivity, Identity, and the Body (Smith), 122, 240 n.1
suicide: autobiography as, xvi, 100, 102–3, 106, 119, 124, 126–27, 240 n.2 n.3; Barbin's, 120, 121; Haydon's, 152, 153; Van Gogh's, 152. *See also* the self in autobiography: erasure of
Sullivan, Louis: *The Autobiography of an Idea*, 163
The Summing Up (Maugham), 67–80; formal structure of, 68–70; hidden fractures in, xv–xvi, 72–76; "pattern" envisioned in, 71–72; Porter's response to, 76–80; resistance to self-disclosure in, xv–xvi, 37, 67–72, 75–76, 81

Tambling, Jeremy, 67
Tate, Allen, 202
The Tempest (Shakespeare), 65
Terence, 171
Through the Flower (Chicago), 163
Thumb, Tom, 153, 165
time: chronological, 104, 114, 131–32, 133, 138, 140, 241 n.1; exilic, 8–9, 10–11, 13, 17–19, 21, 22–24, 26; Gibbon's reflections on, 43, 47, 48; journal writing and, 167, 169, 176, 243 n.3; linear, 21, 23, 27, 87; mythical, 81–82, 85–87, 89–90, 120; Porter's reflections on, 29–32, 51; resistance to, in autobiography, 141, 161, 169–70, 176
'Tis Pity She's a Whore (Ford), 80
Titian, 156, 171, 172
To the Lighthouse (Woolf), 212
To the Palace of Wisdom (Price), 45
Touching the World (Eakin), 37, 38, 54, 224, 240 n.1, 245 n.5
Trapp, Frank, 166, 172
Triple Self-Portrait (Rockwell), 152, 242 n.1
Tropisms (Sarraute), 245 n.6
Troubling Confessions (Brooks), 67–68, 110
truth in autobiography: competing versions of, 216, 218–22, 226; complexity of, 4–8, 9–10, 19, 27; evasion of, 46, 67–71, 223; realization of, 210; scepticism about, 99, 103, 139

Unamuno, Miguel de, 53
Uniontown PA 233, 234
University of California Humanities Research Institute, 128
University of Groningen, 229
Updike, John, 240 n.1

Van Gogh, Vincent, 180; letters of xvi, 149,

150–52, 153, 157, 163; *Letters*, xvi, 149, 150–52, 153, 157, 163; suicide of, 152
Veeser, H. Aram, 237 n.4
Vidal, Gore, 73
The Visionary Company (Bloom), 84
Volpone (Jonson), 66, 145
Voltaire, 171

Waco TX, 77
Waldman, Henry, 198
Wallach, Robert, 234
Wasada University, 77
Waskow, Arthur: *Becoming Brothers*, xvi, 177, 216, 217, 226–29, 232; *Godwrestling*, 177, 228
Waskow, Howard, 231–32; *Becoming Brothers*, xvi, 177, 216, 217, 226–29, 232
Watson, Julia: *Getting a Life*, 80, 146
Weitzman, Chaim, 78
Wellcome, Syrie, 69
Wellington, duke of, 159
The Western Canon (Bloom), xi
West Virginia University, 197, 233–36
Whitman, Walt, 12, 210, 226

A Whole New Life (Price), 241 n.1
Wilson, Edmund: *Classics and Commercials*, 72
Wimsatt, William K., 49; "The Intentional Fallacy," xiii, 237 n.1
Wolf, Howard R., 114, 243 n.1
Wood, Michael: Introduction to Maugham's *Mrs. Craddock*, 70; *The Magician's Doubts*, 23, 26
Woolf, Virginia, 127, 154, 195; *To the Lighthouse*, 212
The Words (Sartre), 221
The Words to Say It (Cardinal), 240 n.1
Wordsworth, William, 87, 155, 160, 163; *The Prelude*, 188, 243 n.3
World Within World (Spender), 90

Yale University, 13, 16, 49, 62, 177
Yeats, William Butler, 96, 232; *Autobiographies*, 95; *Reveries over Childhood and Youth*, 95

Zauhar, Frances Murphy, 237 n.4
Zweig, Paul: *The Adventurer*, 237 n.4